A SECOND COURSE IN COMPUTER SCIENCE WITH PASCAL

Daniel D. McCracken
City College of New York

John Wiley & Sons
NEW YORK   CHICHESTER   BRISBANE   TORONTO   SINGAPORE

To Ruth, Harvey, David, Horace,
and the memory of John

Cover design by Rafael Hernandez

Copyright © 1987, by John Wiley & Sons, Inc.

Library of Congress Cataloging in Publication Data:

McCracken, Daniel D.
  A second course in computer science with PASCAL.

  Bibliography: p. ■■
  Includes indexes.
  1. PASCAL (Computer program language)
I. Title. II. Title: 2nd course in computer science with PASCAL.
QA76.73.P2M363 1987   005.13'3   86-32586
ISBN 0-471-8 1062-1

Printed in the United States of America

10 9 8 7 6 5 4 3 2 1

PREFACE

This is an introductory text on the central subject of computer science—the theory, implementation, and applications of data structures and algorithms.

Key features:

• There is a strong Abstract Data Type (ADT) approach. For each of the major data types the sequence is: a definition in terms of objects and operations, an illustration of usefulness, *then* one or more possible implementations, followed by larger applications and/or an overview of related issues.

• Almost all implementations are informally analyzed using the Big-Oh notation. The concept is introduced in the first chapter, and applied throughout.

• Recursion receives heavy emphasis. One chapter is devoted to its explanation and it offers many examples. Recursion is then used freely in the book, where it makes the presentation of other ideas clearer.

• There is heavy emphasis on program readability as a key feature of good programming style. The point is made explicitly in the first chapter and reinforced by example throughout. All programs have been tested and run, to produce the results shown and explained in the text.

• Program verification, through assertions and loop invariants, is introduced and explained at an informal level.

• The major illustrations are chosen with an eye to making the course serve, among other things, as an overview of what computer science is about. Parsing, simulation, expression simplification, BNF, state transition diagrams, backtracking, the database concept, solving recurrence relations, and several graph algorithms are introduced in this way, at a level appropriate to a second course.

It will be seen that the coverage is that recommended in the Koffman Committee report on a revision for CS2 of the ACM Curriculum 78.

I believe I have written a text that is in the spirit of the best recent work on curriculum revision; I have tried not to fall into the trap of trying to cover everything. The examples, along with their underlying abstract and implemented data structures, provide real-life applications of many theoretical topics. Thus the text complements a separate course in discrete mathematics but can be used separately.

About 15 percent of the entire text is devoted to a variety of exercises. Some test mastery of concepts; some are programming exercises that reinforce the data structures and algorithms covered in the chapter; some extend the mathematics and/or computer science topics of the chapter; and, some are suitable for projects that require consideration of software engineering issues. Many make most sense if programmed and run, but many others will help the student master the material with only paper and pencil to support careful study. About a quarter of them involve discrete mathematics, permitting the instructor to give that emphasis if desired.

Every chapter concludes with a "Suggestions for Further Study" section, which is a selective annotated bibliography. The references chosen include other texts covering about the same material, for comparison and alternative exposition; primary sources; standard works that every student should know (e.g., Knuth); and indications of applications.

An Instructor's Manual will provide answers to exercises, suggestions for teaching the material, a sample syllabus, sample examinations, and ideas for larger projects for those who wish to emphasize the software engineering component of the course. A disk containing all programs and data from the book may be obtained by writing me care of John Wiley & Sons, Inc., 605 Third Avenue, New York, NY 10158.

Daniel D. McCracken
New York, New York
January, 1987

____ACKNOWLEDGMENTS

Many people rendered invaluable help in producing this work, but first on the list must be Doris C. Appleby (Marymount College, Tarrytown, New York). Her primary task was writing most of the exercises and the annotated bibliography, but as the work progressed she did much more. Her help in finding a meaningful presentation of the ADT concept to my chosen readership was especially fruitful. It is a pleasure to acknowledge her contributions.

Charles L. Baker (Science Applications, Inc.) gave me the benefit of reactions from someone who has been a practicing programmer since 1950.

Paul P. Clement (Advanced Systems, Inc.) made a great many helpful suggestions in the early stages of writing, especially on the use of graphics.

Charles Engelke (University of Florida) read every word of every draft, made innumerable suggestions (both large and small) for improvement, and saved me embarrassment by catching many slips in early drafts.

Gene Fisch (New York State Institute for Basic Research in Developmental Disabilities) taught from the manuscript at City College of New York and gave much help and support.

Henry Ledgard (Amherst, Massachusetts) provided a burst of good advice at a very early stage when it was most helpful, and provided a model of programming style that I recommend.

Haim Kilov (Latvian Light Industry Research Institute) also read every word of every draft. He provided reams of detailed suggestions for improved programming and better presentation and never ceased urging more mathematical rigor. I look forward to the day when students in a course at this level will benefit by the advanced approach he would have preferred. I also hope some day to meet him.

James J. Piccarello (formerly City College of New York and now AT&T Information Systems) taught from the manuscript and offered dozens of helpful suggestions of a wide variety of types.

William I. Salmon (University of Utah), my coauthor on other books, solved a troublesome problem in one program at a critical point, and was a supportive colleague in ways too numerous to detail.

Jeffrey R. Sampson (University of Alberta), before his untimely death in 1985, had begun to work on the project and surely would have been at least as helpful as he was on a previous book. He is missed.

Laurie White (University of Florida) taught twice from the manuscript, had many helpful ideas, and passed along the highly useful reactions of her students.

Gregory P. Williams (Woodbury, Connecticut), an old friend from our General Electric days, could be depended on to call within days of receiving anything, with an earful of sharply focused advice. It has been a real pleasure working with him.

My thanks also to Stefan Burr (City College of New York) and David Gries (Cornell University) for many detailed suggestions on Chapter 8.

It is a pleasure to acknowledge the many helpful ideas of the following people who served as reviewers through Wiley. Anonymous to me at the time, they provided both encouragement and valuable criticism. Their inputs made a real difference.

Maria Balogh (Portland State University), George Beekman (Oregon State University), Christopher M. Brown (University of Rochester), Henry A. Etlinger (Rochester Institute of Technology), Arthur C. Fleck (University of Iowa), Gary A. Ford (Carnegie-Mellon University), Raymond Ford (University of Iowa), Paul Gormley (Villanova University), Marc Graham (Georgia Institute of Technology), Adam O. Hausknecht (Southeastern Massachusetts University), Brian L. Johnson (University of New Hampshire), Michael P. Johnson (Oregon State University), John L. Lowther (Michigan Technological University), Louise Moser (California State University at Hayward), Richard E. Pattis (University of Washington), and Justin Smith (Drexel University).

Helen Blumenthal, who is my wife, handled the preparation of the manuscript for submission in magnetic form and many other production matters.

The editorial and production people at Wiley were capable and supportive as they always are, and I am grateful for their efforts.

Finally, it is a pleasure to convey my deep appreciation to my students at City College of New York. They were patient and supportive as, at times, we all learned together. The book would not have been possible without them.

D.D.M.

CONTENTS

CHAPTER 1

THE PROGRAM DEVELOPMENT PROCESS

1.1 TO THE READER: ABOUT THIS BOOK

We begin this text with the assumption that you have had one computer science course on algorithm development, with programming in Pascal. You may, we hope, have had a course in discrete mathematics or you may know other programming languages. You may also know something about how computers operate at a level below programming languages like Pascal. But that you have had one good Pascal-based computer science course in which you wrote five to ten programs and ran them—that is our starting assumption.

Building on that background, study of this book will advance your growth in computer science in four areas:

1. **Abstract data types (ADTs).** You have been introduced to arrays, records, sets, and strings in your previous study. We shall look at those topics afresh, taking a broader viewpoint, and study five others: stacks, queues, linked lists, trees, and graphs. Our major new viewpoint will be to distinguish between the *concept* of a given abstract data type and the various possibilities for its *implementation*. We call this the *abstract data type* (ADT) approach.

2. **Algorithms.** An algorithm is a precisely stated set of steps that terminates in finite time, the execution of which solves a stated problem. You are probably already accustomed to simple algorithms, perhaps when you had to evaluate a polynomial, find the roots of a polynomial, solve a small system of simultaneous equations, or find the greatest common divisor of two integers.

In this book we shall study a number of algorithms for solving some of the "standard" problems that arise frequently in computer science. You have probably seen simple examples of some of these, such as elementary sorting methods or binary search. Here we shall not only investigate sorting and searching in greater depth, but also study a variety of algorithms that arise in connection with the new (to you) ADTs. These involve, for example, ways of "visiting" all the nodes of a binary tree or finding the shortest path between two vertices in a graph. Several of the algorithms will have the dual purpose of illustrating a new ADT and introducing a fundamental area of computer science study.

3. **Better programming.** Computer science is more than the amassing of programming skills and languages, but programming is nonetheless one of the essential tools of a computer scientist. Consequently, in this book we will help you improve your programming skills in a number of ways. One major way is to give you many examples to read and study.

4. **The use of mathematics in computer science.** Computer science as a discipline is in the process of becoming more firmly grounded in mathematics. In various ways, appropriate to your background, we shall demonstrate some of the ways mathematics is useful in computer science and deepen your ability to work with the combination of the two.

In other words, you are going to learn some of the tools of the trade of a computer scientist. Many of these tools have direct application; others are building blocks that will find full value after study of more advanced topics such as compiler construction, database implementation, or computer graphics. A number of the applications that we use to illustrate data structures and algorithms provide "sneak preview" of some of the areas of computer science that you will be studying later.

1.2 THE SOFTWARE DEVELOPMENT CYCLE

In writing programs to this stage, you have probably gone through a process something like this:

1. Get the assignment. The instructor states a problem to be solved.

2. Devise an algorithm. With more or less help depending on your experience, and with more or less difficulty depending on the problem, devise an algorithm for solving the problem.

3. Express the algorithm as a computer program, using the programming language specified for the course. Type the program into the computer.

4. Compile the program. Revise it to correct errors detected by the compiler, run it with sample data for which you know the correct answers, and correct errors discovered in testing. Run the program with actual data and turn in program and results.

And, typically, *never so much as look at the program, ever again.*

This is an acceptable way to start learning about programming, computer science, and software engineering. However, software development outside of the classroom is vastly different. Many organizations develop programs that are far too large to be written by one person or even by one small team. In projects of such size, a majority of the effort may be devoted primarily to communication among team members. Any one team member may be working on a procedure of only a few hundred lines, but that procedure must *interface* (communicate correctly) with other procedures in the program. As a result, interface standards and programming style standards are rigidly enforced. When all the costs have been tallied, including the planning, the waste caused by bad planning, and the meetings to coordinate interface definitions, etc., the cost of a program can easily be in excess of $100 *per line*.

If you have ever written a 200-line program by staying up the night before an assignment was due, you may find this figure incomprehensible. That is because you have seen only a part of the whole job of program development so far.

You are not expected to make the transition from writing ''student-sized'' programs to the industrial world of multi-person projects in one giant leap. For the purposes of this book, you will be writing programs of a few hundred lines, for the most part, and working alone. But one major goal of the book is to help you make several big steps—if not the entire journey—toward your ability to develop software of realistic size.

One of the essentials you will have to acquire is how to become much more systematic about the program development *process*. It won't do, for instance, to approach program development in an informal way. Rather, you will have to start going through a series of well-defined steps, using the intellectual tools that are the main subject of the book, in which the coding is only one phase.

There is no single formula that fits every situation, but we can list a sequence of steps that will provide a starting outlook—a framework that will serve in many cases—and that is a good foundation for discussion of the variations.

Here, then, is a listing of the steps in developing a software system.

1. **User requirements analysis.** The software developer or development team, working closely with the *user* (also called the *client* or *customer*—the person or group requesting the software), produces a definition of the problem. A document called the *user requirements statement* is jointly agreed to by the user and the developer, and becomes a sort of contract stating what the program is to accomplish. However, this document contains essentially nothing about how the requirements are to be met, which is worked out later. ''What, not how'' summarizes this step.

2. **Functional specification.** Next comes a technical statement that shows the major components of the system, data flows between them, required outputs, errors to be checked for and procedures to follow after detection, and any constraints such as required processing rates. A formal document is also produced at this stage, part of which is a first draft of the *User's Guide,* which is what the end users will work from when using the system.

3. **Design.** For each of the major components identified in the functional specification, the developer now chooses data types and algorithms, and breaks

the processing into precisely defined subprograms (procedures or functions, in Pascal). Key algorithms may be subjected to *verification* at this stage, to build confidence that they are correct.

4. **Implementation.** The design is translated into code, usually in a high-level language such as Pascal.

5. **Testing.** The developer then compiles the code and corrects errors detected by the compiler. Next, the compiled programs are run with data for which the correct results are known; errors detected in this stage are also corrected. The programs are then run with data containing all the errors that the requirements ask to be detected. (The programs may also be run with completely random data, to see if they reject unanticipated bad data.) The programs are finally run with real data supplied by the client, which will often disclose errors of understanding of user requirements.

6. **Installation.** The software is placed on the *target computer* (the client's machine, on which the application will run in regular use), which is usually not the one on which development (coding and testing) is done. The client personnel who will operate the system are trained. The system is run in parallel with the one it replaces, if that is the situation. (Discontinuing an old system before its replacement has been thoroughly proven has long been recognized as a recipe for disaster, but it still happens.)

7. **Maintenance.** This is an umbrella term for everything that is done to the software after the user has accepted the initial product—correction of errors not detected earlier, addition of new features, and modifications necessitated by hardware changes. "Maintenance" is a decidedly awkward term for this collection of almost unrelated activities, none of which is similar to the "maintenance" of a car or a TV set, but the terminology is entrenched.

The amount of time devoted to each of these steps obviously varies, but the following percentages of the total effort are generally indicative of what is needed:

User requirements: 10%

Functional specification: 30%

Design: 20%

Implementation: 15%

Testing: 15%

Installation: 10%.

No percentage has been shown for maintenance, which requires further explanation and emphasis. The trouble with trying to pin down a time allotment is that maintenance itself is poorly defined. Pragmatically, it often turns out to cover everything from the time the user accepts the system until an agreement is reached to undertake a major revision. By this definition, maintenance is usually reported as something in the range of 50–90% of the total cost of software development. Astonishing, perhaps, but generally accepted.

Several lessons may be drawn from this discussion.

1. Coding, possibly the only part to which you have given serious attention so far, is a relatively minor part of the job. One reason for this is that real life applications often require a great deal of effort just to get a good definition of what is to be done, in part because the user often doesn't really know at the outset. The user can't write the requirements in isolation, without knowing the constraints imposed by the computer, a subject about which he or she is not expert. Likewise, the software developer obviously can't define the task in isolation. Furthermore, the two people (or two groups) often have quite different vocabularies and areas of expertise, requiring considerable time, effort, and good will just to be sure they are really talking about the same thing. The draft of the User's Guide, which should be written long before coding begins, is an excellent device to help detect misunderstandings early in the development process.

2. Just about anything that can flush out errors of whatever type, *early in the development process,* is beneficial. The earlier an error is caught, the easier and cheaper it is to correct, sometimes even by a huge margin; correcting an error after installation may cost tens or even thousands of times as much as correcting it at the design stage. This is one reason that the percentages of project effort devoted to requirements analysis and functional specification are so much larger than you might have expected: much wasted effort can be saved by getting them right the first time. In sum, delay coding as long as possible.

3. We described this process as a linear sequence of separate steps, but it is really a *cycle:* normally there will be considerable looping back to repeat portions of earlier steps.

4. Because many people are involved in development over periods of months or years, with a great deal depending on an accurate understanding of what is to be accomplished and what has already been done, documentation is a crucial part of the software development process. Documentation does *not* mean a rushed, after-the-fact job that is done carelessly to meet contract requirements. Most of the stages of the development process haven't really been completed at all until an appropriate document has been created. The ability to communicate easily and clearly is a crucial vocational skill for a software developer.

Because so many people of diverse backgrounds and concerns use the computer for so many different applications, it is to be expected that there will be many variations of this process. In fact, some developers feel that there is *so much* variability that it is better not to pretend that there is a ''standard'' ''life cycle'' at all. Such an objection will be viewed with considerable sympathy in these quarters,[1] but you need to have an idea of the traditional approaches before you can deal with the variations. Consequently, we have presented one formulation of the conventional life cycle.

[1]See Daniel D. McCracken and Michael A. Jackson, ''Life-Cycle Concept Considered Harmful,'' *Software Engineering Notes,* **7**, 2 (April 1982).

Whether in this course, in later study, or in a work setting, you may be assured that *some* disciplined series of steps in program development will be required of you. It is inconceivable, for instance, that a chemical engineer would begin the design of a major facility by building one familiar component prior to a feasibility study, cost analysis, siting studies, market and distribution studies, probably a pilot plant, and many other steps. To be sure, there are many differences between a chemical plant and a program. But for the next few months you would do well to concentrate on the similarities in the two development processes—which are greater than you might think—than the differences.

1.3 THE CHARACTERISTICS OF A GOOD PROGRAM

Everybody wants to write good programs, but how do you know if you have done it? What are the characteristics of a good program? As usual, there will be differences of emphasis depending on the circumstances, but the following list will serve as a starting point.

1. **Correctness.** A program that doesn't do what the user expects it to do cannot be a good program. How might this type of program be developed? One way is for the parties to misunderstand each other about the requirements and/or specifications. Are you *sure,* as you design and implement software, that you know what the user expects? Beginners have trouble believing that a major project can reach the installation and acceptance phase only to have the developers and users discover that they really had never been talking about the same thing. Avoiding this most unfortunate situation can be accomplished by carefully documenting your project and devoting great effort to maintaining close communication throughout development.

2. **Reliability.** A good program produces correct output from correct input, produces meaningful error messages from incorrect input, and (as is often required) keeps running in spite of almost anything. Reliability suffers when previously undetected errors (of specifications, design, or coding) turn up, or when bad data causes the program to crash.

3. **Portability.** A good program can readily be moved from one computer to another with a minimum of modification. More often than sometimes expected, a program written for one machine or one operating system turns out to be useful in an entirely different environment; with bad luck—or lack of planning—it can be very difficult to make such a move. Achieving portability usually means staying with languages that are implemented on a wide variety of machines and avoiding non-standard language features.

4. **Maintainability.** Considering that many software products run for years or decades, with great effort and expense devoted to maintenance, it makes sense to write programs that are easy to modify. This is all the more true because maintenance is normally done by people other than the original developers. Indeed, it may be done by a long sequence of people, none of

whom was involved in the original development and whose computing expertise may be a small fraction of that of the developers.

The key feature of a maintainable program, therefore is *readability—by people*. The job of the maintenance programmer, who often works under serious time pressure, is easier if he or she can clearly discern what the program is intended to do. If the program is easily readable it is also less likely that a change will introduce new errors, which also happens all too often.

5. **Readability.** Every characteristic of a good program that we have listed is advanced by readability. A readable program is more likely to be correct in the first place. It is faster and cheaper to test. It is faster and cheaper and safer to modify. In fact, some computer scientists go so far as to say that a program should be designed *primarily* to be readable, with its function of directing the actions of a computer relegated to a secondary consideration.

6. **Use of resources.** All other things being equal, a good program is fast and uses a minimum of storage. This issue will be a primary concern in the chapters that follow.

Because so much depends on the (human) readability of programs, we will now turn to a discussion of how to write a program that is as readable as possible.

1.4 PROGRAMMING STYLE

Writing a readable program is so important to the entire development process that considerable study has been devoted to means for achieving readability. The list that follows is an attempt to summarize some of what has been learned. Bear in mind, however, that it is entirely possible to follow any style manual and still write truly terrible programs. Try to keep the goal at the front of your mind— writing programs that are as easy as possible for *people* to understand. A mental exercise may help. Imagine that every piece of code you write will immediately be turned over to someone else to test, install, and maintain. If that other person can't understand what you wrote, you may as well not have written it. This exercise is much closer to the workplace reality than you might imagine.

Some details are inevitably matters of taste, but most students of software quality would agree with the points presented in the following list.[2]

1. Choose the names of variables and procedures so that they are as meaningful as possible. Pascal wouldn't mind if a variable name like `WordCount`, say, were replaced in all instances with `QqYy1234x9k`, but why do it? Nobody *would* do that, presumably, but `WC` would tempt some; it seems like a natural abbreviation for `WordCount`. But will it be meaningful to someone else two years from now? Will it be meaningful to *you* two years from

---

[2] I have been guided in much of what follows by the discussion in Henry F. Ledgard, *Professional Pascal: Essays on the Practice of Programming*. Reading, MA: Addison-Wesley, 1986.

now? Like most important things, devising good identifiers can take time and effort, but no other one thing can do more to improve program readability.

Ledgard, in the work cited, suggests a useful guideline in choosing names: use nouns for data names, verbs for procedure names, and adjectives for the names of `boolean` variables. Single-letter variable names are defensible only when they follow long-established usage, or when their definition, initialization, and use all fall within a few lines and their function is in a simple loop. Otherwise, use names that are as long as needed to be as clear as you can make them—up to a normal limit of ten or a dozen characters. When a long name makes for clarity, don't devise another name that differs in only one character; it is too hard to distinguish the two names. For a procedure, a fairly long name may be the best way to communicate to a reader what the purpose of the procedure is. However, long procedure names quickly become unintelligible unless there is some way to tell where individual words begin. The convention followed in this book is that the first letter of every word in every identifier is capitalized. In languages that do not permit both uppercase and lowercase letters, hyphens or underscores may sometimes be used to separate words.

Most good programmers agree that meaningful names are worth some extra trouble because of their payoff in program understandability and all the good things that readability promotes.[3] But a lot of judgment is needed to come up with good names, and experience will be a better guide than a set of hard-and-fast rules.

2. With the exception of the numbers zero and one, and *very occasionally* a few others, never write constants anywhere in a program except in the declarations, and then use the `const` declaration for as many of those as possible. The point is that "constants" have a way of changing over the life of the program. Arrays get larger or smaller, we change computers and find a different character representation, and parameters that the client said would never change do change. And, although the value of π can never change, the number of digits we use to approximate it may. When such changes are necessary, it is much easier and far safer to be able to change the one place the constant is defined than to hunt for and hope to find all occurrences of it. Finding all but one can lead to disaster. And even with an interactive text editor there are traps. For instance, if the number 100 occurs dozens of times in a program it is easy enough to change all of them to 200 when an array size is doubled—but what if in two of those occurrences the 100 was a temperature, and the person making the change didn't realize that?

3. Minimize the number of global variables. The reasons for this dictum are various, and some of them will only come out later, but the collective wisdom of the field is that this is good advice. One major reason is that we will be striving to encapsulate related actions into procedures, both to promote clear

---

[3]If you are inclined to resist this advice on the grounds that longer identifiers mean too much typing, *then learn to type better*. Whether for your other work or for its benefit in any programming environment, the time and effort will be repaid many times over.

understanding and to localize the effect of changes. Consequently, it is far easier to be sure that a change affects only one procedure if all variables involved in the change are local to the procedure.

4. Within reason, name everything possible in `type` declarations, including subranges and the definitions of arrays and records. (The alternative, sometimes, is to include them directly in variable declarations.)

5. Use spaces, blank lines, and indentation to promote clarity of meaning. As to spaces within a line, be guided by the usage of ordinary English prose. In writing, you put spaces after commas, colons, and semicolons, but you do not put spaces before them; do the same in your programs.

   There should always be *at least* one blank line between the end of a procedure and whatever comes next; we shall use two. Other use of blank lines is mostly a matter of common sense and simple esthetic judgment.

   It is very important to use indentation to indicate the scope of control of the conditional and loop-control elements of a programming language: there should be some form of indentation to show what the `then` and `else` parts of an `if` control, and what the scope of a `while` or `repeat` is, for example. Beyond that generalization, however, there are many possible forms. You are encouraged to follow the example of the programs in this book, or your instructor may specify some other system. Whatever you decide, *stick to it*. You may not be able to appreciate at this stage how important a consistent indentation style is; however, you will later, so get in the habit now.

6. Use comments intelligently. A line or two near the beginning of a procedure that states the general goal is a good idea if it is not possible to devise a procedure name and parameter names that convey the purpose. Otherwise, use comments only where another competent coder might wonder what your purpose was, or where the programmer might miss an important reason why something works. Don't clutter up your programs with comments that belabor the obvious and don't try to teach programming or explain your language with comments.

   Obviously, finding a middle ground between too few and too many comments can take some practice. The style adopted for this book will not satisfy all instructors, who generally have to threaten violence to get any comments at all. I am sympathetic to such instructors. Since the goal is understandability, however, I believe that a programmer's best efforts should go into devising variable and procedure names that communicate intent instantly. Excessive use of comments is, in my view, an admission that the programmer was unable to do that.

7. Organize your program into procedures, each having a single coherent purpose. The main program should ordinarily consist almost entirely of procedure calls. The primary purpose of this approach is to master program complexity through what is called *top-down design:* we break a task into small pieces, each of which is easier to understand than the total job, and then combine them in strictly controlled ways. If the total job has been broken into pieces in an intelligent way, and if the ways in which they relate are

clean and simple, then understanding the combination of the pieces will be far simpler than understanding a single program that does the whole job.

The key elements are to make each procedure as coherent as possible, and to keep the communications between procedures clean. In this context, "coherent" means that a procedure should carry out only one function or a set of closely related functions. Some have suggested the following test for coherence. If you can describe the action of a procedure with a single English verb, then it probably has a coherent purpose. (Likewise, that verb may as well be the first or only word of the procedure name.) This may be a little too restrictive in some circumstances, but it is an excellent starting point for thinking about the issue. "Clean communication" means that information is transmitted between procedures via parameters, with minimum use of global variables.

This list could be expanded and elaborated. There can be no absolute rules of programming style any more than there can be absolute rules of style in any other area, for programming is partly an art and partly a science. Still, with effort and attention, programs can be made clearer as can writing. Everything we have learned about program development says that the effort is well repaid. Plan to reread this section once for each chapter!

1.5 AN INTRODUCTION TO ANALYSIS OF ALGORITHMS

Other things being equal, we prefer a fast algorithm to a slow one. Consequently, to make intelligent choices about alternative algorithms, we need a way to compare the time they require. And, as with so many other aspects of software development, we seek a technique that focuses on the essentials of a situation. To that end, the technique that we will introduce here, called the *analysis of algorithms,* is one of the fundamental tools of the computer scientist and the software engineer.

An effective way to characterize the speed of an algorithm is to state how its execution time grows as a function of the size of the problem it solves. The "size of the problem," represented by N, might be the number of names to be sorted, elements in a set, or nodes in a circuit to be studied by a graph algorithm. To analyze an algorithm, then, means to find a simple formula that expresses how long it takes to solve problem of size N.

Consider a few examples.

Suppose we have N numbers in random sequence in an array `A[1..N]`, and that we seek the element number of a value X that is known to be in the array. The following piece of code will do that.

```
I := 1;
while X <> A[I] do
   I := I + 1;
```

When the loop terminates (which we are assured that it will because we are told that X occurs in the array), then `A[I]` $= X$, and I is the value we were required to find. The question is, as a function of N, how many times is the loop body executed? If we know nothing about the sequence of the elements in `A`, then it might be any number of times from zero (if $X =$ `A[1]`) to $N - 1$ (if $X =$ `A[N]`). If the element that is equal to X is equally likely to be any of the N elements, then the average number of times is $(N - 1) / 2$.

Dividing through, we get $N/2 - 1/2$. Now comes the first simplification— throw away an unessential detail. We discard the $-1/2$. For large N the $-1/2$ just isn't very important, particularly when all we really want to do is compare the method with one for which the *form* of the formula is entirely different. Having discarded the $-1/2$, we have a formula in which the execution time grows as a linear (first power) function of N. We call this a *linear-time algorithm*.

Compare this with the binary search method. There we start with an array in which the N elements occur in ascending sequence. We first ask whether X is equal to the middle element of the array. If it is, we are done. If not, we ask whether X is greater than or less than the middle element of the array. If it is less, we discard the half of the array holding the larger values from further consideration and repeat the process with the half containing the smaller values. If it is greater, we discard the half holding the smaller values from further consideration and repeat the process with the half holding the larger values. This cutting-in-half process is repeated until we have found the element we seek. How many "halvings" are required to get N down to 1? The answer, as we shall develop in Chapter 9, is about $\log_2 N$, which we shall write as $\lg N$. We accordingly say that binary search is a *logarithmic–time algorithm*.

How do the two algorithms compare? Here are some values.

N	$N/2$	$\lg N$
10	5	4
100	50	7
1,000	500	10
10,000	5,000	14
100,000	50,000	17
1,000,000	500,000	20

The values shown in the $\lg N$ column are actually $\lceil \lg N \rceil$, called the *ceiling* of $\lg N$, which is the actual value rounded up to the next integer.

We see that for small N there is little difference between the two methods, but that for larger N the linear method is a great deal slower. It is *so much slower*, in fact, that for comparison purposes we really don't even care about the divisor of 2. The point is that for any constant factors k_1 and k_2, $k_1 N$ will eventually become larger than $k_2 \lg N$ as N grows.

So, what is at the core? What part is left after we throw away all the non-essential details? The answer is that the dominant term in the formula remains, the part that becomes more important than all others as N grows. Having found that term, we discard any constant multiplier and say that that term characterizes the method. In our example, the dominant terms are simply N (discarding the $-1/2$ and the constant multiplier of 1/2) and $\lg N$.

In the notation that has become standard in the field, we would say that the running time of the linear search method is $O(N)$ (read as "Big Oh of N," or "of the order of N," or just "proportional to N") and that the running time of binary search is $O(\lg N)$. Formally, when we say that the running time $T(N)$ of some program is $O(\lg N)$, we mean that positive constants c and N_0 can be found such that $T(N) < c \lg N$ for $N > N_0$. Informally, we simply mean that for large N nothing else in the formula matters except the $\lg N$ term, not including any constant multiplier.

We shall analyze most algorithms in this book for you, or at least state the results, and offer timing figures for many algorithms to emphasize the importance of the differences in the forms of these formulas. Teaching experience indicates, however, that until you have seen such comparisons yourself, in terms of the actual running time of programs you have written, this kind of discussion will seem very abstract. To demonstrate that very concrete matters are involved, consider the following situation.

Suppose we have a choice between two sorting algorithms, one of which takes $5 N^2$ microseconds and the other of which takes $50 N \lg N$ microseconds. (These are generally indicative of the speeds of sorting on a microcomputer.) Stated otherwise, we have a *quadratic* method (N squared) that has a relatively small multiplier (indicating a simple loop) and an $N \lg N$ method with a much larger multiplier (indicating a more complex method.) How do they compare? Here are the running times for a range of sizes of N.

N	$5 N^2$ μs	$50 N \lg N$ μs
10	0.0005 sec	0.0008 sec
100	0.05 sec	0.016 sec
1000	5 sec	0.24 sec
10,000	500 sec = 8 min	3.2 sec
100,000	50,000 sec = 14 hr	40 sec
1,000,000	5×10^6 sec = 58 days	480 sec = 8 min

The message: For small N, the lesser overhead of the quadratic method results in shorter times. But, for larger values of N, the quadratic term dominates all other considerations and the method becomes useless. Furthermore, the crossover point between the two is at a fairly small value of N, in terms of actual sorting applications.

However, suppose you were stuck with the quadratic method and *had* to sort a big array.[4] Let us also imagine that you obtained access to the largest super-

---

[4]This is less fantastic than it might sound. I wrote a book in 1961, *A Guide to Fortran Programming*, (New York: John Wiley & Sons) in which I used a quadratic sorting method to illustrate loop techniques. In self defense, I will point out that, at that time, only two faster methods were known—merge sort and Shell sort— and both of them would have been much too complex for the programming point I was trying to make. I assumed that anyone who really wanted to sort would find an appropriate reference and look up how to do it properly. All very well except that 25 years later, a man asking for my autograph on a copy of that book told me with a huge smile that for many years he and everyone in the group he was in had used that sorting method—which they referred to as "McCracken's sorting method." Ouch.

computer you could find, and suppose that it was ten thousand times faster than the one that led to the preceding formulas. Well, now you could sort your million records in about the same eight minutes that your old microcomputer would take using the $N \lg N$ method—but at vastly greater expense. The supercomputer, if using the $N \lg N$ method, would sort the million records in considerably less time than it would take you to get your finger off the start button—five hundredths of a second!

We shall return to this subject repeatedly. For now, we close with a comparison showing the growth rates of the most common forms, together with the usual names for them.

Form	Name
$O(k)$	Constant
$O(\lg N)$	Logarithmic
$O(N)$	Linear
$O(N \lg N)$	Nothing generally accepted; say "$N \log N$"
$O(N^2)$	Quadratic
$O(N^3)$	Cubic
$O(2^N)$	Exponential

The growth of these forms as a function of N is depicted in Figure 1.1.

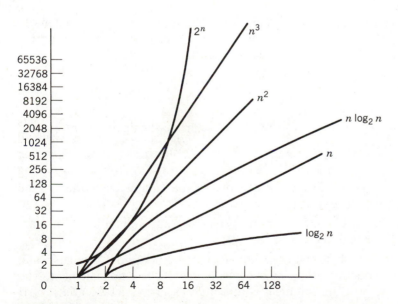

FIGURE 1.1
The growth, for six common forms, of running time as a function of N, the size of the problem.

EXERCISES

1. The following is the first draft of a user requirement statement for a package requested by a small boarding stable that accommodates up to 25 horses. The stable owners want an interactive program to:
    (a) Keep data on horse owners, including:
    1. Name
    2. Home address
    3. Business address
    4. Home telephone number
    5. Business telephone number
    6. Horses owned.
    (b) Keep data on horses, including:
    1. Name
    2. Feed requirements
    3. Services used
    4. Shows entered and prizes won.
    (c) Keep data on service people, including:
    1. Name
    2. Service performed
    3. Address
    4. Telephone number
    5. Prices.
    (d) Keep billing information and print bills, including:
    1. Computation of monthly bill
    2. Indication of date bill was paid.
    Write a draft of a functional specification for the package. Do not write algorithms. Write each procedure as a *stub*. For example, a procedure for finding a veterinarian could be written as follows:

    ```
    FindVet (    Servers: ServiceData;
            var VetList: NameAndPhoneList);
    { Prints list of veterinarians available for emergencies }
    begin  end;
    ```

2. Formulate a program design for one of the four major categories of the user requirement statement in Exercise 1.

3. Reread the discussions of program correctness and reliability. What are their differences and interconnections?

4. Donald Knuth (1974; see bibliographic listing at end of book) suggests that the following code represents an acceptable use of the *goto* statement. The purpose of the program fragment is to search an array, $A[1..M]$, of M distinct values to find where a given value, X, appears. If X is not present, it is to be inserted as an additional entry and the size of the array should be increased. In addition, there is another array, where $Count[I]$ equals

the number of times we have searched for the values in A[I]. (This is essentially a Pascal-like pseudocode.)

```
for I := 1 to M do
    if A[I] = X then goto Found;
{ Not Found }
M := M + 1;
A[M] := X;
Count[M] := 0;
Found:  Count[I] := Count[I] + 1;
```

(a) Rewrite the code above using a `while` loop to eliminate the `goto`.
(b) Do you agree with Knuth that the code with a `goto` is clearer to read than that without?

5. Kernighan and Plauger (1974) list the following three loops, which accomplish the same thing.

```
1.  for I := 1 to N do
        for J := 1 to N do
            A [I,J] := (I div J) * (J div I);

2.  for I := 1 to N do
        for J := 1 to N do
            if I = J then A [I,J] := 0.0
            else A [I,J] := 1.0

3.  for I := 1 to N do
    begin
        for J := 1 to N do
            A [I,J] := 0.0;
        A [I,I] := 1.0
    end;
```

(a) What do the loops do?
(b) Which reads the most clearly?
(c) Which is the most efficient? (Consider the number of operations that must be performed in each loop, as well as the number of times the loop executes.)

6. Suggest suitable variable names for the following (see Exercise 1).
(a) A procedure to compute the amount of hay eaten by one horse in a week.
(b) A function to compute the cost for all food consumed by a single horse in a week.
(c) A procedure to compute the monthly bill for an owner.
(d) A record type for data on one horse.
(e) A variable of the type in (d).
(f) A variable to record whether a bill has been paid.
(g) A package containing all the stable procedures.
(h) The coordinates of a point on the cartesian plane.
(i) Vertices of a triangle, a square, and a parallelogram.

7. If you were to read quickly through an unfamiliar program, what would you think the following variable names designate? Which are ambiguous?
   (a) `Flag`
   (b) `X, Y, Z`
   (c) `A, B, C`
   (d) `Temp`
   (e) `Ave`
   (f) `TxDllrs`
   (g) `Num5`
   (h) `InFile, OutFile`

8. One suggestion for the use of uppercase and lowercase in identifiers is:
   1) use lowercase for keywords such as `begin, end` and `if`;
   2) use uppercase for user-defined variables and types; and,
   3) use uppercase and lowercase for comments.

   (a) Give pros and cons for these suggestions.
   (b) Defend the convention you use (or intend to use) when writing programs.

9. When analyzing algorithms, certain integer sums often appear. Use induction to prove the following equalities. (If you don't know how to do a proof by induction, consult one of the references suggested at the end of the chapter, or ask your instructor for help.)
   (a) $1 + 2 + \cdots + n = n(n+1)/2$
   (b) $1^2 + 2^2 + \cdots + n^2 = n(n+1)(2n+2)/6$
   (c) $2^0 + 2^1 + \cdots + 2^n = 2^{n+1} - 1$
   (d) $1/2^0 + 1/2^1 + \cdots + 1/2^n = 2 - 1/2^n = (1 - (1/2)^{n+1})/(1 - 1/2)$
   (e) $a^0 + a^1 + \cdots + a^n = (1 - a^{n+1})(1 - a) \ (a > 0)$

10. Rules of big O arithmetic include the following:
    $$O(N) + c = O(N) \qquad (c \text{ is a constant})$$
    $$O(cN) = O(N) \qquad (c \text{ is a constant})$$
    $$O(N) + O(M) = O(M) + O(N)$$
    $$O(N) + O(M) = O(N) \qquad (M \leq N)$$
    Given these rules, replace the "?" with $<, >$ or $=$.
    (a) $O(5) \ ? \ O(23)$
    (b) $O(N + 4) \ ? \ O(N - 1512)$
    (c) $O(\lg N) \ ? \ O(N)$
    (d) $O(N^2 + N) \ ? \ O(N^3)$
    (e) $O(N \lg N + N^3) \ ? \ O(2^N)$
    (f) $O(N) + O(\lg 2^N) \ ? \ O(N)$
    (g) $O(2^N) \ ? \ O(5^N)$
    (h) $O(\lg N) \ ? \ O(\log_{10} N)$
    (Note: (f) and (g) require conversion to a common base.)

SUGGESTIONS FOR FURTHER STUDY

Note: Complete bibliographical references, listed by author, are at the back of the book. In the notes that follow, references are cited by author and year of publication.

The reader should be warned that analyzing algorithms and proving correctness may require considerable knowledge of discrete mathematics and methods of proof, especially proof by induction.

Although Baase (1978) is written for a third or later course in computer science, the introductory chapter, "Data Structures and Mathematical Background," provides an excellent summary of notation and essential combinatorial methods at an elementary level. Johnsonbaugh (1984) also presents order arithmetic and induction in a clear manner. The three volumes of Knuth (1973a, 1973b, and 1981) also detail the mathematics necessary for algorithmic analysis.

Communicating and reading proofs plague almost any student of mathematics, and those in related fields such as the natural sciences or computer science often have even more difficulty. Solow (1982) believes proof methods can be taught systematically so a student can read, understand, and create both formal and informal proofs. A student who finds and reads this small book early in his or her educational career will be fortunate indeed.

An entire issue of *Computing Surveys,* edited by Kernighan and Plauger (1974), is concerned with programming style. Due to the fact that the first Pascal compiler had been available for only three years at that time, the articles focus on Fortran, PL/I and occasionally on Algol-60. Thus, some of the material may seem dated, but the spirit of what comprises good programming style remains applicable. Included is an extensive bibliography on the development of both good programming style and languages to support it.

(Any serious student of computer science should become familiar with *Computing Surveys,* which has students as a primary intended readership, and which has long been the most popular of the optional publications of the Association for Computing Machinery.)

Ledgard (1986) has collected a more recent series of essays to aid the novice in becoming a professional programmer. He considers clear, readable style, documentation, use of procedures, program structure, and naming conventions. There are also three sections discussing the idiosyncracies of Pascal, which should be a godsend to Pascal programmers, and a long annotated program intended as an example of good programming practices.

One of the landmarks in the systematic study of program structure is Dijkstra (1968), which was published as a letter to the editor, with the title "Go To Statement Considered Harmful." As a result, structured programming has often wrongly been equated with "goto-less programming." However, Dijkstra's letter does not use the term "structured programming," and it should be noted that the title was supplied by the Letters Editor, not Dijkstra.

Knuth (1974) defends the use of judiciously chosen goto's, when program clarity and/or efficiency results.

CHAPTER 2

ARRAYS AND RECORDS

2.1 INTRODUCTION: THE ABSTRACT DATA TYPE (ADT) APPROACH

The first data type we shall study is the array because arrays are found in essentially all programming languages and they are presumably the most familiar to you of the data types we shall consider.

We approach the array the way we shall approach all the other data types: as an *abstract data type* (ADT). The intent of the ADT approach is to clarify the concept and the usefulness of a data type by concentrating on *what it is and what one can do with it,* which is totally independent of *how it is implemented.* This approach, which was developed in theoretical terms in the 1960s and early 1970s, has recently come into wide acceptance as its practical benefits have been demonstrated. It has also been shown that once the idea is accepted, students have no difficulty with the approach. Indeed, understanding is both speeded and improved with its use.

In keeping with the intent of the approach, the pattern for our study of every ADT—modified only to take occasional advantage of your prior experience with some of the data types—will consist of the following:

1. A definition of the abstract data type, in the form that will be described shortly.
2. Examples of its usefulness, which will also clarify the definition as needed.
3. A discussion of one or more possible implementations. In the early chapters there may be only one or two implementations for an ADT, with other possibilities appearing in later chapters.

Definition: *An* ADT *is a collection of data objects, together with a set of operations.*

In specifying an ADT, we keep the description of the data objects as abstract as possible. The key idea is the centrality of a precise definition of the *operations*. In fact, we shall see that it is the operations that characterize an ADT. This point of view is not usually emphasized in a first course in computer science and may be new to you. We shall return to the issue repeatedly.

A note on terminology is necessary at this point. The definitions of the terms *data type, data structure,* and *abstract data type* have not completely stabilized. We shall use the term "ADT" to mean the array, record, set, string, stack, queue, linked list, tree or graph, in the abstract, as characterized by the operations for manipulating the data objects in the ADT. "Data type" will mostly be reserved for its meaning in Pascal. "Data structure," which has been the conventional term in the field, will be used occasionally, to mean a particular implementation of an ADT.

2.2 THE ADT ARRAY

Let us see the ADT approach in action, as applied to the *array*.

Definition: *An* array *is a collection of elements, an index set, an operation called* Store *that defines a (partial) mapping from the index set to the elements, and an operation called* Retrieve *that utilizes that mapping.*

A member of the index set for an array may be a single index, such as 11, or an n-tuple of indices, such as (17, 4). In this book we generally speak of "the index" to mean as many indices as there are, whether that be one or many.

The elements must all be of the same type, but are otherwise completely abstract prior to implementation. In this book we will deal with arrays of integers, reals, booleans, characters, records, and linked lists, among others.

Each of the one or more indices of an array has a specified set of permissible values. The set of values is most commonly a subset of the integers, but for a Pascal array it may be any ordinal type.

The Store operation takes the name of an array, a value for its index, and an element value. It defines a mapping from the index value to the element value.

Thus, an array is a mapping, in the ordinary mathematical sense, but the mapping is partial until such time as a Store has been executed for each value of the index set.

A Store is most frequently accomplished, in programming terms, by an assignment statement or an input operation, in which we write the name of the array followed by square brackets (or parentheses, in some languages) enclosing expressions that give values for the indices. Thus, if A is an array of reals with three integer indices, then in Pascal notation

```
A[2, 7, 4] := 16.7
```

establishes a mapping from the index value (2, 7, 4) to the element value 16.7.

The mapping may be many-to-one: the index value (1, 8, 1), or any other permissible index, might also map to the element value 16.7.

The index-to-element correspondence defined by a Store operation stays in effect so long as the array exists, but may be changed by a subsequent Store.

The Retrieve operation takes the name of an array and an index value, and returns the element value most recently Stored in that array for that index value. If a Retrieve is attempted with an index value for which no Store has been executed within the existence of the array, the Retrieve operation should return an error indication. Some operating systems do so.

The Retrieve is most commonly accomplished by writing the name of the array together with brackets enclosing index expressions. This may be done anywhere the name of a variable is permitted, such as the right-hand side of an assignment statement or in the list of an output statement.

This definition is incomplete in that it does not explicitly say what happens if a Retrieve is attempted with an index value for which no prior Store has been performed. In programming terms, we would like an error indication. Some systems provide this. We shall generally omit this detail, important as it is, because enforcement of it cannot usually be assumed. It is, rather, the responsibility of the programmer.

For completeness we should define an operation called Create, which brings the array into existence. In Pascal programming terms, this is accomplished for an array by declarations, and is not under programmer control at execution time. This being the case, we shall not emphasize the Create operation. (Things will be different when we get to ADTs implemented with dynamic storage, a subject that is introduced in Chapter 6.)

Let us now see if we can relate the foregoing, somewhat abstract discussion, to the way arrays are usually presented in a first programming course.

The conventional way to picture an array is as a linear sequence, like the following picture of a one-dimensional array having ten elements indexed by the integers from one to ten.

Element values:			16.7							
Index values:	1	2	3	4	5	6	7	8	9	10

The array A

A value is shown for A[3], assuming that the assignment statement

```
A[3] := 16.7
```

has been executed, but not for any of the others. The value of an array element is undefined until something has been stored in it.

If you know the rudiments of how computers work at the machine level, you may be objecting to the earlier definition of an array. Everybody knows, you might be saying, that an array is a way of assigning elements to consecutive storage locations for fast and easy access. Why not just say so?

Well, the answer is yes and no. It is certainly true that the sequential storage assignment technique is commonly used and that many working programmers never realize that there is any other way to implement an array. However, as you deepen your understanding of computer science, it is essential that you take a more abstract point of view.

The word "abstract" carries a number of meanings in ordinary usage, among them "difficult to understand" and "insufficiently factual." Quite contrary to either of these, we intend the meaning to be "disassociated from any specific instance." Indeed, one of the goals of abstraction is precisely to make a topic *easier* to understand, by concentrating on certain aspects and ignoring others. The Latin root of the word "abstract" means "to draw away." We take that in the sense of "standing back" from the details, so as to see the concept more clearly. By way of analogy, if you are in the right position to study the shape of the branches of a tree, you are in a poor position to study either the shape of its leaves or the shape of the mountain on which it is growing. We pick a level of abstraction that is appropriate to our work at a given time.

Consider an example. From your programming experience you have at least an intuitive notion of what an integer is—a signed whole number. If you have studied the appropriate mathematics, your understanding of the characteristics of the integers is, of course, more precise than that. But either way, you may not have given much thought to the distinction between what an integer *is* and how it is *represented*. It might surprise you to learn that in one widely used family of computers integers may be represented in any one of *five* quite different ways, and converting among them takes some effort. And even if we think only of the representation as a binary number, which is available in essentially all machines and is the only form in some, the computer designer must still choose among three ways of representing negative numbers.

Similarly with arrays. You have done your programming on the basis of an intuitive notion of what an array is—and your notion was not wrong, just too narrow. Your increasing skills will lead you into applications where the usual way of implementing a particular ADT may be too slow or require too much storage to permit the application to be done effectively. Then you need to know what the other possibilities are, what their advantages and disadvantages are in various contexts, and how to choose among them. And if you are ever going to write a compiler or any other kind of software that works below the level of a procedural language like Pascal, you need to know how arrays can be represented and manipulated "underneath" the Pascal level.

This then is the heart of the abstract data type approach: separate the *semantics* (the meaning) from the *implementation*.

2.3 STORAGE ALLOCATION FOR SEQUENTIAL REPRESENTATION OF ARRAYS

We now take up the most common implementation of arrays, which is indeed based on assigning elements to sequential storage locations. The advantages of sequential storage are simplicity, economy of storage if all or most of the locations are used, and the *random access* feature, meaning that any location can be accessed in the same time as any other. The disadvantage of sequential storage is that it wastes storage space if only a small fraction of the locations are used. Other methods (linked lists, in particular) will be studied in later chapters when the techniques needed for them have been presented, and at that time their advantages and disadvantages will be discussed.

The process that a compiler or other language processor goes through in setting up sequential storage for an array consists of two parts. First, the compiler must decide where the storage for the array starts, as an address in the computer's main storage. When and how this is done is something of a long story since there are many possible variations. In Pascal, it is done at the time that the program block in which the array is declared becomes active. That could be at the time the program is loaded, for a global array, or could be at the beginning of invocation of a procedure for a local array.[1] We shall not be concerned about this problem, but shall look only at the second issue: relative to the address of the first element, where are the others to be found?

This question is answered by an *index function,* also called a *storage allocation function*. This is a formula that converts the value of the index or indices of an array to an address. For example, suppose we are working with the array declared by

```
var
   X: array [0..99] of real;
```

Let us also suppose that we have a computer in which a real number takes one storage location. Then, if the compiler (or other software) selects storage location 1200 for the first element of the array, the 100 elements of the array would be stored in locations 1200, 1201, . . ., 1299. If we adopt the notation $Loc(X)$ for the location at which X is stored and if i is the value of the index for an element, then we have the equation:

$$Loc(X[i]) = Loc(X[0]) + i$$

As a picture, for $Loc(X[0]) = 1200$

1200	1201	1202	1203	1204	1205	1206
X[0]	X[1]	X[2]	X[3]	X[4]	X[5]	X[6]

This, of course, is valid only if the lower bound of the array is zero. For the more general case where the lower and upper array bounds are L and $U,$ the index function is

$$Loc(X[i]) = Loc(X[L]) + i - L$$

For example, if $L = 7, Loc(X[L]) = 1200,$ and $i = 11,$ then

$$Loc(X[11]) = Loc(X[7]) + 11 - 7 = 1200 + 11 - 7 = 1204$$

1200	1201	1202	1203	1204	1205	1206
X[7]	X[8]	X[9]	X[10]	X[11]	X[12]	X[13]

[1] The word "procedure" will be used in this kind of context to mean either a Pascal procedure or a Pascal function, since the distinction between the two is immaterial for the purposes of this discussion.

Finally, suppose that each array element requires m units of storage. In a machine in which the fundamental unit of storage is the byte (eight bits), this might be four bytes for a real number, two for an integer, or some large number for a complicated record. Or, in a machine in which the smallest addressable unit of storage is one word of 32 bits, an integer might require one word and a real number might require two. In any event, the equation now is

$$Loc(X[i]) = Loc(X[L]) + (i - L) m$$

For example, if $L = 5$, $Loc(X[5]) = 1200$, $i = 8$, and $m = 4$, we have

$$Loc(X[8]) = Loc(x[5]) + (8 - 5) * 4 = 1200 + 3 * 4 = 1212$$

1200	1204	1208	1212	1216	1220	1224
X[5]	X[6]	X[7]	X[8]	X[9]	X[10]	X[11]

For simplicity, in the remainder of this section we shall assume that all lower bounds are zero and that an array element requires one storage location. We will do this because we have seen that handling the more general cases involves only simple modifications of the formulas for the index functions.

For arrays of more than one dimension, the task becomes only a little more complex. We can still lay out the elements sequentially after the location chosen for the first element, but now we must deal with the problem of converting from the values of several indices (and their corresponding bounds) to a sequential layout. Let us consider the case of a two-dimensional array.

Suppose the declaration is

```
var
    X: array [0..m, 0..n] of element-type
```

The usual procedure is to assign the elements of the first row to sequential locations, followed by the elements of the second row, and so forth. The index function can be derived informally, as follows. The elements of the first row are assigned to sequential locations. Relative to the address of the first element, these will be 0, 1, . . ., n. Now the first element of the second row will follow immediately, which is location $n + 1$. The elements of the second row are therefore in locations $n + 1, n + 2, . . ., n + 1 + n$. The first element in the third row goes in $n + 1 + n + 1$, which can be written $2(n + 1)$. The pattern is simply to multiply the first index by $n + 1$ and add the second index; $n + 1$ is, of course, the number of elements in a row. As an equation for the index function we have

$$Loc(X[i, j]) = Loc(X[0, 0]) + i (n + 1) + j$$

Suppose $m = 1$ (two rows), $n = 4$ (five columns), and $Loc(X[0, 0]) = 1200$. Then the mapping from the two-dimensional index form to a one- dimensional index function can be visualized this way:

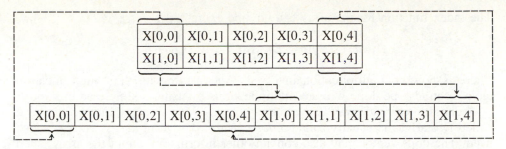

This method of allocating the elements is called *row-major* order because all of the elements of the first row are allocated before any of the elements of the second row, and so on. It is also called *lexicographic* order because it places the indices of the elements into the sequence in which they would appear if sorted into increasing sequence. For example, suppose the declaration is

```
var
   X : array [0..2, 0..3] of integer;
```

The elements of this array, in row-major order, would be assigned in the sequence: X[0, 0], X[0, 1], X[0, 2], X[0, 3], X[1, 0], X[1, 1], X[1, 2], X[1, 3], X[2, 0], X[2, 1], X[2, 2], X[2, 3]. If you study the index pairs in this listing, you will see that, considered as two-digit numbers, they are listed in increasing sequence; hence, the term lexicographic order.

Another way of describing row-major allocation is to note that as we move from one element's storage location to the next, it is the *rightmost* index that varies most rapidly. In a few languages, most notably Fortran, *column-major* order is used, in which the *leftmost* index varies most rapidly.

Looking back at the formula for the index function for a two-dimensional array, we see that it involves multiplying the first index by the number of elements in a row and adding the second index. This is readily enough done, and in one of the programs at the end of the chapter we shall see such a function in action. But suppose we are working with a machine that does not have a built-in multiply instruction? (And there *are* such machines, even at this late date. Many microprocessors do not have built-in multiply or divide instructions.) Naturally, the subroutine libraries for such machines provide routines to do multiplication, but such a routine could take much longer to execute than the computation we have to do with the element once we find it. There must be an answer, especially since this problem has existed since the earliest days on computers, when even what were then the large machines did not always have a divide instruction, and multiplication could be terribly slow.

The answer is to set up a separate one-dimensional array containing the multiplication table for the product $i * (n + 1)$. Suppose we have an array where the row numbers (the first index) run from 0 to 5, and there are eight elements in a row. Then we set up an array, call it D, with the following elements:

```
D[0] = 0            D[3] = 24
D[1] = 8            D[4] = 32
D[2] = 16           D[5] = 40
```

The index function for the array can now be expressed as

$$Loc(X[i, j]) = Loc(X[0, 0]) + D[i] + j$$

There is now no multiplication involved. And, setting up the "multiplication table" can also be done without multiplications by using a simple adding loop.

A one-dimensional array is the underlying ADT for a vector and the array we called D, earlier, is usually called a *dope vector*. The term *access vector* is also used. The dope vector may also contain other information about the array, such as the upper and lower bounds, to permit run-time checking for validity of index values.

Arrays of more than two dimensions lead to storage allocation functions that are slightly more complex, but which can be derived and processed in ways entirely analogous to what we have already done.

2.4 NON-RECTANGULAR MATRICES

Some computer applications lead to two-dimensional arrays that are too large to fit in storage, but in which many or even most of the elements are zero. (In mathematical terminology we speak of a *matrix,* which is implemented with a two-dimensional array.) If the non-zero elements occur in a regular pattern, it is often possible to store them in a one-dimensional array and devise a specialized index function to convert from the two-index form that is natural and convenient for the application, to the one-index form in which we actually store the non-zero elements. Let us look at two representative examples.

Figure 2.1 shows, in schematic form, a *lower triangular* matrix and a *tri-diagonal* matrix. In a lower triangular matrix, the non-zero entries occur only on or below the main diagonal; in a tri-diagonal matrix they occur on the main diagonal and on the diagonals above and below it.

For a simple example of how a triangular matrix can arise, consider a computation involving the distances between pairs of cities. For N cities we can set up an N by N matrix in which the entry in row i and column j is the distance from city i to city j. But this is also the distance from city j to city i, so there is no need to store the same value in matrix row j, column i.[2] Storing the distance only once results in a triangular matrix. A little more space could also be saved by not storing the diagonal elements, because the distance from a city to itself is always zero.

If we store a triangular matrix in a regular two- dimensional array, we waste about half the space storing elements that are always zero (and are never used). In the case of a tri-diagonal matrix we waste nearly all the space. In many applications in which such matrices arise, the full matrix (including the zeros) would be very much too large to fit in storage, and we have no choice but to find an alternative.

---

[2]This seemingly self-evident statement is not always true in related problems of this type. If for simple distance we substitute airline flying time, then the flying time between two cities can be quite different because of prevailing wind patterns.

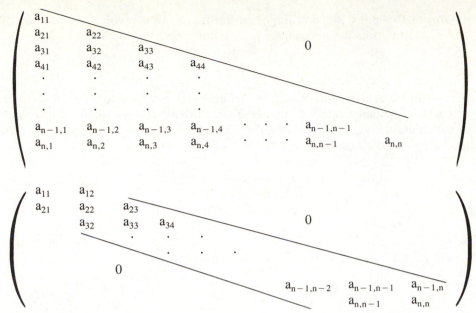

FIGURE 2.1
Lower triangular and tri-diagonal matrices.

Fortunately, it is not hard to do so. Looking first at the lower triangular matrix, let us call the row index r and the column index c. Further, let us assume that the lower bound on each index is 1, since the algebra is a bit simpler that way. Our goal is to map these indices onto the integers beginning with 1, so that we can assign each element of our lower triangular array to an element in a one-dimensional array. Thus, if t_{rc} is an element of the lower triangular array and L is the one-dimensional (or linear) array in which we actually wish to store these elements, then t_{11} goes in L[1], t_{21} goes in L[2], t_{22} goes in L[3], t_{31} goes in L[4], and so forth.

With the numbering we have chosen (indices starting at 1), it is obvious that row r contains r elements, so the number of elements preceding the first element in row r is $1 + 2 + \ldots + r - 1$. The sum of this familiar series is $r \times (r - 1) / 2$. Therefore the first element in row r must be in location $r \times (r - 1) / 2 + 1$, and the cth element in row r is in location $r * (r - 1) / 2 + c$. This is the index function we seek. If the multiplication involved is a problem, we can set up a dope vector containing 0, 1, 3, 6, 10, and so forth, indexed by the row number. Setting up this dope vector may also be done with a simple loop, without multiplication.

The index function for the tri-diagonal case could be found in a similar informal way, but let us instead see how it can be derived formally. If all indices begin at 1 and the rows of the tri-diagonal matrix T are stored in consecutive locations of the linear array L, then t_{11} goes in L[1], t_{12} goes in L[2], t_{21} goes in L[3], and so on. We begin by making the assumption that, because the number of elements in a row is always three except for the first and last rows, the *form* of the index function might be linear, i.e., not involve the product of *r* and *c*. Writing this assumption as an equation, we have

$$I = r x + c y + z$$

where *r* and *c* are the indices of the tri-diagonal matrix and *x, y,* and *z* are unknowns to be determined. In this case (and it isn't always so simple) we can just substitute the values of the first three elements, leading to a system of three simultaneous equations, as follows.

$$x + y + z = 0 + Loc(X[1,1])$$
$$x + 2y + z = 1 + Loc(X[1,1])$$
$$2x + y + z = 2 + Loc(X[1,1])$$

The solution is $x = 2$, $y = 1$, and $z = -3$, so the index function for storing the elements of the tri-diagonal array in a linear array is

$$Loc(X[r, c]) = Loc(X[1, 1]) + 2r + c - 3$$

Many other types of specialized arrays arise in practice, typically where storage limitations make it mandatory to find a way to avoid storing meaningless zeros. The techniques studied in this section, which amount to storing parts of a multidimensional array in a linear array, are often useful.

2.5 THE ADT APPROACH TO ARRAYS AGAIN

We began by defining an array in a way that was probably unfamiliar to most readers, in terms of a mapping from an index set to an element set. Let us see how that functional approach could pay off.

Suppose we have programmed an application that makes heavy use of a square array and that we have found that the size of the array must be increased to a size that is beyond the storage capacity of our computer. Suppose further, that in seeking a way out of the impasse, we realize that the array has some special form, such as lower triangular or any of many others, that does not require the storage of every element. By now we know how to store such an array in a linear array, with an index function to convert from row and column number to a single index for a linear array. But do we also have to go back and completely reprogram the application? Perhaps not.

Assume that the two-dimensional array was named `A`. We set up a linear array, named `ALinear`, large enough to hold all the elements in whatever specialized form we can employ. We now set up a *function* named A that takes two arguments, converts their values to an index value in `ALinear`, and returns the value associated with that index. Finally, we use an editor to change all instances of `A[I, J]` to `A(I, J)`, assuming Pascal syntax. The array reference has become a function call, and the program works unchanged.

Well, almost. What we have implemented is the `Retrieve` operation of the array ADT. Writing `A(I, J)`, which is now a function call, on the left side of an assignment statement will surely not result in a `Store`, but rather in a compiler error message. This brings out the distinction between what a variable means when written on the right side of an assignment (a `Retrieve`), versus what it means written on the left (a `Store`).

To implement the `Store` for our hypothetical case, we would need a procedure, called something like `StoreA`, which would take two indices and an element value, and place the value in the correct position in the linear array.

In certain rare cases the ADT approach may be used to circumvent the need for any array storage. The *Hilbert matrix*, for example, has elements that are defined as $1 / (R + C - 1)$, where R and C are row and column numbers starting at 1. There would be no need for a `Store` operation in this case, and the `Retrieve` could be handled by the following simple function.

```
function Hilbert (R, C: integer): real;
begin
    Hilbert := 1.0 / (R + C - 1.0)
end;
```

In a great many programming tasks, it is perfectly adequate to think of an array in terms of sequential storage using only the features provided by ordinary programming languages. In other cases, however, the serious student of computer science needs a broader viewpoint, and the functional or mapping view of the array ADT takes on considerable importance.

2.6 RECORDS

A record, in ADT terms, is a collection of *fields*, each identified by a field name, together with the operations of `Store` and `Retrieve`. Each of the fields in a record may be any ADT available; the fields are not all required to be of the same type. The field names are formed by following the same rules as for any other identifiers. There is no analogy with the ordinal type requirement of indices of arrays. A record has a name, which applies to the entire collection of fields.

Arrays and records are similar in that they both refer to a collection of data by a single name, and in that they are both built on `Store` and `Retrieve` operations. They are different in that the elements of an array must all be of the same type whereas there is no such requirement on the fields of a record, and in the differences between an index and a field name. The similarities are strong enough that we shall not restate the operations in record terms.

Pascal provides the record type, as do some other languages, such as PL/I and C. There is no practical way to implement the record ADT in a language that does not provide it, so we shall not present an implementation. What would be required, if it were possible, would be to take any collection of diverse ADTs available to us, and to give the entire collection a single name by which the assemblage could be manipulated. Furthermore, it would be necessary to be able to define such a collection and then use it as a component in other ADTs. We shall make heavy use, for example, of arrays in which the elements are records.

With arrays, we saw that the conventional way to implement the ADT at the machine level (in the absence of strong reasons to do otherwise) was with sequential storage locations for the elements. With records, the usual method is also to assign the fields to sequential locations. Machine architecture influences the details heavily, in particular the question of the smallest individually addressable unit of storage. We shall not pursue this topic, which would require more background in machine-language programming than you are assumed to have, and which would take us further into compiler construction complexities than is reasonable in a second course.

You are assumed to have seen the Pascal features for defining and using records in your previous study and, as usual, we shall not review the Pascal syntax. However, one Pascal feature that is often omitted in a first course should be mentioned: the variant record, more precisely called a record variant.

A variant record in Pascal has a *fixed part,* which may be empty, together with a *variant part* that can take any of the forms that we specify in the record type definition. Here is an example. In this case the fixed part is empty.

```
type
    FormOfRep = (Rectangular, Polar);

    Complex = record
                case Form: FormOfRep of
                Rectangular: (X, Y: real);
                Polar: (R, Theta: real)
            end;
```

In this case, `Form` is the *tag* of the variant record. Because `FormOfRep` is defined as an enumerated type (it could have been any ordinal type), `Form` can take on only the values `Rectangular` and `Polar`. If the tag has the value `Rectangular`, then the record consists of two real fields named `X` and `Y`; if it has the value `Polar`, the record consists of two real fields named `R` and `Theta`. There is no requirement that the variants have the same structure, as with the two real fields in this example, or that the total storage required be the same in every case.

No use may be made of a variant part of a record variable until a value has been given to the tag field. After the tag field has a value, it is as though the record consists only of the definition given for that tag value. The tag value, and therefore the effective record definition, may change during program execution.

Here is a procedure that uses a record as we have just defined it. The purpose is to permit a user to store complex numbers in the most convenient form.

```
procedure ReadCpx (var Z: Complex);
var
    FormCode: char;
    A, B: real;
```

```
begin
   ReadLn (FormCode, A, B);
   if FormCode = 'R' then
   begin
      Z.Form := Rectangular;
      Z.X := A;
      Z.Y := B
   end
   else if FormCode = 'P' then
   begin
      Z.Form := Polar;
      Z.R := A;
      Z.Theta := B
   end
   else
      WriteLn ('bad data')
end;
```

If Z is a variable declared to be of the user-defined type `Complex`, then we could write

```
ReadCpx (Z)
```

In this case, depending on the data, the two real input values would be interpreted either as the real and imaginary part of a complex number represented in rectangular form, or as the magnitude and angle of a complex number represented in polar form. At different times during the execution of a program using such a variable, Z could hold a complex number in either form.

The tag field is used to determine which variant is in effect at any given time, but it may also be used as a value in its own right. For example, we might wish to add two complex numbers represented this way. To do so, we need to be able to determine which form the operands have. On the assumption that we want the result to be in rectangular form, the following procedure does the job.

```
procedure AddCpxRect (Z1, Z2: Complex; var ZSum: Complex);
{ Add two complex numbers, each of which may be represented
  in either rectangular or polar form, and produce their
  complex sum in rectangular form. }

var
   X1, Y1, X2, Y2: real;
begin
   if Z1.Form = Rectangular then
   begin
      X1 := Z1.X;
      Y1 := Z1.Y
   end
   else
   begin
      X1 := Z1.R * Cos (Z1.Theta);
      Y1 := Z1.R * Sin (Z1.Theta)
   end;
```

(Continued)

(Continued)

```
if Z2.Form = Rectangular then
begin
   X2 := Z2.X;
   Y2 := Z2.Y
end
else
begin
   X2 := Z2.R * Cos (Z2.Theta);
   Y2 := Z2.R * Sin (Z2.Theta)
end;

ZSum.Form := Rectangular;
ZSum.X := X1 + X2;
ZSum.Y := Y1 + Y2
```

```
end;
```

Exercise 12 at the end of this chapter asks you to modify this procedure so that it produces the sum in polar form if both operands are polar, and *coerces* a polar number to rectangular only if the other operand is rectangular.

Storage allocation for variant records is complicated. The most straightforward approach is to set aside as much storage as is required for the longest variant. The details are far beyond the scope of this book.

2.7 APPLICATION: LETTER-SEQUENCE FREQUENCIES AND A PERFORMANCE PROBLEM

Let us now apply some of the ideas we have discussed in this chapter. We shall use the application to explore some of the ideas of software engineering.

One software engineering issue particularly applicable at this time is the adequacy of the user requirements definition, and what we might do if—as commonly happens— their initial form is not suitable for our purposes. A second important issue is managing the fundamental resources of storage space and program execution time, one of the fundamental tasks of the software engineer. We shall also take the opportunity to discuss the speed issue.

Our application here is to produce a table of the most frequently occurring two-letter sequences in a body of text read as input. This might be useful in a military intelligence operation—for example, in scanning radio traffic for messages of possible interest. As the results shown at the end of the chapter will suggest, useful guesses can be made about the text based only on the results that our program will produce.

2.8 THE USER REQUIREMENTS STATEMENT

Here is a description of the task as we might get it from the user.

Given a file of text in the language one might find in a military dispatch or a business communication, we are to produce a table showing the frequency of occurrence of sequences of two adjacent letters. The text contains both uppercase and lowercase letters, but we are not to distinguish between them, as we are to display the frequencies only in upper-case form. Furthermore, we are not to display all sequences, but only those that exceed 1% of the total number of sequences. The output is also to be arranged in decreasing order of frequency. Finally, the program must begin to display the results on the screen of a typical microcomputer within a second or two of reading the last character of the text.

What do you think of that paragraph, considered as a requirements definition? Is it complete? Is it precise? Well, hardly. The first form in which a user presents the needs for a program will seldom be complete or precise. Part of the job of the software engineer is to ask the questions that will lead to a precise statement of what the program must do—the functional specifications.

Here are some of the questions that you might ask. The user's responses are in parentheses.

1. What is the size of the text file, which we need to know to set up fields large enough to hold the maximum counts? (On the order of a few typewritten pages, never more than ten.)

2. What should I do if the input contains *no* two-letter sequences? (Tell me so.)

3. What is the definition of a letter sequence and, in particular, do you want counts of two-letter sequences extending across the break between words? (A letter sequence is two contiguous letters; no. Thus, the two-letter sequences in the words THE CAT would be TH, HE, CA, and AT; EC in this text is not a letter sequence by this definition.)

4. Is the text one continuous stream, or is it broken into lines? And if it is broken into lines, does a word ever continue across the End-Of-Line (EOLN) mark? (It is broken into lines; words never continue across the line break.)

5. May we assume that the text consists only of correctly spelled English words, and that certain combinations—QQ, for example—never occur? (You may not assume that.)

6. Could that 1% figure ever change, or should we make it an input parameter? (It could change, but not often enough to justify entering it every time the program is run.)

7. Can you be more precise about that phrase "within a second or two"? (No, I can't. It's something like that, but otherwise I'll just have to try out your program and see if it's fast enough.)

This is not a complete list. In a certain sense no specification can ever be complete, to the extent of saying what should be done in literally *every* circumstance that could ever occur. We haven't asked, for example, about diacritical marks (umlauts in German and tildes in Spanish, for example), or whether there might ever be an extended alphabet with more than the 26 letters of the English alphabet, or whether we are required to detect letter sequences in subscripts. In some applications it might be necessary to get precise answers to many questions like these, which could be a major fraction of the total effort in developing the program. For our purposes here, we shall assume that what we have done is enough for our example.

The highly unsatisfying answer to Question 7 is the kind of thing that will sometimes happen. Your programming assignments up to now have, for the most part, been carefully designed by your instructors *not* to have any loose ends of this sort—or so he or she hopes. In the so-called real world, things aren't always like that, and a design process that responds gracefully to such uncertainties is one of the things we seek.

2.9 THE FUNCTIONAL SPECIFICATION

A functional specification for this task might be as follows.

Read text from a file that may or may not contain *two-letter sequences*. A letter sequence is two adjacent letters of the English alphabet, with uppercase and lowercase not distinguished. A sequence cannot extend across a blank or across the end of line. If the text contains no sequences, report that fact and do nothing else.

If the number of letter sequences is non-zero, produce a table showing the most frequent letter sequences, in decreasing order of frequency, together with the percentage that each sequence represents of the total number of sequences. Print a sequence and its frequency only if the frequency exceeds a threshold value, taken to be 1%. After the table of frequencies has been printed, print a line showing what percentage of the total number of sequences those in the table represent. The exact format of the table is not critical, but it should be easy to read. The table must begin printing within 1–2 seconds of the completion of reading the data.

This functional specification is, in part, a restatement of the user requirements but in a more precise form, and with some of the gaps in the user's description filled in. It does *not*, however, say anything at all about how the processing will be done. There is nothing whatsoever about ADTs or algorithms. This is intentional. *What* to do is the job of the functional specification; *how to do it* is the function of the design. Two software engineers working from these specifications might produce very different designs and implementations; a user inspecting two such implementations ideally should not be able to tell them apart just by watching the programs run and inspecting the output.

With this understanding of what the task is, we proceed to a program design.

2.10 THE PROGRAM DESIGN

1. The overall program operation is to read the text, identifying sequences in which both characters are letters and, when a letter sequence is found, to increment the corresponding entry in a two-dimensional table of letter-sequence

counts. At the same time, a total of the number of letter sequences is developed. When the end of the text is reached, we transfer the counts to a one-dimensional array, placing in each record the two letters of that sequence and a count of the number of times it occurred in the text. This table is sorted into decreasing sequence on the counts, and then those that exceed 1% of the total are printed.

The major actions here are easily parceled out to procedures, which will be named `Initialize`, `BuildCountTable`, `MoveTo-ResultTable`, `Sort`, and `Print`.

One way to depict the program design is with a *hierarchy chart,* as shown in Figure 2.2. The top box represents the action of the entire program. This is the main program, in Pascal terms. It calls procedures, shown as boxes on the second level of the hierarchy; these are the major procedures in the program. This top-down description can be carried as far as necessary and useful. We might or might not choose to show details such as the fact that the sort procedure calls an auxiliary procedure to swap two records. The operations shown on the third level in this case are parts of one procedure, not separate procedures. A graphical presentation of this type is often the quickest way to communicate the overall structure of a program design.

2. One ADT will be a two-dimensional array having 26 rows and 26 columns, indexed by the character sub-range `'A'..'Z'`. Each element of the array will be an integer giving the count of occurrences for one sequence.[3] In the

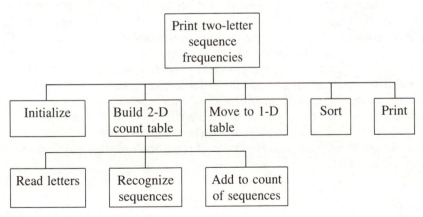

FIGURE 2.2
Hierarchy chart showing the top-level design of a program for letter-sequence frequency analysis.

---

[3]This presentation assumes that we are using a computer with ASCII coding of the characters. In an EBCDIC machine there are seven non-letters between I and J, and eight between R and S, for a total of 41.

microcomputer we plan to use, the maximum size for an integer is 32,767. A little arithmetic shows that even for extreme cases this is large enough for a text file corresponding to dozens of pages of typewritten text.[4] The elements of this table must be initialized to zero.

3. A second ADT will be a one-dimensional array of records, $26 \times 26 = 676$ of them. Each record will consist of two characters defining the letter sequence and an integer for the count for that sequence. Because of the way the program works, the initialization of this table is handled during loading, so no separate initialization is required.

With this design, the game has already been lost: it will be impossible to meet the speed requirement on the microcomputer chosen. Can you see the problem?

2.11 THE IMPLEMENTATION: A PROGRAM

The program shown in Figure 2.3 implements this design. The program description will be limited mostly to the issues studied in the chapter and a few features that might not be familiar to all readers.

The `program` declaration shows that the input comes from the pre-defined file `input` and that the output goes to the pre-defined file `output`. This will be the pattern in all programs in the book. Normally, if you do nothing to indicate otherwise, this means that input comes from the keyboard and output goes to the screen. It is not difficult to specify that the input should come from a disk file and/or that the output should go to disk, but because the details vary tremendously and involve features that are not standard Pascal, we shall simply use the pre-defined files and leave you to handle the more realistic situation of disk files.

The brief comment at the beginning of the program is intended to give an overall picture of what the program does: input, processing, and output. But *brief,* with no attempt to give all the details. We assume that a reader of the program has the functional specifications and is generally aware of what the application is, so we do not give a detailed analysis of the function and operation of the program. There are circumstances where a more complete description than this one would be appropriate. However, it is difficult to give hard-and-fast rules about program style.

---

[4]Making "back of the envelope" estimates of this type is a skill worth developing. Great accuracy is not required; in this case an estimate within 20% is probably good enough; sometimes an estimate that is within an order of magnitude is good enough.

Here is the argument for this case. The limit was said to be ten typewritten pages. A double-spaced typewritten page has about 250 words. A "word," in this context, is five characters; add one for the space between words, and we have $6 \times 250 = 1500$ characters per page. Ten pages makes it 15,000. A Pascal integer, in the machine to be used, can be as large as 32,767. We clearly have no problem, unless, of course, the user meant *single*-spaced pages, in which case we are dangerously close to our machine's maximum. It might be a good idea to check with the user on that. On the other hand, we would not be in trouble even then unless the text could contain a great many strings of the same character, which is presumably unlikely.

```
program LetterSequences1 (input, output);

{ First version of program to print frequencies of two-letter
  sequences: after reading text and building count table,
  move all sequence records to a one-dimensional array,
  sort them, then print those that exceed a 1% Threshold. }


const
    ResultTableSize = 676;    { 26 letters;  676 = 26 * 26 }
    Threshold = 1.0;

type
    NonNegInt = 0..MaxInt;
    Letter = 'A'..'Z';

    SeqCountArray = array [Letter, Letter] of NonNegInt;

    SeqRecord = record
                    Letter1, Letter2: Letter;
                    Count: NonNegInt
                end;

    ResultIndex = 1..ResultTableSize;

    ResultTableArray = array [ResultIndex] of SeqRecord;


var
    SeqCount: SeqCountArray;
    ResultTable: ResultTableArray;
    TotalSeqs: NonNegInt;


procedure Initialize (var SeqCount: SeqCountArray);
var
    I, J: Letter;
begin
    for I := 'A' to 'Z' do
        for J := 'A' to 'Z' do
            SeqCount[I, J] := 0
end;


procedure BuildCountTable (var SeqCount: SeqCountArray;
                           var TotalSeqs: NonNegInt);
{ Read text, build a two-dimensional table of letter-sequence
  counts, and compute total number of letter sequences. }

const
    Blank = ' ';
    ASCIICaseConvert = -32;   { Make this +64 for EBCDIC }
var
    PrevCh, CurrCh: char;
```

(Continued)

(Continued)

```
begin
    PrevCh := Blank;
    Read (CurrCh);
    TotalSeqs := 0;

    while not EOF do
    begin
        if CurrCh in ['a'..'z'] then
            CurrCh := Chr(Ord(CurrCh) + ASCIICaseConvert);
        if (PrevCh in ['A'..'Z']) and (CurrCh in ['A'..'Z']) then
        begin
            SeqCount[PrevCh, CurrCh] := SeqCount[PrevCh, CurrCh] + 1;
            TotalSeqs := TotalSeqs + 1
        end;
        PrevCh := CurrCh;
        Read (CurrCh)
    end
end;


procedure MoveToResultTable (var SeqCount: SeqCountArray;
                             var ResultTable: ResultTableArray);
var
    I, J: Letter;
    K: NonNegInt;
begin
    K := 1;
    for I := 'A' to 'Z' do
        for J := 'A' to 'Z' do
        begin
            ResultTable[K].Letter1 := I;
            ResultTable[K].Letter2 := J;
            ResultTable[K].Count := SeqCount[I, J];
            K := K + 1
        end
end;


procedure Swap (var X, Y: SeqRecord);
{ Exchange two records -- used by Sort procedure }
var
    Temp: SeqRecord;
begin
    Temp := X;
    X := Y;
    Y := Temp;
end;
```

```
procedure Sort (var ResultTable: ResultTableArray);
{ Sort records into descending sequence on Count. }
var
   I, J, Big: ResultIndex;
   Temp: SeqRecord;
begin
   for I := 1 to ResultTableSize - 1 do
   begin
      Big := I;
      for J := I + 1 to ResultTableSize do
         if ResultTable[J].Count > ResultTable[Big].Count then
            Big := J;
      Swap (ResultTable[I], ResultTable[Big])
   end;
end;




procedure Print (var ResultTable: ResultTableArray;
                 TotalSeqs: NonNegInt);
const
   NumColumns = 7;
var
   I: ResultIndex;
   SubTotal: NonNegInt;
begin
   WriteLn ('Letter-sequence frequencies in a sample of text.');
   WriteLn ('Only sequences representing more than ',
            Threshold:4:2, '% of total are shown.');
   WriteLn;

   SubTotal := 0;
   I := 1;
   while (ResultTable[I].Count / TotalSeqs)*100 > Threshold do
   begin
      Write (ResultTable[I].Letter1, ResultTable[I].Letter2,
             (ResultTable[I].Count / TotalSeqs)*100:5:2, '%  ');
      SubTotal := SubTotal + ResultTable[I].Count;
      if I mod NumColumns = 0 then
         WriteLn;
      I := I + 1
   end;

   WriteLn;
   WriteLn;
   WriteLn ('The sequences shown represent ',
            (SubTotal / TotalSeqs) * 100:5:2,
            '% of the total of ', TotalSeqs:1, ' sequences.')
end;
```
(Continued)

(Continued)

```
begin
    Initialize (SeqCount);
    BuildCountTable (SeqCount, TotalSeqs);
    if TotalSeqs = 0 then
        WriteLn ('Data contains no two-letter sequences')
    else
    begin
        MoveToResultTable (SeqCount, ResultTable);
        Sort (ResultTable);
        Print (ResultTable, TotalSeqs)
    end
end.
```

FIGURE 2.3

The first version of a program for letter-sequence frequency analysis.

The size of the table of results, a linear array, is $26^2 = 676$. This conceivably could change if we were to handle numbers as well as letters, or were required to process a different alphabet, so we put it in a `const` declaration. It is fairly clear that `Threshold` should be placed in a `const` declaration rather than being embedded as a constant in the program. An experienced programmer would automatically assume that the user will have a change of heart on that figure sooner or later. Actually, we will not stop to justify every use of a `const` declaration; *all* constants will be given names, with the exception of zero, one, and a very few others.

We see the definition of a two-dimensional array type to hold the sequence counts, indexed by a sub-range of the characters. We could easily program the conversion from a letter to an integer index, but because Pascal provides the convenience of using a letter as an index we may as well use it.

Next we have the definition of a simple record type consisting of two fields of the type `Letter,` and a count that is a non-negative integer (`NonNegInt`). For run-time checking, `ResultIndex` gives a name to the valid values of a variable. With this record type defined and named, it is now possible to define an array of such records.

Next come the declarations of the variables are terms of the types just defined, but without any information about array bounds, and so forth. This will be the usual pattern. All of these variables are global in the sense that they are *declared* outside of any procedure, but not one of them is ever *referenced* in a procedure in which it is not a parameter. They are declared here only to "anchor" the variables, so to speak, in a place where they will not cease to exist between procedure invocations (which they would do if declared in a procedure). But they will always be named as parameters in any procedure that uses them.

Now we have the procedures of the program, shown in the order in which they are invoked by the main program. Pascal does not require this order—all it asks is that a procedure be defined before it is used—but anything we can do to help the reader is a plus. A program of realistic size would be dozens or hundreds of pages long, and we would need some kind of index to find a given procedure.

The procedure `Initialize` is unremarkable.

`BuildCountTable` carries out the closely related functions of reading the text, deciding if two adjacent characters are both letters, and, if so, updating the count for that letter sequence and the count of total sequences.

Two constants are given names here, `Blank` and `ASCIICaseConvert`. The character "blank" is given a name simply to make the reading and understanding of the program simpler. `ASCIICaseConvert` is used to convert lowercase letters to uppercase. As the name indicates, this is the constant needed for the ASCII character representation used on the IBM Personal Computer with which most of the programs for this book were developed. The comment shows what would be needed for EBCDIC,[5] the other major character representation.

`PreviousCharacter` and `CurrentCharacter` would unquestionably be more descriptive names than the ones used in our program, `PrevCh` and `CurrCh`. However, the longer names would lead to statements that would not fit on one line, and would thus impair program readability. Such compromises are routine; making them is a matter of experience and, to a degree, personal taste.

The logic of determining if two adjacent characters are both letters is handled by initializing `PrevCh`, the left member of the sequence, to blank, then reading the first character into `CurrCh`. Naturally, the first time through the loop we will not find a letter sequence. After that, we always move the contents of `CurrCh` into `PrevCh` and then read another character into `CurrCh`. This means that we will execute a `Read` when the file pointer is on the `EOLN` mark, but that is what we want, because, in such a case, a blank is returned. This satisfies the requirement that words are not be considered to continue across lines.

The test for a lowercase letter is a Pascal set membership operation, but if you haven't seen Pascal's set operations before don't worry about it: the meaning is just what it looks like.

`MoveToResultTable` moves the sequences and their counts to a one-dimensional array for sorting and subsequent printing. Its operation is simple, but you should study the handling of indices and the specification of record fields carefully if anything here is new to you.

Note that `SeqCount` has been made a `var` parameter although it is an input parameter and is not modified by the procedure. This is to avoid the operation of making a copy of the array when the procedure is invoked, which is how Pascal works with value parameters. The copying buys us nothing and wastes both time and storage. Pascal provides no means of specifying call-by-reference but restricting usage to input, which is what we would like here. We shall frequently use the `var` mechanism this way, noting the obligation it creates not to change arguments that are intended as input only.

---

[5]ASCII stands for American Standard Code for Information Interchange, and EBCDIC stands for Extended Binary Coded Decimal Interchange Code. The story of how the computer industry arrived at two "standards" for character coding is long and involved.

A diagram will clarify the operation of the program to this point. Suppose that our alphabet were just the first four letters, and that we have processed the following text:

```
abcd
BCD
AaAbBcA
```

Then, the array `SeqCount` would look like this

	A	B	C	D
A	2	2	0	0
B	0	1	3	0
C	1	0	0	2
D	0	0	0	0

After the execution of `MoveToResultTable, ResultTable` would be

1	2	3	4	5	6	7	8
A A 2	A B 2	A C 0	A D 0	B A 0	B B 1	B C 3	B D 0

9	10	11	12	13	14	15	16
C A 1	C B 0	C C 0	C D 2	D A 0	D B 0	D C 0	D D 0

`Sort` does its job by one of the simplest (and slowest) methods: selection sorting. We shall devote all of Chapter 8 to a systematic study of sorting, but this preview gives us an early look at some fundamental issues. We begin by finding the largest element in the entire array; its element number will be in `Big` when the inner loop terminates the first time. The first element is exchanged with element number `Big`, using a procedure named `Swap`. We may now forget about the first element of the array because we have selected the largest element in the entire array and placed it there. We now do the same thing with the second element, and so on. When this process has been carried out with the index of the outer loop being 675 and that of the inner loop being 676, the array has been sorted into non-ascending order.

The procedure `Print` handles the formatting of the report as well as the selection of those sequences that exceed the threshold of 1% for printing. A count of those sequences is maintained with the index `I` so that we can use the `mod` function to determine when a line has been filled. (`I mod NumColumns` is zero only when `I` is a multiple of `NumColumns`.)

We give a name to the constant that determines the number of columns per line, but not to 100. "Per cent" means "for each hundred," and that can't change. The numbers in the output are formatted using Pascal's facilities; recall that specifying one position for an integer tells the compiler to print it in as many columns as its width, whatever that number may be.

The main program is typical of what you will see in this book: it consists mostly of the invocation of procedures. The names of the these procedures, and of their parameters, have been carefully chosen with the intention that the main program should provide a quick top-level overview of the organization and functioning of the program. When looking at a new program for the first time, it is always a good idea to look at the main program first.[6]

2.12 TESTING

The next stage in the development of the program is to test it with sample data.

The first set of sample data should be something very simple, for which the correct results are easily determined. Even in a program like ours where the output is an approximate statistical summary, we want the assurance of knowing that the program is exactly correct. A good practice would be to test the building of the count table and the sorting by running a modified version that prints the actual counts rather than the percentages. One test case should demonstrate that the end-of-line specification is handled correctly. Another should be designed to satisfy ourselves that every character in the input is processed, under various combinations of possibilities. For example, is a line consisting of a single two-letter word handled correctly, and does the program crash if a line consists of a single letter?

Many modified versions of the program may be run in the course of this testing. These versions, together with any programs that generate test data and do various other chores, are sometimes called *scaffolding*.[7] They are needed by the program developer during development, but are removed before the finished product is delivered to the client.

All this having been done, and no errors discovered, we ran the program with text consisting of the first two sections of this chapter. Simple operating system commands were used to direct the output to disk for later printing; as usual, these operations will not be shown because they are not part of Pascal and because they are highly dependent on the particular operating system. The output is shown at the top of the next page.

---

[6]This being the case, it would be nice if the main program came *first*, not last. Placing it last simplifies the work of the compiler writer slightly at the expense of making the program harder to read. Very few other languages impose this requirement.

[7]The term was introduced by Frederick P. Brooks, Jr., in *The Mythical Man-Month*, Reading, MA: Addison-Wesley, 1975. This small book is a masterpiece of condensed and wittily-presented wisdom, based on the author's experience as manager of the first very large operating system, OS 360 for the IBM System/360 series of computers and their successors. Anyone who is involved in developing large software systems, or who expects to be, should read this book once a year. The lessons it contains were learned in work done more than 20 years ago, but the message is timeless.

```
Letter-sequence frequencies in a sample of text.
Only sequences representing more than 1.00% of total are shown.

TH 3.73%   IN 2.96%   HE 2.88%   AN 1.92%   AT 1.82%   ER 1.80%   ON 1.77%
EN 1.62%   RA 1.57%   NT 1.49%   RE 1.46%   TI 1.46%   IS 1.41%   ST 1.31%
AR 1.29%   TE 1.29%   OF 1.28%   OR 1.26%   ND 1.24%   AL 1.24%   HA 1.21%
IT 1.10%   DE 1.06%   NG 1.06%   ME 1.06%   TO 1.06%

The sequences shown represent 41.39% of the total of 6106 sequences.
```

The good news is that the program seems to give correct answers. The bad news is that after completing the building of the table, it took 33 seconds to begin printing.[8] We have clearly not met the specifications. What happened?

2.13 AN ATTEMPT TO RESCUE PERFORMANCE

Perhaps you saw this time problem long ago, but let's pretend we are beginning programmers with a deadline and no time to think. (A recipe for disaster, that combination.) Our first thought might be that since there are faster sorting methods, why not try them? Given that fact, we reran the program with the fastest sorting method known, QuickSort, substituted for the procedure Sort. This is not the time for the details on this topic, which is covered in Chapter 8. Well, we found that there certainly are differences in sorting methods. This time the delay between reading the last character and the start of printing was only five seconds. But this does not meet the specs either.

Still operating in desperation mode, we might also think about the transfer of the frequencies from SeqCount to ResultTable. There are 676 records to transfer, after all, and that takes time. Why not use a one-dimensional array in the first place, with a programmed index function to find the correct location for each letter sequence, and then start sorting immediately when the last character has been read?

This might actually be a useful technique in some circumstances and it lets us practice with an index function, so let's try it. Figure 2.4 shows the modified portions of the earlier program. (The Sort and Print procedures and the main program are changed in only trivial ways.) The only array is now the one-dimensional version, ResultTable.

---

[8]Running on an IBM Personal Computer AT. The program was written in Turbo Pascal, and run-time range checking was enabled. The timings quoted in this book are for general comparison purposes only; with different computers and different compilers the results could be vastly different.

```
program LetterSequences2 (input, output);

{ Second version of program to print frequencies of two-letter
  sequences: the count table is a linear array accessed by an
  index function, eliminating the procedure MoveToSortTable.
  ResultTable is the only array. }


const
    ResultTableSize = 676;    { 26 letters;  676 = 26 * 26 }
    Threshold = 1.0;

type
    NonNegInt = 0..MaxInt;
    Letter = 'A'..'Z';

    SeqRecord = record
                    Letter1, Letter2: Letter;
                    Count: NonNegInt
                end;

    ResultIndex = 1..ResultTableSize;

    ResultTableArray = array [ResultIndex] of SeqRecord;


var
    ResultTable: ResultTableArray;
    TotalSeqs: NonNegInt;


function ArrayIndex (Row, Column: Letter): ResultIndex;
{ Convert a two-letter sequence into an index
  to a one-dimensional array }
begin
    ArrayIndex := 26 * (Ord(Row) - Ord('A'))
                     + (Ord(Column) - Ord('A')) + 1
end;


procedure Initialize (var ResultTable: ResultTableArray);
var
    I, J: Letter;
    Index: ResultIndex;
begin
    for I := 'A' to 'Z' do
        for J := 'A' to 'Z' do
        begin
            Index := ArrayIndex(I, J);
            ResultTable[Index].Letter1 := I;
            ResultTable[Index].Letter2 := J;
            ResultTable[Index].Count := 0
        end
end;
```

(Continued)

(Continued)

```
procedure BuildCountTable (var ResultTable: ResultTableArray;
                           var TotalSeqs: NonNegInt);
{ Read text, build a one-dimensional table of letter-sequence
  counts, and compute total number of letter sequences. }

const
    Blank = ' ';
    ASCIICaseConvert = -32;    { Make this +64 for EBCDIC }
var
    PrevCh, CurrCh: char;
    Index: ResultIndex;

begin
    PrevCh := Blank;
    Read (CurrCh);
    TotalSeqs := 0;

    while not EOF do begin
        if CurrCh in ['a'..'z'] then
            CurrCh := Chr(Ord(CurrCh) + ASCIICaseConvert);
        if (PrevCh in ['A'..'Z']) and (CurrCh in ['A'..'Z']) then
        begin
            Index := ArrayIndex(PrevCh, CurrCh);
            ResultTable[Index].Count := ResultTable[Index].Count + 1;
            TotalSeqs := TotalSeqs + 1
        end;
        PrevCh := CurrCh;
        Read (CurrCh)
    end
end;



{ Swap, Sort, and Print not shown. }


begin
    Initialize (ResultTable);
    BuildCountTable (ResultTable, TotalSeqs);
    if TotalSeqs = 0 then
        WriteLn ('Data contains no letter sequences')
    else
    begin
        Sort (ResultTable);
        Print (ResultTable, TotalSeqs)
    end
end.
```

FIGURE 2.4

Second version of a program to produce a table of letter-sequence frequencies.

The most interesting new feature is the procedure named `ArrayIndex`, which accepts row and column indices, both letters, and returns an index to `ResultTable`. This is essentially the formula shown earlier in the chapter, except that we have to convert from a letter to an integer in the range of 0 to 25 before doing the arithmetic, and we have to add 1 because `SeqCount` is numbered from one, not zero. Now, everywhere else in the program that we have two letters and need to find the corresponding index to `SeqCount`, we first invoke `ArrayIndex`. (Actually, the invocation of the function could have been written in place of every occurrence of the local variable `Index`, but this would have meant multiple invocations of the function for the same arguments. We shall not place excessive emphasis on such ''micro-efficiency'' issues in this book but, in this case, using the one extra local variable with a single invocation saves time and improves clarity.)

The result? Alas, no improvement. This version takes just as long, measured to the nearest second, as the previous version. This was evidently not the problem.

2.14 INFORMAL ANALYSIS OF SELECTION SORTING

Something is taking hopelessly too much time. We have clearly implicated the sorting operation even without studying of execution speeds on our computer, because the other obvious suspects have been eliminated. To approach this problem sensibly, let us see if we can get a quantitative description of how long selection sorting takes, as a function of the number of records to be sorted.

Here is the crucial piece of code, modified slightly to use N as the number of records, and with the exchanging shown in shorthand form.

```
for I := 1 to N - 1 do
begin
    Big := I;
    for J := I + 1 to N do
        if ResultTable[J].Count > ResultTable[Big].Count then
            Big := J;
    Swap records J and Big
end;
```

We adopt this informal style to focus on the key question: how many times is the inner loop executed? That is, how many times is the `if` statement executed? It turns out that this is not very hard to determine, and it is something that you need to learn how to do comfortably.

The first time through the outer loop, when I is 1, the inner loop is executed with values ranging from 2 to N. The next time through the outer loop, when I is 2, the inner loop is executed with values ranging from 3 to N. Continuing in this way, on the last time through the outer loop, when I is $N - 1$, the inner loop is executed once. Now, look at these numbers in reverse order.

We have an inner loop that is executed once, twice, three times, . . ., ending with $N - 1$ times. Do we know a formula for the sum of this series? Of course! $N(N - 1)/2$, which we can rewrite as $N^2/2 - N/2$.

As introduced briefly in Chapter 1, all that really matters for our present purposes is the N^2 term. N in this case is 676; the square of that is 456,976; half of that is 228,488. Compared to 228,488, $N/2$, which is 338, is entirely negligible for our present purposes. Whatever our problems are here, it's obvious they aren't going to be solved by reducing 228,488 to 228,150. Furthermore, the divisor of 2 isn't very interesting either. (We have already seen that the fastest sorting method currently known is inadequate to rescue this design.) What really matters is the N^2 term. Because the N^2 term is the dominant one in determining the running time, we call selection sorting a *quadratic* method. Or, in the "Big Oh" notation, the running time of the algorithm is $O(N^2)$.

The intent of the Big Oh notation is simply to say that, to within a multiplicative constant, the method will take *about* N^2 steps. We cannot claim that the sorting method takes *exactly* N^2 steps. If there is an alternative that takes only N steps, or only $N \lg N$ steps, then the multiplicative constant and all the other details are completely insignificant.[9]

So why didn't QuickSort solve the problem? Is it also quadratic? Not at all. Its average execution time, as a function of N, the number of records, is $O(N \lg N)$. (Remember that lg means logarithms to the base 2.) In our case N is 676 and, to the next larger integer, the base 2 logarithm of that is 10. Ten times 676 is a truly smaller number than 676 squared. Furthermore, QuickSort is the fastest $N \lg N$ method known, and it is unlikely that anything significantly faster will be discovered. Is there any chance of finding a sorting method for which the execution time is $O(N)$? Such methods do exist, but only if very stringent restrictions can be placed on the key. (The key in this case is the `Count` field.) The conditions are too restrictive for our purposes.

2.15 SOLVING THE PERFORMANCE PROBLEM

What's left? Perhaps you saw it long ago: *reduce N*. The specifications require us to print only those letter sequences that represent more than 1% of the total number of letter pair sequences. The design chosen earlier said to sort all the pair counts, then print only those that exceed the threshold. Why not limit the sorting to those few that meet this test? With a 1% threshold, even in the extreme case of 99 sequences all having the same frequency, there would be 99 records to sort, not 676. And even if we stay with a quadratic sorting method, 99 squared is roughly 50 times smaller than 676 squared. (That is in the extreme case; the

---

[9]But be careful. If we say that a method that takes $N^2 + N$ steps is $O(N^2)$ and another that takes N^2 steps is also $O(N^2)$, does that permit us to apply transitivity and write $N^2 + N = N^2$? *Very interesting* if so, because with the slightest bit of algebra we have that $1 = 0$ and, given that premise, it is possible to prove *absolutely anything*. It is because of possible confusion along these lines that we avoid using the equal sign in connection with Big Oh notation.

sample output reproduced earlier suggests that with ordinary English text, there might be no more than 20–40 records to sort.) The square of numbers in this range is hundreds of times smaller than the square of 676.

The final version of the program is shown in Figure 2.5. The most significant change is in `MoveToResultTable`, where only those letter sequences that exceed the threshold are moved to `ResultTable`. Also, the computation of the number of sequences that correspond to 1% of the total is done before entering the loop. The number moved now needs to be known to the procedures `Sort` and `Print`, so `NumMoved` has become a parameter.

```
program LetterSequences3 (input, output);

{ Third version of program to print frequencies of two-letter
  sequences: arrays are as in LetterSequences1, but only those
  sequences with counts exceeding the threshold are moved to the
  sort array and sorted. }

const
    ResultTableSize = 676;    { 26 letters;  676 = 26 * 26 }
    Threshold = 1.0;

type
    NonNegInt = 0..MaxInt;
    Letter = 'A'..'Z';

    SeqCountArray = array [Letter, Letter] of NonNegInt;

    SeqRecord = record
                    Letter1, Letter2: Letter;
                    Count: NonNegInt
                end;

    ResultIndex = 1..ResultTableSize;

    ResultTableArray = array [ResultIndex] of SeqRecord;


var
    SeqCount: SeqCountArray;
    ResultTable: ResultTableArray;
    TotalSeqs: NonNegInt;
    NumMoved: NonNegInt;


procedure Initialize (var SeqCount: SeqCountArray);
var
    I, J: Letter;
begin
    for I := 'A' to 'Z' do
        for J := 'A' to 'Z' do
            SeqCount[I, J] := 0
end;
```

(Continued)

(Continued)

```
procedure BuildCountTable (var SeqCount: SeqCountArray;
                              var TotalSeqs: NonNegInt);
{ Read text, build a two-dimensional table of letter-sequence
  counts, and compute total number of letter sequences. }

const
    Blank = ' ';
    ASCIICaseConvert = -32;    { Make this +64 for EBCDIC }
var
    PrevCh, CurrCh: char;

begin
    PrevCh := Blank;
    Read (CurrCh);
    TotalSeqs := 0;

    while not EOF do
    begin
        if CurrCh in ['a'..'z'] then
            CurrCh := Chr(Ord(CurrCh) + ASCIICaseConvert);
        if (PrevCh in ['A'..'Z']) and (CurrCh in ['A'..'Z'])then
        begin
            SeqCount[PrevCh, CurrCh] := SeqCount[PrevCh, CurrCh]+ 1;
            TotalSeqs := TotalSeqs + 1
        end;
        PrevCh := CurrCh;
        Read (CurrCh)
    end
end;




procedure MoveToResultTable (var SeqCount: SeqCountArray;
                                var ResultTable: ResultTableArray;
                                var NumMoved: NonNegInt);
{ Move only those exceeding the threshold }
var
    I, J: Letter;
    K: NonNegInt;
    CutoffValue: NonNegInt;
begin
    CutoffValue := Trunc (TotalSeqs * Threshold / 100);

    K := 0;
    for I := 'A' to 'Z' do
        for J := 'A' to 'Z' do
            if SeqCount[I, J] > CutoffValue then
            begin
                K := K + 1;
                ResultTable[K].Letter1 := I;
                ResultTable[K].Letter2 := J;
                ResultTable[K].Count := SeqCount[I, J]
            end;

    NumMoved := K
end;
```

```
procedure Swap (var X, Y: SeqRecord);
{ Exchange two records -- used by Sort procedure. }
var
   Temp: SeqRecord;
begin
   Temp := X;
   X := Y;
   Y := Temp;
end;


procedure Sort (var ResultTable: ResultTableArray;
                NumMoved: NonNegInt);
{ Sort records into descending sequence on Count. }
var
  I, J, Big: ResultIndex;
  Temp: SeqRecord;
begin
   for I := 1 to NumMoved - 1 do
   begin
      Big := I;
      for J := I + 1 to NumMoved do
          if ResultTable[J].Count > ResultTable[Big].Count then
             Big := J;
      Swap (ResultTable[I], ResultTable[Big])
   end;
end;


procedure Print (var ResultTable: ResultTableArray;
                 NumMoved: NonNegInt;
                 TotalSeqs: NonNegInt);
const
   NumColumns = 7;
var
   I: ResultIndex;
   SubTotal: NonNegInt;
begin
   WriteLn ('Letter-sequence frequencies in a sample of text.');
   WriteLn ('Only sequences representing more than ',
            Threshold:4:2, '% of total are shown.');
   WriteLn;

   SubTotal := 0;
   for I := 1 to NumMoved do
   begin
      Write (ResultTable[I].Letter1, ResultTable[I].Letter2,
            (ResultTable[I].Count / TotalSeqs)*100:5:2, '%  ');
      SubTotal := SubTotal + ResultTable[I].Count;
      if I mod NumColumns = 0 then
          WriteLn
   end;

   WriteLn;
   WriteLn;
   WriteLn ('The sequences shown represent ',
            (SubTotal / TotalSeqs) * 100:5:2,
            '% of the total of ', TotalSeqs:1, ' sequences.')
end;
```

(Continued)

(Continued)

```
begin
    Initialize (SeqCount);
    BuildCountTable (SeqCount, TotalSeqs);
    if TotalSeqs = 0 then
        WriteLn ('Data contains no letter sequences')
    else
    begin
        MoveToResultTable (SeqCount, ResultTable, NumMoved);
        Sort (ResultTable, NumMoved);
        Print (ResultTable, NumMoved, TotalSeqs)
    end
end.
```

FIGURE 2.5
Final version of a program to produce letter-sequence frequencies.

The response time, from reading the last character to the start of printing, is now less than one second. Substitution of QuickSort for selection sort produces no noticeable change in the response.

Having put this much effort into the program, let's see it in operation a little more. Figure 2.6 shows the output when the program was run with six selections of text. The output has been edited slightly to fit on the page, and identifications have been added for easier study.

The final case reminds us of a fundamental issue in computer science: a program is a set of commands to a computer to carry out processing, but it can also be—at other times—treated as data.

2.16 CONCLUSION: THE LESSON OF THIS EXAMPLE

In this book, we devote considerable effort to the analysis of the time and space requirements of algorithms. This is a fundamental part of computer science, which you need to know. But never lose track of your common sense. The fastest method known, when applied to a file that is 50 times larger than it needs to be, may not have a chance against the slowest method known.

```
-- First two sections of this chapter:

Letter-sequence frequencies in a sample of text.
Only sequences representing more than 1.00% of total are shown.

TH 3.73%   IN 2.96%   HE 2.88%   AN 1.92%   AT 1.82%   ER 1.80%   ON 1.77%
EN 1.62%   RA 1.57%   NT 1.49%   RE 1.46%   TI 1.46%   IS 1.41%   ST 1.31%
AR 1.29%   TE 1.29%   OF 1.28%   OR 1.26%   ND 1.24%   AL 1.24%   HA 1.21%
IT 1.10%   DE 1.06%   NG 1.06%   ME 1.06%   TO 1.06%

The sequences shown represent 41.39% of the total of 6106 sequences.
```

```
-- Three arias from Gounod's Faust:

DE 2.89%   ER 2.74%   OI 2.45%   RE 2.45%   ES 2.31%   ME 2.31%   LE 2.16%
NE 2.16%   CE 2.02%   TE 2.02%   UR 1.88%   ET 1.73%   AI 1.73%   TO 1.73%
ON 1.59%   OU 1.59%   SE 1.59%   ST 1.59%   LU 1.44%   EU 1.44%   IR 1.44%
LA 1.30%   IN 1.30%   IE 1.30%   EN 1.30%   EL 1.30%   RO 1.15%   SA 1.15%
LL 1.15%   RA 1.15%   IT 1.15%   CH 1.01%   RI 1.01%   GE 1.01%   UT 1.01%

The sequences shown represent 57.58% of the total of 693 sequences.


-- Three arias from Mozart's Don Giovanni:

NT 2.22%   TO 2.22%   AN 2.06%   AR 2.06%   IN 2.06%   IO 1.90%   ON 1.90%
TE 1.90%   EL 1.74%   EN 1.74%   DI 1.58%   IA 1.58%   AT 1.58%   MI 1.58%
RE 1.58%   SE 1.58%   TA 1.58%   CH 1.58%   ES 1.43%   RA 1.43%   CA 1.27%
NO 1.27%   AD 1.27%   CE 1.27%   OR 1.27%   QU 1.27%   LE 1.27%   HE 1.27%
DA 1.27%   SO 1.27%   IL 1.27%   ER 1.27%   AL 1.27%   LL 1.11%   OG 1.11%

The sequences shown represent 54.04% of the total of 631 sequences.


-- Three arias from Bach's St. Matthew's Passion:

IN 3.92%   EN 3.74%   CH 3.57%   EI 3.21%   ER 3.21%   ES 2.67%   DE 2.50%
SE 2.32%   HE 2.14%   BE 2.14%   IC 1.96%   ME 1.96%   LL 1.78%   ST 1.78%
EL 1.60%   AU 1.60%   SU 1.60%   SS 1.43%   UN 1.43%   UR 1.43%   US 1.43%
WE 1.43%   GE 1.25%   IL 1.25%   FU 1.25%   EH 1.25%   AS 1.25%   WI 1.25%
AB 1.07%   NE 1.07%

The sequences shown represent 58.47% of the total of 561 sequences.


-- Jerome Kern's "All the Things You Are":

TH 4.97%   IN 3.87%   HE 3.59%   RE 3.59%   AR 3.31%   NG 3.31%   OU 3.04%
AT 2.49%   YO 2.49%   VE 2.21%   HA 2.21%   LO 1.93%   EA 1.93%   ME 1.66%
ON 1.66%   LL 1.66%   NE 1.38%   EN 1.38%   NT 1.38%   OM 1.38%   AN 1.38%
ND 1.38%   ES 1.10%   SO 1.10%   ST 1.10%   AL 1.10%   UR 1.10%   ER 1.10%
HI 1.10%

The sequences shown represent 59.94% of the total of 362 sequences.


-- The source code for the final version of the program:

RE 3.42%   TA 2.93%   SE 2.69%   ES 2.54%   LE 2.54%   NT 2.49%   EQ 2.39%
TT 2.39%   IN 2.34%   CO 2.29%   EN 1.86%   TE 1.81%   AR 1.76%   SU 1.76%
TO 1.76%   BL 1.56%   LT 1.51%   OU 1.51%   UL 1.51%   UN 1.51%   AB 1.46%
OR 1.27%   RR 1.27%   GI 1.27%   EG 1.27%   AL 1.22%   ON 1.22%   ER 1.17%
ED 1.12%   TH 1.07%   ET 1.07%   ND 1.07%   CE 1.07%   OT 1.07%

The sequences shown represent 59.23% of the total of 2048 sequences.
```

FIGURE 2.6
The output of the letter-sequence program, with six sets of text as identified in the edited output.

EXERCISES

1. An abstract data type (ADT) for families could have families as its data objects and the following operations.

   `Create`: Establishes an instance of the `Family` type.

   `FatherOf`: Given a family, `FatherOf` returns its father.

   `MotherOf`: Given a family, `MotherOf` returns its mother.

   `IsInFamily`: Given an individual and the name of a family, `IsInFamily` returns `true` if the individual is in the given family. For example, `IsInFamily (Luciano, Paverotti)` would be `true` if `Luciano` is in the `Paverotti` family.

   `IsChildInFamily`: Given an individual and a family, `IsChildInFamily` returns `true` if the individual is a child in the given family.

   (a) An error might occur if `IsChildInFamily` were implemented and then called for a family with no children. What other sorts of errors might occur in an implementation of the ADT? How might you program the detection of these errors?

   (b) What other procedures might be appropriate for an ADT `Family`?

   (c) Suggest Pascal data structures to implement the objects of the ADT `Family`. You will need types for `Individuals`, as well as a definition for `Create`.

   (d) Using your structure for (c), complete the implementation of the ADT `Family` by writing Pascal procedures for each of the operations listed. If a procedure is not needed for `Create`, state in plain English how your `Family` ADT would be "created" in Pascal.

2. Using the style of Exercise 1, define an ADT `ClassList`. Your ADT should not specify a particular Pascal implementation for a `ClassList`, but should include any operations for which you think one would want to access a `ClassList`. For example, one operation on a `ClassList` might return the course number.

3. Write a Pascal program, compile it, and test it with sample data for the ADTs of either Exercises 1 or 2. The program should consist of type declarations, the ADT procedures, and a main program to *drive* the procedures, that is, invoke them for testing.

4. Extend the ADT `Array` to include a procedure to initialize an `Array` so that each array location contains the same element. How could you program an error check to eliminate the potential for attempting to `Retrieve` an element where no `Store` had been performed? (Be careful; this one is harder than you might think.) Some languages provide for initialization in a variable declaration, or even (as in Ada) in a type declaration. Is this an improvement on Pascal?

5. Rational numbers are defined as ratios of integers, with non-zero denominators. If we write $X := 1/3$, a real number, $0.3333..3$, will be stored at the location for `X`, which is not exactly the one-third we had in mind.

(a) Define an ADT Rational and include the necessary operations. Be sure to include an equality operator on two rationals.

(b) Implement your ADT as a record, and write Pascal procedures for the operations.

6. Peano's Axioms have been used since the end of the nineteenth century to characterize the natural numbers. They are:

P1: 1 is a natural number.

P2: If n is a natural number, then Successor(n) is a natural number.

P3: $1 \neq$ Successor(n) for any natural number, n.

P4: If Successor(n) = Successor(m), then $n = m$.

P5: **(A)** If P is a predicate, such that $P(1) =$ true;
　　　(B) If $P(n) =$ true, then $P(n+1) =$ true, for all natural numbers; then, $P(m) =$ true, for all natural numbers m.

P5 is the *principle of induction,* which is a powerful tool for proving statements about natural numbers.

(a) Construct an ADT NaturalNumber using P1–P4, that is, describe the essential operations on natural numbers.

(b) If we equate Successor(n) with $n + 1$, where "$+$" is the symbol for integer addition, do you think that any computer implementation of the positive integers obeys P1–P4?

7. (a) Suppose a one-dimensional array, A, has indices 1..50, and that each element of the array requires two storage locations. If the array begins at location 1540, what are the starting addresses of A[1]? A[50]? A[23]?

(b) Redo (a) if each element occupies eight storage locations.

(c) Suppose an array named Inventory is used to store a wine inventory, with indices (Chablis, Madeira, DrySherry, MediumSherry, CreamSherry, Chardonnay, Zinfandel, Burgundy, Tokay). The array elements are integers, each occupying one word of two bytes (storage locations). Again, suppose the array starts at location 1540. What is the starting address for Inventory [MediumSherry]?

(d) Suppose further that the wine steward has the wines listed in (c) from France, Italy, Spain and/or California. Change the Inventory array so that Inventory [Spain, DrySherry] represents the number of bottles of Spanish DrySherry on hand. What is the starting address of Inventory [Spain, DrySherry]? Of Inventory [California, Zinfandel]? Assume row-major allocation order and the same starting address.

(e) What are the answers to (c) and (d) if column-major order is used?

(f) Would knowing which storage allocation method (row-major vs. column-major) is used for arrays influence the way you wrote any procedures? Which ones?

8. If we have a three-dimensional array (for example, $X[0..5, 0..3, 0..7]$) we will need two dope vectors, $D1$ and $D2$, to provide rapid computation of the location of $X[I, J, K]$. If each array element occupies one storage location, and if $D1$ and $D2$ are

D1			D2	
0	0		0	0
1	32		1	8
2	64		2	16
3	96		3	24
4	128			
5	160			

then $Location(X[I, J, K]) = Location(X[0, 0, 0]) + D1[I] + D2[J] + K$.

(a) Write Pascal procedures to:

(i): Compute $D1$ and $D2$, given the upper and lower limits of I, J and K.

(ii): Compute the location of $X[I, J, K]$, given I, J, and K, using $D1$ and $D2$ from (i).

(b) Can you generalize this to n dimensions ($n > 3$)? *yes*

(c) What changes should be made to compute dope vectors for arrays with elements requiring s units of storage? *MULTIPLY BY S*

9. The following table represents distances between mid-Atlantic cities.

(a) Devise a conversion function so that the distances can be kept as linear array. Do you need to store all 144 distances listed?

(b) Write Retrieve and Store procedures using your conversion function so that Retrieve (Store (Dist (I, J)), (I, J)) = Dist (I, J).

	BMD	BVA	CWV	CVA	CMD	DDE	HMD	NVA	RIV	ROV	SMD	WDC
BMD	0	405	370	150	130	80	75	210	145	265	105	40
BVA	405	0	205	260	370	470	370	400	315	140	495	360
CWV	370	205	0	250	260	445	310	405	310	170	475	320
CVA	150	260	250	0	165	205	140	160	65	115	230	110
CMD	130	370	260	165	0	215	60	300	210	230	240	135
DDE	80	470	445	205	215	0	150	190	195	320	60	95
HMD	75	370	310	140	60	150	0	260	175	225	175	80
NVA	210	400	405	160	300	190	260	0	85	245	130	190
RIV	145	315	310	65	210	195	175	85	0	165	195	105
ROV	265	140	170	115	230	320	225	245	165	0	350	225
SMD	105	495	475	230	240	60	175	130	195	350	0	120
WDC	40	360	320	110	135	95	80	190	105	225	120	0

(Note: BMD = Baltimore, MD; BVA = Bristol, VA; CWV = Charleston, WV; CVA = Charlottesville, VA; CMD = Cumberland, MD; DDE = Dover, DE; HMD = Hagerstown, MD; NVA = Norfolk, VA; RIV = Richmond, VA; ROV = Roanoke, VA; SMD = Salisbury, MD; WDC = Washington, DC.)

(c) Thought question: How would you get from Roanoke, Virginia, to Cumberland, Maryland, traveling the shortest distance?

10. Statistical analysis of data makes heavy use of arrays. Techniques have been developed, and are a part of almost all statistical packages, to *crosstabulate* data. The purpose of a crosstabulation is to help decide whether there is some relationship between two or more variables and a third variable of interest. For example, the following data taken from Twaite and Monroe[10], represents results from an opinion survey on the Equal Rights Amendment to the US Constitution.

		Sex		Row
		Male	Female	Total
Opinion	In favor	33	31	64
	Opposed	53	23	76
	No opinion	15	8	23
	Column totals	101	62	163

(a) A user of a statistical package might enter data as three rows: (33, 31), (53, 23), and (15, 8). He or she might also enter row and column labels: 'In favor', 'Opposed', 'No opinion', 'Male', 'Female'.

(b) Write a Pascal procedure to accept the data given in (a), and print out a `CrossTabs` matrix including:

(i)   Row totals;

(ii) Column totals;

(iii) Percentage in each category (e.g., the 15 males with no opinion above represent 14.85% of all males, and the 23 of either sex are 14.11% of the total.) Try to make your output attractive enough to be included in a user's research paper.

11. Suppose you are charged with setting up the personnel record system for the US Navy. The Navy employs some civilians, some enlisted persons, and some officers. Devise a variant record, `Personnel,` to accommodate this data. (In Pascal, only the last field can be a variant, but any one of the fields of this variant can be a variant record. There is no limit on the degree of nesting of variant records.)

12. Modify the `AddCpxRect` procedure so that the result is in polar form if both operands are polar, but is in rectangular form if either operand is in rectangular form.

13. Complex numbers can be multiplied as well as added. Write a Pascal procedure `MultCpxRect` that returns the product of two complex numbers in rectangular form.

14. Modify your procedure in Exercise 13 to conform with the complex addition procedure of Exercise 12.

[10]Twaite, J., and Monroe, J., *Introductory Statistics*. Glenview, IL: Scott, Foresman, 1979.

15. The difference of two complex numbers, `Cpx1 - Cpx2`, can be implemented using either of the `AddCpx` procedures if we write a new procedure, `NegCpx` that, given a complex number, returns its additive inverse, i.e., `NegCpx (C) = -C`. Then, `Cpx1 - Cpx2 = AddCpx (Cpx1, NegCpx (Cpx2), Sum)`. Write a Pascal procedure for `NegCpx` that returns the negative in the same form as its argument.

16. Our complex arithmetic package will be complete if we provide a procedure to perform complex division. This can be accomplished in a manner similar to that suggested for complex subtraction in Exercise 17. We will need a procedure, `InvCpx`, to compute the multiplicative inverse `1/Cpx`, for any non-zero complex number `Cpx`. Then `Cpx1 / Cpx2 = Q`, where `MultCpx (Cpx1, InvCpx (Cpx2), Q)` computes `Q`. Write the Pascal procedure `InvCpx (Cpx, Inv)`.

17. Embedded in `LetterSequences` is a (not very efficient) sort routine called selection sort. When records are sorted, we must decide which field will be the *key,* and then sort on that field. Use your Navy personnel record, devised in Exercise 11, to generate a file of 25 or so records. Sort the data twice: once by last name, and once by social security number (or any other suitable field).

18. A sort is called *stable* if duplicate keys remain in the same order after sorting as in the original data. Is selection sort stable?

19. A change in the procedure `MoveToResultTable` improved the runtime performance of `LetterSequences2` by a factor greater than 33. Build some "scaffolding" into the final `MoveToResultTable` procedure to provide a *trace* of just what the procedure does. A trace often prints out the values of input and output parameters to a procedure with some suitable messages, such as "`Entering MoveToResult-Table,`" and "`Leaving MoveToResultTable.`" You may, of course, and normally should, print intermediate results as well. Run `LetterSequences3`, including your trace, on a small text file.

20. Modify `LetterSequences3` so that it reports on the frequencies of three-letter sequences. (If you are working on an EBCDIC machine you may have to modify the arrays to make the program fit in storage.) Make an informal analysis of your program. For example, how many times is the assignment statement in `Initialize` executed? What fraction of the elements of your sequence count array ever contain anything but zero?

SUGGESTIONS FOR FURTHER STUDY

Material on properties of numbers can be found in various references. Two of the most tractable are Cohen and Ehrlich (1963) and Suppes (1960). The first is an excellent little volume building up the real numbers from the natural numbers, *N*, through integers, *Z*, the rationals, *Q*, and ending with the field of complex numbers, *C*. Along the way one can pick up groups, rings, relations, metrics, and the notions of completeness and uncountability. Long a classic in the field, the Suppes undergraduate text includes all of Cohen & Ehrlich, plus material on sequences, transfinite arithmetic, well-ordered sets, and equivalents to the Axiom of Choice. The introduction to Peano (1894) provides the original notation for natural number arithmetic, with n′ representing what we have called *Successor (n)*.

Work on stepwise (top-down) refinement of programs suggests that a wise programmer will defer the selection of a representation for data until a complete algorithm, expressed as an abstract program, has been designed. Hoare (1972) suggests a method for transforming an abstract program including ADTs into a concrete program and also a method for proving its correctness. Gerstmann and Ollongren (1980) begin with ADTs in bare-bones form, then develop a method for refining the basic ADT to support other features a programmer might desire.

Liskov and Zilles (1974) investigate ADTs in conjunction with the development of the CLU programming language. An introductory text, Liskov and Guttag (1986), provides a method for writing careful informal specifications for data and shows how to formalize them. Although the sample programs are written in CLU, Pascal programmers can gain much from the methods presented for decomposing programs into smaller units.

Cardelli and Wegner (1985) look at types in general, including ADTs. They provide a brief history of types starting with their uses in mathematics to ''prevent objects from inconsistent interaction with other objects.'' Polymorphic types are defined as ''types whose operations are applicable to operands of more than one type.'' A theoretical language called *Fun* is used to model various data type considerations, and examples are given using real programming languages.

An excellent source for algorithms written in Pascal code is Sedgewick (1983). The stated goal for the book is ''to bring together the fundamental methods [on sorting, searching, string processing, geometry, graphs, and others] to provide access to the best methods that we know for solving problems by computer.'' Hundreds of practical algorithms are organized into 40 chapters.

CHAPTER 3

SETS AND STRINGS

3.1 INTRODUCTION

Sets and strings are useful in many applications of computers, either because an application actually deals primarily with such objects or because they are convenient for doing other things. For example, sets are primary objects in the following program, which finds prime numbers, but they also provide a simple way to test whether a character is a lowercase letter. Strings of characters are primary objects when we process names and addresses of people, but they are also useful simply as column headings or as identifiers of vertices of a graph.

Following our usual approach, we first define an ADT and show examples of its use, then consider an implementation and analyze it as to time and space required. In the case of sets we also consider a different implementation, which is essentially the way the Pascal set feature operates.

3.2 THE ADT SET

As with any other ADT, the ADT *set* is defined in terms of objects and operations. The objects are just sets in the mathematical sense, with the representation unspecified. Numerous representations are possible; we consider two later in the chapter, and see two others in Chapters 6 and 10. The operations in the set ADT, as we shall define it, are as follows. The names are those of the procedures and functions discussed in the next section. The brief descriptions are informal statements of the axioms that, if put into more precise form, would be a mathematical definition of the ADT.

1. `MakeSetEmpty`. Takes a set; returns the same set with no elements.

2. `MakeUniversalSet`. Takes a set; returns the same set with all elements present, "all" meaning "as defined in the program declarations."

3. `AddElementToSet`. Takes an element and a set; returns the same set with the element included. Immaterial whether the element was in the set previously.

4. `DeleteElementFromSet`. Takes an element and a set; returns the same set with the element not present. Immaterial whether the element was in the set previously.

5. `SetIsEmpty`. Takes a set; returns the boolean value `true` if the set is empty, and `false` otherwise.

6. `ElementIsInSet`. Takes an element and a set; returns the boolean value `true` if the element is in the set, and `false` otherwise.

7. `SetsAreEqual`. Takes two sets; returns the boolean value `true` if they contain the same elements, and `false` otherwise.

8. `IsSubset`. Takes two sets; returns the boolean value `true` if all of the elements in the first set are also in the second set, and `false` otherwise.

9. `Union`. Takes two sets; returns a set that contains every element that is in either of the two sets.

10. `Intersection`. Takes two sets; returns a set that contains every element that is in both of the two sets, and no others.

11. `Difference`. Takes two sets; returns a set that contains every element that is in the first set but not in the second, and no others.

We can see some of these operations in action by considering a program to find prime numbers by an ancient and elegant method, the Sieve of Eratosthenes. It is of no practical importance to the applications that require knowledge of whether large numbers are primes or not (cryptanalysis, especially), because it is hopelessly slow, but it is a pleasant application of sets. The program is shown in Figure 3.1.

`Sieve` is a set initialized to contain all the integers from 1 to the largest element that our implementation can handle. This latter number is specified in the declarations for the main program, which is not shown. For our purposes, this is the universal set. We now delete 1 from `Sieve`, because, by the usual definitions, 1 is not a prime. From now on, the smallest element remaining in `Sieve` is the next prime.

Now we have a loop that is repeated until `Sieve` is empty. The first statement in this loop is a `while` that increments `Next` so long as its value is not a member of the set `Sieve`. The first time this loop is executed, it will stop with `Next` = 2.

```
procedure SieveOfEratosthenes;
var
    Sieve: SetType;
    Next: integer;     { the next prime }
    J: integer;

begin
    MakeUniversalSet (Sieve);
    DeleteElementFromSet (1, Sieve);
    Next := 1;

    repeat

        { Smallest element still in Sieve is the next prime }
        while not ElementIsInSet (Next, Sieve) do
            Next := Next + 1;
        WriteLn (Next);

        { Delete Next and all its multiples from Sieve }
        J := Next;
        while J <= MaxElementNumber do
        begin
            DeleteElementFromSet (J, Sieve);
            J := J + Next
        end

    until SetIsEmpty (Sieve)

end;
```

FIGURE 3.1
A procedure to find primes, using the Sieve of Eratosthenes.

The next task is to remove 2 from `Sieve` (we know it is a prime) along with all its multiples (which are obviously not primes, since they have a factor of 2). The generation of the multiples can be done without multiplication. We simply start another variable (`J`) at the value of `Next` and repeatedly add `Next` to this variable.

At this point the smallest number in `Sieve` is a prime, because it is not 1 and it is not a multiple of any prime found so far. Returning to the beginning of the `repeat` loop, the `while` will determine what the smallest remaining element is and then write it.

The `repeat` continues until `Sieve` is empty, at which point all the primes it originally contained have been identified.

It is possible for a program that implements the Sieve of Eratosthenes to be considerably more efficient than the one shown, particularly by considering only the odd candidates after 2, but since the method is not really a practical way to test for primality, we shall not pursue this line of investigation.

3.3 AN IMPLEMENTATION OF SETS USING ARRAYS

The concept of a set is familiar to you from your study of mathematics, and we know that Pascal provides a data type for sets, together with most of the operations in our ADT for sets. Now it is time to see how sets can be implemented without the Pascal set data type.

We begin with a decision to make the elements of our sets integers in the range of 1 to some maximum specified in a `const` declaration for `MaxElementNumber`. This is less of a loss of generality than it might seem, because any ordinal type can be mapped into the integers. In practice the mapping, using search techniques that will be developed in later chapters, might become a bit of a chore. But, because we know it can be done, we shall deal with integer elements only.

Our basic approach is to set up a boolean array in which a value of `true` for element `I` means that `I` is present in the set. The required declarations are as follows:

```
const
    MaxElementNumber = 1000;   { or whatever }

type
    SetElement = 1..MaxElementNumber;
    SetType = array [SetElement] of boolean;
```

We prefer to avoid devising names for types by mechanically adding ''Type'' as a suffix, but, unfortunately for this point of view, ''set'' is a reserved word in Pascal.

Here now are the procedures and functions for carrying out the operations that we specified in the previous section as defining our ADT set. For the most part they are quite straightforward and will require little explanation.

The first four follow directly from the definition of a set and the chosen representation.

```
procedure MakeSetEmpty (var S: SetType);
var
    I: integer;
begin
    for I := 1 to MaxElementNumber do
        S[I] := false
end;


procedure MakeUniversalSet (var S: SetType);
var
    I: integer;
begin
    for I := 1 to MaxElementNumber do
        S[I] := true
end;
```

```
procedure AddElementToSet (E: SetElement;
                              var S: SetType);
begin
   S[E] := true
end;


procedure DeleteElementFromSet (E: SetElement;
                                  var S: SetType);
begin
   S[E] := false
end;
```

Next, the boolean function `SetIsEmpty` must examine array elements until finding one that is `true` or until all elements have been tested. We use a `var` parameter here, and in all other such cases, to circumvent the Pascal action of making a copy of a value parameter. With large sets, such copying could waste a great deal of time. In using the `Sieve` program to find the primes less than 5000, for example, just making the set name a `var` parameter in the `SetIsEmpty` procedure speeds up program execution by a factor of three (on my computer), compared with using it as a value parameter.

```
function SetIsEmpty (var S: SetType): boolean;
{ var parameter used to prevent copying array. }
var
   I: integer;
   EmptySoFar: boolean;
begin
   EmptySoFar := true;
   I := 1;

   while (I <= MaxElementNumber) and (EmptySoFar) do
      if S[I] then
         EmptySoFar := false
      else
         I := I + 1;

   SetIsEmpty := EmptySoFar
end;
```

`ElementIsInSet` is simpler and faster.

```
function ElementIsInSet (E: SetElement;
                           var S: SetType): boolean;
begin
   ElementIsInSet := S[E]
end;
```

`SetsAreEqual` is similar, from a coding standpoint, to `SetIsEmpty`.

```
function SetsAreEqual (var S1, S2: SetType): boolean;
var
   I: integer;
   EqualSoFar: boolean;
begin
   EqualSoFar := true;
   I := 1;

   while (I <= MaxElementNumber) and (EqualSoFar) do
      if S1[I] <> S2[I] then
         EqualSoFar := false
      else
         I := I + 1;

   SetsAreEqual := EqualSoFar
end;
```

The definition of a subset says that every element in the first set must also be in the second set, so one element pair that fails this test allows us to give `IsSubset` the value `false`. To give it the value `true`, we must examine all pairs of elements in the two arrays.

```
function IsSubset (var S1, S2: SetType): boolean;
var
   I: integer;
   SubsetSoFar: boolean;
begin
   SubsetSoFar := true;
   I := 1;

   while (I <= MaxElementNumber) and (SubsetSoFar) do
      if S1[I] and not S2[I] then
         SubsetSoFar := false
      else
         I := I + 1;

   IsSubset := SubsetSoFar
end;
```

`Union` applies the definition of set union to each pair of elements in the two sets, and similarly for `Intersection` and `Difference`.

```
procedure Union (var S1, S2, UnionSet: SetType);
var
   I: integer;
begin
   for I := 1 to MaxElementNumber do
      UnionSet[I] := S1[I] or S2[I]
end;
```

```
procedure Intersection (var S1, S2, IntersectionSet: SetType);
var
    I: integer;
begin
    for I := 1 to MaxElementNumber do
        IntersectionSet[I] := S1[I] and S2[I]
end;
```

```
procedure Difference (S1, S2, DifferenceSet: SetType);
var
    I: integer;
begin
    for I := 1 to MaxElementNumber do
        DifferenceSet[I] := S1[I] and not S2[I]
end;
```

Finally, for convenience, here are two procedures to handle input and output, at least in simple cases.

```
procedure ReadSet (var S: SetType);
var
    I: SetElement;
begin
    while not EOLN do
    begin
        Read (I);
        S[I] := true
    end;
    ReadLn
end;
```

```
procedure WriteSet (var S: SetType);
var
    I: integer;
begin
    for I := 1 to MaxElementNumber do
        if S[I] then
            Write (I, '   ')
end;
```

3.4 ANALYSIS OF THE ARRAY IMPLEMENTATION OF SETS

Analysis of the algorithms for processing sets with an array implementation is simplicity itself: they are all linear or faster. Union, Intersection, and Difference are clear: each contains a single loop that is executed N times, where N, in programming terms, is the value of MaxElementNumber. Considered as a polynomial in N, this expression is obviously linear, for the highest power of N is one. The running time of all of these procedures is $O(N)$.

The boolean functions to test for set empty, equal, or subset are also linear, because they have to test all corresponding pairs of elements to establish the true result. Of course, this is a worst case. If the first element of a set is present, for example, SetIsEmpty can answer "false" after examining that one element. The average is something in between, depending on the average number of set elements during execution.

If we know something about the nature of the set, it may be possible to speed up these operations. In the Sieve procedure, for example, SetIsEmpty starts testing at 1. We are deleting small elements first, so this guarantees that toward the end of the operation, program execution will slow to a crawl. A solution in this case is to start the testing with MaxElementNumber and work backwards. In that case, the average number of array positions that have to be tested to discover that the set is not empty is very much smaller.

The procedures to add or delete an element, as well as to test set membership, execute in constant time. That is, their execution time does not depend on the size of the set (assuming, of course, that here too we use var parameters in Pascal).

As for storage space, this implementation requires one boolean variable for each possible element, i.e., as many booleans as the size of the universal set. In many computers a boolean variable is stored in one byte (eight bits), but in some it requires 16, 32, or 36. This is somewhat painful when we consider that a boolean variable, since it holds only a true/false value, can be stored in *one* bit. We use a full boolean variable of eight or more bits because, in Pascal, we have no way to decompose a variable into any smaller component. If we had a serious amount of work to do with sets we would probably turn to a representation in which a boolean value is stored in a single bit and use machine language or some higher level language other than Pascal. This is precisely what happens when a Pascal compiler encounters the predefined type set, the topic of the next section.

3.5 THE PASCAL IMPLEMENTATION OF SETS

Our basic operating premise is that we allocate one bit to represent each set element. If the bit is one, the element is present in the set, and if the bit is zero, it is not. In the architecture of many computers, eight bits make one *byte;* no computer directly addresses less than one byte, and many permit 16, 32, 48, 64, or some other number of bits to be manipulated with one machine instruction.

Thus, we stand to save considerable time with this method, as compared with the array implementation. And, in any Pascal system in which the elements of a boolean array are stored in the space of one or more bytes, we also save space.[1]

The method of the last section used an array of `boolean`; the method we are investigating now uses a collection of bits. A collection of bits in a word can be thought of as an array of bits (although it is not literally that in Pascal programming terms). And, because an array is the programming analog of a vector, this method for handling sets is usually called a *bit-vector* implementation.

When a universal set contains more elements than there are bits in a word in the machine in question, then more than one word is used. A formula, described later, determines which bit of which word represents a given element.

The bit-vector approach is attractive because at the machine level, all the corresponding pairs of bits in two words can be operated on with single instructions that give the effect of union and intersection. Suppose, for example, that we have two sets, each of which has a maximum of eight elements, namely the integers from 0 to 7. We can represent such a set by making each element correspond to one bit of one byte. If the bits of a byte are numbered from 0 to 7 from the left, which is one way it is done, then the set {0, 3, 5, 6, 7} would be represented by the byte `10010111,` and the set {2, 3, 4, 5} would be represented by `00111100.`

With these representations, the union of the two sets can be found with a single machine instruction that carries out the bit-wise logical operation `or` on each pair of bits in the two bytes. This yields `10111111,` the representation of the union of the two sets, {0, 2, 3, 4, 5, 6, 7}. Similarly, the intersection of the two sets could be found with a bit-wise `and` operation in one instruction, giving `00010100,` which is the representation of {3, 5}. The subset operation is almost as simple. We *complement* the second byte (change all 1s to zeros and vice versa), which takes one instruction, then `and` that with the first byte. If the result is all zeros, which can be tested in a single instruction, then there is no bit pair in which the bit from the first byte was one and the bit from the second (original, un-complemented) byte was zero.

In most computers it is possible to carry out these bit-wise boolean operations on words of at least 16 bits and, in many cases, 32 or more. For sets of up to these numbers of bits, therefore, the various set operations are very fast indeed. When the number of set elements exceeds the number of bits in a word, more words must be used and the process is slowed. A simple way to assign an element to a bit-location follows. Assume that the set elements are integers starting at zero and that there are B bits per machine word. Then the bit for set element I is found in word `I div B`, bit `I mod B`. Suppose, for example, that the word length is 32. Then element 3 is in word 0, bit 3; element 32 is in word 1, bit 0; element 69 is in word 2, bit 5.

If we wish to use Pascal's set operations for their speed and notational convenience but find that our sets are larger than the maximum allowed by our compiler, then it is possible to establish an array of sets, using some modification of a formula like that just shown, to decide which set in the array holds the element of interest.

---

[1]But in some implementations, a `packed array of boolean` results in precisely the one-bit-per-element technique we are discussing.

3.6 ANALYSIS OF THE BIT-VECTOR IMPLEMENTATION OF SETS

If the maximum number of elements in a set is not larger than the number of bits that can be processed in a single `and` or `or` instruction, then the time required for the set operations with a bit-vector implementation is constant. That is, whether we have three elements in a set or 16 (assuming our machine has a word length of at least 16 bits), the time required to form the union of two sets, or to determine if one is a subset of another, takes the same amount of time. It does not depend on N. This is obviously much more desirable than the linear time of the array method.

On the other hand, if the maximum number of elements, N, is greater than the number of bits in a word, B, then the logical operations to find the union or to test for subset have to be executed about N/B times. This is approximately B times faster than for the array implementation. We have to add the qualification "approximately" because we must consider loop overhead. However, the bit-vector approach is still faster.

Here, then, is a case where we care about the proportionality constant in the analysis of running time. If we have one method that is $O(N^2)$ and another that is $O(N)$, then we just don't care about the proportionality constants. At some point, whenever N gets big enough, the linear method has to be faster. However, when we are comparing two linear methods and one is 16 times faster than the other, then naturally we prefer the faster one, other things being equal.

This comparison between these two methods of implementing sets provides an interesting counter-example to a generalization that is true more often than not: in choosing algorithms we usually have a trade-off between speed and storage space. Fast methods take lots of storage; slow methods conserve storage. However, this is not always true: the bit-vector method is both faster in execution time *and* more economical of storage than the array method.

Then, would anyone except a textbook author with a point to make ever actually use the array method? Certainly. A programmer using a language without set features and without any way to do bit-wise logical operations might find it the best choice. Likewise, a Pascal programmer with sets too large for the limits imposed by the compiler might find it faster to program an array implementation, as in the previous section, than to get into the complexities of arrays of sets. This brings us to a third factor in comparing implementations: programming time. On a small job that is expected to run only a few times and where there is plenty of storage, the best algorithm is often the one you know best.

Anyone who is willing to tell you "The best method for X is Y," where X is sorting, searching, symbol table manipulation, or most anything else of the type considered in this book—that person can be marked down as inexperienced. The best method for one circumstance may be hopeless in another. Space, execution time, and programming time are three factors that such choices depend on, and we shall see others. A major purpose of this text is to help you understand the trade-offs involved in picking a data structure and an algorithm for a particular problem, so that you can make intelligent decisions about choices of methods.

As we leave sets for the time being, consider this tantalizer: wouldn't it be nice if we could find a method that would handle the set operations in constant time, regardless of the size of the sets? And wouldn't it be nice it we didn't have to know at the time we program an algorithm how big the sets might get, just so we have enough storage available in the computer? Such a thing is quite impossible with the methods of this chapter. But we shall see in Chapter 10, in connection with a graph algorithm, that if we need only the union and set membership operations, then with the expenditure of some extra storage we can do exactly that.

3.7 THE ADT STRING

Our second major topic for this chapter is the ADT string.

A *string,* for our purposes, is a linear sequence of zero or more of the characters representable in the machine, together with the following operations. The names are those of procedures and functions in the string package that will be developed later.

`MakeStrEmpty` sets the length of the string named as its argument to zero. Any previous value is lost.

`StrLength` returns the length (number of characters) in the string named as its argument.

`AppendChar` appends the value of its second argument, which must be a string constant, to the right end of the string that is its first argument.

`ReadLnStr` reads characters from the current position of the file pointer to the end of line, and makes its string argument equal to the characters read. The "`Ln`" is included in the name to indicate that the operation reads to the end of the current line and then leaves the file pointer positioned at the start of the next line.

`WriteStr` writes the value of its argument. It does *not* move the output file pointer to the beginning of the next line. This permits you to invoke `WriteStr` several times to get several strings on the same line of output. Moving the file pointer to the next line is done with the ordinary Pascal `WriteLn` statement.

Some fairly arbitrary decisions have been made in devising these operations, based on convenience in expected use. The ADT string could reasonably be defined in ways that would differ in many details.

`ConcatStr` *concatenates*[2] the string named as its second argument to the right end of the string named as its first argument. This is a fundamental string operation, analogous to addition for numbers and union for sets. Most programming languages that have a string capability have a concatenation operator; *overloading* + for this purpose is one possibility. (Overloading an operator means that it specifies different operations with different ADTs, just as + already means integer addition or real addition, depending on the type of its operands.) Another way this procedure could be set up would be with three arguments. In that case, the first argument gets the concatenation of the second and third.

[2]The Latin root *catena* means "chain." The idea is that we are "chaining" two strings together.

`DeleteStr` accepts a string, together with arguments defining the starting point and the number of characters to be deleted. The deleted portion is not saved. For example, if the value of string `Name` is `John Q. Public` when we execute `DeleteStr (Name, 6, 3)`, then the new value of `Name` will be `John Public`.

`InsertStr` is the inverse of `DeleteStr`: the value of the string that is its first argument is inserted into the string that is its second argument, beginning at the position given by its third argument. Thus, if the value of `Name` is `John Public` and the value of `MiddleName` is `Quincy` (seven characters including final blank), then executing `InsertStr (MiddleName, Name, 6)` gives `Name` the value `John Quincy Public`.

`CopyStr` takes a string as its first argument, together with arguments giving the starting position and length of a substring; the fourth argument specifies where to place the substring (which is not deleted.) Thus, if the value of `Name` is `John Q. Public`, then executing `CopyStr (Name, 1, 4, FirstName)` leaves `Name` unchanged and gives `FirstName` the value `John`.

`SearchStr` is a function that accepts as arguments two strings called `Pattern` and `Source`. If `Pattern` occurs in `Source`, the character position of the first such occurrence (first from the left) is returned as the value of the function. If there is no such occurrence, zero is returned as the function value. Thus, with `Name` having the value `John Q. Public` and `LastName` having the value `Public`, then `SearchStr (LastName, Name)` returns 9 as the value of the function. `Name` is unchanged. Searching for `Quincy` would return zero, because that string does not occur in `John Q. Public`.

`CompareStr` is a function that determines whether its first argument is less than, equal to, or greater than its second argument. It returns one of the characters `<`, `=`, or `>`. We are forced to provide some such mechanism because we cannot overload the relational operators any more than we can overload the arithmetic operators.

What exactly do we mean when we say that the value of one string of characters is "less" than that of another? First, we mean that individual characters are compared according to the *collating sequence* of the machine being used, that is, the sequence into which the allowable characters are ordered by a comparison.[3] A comma, for instance, is "less" than any letter in my machine, because that is how the character set was designed.

The other question about string comparison is what is the answer when the two strings are of unequal length and all the characters match, up to the length of the shorter? Are they equal? The usual answer, adopted here, is based on what people typically want to do with strings. In such a case the shorter string is taken to be smaller. The situation where two strings match in some number of characters at the left and then differ, is clearcut: the entire comparison then depends

---

[3]The Latin root of the term "collating" has to do with "bringing together," and "comparison." In the decades before the widespread arrival of computers, roughly the 1950s, the fastest way to do the kinds of things we now do with computers involved a great deal of movement of punched cards. A device called a *collator* was used to compare values on two decks of cards and carry out various data processing operations on the cards based on the result of the comparison.

on just the first two differing characters. Both of these decisions are normal practice in alphabetization: Smith comes before Smithers, and McCracken comes before McDuff.[4] This is lexicographic ordering, of which we encountered a special case in Chapter 2 in the discussion of arrays.

3.8 TWO ILLUSTRATIONS OF THE USE OF THE ADT STRING

Before looking into the implementation of these operations, let us pause to see them in action. Although you have not yet seen the precise definition of their parameters, the carefully chosen names we use will allow you to read and understand the code anyway.

Figure 3.2 is a procedure that illustrates the use of some of these operations in a simple task of determining whether the strings in the file it reads are people's addresses in the filing system for my correspondence. A person's address, for my purposes, is a string of at least four but not more than eight characters, the last three of which are ADD. Thus, HENRYADD is an address, but HENRY723, ADDING, BINADDER, and ADD are not.

In this procedure, `IdentifyAddresses`, we first build up the constant `ADD` for use in the `SearchStr` operation. Within the `while not EOF` loop, we first search for the substring `ADD`. Then, an `if` statement checks for satisfaction of the various parts of my definition of an address. The procedure could have been set up in many other ways, such as by testing each of the last three characters individually and not using the constant `ADD`. Fig. 3.3 shows the output when this program was run. Observe that a blank line was handled correctly. A file name can't be all blanks, of course, but unless such a case is to be reported as an error it should be handled gracefully.

For a second illustration of our string package, let us examine procedures to sort a group of names and to reformat them. The names will be entered in a last-name-first format: "Adam Q. Smith," for example, would be entered as "Smith,Adam Q.". This is done because names in this form alphabetize correctly. "Smith,Adam Q." alphabetizes before "Smith,Maggie" because, although the first six characters match, A is less than M. "Smith,John" comes before "Smithers,John" because a comma (in the collating sequence of essentially all current computers) is less than any letter. With a few more conventions, such as semicolons setting off prefixes (Ms., Dr.) and suffixes (Jr., IV), names can be sorted in this form with no extra work. In a system intended primarily for data processing, a name in such a form should be a separate data type, with simple ways to convert to any reasonable output form.

---

[4]Which is not to say that all the alphabetization rules in common practice would be correctly handled by CompareStr. Knuth, in *The Art of Computer Programming*, Vol. 3 (Sorting and Searching), Reading, Ma: Addison-Wesley, pp. 8–9, gives an amusing listing of the way about 50 book titles would be "alphabetized" by the rules of the American Library Association. "1812, ein historischer roman," would be filed with the "As," because numbers are spelled out, and in German, 1812 is *Achtzehnhundert zwölf;* but "1812 ouverture" would go under "D" because 1812 in French is *Dix-huit cent douze.*

```
procedure IdentifyAddresses;

{ An "address," the way I devise file names for my word
  processing system, is four to eight characters, inclusive,
  the last three of which are ADD. }

var
   StringIn: StrType;
   Pos: StrIndex;
   ADD: StrType;    { to hold a constant }
begin
   MakeStrEmpty (ADD);
   AppendChar (ADD, 'A');
   AppendChar (ADD, 'D');
   AppendChar (ADD, 'D');

   while not EOF do
   begin
      ReadLnStr (StringIn);
      WriteStr (StringIn);
      Pos := SearchStr (ADD, StringIn);
      if (Pos > 1) and (Pos < 7)
           and (Pos = StrLength(StringIn) - 2) then
         WriteLn ('   is an address')
      else
         WriteLn ('   is not an address')
   end
end;
```

FIGURE 3.2
A procedure to identify "addresses" in a filing system, using the string procedures shown later.

```
HENRYADD    is an address
HENRY522    is not an address
JANADD    is an address
PAULADD    is an address
DADD    is an address
ADD    is not an address
Q    is not an address
     is not an address
BINADDER    is not an address
ILLEGALADD    is not an address
WSDADD    is an address
```

FIGURE 3.3
The output when the procedure of Figure 3.2 was combined with string procedures and a main program, and then run.

ReformatName, shown in Figure 3.4, is a procedure that is called by SortAndFormatNames, shown in Figure 3.5. The purpose of ReformatName is to convert a name from a form like "Smith,Adam Q.", to a more conventional form like "Adam Q. Smith". ReformatName begins by setting up a comma as a constant and then searching for the first instance of a comma in NameIn. If there is no comma, the name is sent back unchanged. Otherwise, we form a substring consisting of all the characters preceding the first comma, which is taken to be the last name. Then we delete everything up to and including the first comma, append a blank, and finally concatenate the last name to the rest.

SortAndFormatNames, shown together with the procedure Swap in Figure 3.5, declares the local variable Name to be an array of strings. Strings are read into this array and then sorted using selection sort. They are printed as read, with line numbers, so that you can see the before-and-after picture on sorting. The sorting method is the same used in Chapter 2, although here we use CompareStr for the comparison.

```
procedure ReformatName (NameIn: StrType;
                        var NameOut: StrType);

{ Convert a name in the form Smith,Adam Quincy to the form
  Adam Quincy Smith. If NameIn does not contain a comma,
  NameOut gets NameIn unchanged.
  Note that NameIn is NOT a var parameter. }

var
    Comma: StrType;        { to hold a constant }
    CommaPos: StrIndex;
    LastName: StrType;

begin
    MakeStrEmpty (Comma);
    AppendChar (Comma, ',');

    CommaPos := SearchStr (Comma, NameIn);
    if CommaPos <> 0 then
    begin
        CopyStr (NameIn, 1, CommaPos - 1, LastName);
        DeleteStr (Namein, 1, CommaPos);
        AppendChar (NameIn, ' ');
        ConcatStr (NameIn, LastName)
    end;

    CopyStr (NameIn, 1, StrLength (NameIn), NameOut)
end;
```

FIGURE 3.4
A procedure to convert a person's name from a form in which it is easy to alphabetize, to a conventional form.

```
procedure Swap (var A, B: StrType);
var
   TempStr: StrType;
begin
   CopyStr (A, 1, MaxStrLength, TempStr);
   CopyStr (B, 1, MaxStrLength, A);
   CopyStr (TempStr, 1, MaxStrLength, B)
end;


procedure SortAndFormatNames;
type
   SortIndex = 1..100;
   NameArray = array [SortIndex] of StrType;
var
   Name: NameArray;
   TempStr: StrType;
   I, J, N, Small: SortIndex;

begin

   { Read and echo input }
   I := 1;
   while not EOF do
   begin
      ReadLnStr (TempStr);
      Write (I:4, ':    ');
      WriteStr (TempStr);
      WriteLn;
      CopyStr (TempStr, 1, MaxStrLength, Name[I]);
      I := I + 1
   end;
   N := I - 1;
   WriteLn;

   { Sort names }
   for I := 1 to N - 1 do
   begin
      Small := I;
      for J := I + 1 to N do
         if CompareStr (Name[J], Name[Small]) = '<' then
            Small := J;
      Swap (Name[I], Name[Small])
   end;

   { Write sorted output }
   for I := 1 to N do
   begin
      Write (I:4, ':    ');
      WriteStr (Name[I]);
      for J := 1 to 30 - StrLength (Name[I]) do
         Write (' ');
```

```
        ReformatName (Name[I], TempStr);
        WriteStr (TempStr);
        WriteLn
     end

end;
```

FIGURE 3.5
A procedure to sort names, then reformat them using the procedure of Figure 3.4.

The remainder of the procedure prints each unformatted name in a fixed width of 30 columns, by writing as many blanks as the difference between 30 and the length of the unformatted name, and then prints the formatted name. Here is output from the program that contains these procedures, when run with suitable data.

```
 1:    Truman,Harry S
 2:    Smithers,Maggie
 3:    Smith,Maggie
 4:    Smith,Adam Quincy
 5:    Jonson,Oh, Rare Ben
 6:    Pisa (Fibonacci),Leonardo of
 7:    Wolverton,Van
 8:    McCracken,Daniel D.
 9:    McDuff,Daniel D.
10:    Von Neumann,John
11:    Knuth,Donald Ervin
12:    Snavely
13:
14:    Blumenthal,Helen E.
15:    Gooden,Dwight "K"
16:    Cohen,Michael S.
17:    McCracken,Aliza Blanche

 1:
 2:    Blumenthal,Helen E.            Helen E. Blumenthal
 3:    Cohen,Michael S.               Michael S. Cohen
 4:    Gooden,Dwight "K"              Dwight "K" Gooden
 5:    Jonson,Oh, Rare Ben            Oh, Rare Ben Jonson
 6:    Knuth,Donald Ervin             Donald Ervin Knuth
 7:    McCracken,Aliza Blanche        Aliza Blanche McCracken
 8:    McCracken,Daniel D.            Daniel D. McCracken
 9:    McDuff,Daniel D.               Daniel D. McDuff
10:    Pisa (Fibonacci),Leonardo of   Leonardo of Pisa (Fibonacci)
11:    Smith,Adam Q.                  Adam Q. Smith
12:    Smith,Maggie                   Maggie Smith
13:    Smithers,Maggie                Maggie Smithers
14:    Snavely                        Snavely
15:    Truman,Harry S                 Harry S Truman
16:    Von Neumann,John               John Von Neumann
17:    Wolverton,Van                  Van Wolverton
```

Observe that a name with no comma was handled correctly, as was a blank line, and that in the case of two commas, processing was based on the first one.[5]

3.9 DESIGN CONSIDERATIONS IN IMPLEMENTING THE ADT STRING

There are two main design decisions in implementing the ADT string—how to store the characters, and how to treat errors in the use of the procedures.

We choose an array to hold the characters because it is one reasonable choice and because we have not yet discussed another reasonable choice, a linked list (see Chapter 6). For the number of characters in a string to be variable, given the rules of standard Pascal, we have no choice but to declare our[6] strings to be a fixed-size array of characters, and then to provide a separate means of letting our procedures set and test the actual length. We shall set up our string type as a record, with one field being an array that contains the characters of the string and with a separate field that gives the length. The maximum size of a string will be specified in a `const` declaration. Eighty is used in the following implementation because 80 is about the maximum line length we can read from a terminal. However, the program could work with shorter or longer strings as might be needed.

Two other ways to represent the length, both used in actual Pascal string extensions, would be to store the string length in element zero of the array or to place a special string-end character after the last character of data.

It should be clearly understood what is meant by ''variable-length strings'': *every* string variable is of variable length. We have no way to say ''I want this particular string to be 40 characters long, always, and if I assign something shorter to it, please pad out the right-hand side with blanks.'' Sometimes, especially in data processing applications, that is the normal way of doing things— but a variable set up that way isn't a variable-length string in Pascal. We have already seen, in the illustrative program to reformat names, one way that fixed-length fields on reports can be produced with our package.

The second major design consideration is how to handle errors in the use of the string procedures. If a user specifies deleting 20 characters starting at position −34, we obviously can't do it, and it is poor design to ignore the issue. If we let our `DeleteStr` procedure try to operate on such an argument, we can't even say exactly what will happen without knowing which operating system will be used. In some cases the operating system will catch the error and stop program execution, giving an error message that may tell the user very little about the

---

[5]''Harry S Truman'' has no period after the initial because that is how he preferred it: the ''S'' did not stand for anything. Another reminder of the vast range of exceptions that can crop up in commercial data processing, a factor that can overwhelm computer science graduates going into that field without adequate preparation.

[6]We say ''our'' strings because standard Pascal does, after all, provide strings—but they are the type that must be greater than one character, with no type compatibility except between strings of the same length. In all of what follows, unless stated otherwise, when the word ''string'' is used we mean the new type, not part of Pascal, that we are developing.

true source of the trouble. (''Run-time error 91—execution halted'' doesn't convey much information.) Worse, the procedure may lead to no error indication, but just produce wrong results.

In other cases it is not even clear what should be considered to be an error. Suppose the user asks for ten characters to be deleted, starting at position six, from a string that has only nine characters? Taken literally, this is an error in the sense that the instruction cannot be carried out. But we could take the view that the user might have intended simply to delete as many characters as remain in the string.

To approach this issue sensibly it may help to try to categorize the kinds of errors that we might encounter. Naturally, the worst are programming or design errors in the procedures themselves, such that for correct input they give incorrect results and no error message. But that is an issue in design, verification, implementation, and testing. Here, we focus on the specification issue. What constitutes an error, and what checking and error diagnostics shall we provide?

1. There may be errors that we cannot catch before they cause a run-time diagnostic and termination of program execution. The degree to which this happens depends on the type of operating system. A total program crash due to this sort of thing would be unacceptable in a production program. In such an environment, the operating system should provide options to let us diagnose such a fault before it might cause the whole program to crash.

2. There are errors that result from bad argument values, for which no reasonable interpretation is possible. An example would be a concatenation leading to a new string longer than the array size. The specification of a negative number of characters also falls in this category.

3. Finally, there are cases where it is essentially a matter of taste whether a given case is an error or not. An example was given above: deleting nonexistent characters at the end of a string. Another example would be an insertion specified to start beyond the end of the destination string. This could be treated either as an error, or as a *de facto* concatenation.

Other defensible design decisions about these issues are possible. Factors to be considered include the nature of the application (student program checkout or air traffic control?), the basic design approach to programming errors (assume the best or the worst about the programmer's intentions?), and perhaps performance requirements that would argue against run-time testing of a time-sensitive program than has been very thoroughly tested. For our purposes here, which are most heavily influenced by the educational value of what we do, we shall develop a package that will not crash at run time but which generally assumes the best about the programmer's intentions in situations where a strict literal interpretation based on the argument values is not possible.

In carrying out this plan, we encounter an interesting problem: under certain circumstances the error-checking built into some Pascal compilers and operating systems can defeat our purpose in the following way. The programs so far in this book have generally used type declarations that make it possible to do run-time range checking of values that are about to be assigned to variables (if the

Pascal system you are using has this capability.) For example, if we declare the type StrType = 0..MaxStrLength, then any attempt to assign a negative value to a variable of that type will result in a run-time diagnostic.

Now suppose that we specify StrType as the type of such parameters as StartPos in InsertStr or DeleteStr. If range-checking is in effect, then a procedure call with a negative value will cause the program to abort before any testing within the procedure can be carried out. The run-time message will be of the unhelpful ''value out range, PC = 38FA'' variety.

It is actually worse, in some cases, if we have specified such a type and range-checking is *not* in effect. Then, depending on how the compiler and the operating system have been set up, a negative number may be converted to a complement form, which will look to our procedures like a large positive number!

For this reason we shall use integer types on such parameters, which will bypass all run-time checking by the system, and make our own explicit checks.

3.10 IMPLEMENTATION OF A PACKAGE OF PROCEDURES FOR THE ADT STRING

Let us now investigate the procedures in this package, both as to how they are used and how they work. With two or three exceptions, the procedure bodies involve relatively straightforward array processing, which need not be explained in excruciating detail.

Note that in setting up a string package with standard Pascal, however, we are forced to do some rather awkward things. There is no way to use standard Pascal's string constants, for example, because a Pascal string is compatible only with another string of the same length. We are forced to the rather clumsy expedient of providing a procedure MakeStrEmpty that sets the length of a string to zero, along with a procedure AppendChar that appends a single-character constant to a string. A string constant for use with our procedures must be built up by multiple invocations of AppendChar. If we were building a string extension package to run with a modified Pascal compiler, we would simply add to the definition of the language, possibly using double quotes to signify our string constants.

With these considerations in mind, the following declarations must be present:

```
const
   MaxStrLength = 80;   { or whatever }

type
   StrIndex = 0..MaxStrLength;
   StrType = record
               Ch: array [1..MaxStrLength] of char;
               Length: StrIndex
             end;
```

Here now are the procedures and functions that implement the string operations defined at the beginning of our study of the string ADT. Each will be shown and briefly discussed.

`MakeStrEmpty` sets the length field of its argument to zero. Why make a procedure out of something so simple? *Because we want to hide the data structure*. Furthermore, giving the operation a name is in the spirit of the ADT approach: every operation that is part of an ADT has a name, and the user need know nothing about implementation.

```
procedure MakeStrEmpty (var S: StrType);
begin
    S.Length := 0
end;
```

`StrLength` is a function that returns the length of the string sent to it. We choose to make `StrLength` a function because it is so frequently needed as a parameter when another procedure is called. If it were a procedure, a separate statement would be needed to get the length. This would be no great problem, but the function approach improves the readability of a program that uses this package.

```
function StrLength (var S: StrType): StrIndex;
{ var parameter used to prevent copying array. }
begin
    StrLength := S.Length
end;
```

The use of a `var` parameter here does not save as much time, ordinarily, as it does with sets. We shall, however, make a general practice of writing all arrays as `var` parameters unless there is some specific reason not to do so.

`AppendChar` appends a character at the right end of a string. If this is attempted with a string that is already of maximum length, no reasonable error recovery is possible. We note this fact with an *assertion* about the operation of the procedure, which we write as a comment. There are programming languages in which such an assertion would automatically be checked at run time; here, it is a statement about what we expect of the data the procedure processes, which we will explicitly test. We shall see more about assertions as a tool for producing correct programs in Chapter 8. Until then, we shall use them simply as another form of documentation.

```
procedure AppendChar (var S: StrType;
                         Ch: char);

{ Append Ch to right end of S. }

{ Assert: S.Length + 1 <= MaxStrLength. }

begin
    if S.Length = MaxStrLength then
        StrError (1)
    else
    begin
        S.Length := S.Length + 1;
        S.Ch[S.Length] := Ch
    end
end;
```

Exactly what is done when the error condition is detected is a design decision. Perhaps the program should be halted with as much information about the cause of the trouble as possible. In that case we might wish to print the offending string. Perhaps the program that invoked `AppendChar` should be sent an error code and given the opportunity to take its own corrective measures. We shall not try to settle this issue, which has different answers in different circumstances. We shall just prevent a run-time crash by testing for the possibility first and then simply issuing a diagnostic message. `StrError` is such a procedure.

```
procedure StrError (ErrorNumber: integer);
begin
   case ErrorNumber of
   1: WriteLn ('AppendChar attempting to exceed MaxStrLength');
   2: WriteLn ('ReadLnStr attempting to exceed MaxStrLength');
   3: WriteLn ('ConcatStr attempting to exceed MaxStrLength');
   4: WriteLn ('DeleteStr number of characters < 0');
   5: WriteLn ('InsertStr attempting to exceed MaxStrLength');
   6: WriteLn ('CopyStr number of characters < 0')
   end
end;
```

This procedure also shows the other errors that we shall diagnose and report. Most of them, it may be noted, would be either the result of programming errors, which should be caught in testing, or run-time problems with unexpected data, for which the calling program could check. For example, if there is the possibility that a concatenation could produce a result that is too long, a test could be made of the lengths of the strings being concatenated. The one exception to this generalization is `ReadLnStr`, to which we now turn.

```
procedure ReadLnStr (var S: StrType);

{ Read from position of file pointer to EOLN, then ReadLn.
  Discard any previous contents of S. }

{ Assert: MaxStrLength not exceeded. }

var
   I: StrIndex;
begin
   I := 0;
   while (not EOLN) and (I < MaxStrLength) do
   begin
      I := I + 1;
      Read (S.Ch[I])
   end;

   S.Length := I;
   if not EOLN then
      StrError (2);
   ReadLn
end;
```

`ReadLnStr` begins with the character currently pointed to by the file pointer, and reads to the end of the line. It then carries out a `ReadLn` statement to position the pointer at the start of the next line. This is a strictly *ad hoc* decision for an illustrative program. It permits us to read other things before reading the last part of the record into one of our strings. The alternative would be to define some character in the input as designating the end of a string, or perhaps to permit the user to specify a set of such characters. Because all we actually do with the package is read data for a few programs that illustrate string operations, we will not go to this trouble.

The program that invokes `ReadLnStr` clearly cannot test in advance for excessive string length, because that depends on the data encountered by `ReadLnStr`. This kind of testing is needed even in the most carefully designed program: there is no way for the program designer to guarantee that wrong data will never be supplied to the program.

`WriteStr` is simpler. We will often wish to write other things on a line after writing a string, so this procedure does not do a `WriteLn`.

```
procedure WriteStr (var S: StrType);

{ Write the string, but do NOT execute a WriteLn. }

var
   I: StrIndex;
begin
   for I := 1 to S.Length do
      Write (S.Ch[I])
end;
```

`ConcatStr` makes two strings into one. This procedure, like `Append-Char`, could cause a run-time error if it caused a string index to exceed `MaxStringLength`.

```
procedure ConcatStr (var Left, Right: StrType);

{ Left gets concatenation of Left and Right. }

{ Assert: Left.Length + Right.Length <= MaxStrLength. }

var
   I: StrIndex;
begin
   if Left.Length + Right.Length > MaxStrLength then
      StrError (3)
   else
   begin
      for I := 1 to Right.Length do
         Left.Ch[Left.Length + I] := Right.Ch[I];
      Left.Length := Left.Length + Right.Length
   end
end;
```

For `DeleteStr` we decided that it is not wrong to try to delete more characters from the end of a string than exist. We simply delete as many characters as remain. This also means that if the user says to delete more characters than there are in the string, starting at position 1, the result is the empty string. Following this design philosophy, namely that the user knows what he or she is doing, we simply do nothing if the specified starting position is outside the string. Specification of a negative numbers of characters, on the other hand, is hard to imagine as intentional, and is flagged as an error. Always keep in mind that other designs could lead to different answers to these kinds of questions.

```
procedure DeleteStr (var S: StrType;
                         StartPos: integer;
                         NumChars: integer);

{ Starting at StartPos, delete NumChars or to end of string.
  If StartPos < 1 or > S.Length, do nothing. }

{ Assert: NumChars >= 0. }

var
   I: StrIndex;
begin
   if (StartPos < 1)
        or (StartPos > S.Length) then    { do nothing }
   else if NumChars < 0 then
      StrError (4)
   else
   begin
      I := StartPos;
      while I + NumChars <= S.Length do
      begin
         S.Ch[I] := S.Ch[I + NumChars];
         I := I + 1
      end;

      if StartPos + NumChars > S.Length then
         S.Length := StartPos - 1
      else
         S.Length := S.Length - NumChars
   end

end;
```

The work of `InsertStr` is a little more complicated than that of `DeleteStr` because we have to make room for the string to be inserted before actually inserting it. This must be done working from right to left to avoid writing over, and thus destroying, characters that have not yet been moved. Our design philosophy leads to interpreting a starting position outside the range of the destination string as meaning that the two strings should be concatenated. But any attempt to exceed the maximum string length is still an error from which we cannot recover.

```
procedure InsertStr (var Source, Dest: StrType;
                     StartPos: integer);

{ Insert Source into Dest, with the first character of Source
  becoming character number StartPos of the modified Dest.
  If StartPos < 1, effect is like ConcatStr (Source, Dest);
  if StartPos > Dest.Length, effect is like
  ConcatStr (Dest, Source). }

{ Assert: Dest.Length + Source.Length <= MaxStrLength. }

var
   I: StrIndex;
begin
   if StartPos < 1 then
      StartPos := 1;
   if StartPos > Dest.Length then
      StartPos := Dest.Length + 1;

   if Dest.Length + Source.Length > MaxStrLength then
      StrError (5)
   else
   begin
      { Make room, working from right
        so as not to destroy characters to keep }
      for I := Dest.Length downto StartPos do
         Dest.Ch[I + Source.Length] := Dest.Ch[I];

      { Insert Source into the space made available in Dest }
      for I := 1 to Source.Length do
         Dest.Ch[StartPos + I - 1] := Source.Ch[I];
      Dest.Length := Dest.Length + Source.Length
   end
end;
```

CopyStr is used to copy part or all of a source string to a destination string. A starting position outside the source is not treated as an error, but simply results in an empty destination string. Likewise, any attempt to copy past the end of the source is simply terminated when no more characters remain. A negative number of characters, on the other hand, is still reported as an error.

```
procedure CopyStr (var Source: StrType;
                       StartPos: integer;
                       NumChars: integer;
                       var Dest: StrType);

{ Starting at StartPos in Source, copy characters to Dest.
  Copy NumChars or until end of Source.
  If StartPos < 1 or > Source.Length, make Dest empty. }

{ Assert: NumChars >= 0. }

var
   I: integer;
begin
   if (StartPos < 1) or (StartPos > Source.Length) then
      Dest.Length := 0
   else if NumChars < 0 then
      StrError (6)
   else
   begin
      I := 1;
      while (I <= NumChars)
         and (StartPos + I - 1 <= Source.Length) do
      begin
         Dest.Ch[I] := Source.Ch[StartPos + I - 1];
         I := I + 1
      end;
      Dest.Length := I - 1
   end
end;
```

The main design issue with the function `SearchStr` is what to do if the string being sought is empty. To return a zero would be to say ''nothing doesn't exist,'' which strains both language and logic. Our decision is to report character position 1 in this case; any user who finds that choice unsatisfactory is free to test the length of the search pattern before invoking `SearchStr`. A search pattern longer than the source obviously cannot exist in the source, and this is tested before going into the search loop.

```
function SearchStr (var Pattern, Source: StrType): StrIndex;

{ Return the character position where Pattern starts in Source,
  if it does, and otherwise zero. If Pattern is the empty
  string, return 1. }

var
   P: integer;     { position in Pattern }
   S: integer;     { position in Source }
begin
   if Pattern.Length = 0 then
      SearchStr := 1
   else if Pattern.Length > Source.Length then
      SearchStr := 0
   else
   begin
      P := 1;
      S := 1;
      repeat
         if Pattern.Ch[P] = Source.Ch[S] then
         begin
            P := P + 1;
            S := S + 1
         end
         else
         begin
            S := S - P + 2;
            P := 1
         end
      until (P > Pattern.Length) or (S > Source.Length);

      if P > Pattern.Length then
         SearchStr := S - Pattern.Length
      else
         SearchStr := 0
   end
end;
```

The searching is done with two indices, one for each string. If they point at matching characters, both indices are incremented. If the characters don't match, the index to the source string is reset to the next character and the index to the pattern is reset to 1. Eventually we will reach the end of one string or the other; if the termination is caused by reaching the end of the search pattern, we have found a match.

An example is in order. Suppose we are looking for the search pattern "lamp" in the source string "Aladdin's lamp is mine."

```
P:  1 2 3 4
    l a m p

S:  0 0 0 0 0 0 0 0 0 1 1 1 1 1 1 1 1 1 1 2 2 2
    1 2 3 4 5 6 7 8 9 0 1 2 3 4 5 6 7 8 9 0 1 2 3
    A l a d d i n ' s   l a m p   i s   m i n e
```

We start with P = 1 pointing to "l" and S = 1 pointing to "A". These characters are not equal, so the statement S := S − P + 2 increases S to 2, and P is reset to 1. The "l" in "lamp" now matches the "l" in "Aladdin's", so P is increased to 2 and S to 3. The "a" in "lamp" matches the "a" in "Aladdin's", so P is increased to 3 and S to 4. But now "m" does not match "d," so S is reset to 3 and P to 1. Nothing matches for the next eight repetitions of the loop until S = 11 and P = 1. Now the pairs of characters match through the end of the search pattern, and the repeat terminates because P has been incremented to a value greater than the length of the search pattern. At this point S is 15 and P is 5. Fifteen minus the length of "lamp" gives 11, the starting point of the string "lamp" within "Aladdins's lamp is mine." If we were to search for "lantern," say, then the termination of the repeat would be caused by S becoming greater than the length of the source pattern, meaning that the search pattern was not found. In this case, SearchStr returns zero.

This is one version of a classical problem in computer science called *pattern matching*. It turns up in many applications. One frequent use is the kind of thing just illustrated, searching for a string of characters in a body of text in a word processing system. This chapter, for example, contains about 67,000 characters at this point. I might wish, for example, to begin at the start of the chapter and find all instances of the string "signalled," which I have just looked up and found to have a preferred spelling of "signaled." And I don't want to wait several minutes while an inefficient algorithm plods through the text. It turns out that there are algorithms that are much faster than the brute force method used here for searching. In some the "alphabet" (the set of possible characters) is reduced, such as searching in a string of binary digits. The interested reader is referred to the treatment in Sedgewick (1983), which includes a fascinating summary of the history of development of pattern matching algorithms. (His moral to the story: there can be *much* better algorithms waiting to be discovered in situations where most of us might think the obvious way is the only one possible; such discoveries can come through both theoretical and practical investigations.)

Before moving on, note that the variables P and S were declared to be of type integer, not StrIndex. Why is that? The problem is that if the search pattern matches at the very end of a string that is of length MaxStr-Length, S legitimately gets a value one greater than MaxStrLength. If this variable had been declared to be of type StrIndex, then run-time checking would report an "error" that, in fact, is not an error. This is not as bad as failing to report an actual error, but is obviously to be avoided.

CompareStr uses logic that is simpler than SearchStr in one way—
it needs only one index to work through both strings. However, it is more
complex in another: if the while loop terminates because the end of one string
has been reached, there are still three possible outcomes of the comparison. The
while is set up to terminate either because MatchSoFar becomes false
or because the end of either string is reached. If, as we work across the two
strings, comparing a character from one against a character from the other, the
two characters do not match, then we know that the strings are not the same and
a simple test decides which is larger. When this occurs MatchSoFar is set to
false, which bypasses the rest of the logic. If the while terminates because
the strings are not the same length, then all the characters checked must have
matched. If the two strings are of the same length, then they are equal. Otherwise,
the shorter string is smaller.

```
function CompareStr (var S1, S2: StrType): char;

{ Compare S1 and S2. Return the character
  '<' if S1 < S2, '=' if S1 = S2, and '>' if S1 > S2.
  Two strings are equal if they are of same length and all
  characters match; if all characters match up to the length of
  the shorter, then the shorter is smaller. }

var
   I: integer;
   MatchSoFar: boolean;
begin
   I := 1;
   MatchSoFar := true;

   while MatchSoFar and (I <= S1.Length) and (I <= S2.Length) do
      if S1.Ch[I] = S2.Ch[I] then
         I := I + 1
      else
      begin
         MatchSoFar := false;
         if S1.Ch[I] < S2.Ch[I] then
            CompareStr := '<'
         else
            CompareStr := '>'
      end;

   if MatchSoFar then
      if S1.Length = S2.Length then
         CompareStr := '='
      else if S1.Length < S2.Length then
         CompareStr := '<'
      else
         CompareStr := '>'

   end;
```

3.11 ANALYSIS OF THE ARRAY IMPLEMENTATION OF STRINGS

The analysis of this implementation of strings is almost too simple to be very interesting. A few of the operations execute in constant time (`MakeStr-Empty, StrLength, AppendChar`). Most of the rest are linear in the length of their operands. Our `SearchStr` has a worst-case performance that is of the order of the product of the search pattern length and the source string length. To see this, try searching for `AAAAAB` in `AAAAAAAAAAAAAAAAAAAAAAAAB`. In word processing applications, however, such a case would be almost pathological. In such use the algorithm is ordinarily only slightly worse than linear in the length of the search pattern. As noted, faster algorithms exist.

In terms of space, every string in this implementation takes the same amount of space—as many characters as the longest string permitted, plus one integer. If many actual strings are shorter than this maximum, then obviously some space is being wasted. To conserve space, one solution might be to establish several different maximum string lengths possibly distinguished by another parameter, but this would rapidly become awkward. The other solution would be to use linked lists, as described in Chapter 6.

3.12 CONCLUSION

Our investigation of sets and strings has provided you with an opportunity to see the ADT approach in action, where many more operations are needed than with arrays and records, and where a number of design decisions are required in the implementation. In both cases there are other reasonable implementations, depending on the circumstances, and we shall see some of them later.

Sets are provided in a few programming languages and strings are provided in most. String features, however, are far from standardized. And, because Pascal provides strings that are so rudimentary as to be of little use, implementers have designed their own string extensions—and they, too, differ widely, which impedes portability.

If you wish to use the set and string ADTs as implemented here, you will likely need to modify them in major or minor ways to fit your application, language, and operating system, but you have a solid beginning for such work.

PROGRAM

EXERCISES

1.

 If we wish to implement the ADT `Set`, using the built-in Pascal set type but keeping the same 11 operation names listed at the beginning of the chapter, we must write a Pascal procedure for each operation. For example

```pascal
procedure MakeSetEmpty (var S: SomeSetType);
begin
   S := []
end;
```

STARTING := CLOCK
SIEVEOFERATOSTHENES;
ENDTIME := CLOCK
WRITELN (TOTAL TIME := 1 , (ENDTIM-
STARTIME / NO 'SECO'

 would do for the first operation.
   (a) Write Pascal procedures for each of the other ten set operations.
   (b) Compile and run `SieveOfEratosthenes`, substituting your procedures for those used in the array implementation. (You may have to use a sieve considerably smaller than 1000 elements. Check your Pascal compiler for the maximum set size allowed.)

} CHECK NOTE AND p80-90

   (c) If you are able to access a `TIME` function in your operating system, run both versions of `SieveOfEratosthenes` and compare running times.
   (d) To get around the set size limit, `Sieve` could be implemented as an array of sets, with the first k elements in `Sieve [1]`, the second k elements in `Sieve [2]`, and the nth k elements in `Sieve [n]`. Well, almost. Check your Pascal compiler for limitations on set elements, and implement `SieveOfEratosthenes` to accommodate up to 1000 integers. Once again, the only changes necessary should be in the data declarations and the associated operations.

2. Much of formal set theory was developed in the nineteenth century by the English mathematician, George Boole. A collection of elements, B, with two operations, `Union` ($\cup$) and `Complement` ($'$), that satisfy the following axioms is called a *Boolean Algebra*.

   (i) $a \cup b = b \cup a$ $\qquad\qquad\qquad$ $(a, b \in B)$
   (ii) $a \cup (b \cup c) = (a \cup b) \cup c$ $\qquad$ $(a, b, c \in B)$
   (iii) $(a' \cup b')' \cup (a' \cup b)' = a$ $\qquad$ $(a, b \in B)$

(These axioms were developed by the American mathematician, E. V. Huntington.)

   (a) Draw a Venn (circle) diagram to convince yourself of the reasonableness of (iii) if B is a collection of sets.
   (b) Write a Pascal procedure to implement the complement operation, using the boolean array set implementation of this chapter.
   (c) Repeat (b) using the built-in Pascal set operations.
   (d) Notice that the operation of `Intersection` is not mentioned in the axioms. How could you define `Intersection` using only `Union` and `Complement`? (Hint: A Venn diagram or two might be helpful.) Write a Pascal procedure, `Intersection2`, to implement this operation and use only `Union` and `Complement`. Use the boolean array `SetType`.
   (e) Repeat (d) using the built-in Pascal set type. (Don't use "`*`", because that is what we are re-defining.)

3. Perhaps you have heard of the elements of a Boolean Algebra as being `true` and `false,` instead of as sets. In this interpretation ∪ is thought of as "Or" and ′ is thought of as "Not."

   (a) Rewrite the three axioms above, replacing ∪ with `Or` and ′ with `Not`. Show that the axioms hold for all assignments of *a, b, c* to `true` and `false`.

   (b) `true` can be implemented as 1 and `false` as 0. Then `Not(1) = 0`, and `Not(0) = 1`. And, `a Or b = 1` if `(a = 1)` or `(b = 1)`. Show that the axioms hold for this interpretation.

4. An ADT `BooleanAlgebra` would include two operations `BooleanOr` and `BooleanNot,` as described above. Implement the ADT using the truth functional scheme described in Exercise 3. An implementation consists of deciding on something to represent the type itself, e.g. 0..1, and then writing procedures for the operations. You can prove your `BooleanAlgebra` implementation correct, by showing that the implemented operations satisfy the axioms listed in Exercise 2.

5. A second limitation on sets in Pascal, in addition to set size, is that set elements must be ordinal types, such as positive integers or characters. In some applications, the natural data type might be a set of records or some other structured type. The array implementation of sets can be used here if we maintain an additional array of set values that contain the records themselves. $S = \{1, 4, 5\}$ would thus indicate that `Value [1]`, `Value [4]` and `Value [5]`, were in set `S`.

   (a) Rewrite the procedures `ReadSet` and `WriteSet` to accommodate sets of records.

   (b) We might also want to change `MakeUniversalSet` to initialize the `Value` array. Would any other set procedures need changes?

6. Rewrite the function `SearchStr` to search the source string from right to left for occurrences of the pattern string.

7. A *haiku* is a Japanese poem containing exactly 17 syllables. Write a Pascal program, using the ADT `string,` to generate haiku (in English, unless you are comfortable in Japanese). You may want to start with an initial set or array of syllables, and may wish to exclude illegal words or combinations of syllables.

8. The program in Figure 3.5 sorts names with the entire name as key, but with last name most significant. After sorting, names are reformatted and printed, using `ReformatName,` in conventional first-middle-last style. Modify `SortAndFormatNames` so that the sort is performed with the reformatted name as as key. Test your modification with the 17 names of the example in the text. If your program is correct, Adam Q. Smith should be first, and Van Wolverton should retain his last position. (Hint: You might consider naming your modification `FormatAndSortNames.`)

9. You may have noticed that some operating systems do not report an error if you try to assign a file a name that is too long. Some systems allow a six-character name, while others allow eight with a three-character extension. If you tried to name a file `Bibliography.txt`, it might be

assigned `Biblio.txt`, or `Bibliogr.txt`, depending on the system. The system truncates overly long names rather than asking the user to rename the file.

(a) What are the merits of such automatic name revision? What might happen if a system used six-character file names, and a user, who already had a file called `Myprog.pas` in his or her account, attempted to save `Myprog2.pas`?

(b) Write a file naming procedure that 1) returns a truncated name if the input name is too long and there is no active file with the new name; 2) returns an error if there already is an active file with the proposed name; and 3) returns the input name otherwise. Consider your policy for file name extensions and include it in the procedure.

10. We presented two procedures in this chapter that could test for equality of strings: `CompareStr (S, S) = "="`, and `SearchStr (S, S) = 1`. Let `S = "AAAAAAB"`. Trace both functions, counting the number of comparisons. Is one more efficient than the other in doing this job?

11. When you traced the operation of `SearchStr (AAAAB, AAAAAAAAAAAAAAAAAAAAAAAAAAB)`, it may have become apparent that a matching procedure that "remembered" that the first four `A`'s had matched before the failure occurred at $S = P = 5$, would have been more efficient than the 5*27 comparisons reported. One of the famous algorithms that does exactly this is the Knuth-Morris-Pratt (KNP) algorithm. Look up this algorithm (See *Suggestions For Further Study* at the end of the chapter) and trace it through for the patterns above.

12. There are many useful string operations other than those implemented in this chapter. Two of these are `GetChar (Str, N)` and `SubString (Str, N, M)`. `GetChar` returns the character at position `N` in string `Str`, and `SubString` returns the substring of `Str` of length `M`, beginning at position `N`. Write Pascal procedures for these two functions, using the `StringType` of this chapter. Consider what should constitute an error in each of these functions, and include error-handling routines. You may extend the error list in `StrError` if necessary.

13. Write Pascal procedures for the following often-used word processing operations.

(a) Given a string, return it in all capital letters. Be careful about punctuation and blanks.

(b) Given a string of 80 characters or less, return a string with the same text, but centered in 80 characters (one line).

(c) Word processors usually let the user vary the line length. Modify your procedure in (b) to allow for different line lengths.

(d) Write a Pascal procedure `Substitute (Str1, Str2, Str3)` that substitutes `Str1` for the first occurrence of `Str2` in `Str3`, and returns an appropriate message if there are no occurrences of `Str2` in `Str3`. You will probably want to use the function `SearchStr` from this chapter.

14. One area of literary analysis is resolving disputed authorship. Writers tend to develop a style, including consistent frequencies of words of different lengths.

   (a) Write a Pascal procedure that reads text and counts the number of occurrences of words of each length. That is, its output will be a frequency table of word lengths. You may assume that 1) A space precedes every word; 2) a period, comma, colon, semicolon, question mark, or exclamation mark is not part of a word; and, 3) any other character is part of a word.

   (b) Add the computation of the mean and standard deviation of the word lengths to the procedure of part (a). A formula for the mean is

   $$Xbar = (\Sigma\ wordlength * frequency) / (\Sigma\ frequencies)$$

   A formula for the standard deviation is

   $$SD = (\Sigma\ frequency * (wordlength - Xbar)^2 / (\Sigma\ frequencies - 1))^{1/2}$$

   (An alternative formula for *SD*, which is more efficient in that *Xbar* need not be computed first, is

   $$SD = ((N * \Sigma f * X^2 - (\Sigma f * X)^2) / N * (N - 1))^{1/2}$$

   where *f* stands for frequency, and *N* stands for Σ frequencies.

SUGGESTIONS FOR FURTHER STUDY

The axioms describing a boolean algebra were first published in Huntington (1904).

Ide (to be published 1987) has written a Pascal text for the beginning programmer with a non-mathematical, liberal arts background. All programming projects focus on tasks commonly performed in computer-aided literary and linguistic analyses. Thus the pervasive data type is string. In addition to surveying uses of computing in the humanities, Hockey (1980) has collected key articles documenting the building of concordances, literary analysis of Greek testaments, computer art, and so forth. Either volume provides extensive examples of string processing.

The original linear matching algorithm was reported in Morris and Pratt (1970). A more easily understood version is given in Baase (1978). Sedgewick (1983) also discusses a variety of pattern-matching algorithms, including a faster variation (KNP) originally published in Knuth, Morris, and Pratt (1977).

CHAPTER 4

STACKS AND QUEUES

4.1 INTRODUCTION

With stacks and queues we come to the first ADTs not usually covered in a first course in computing. Both are reasonably familiar concepts from everyday life, but neither is provided in Pascal (or in other common languages) so we shall have many implementation details to study.

We thus have an opportunity to minimize potential confusion by adhering strictly to the ADT discipline: to separate concept from implementation details. In each case (stack and queue) we first define the ADT in terms of data objects and operations, then show an example in use, *then* look into how it can be implemented in Pascal. Finally we study a significant application of the ADT in computer science. These application studies, involving postfix expressions and simulation, are important in their own right.

4.2 THE ADT STACK

Definition: *A stack is a collection of data items organized in a linear sequence, together with the following five operations:*

1. `CreateStack` brings a stack into existence.
2. `MakeStackEmpty` deletes all items, if any, from a stack.
3. `Push` adds an item at one end, called the top, of a stack.
4. `Pop` removes the item at the top of a stack and makes it available for use.
5. `StackIsEmpty` tests whether a stack contains any items.

The items in a stack might be integers, real numbers, characters, or complete records about employees—in other words, any simple or structured data type. The examples we will study later in this chapter involve integers and characters, but the concept is not restricted to such simple types.

Central to the concept of a stack is the restriction to operating only on the item that is currently at the top of the stack.

The terms *stack, push,* and *pop* come from the image of a stack of plates in a cafeteria. We start with an empty place on a table, labeled "the stack." If we place a plate on the stack, we may immediately remove it, if we wish. If we leave it there and then add another, the only one we may remove is the top one. Another way of expressing the situation is to describe the "discipline" we impose on ourselves in accessing the stack. At any point we may either add a plate to top of the stack or we may remove the top one.

"Discipline" as used here means that we *choose* to restrict ourselves to dealing only with the top of the stack. You might say, "Well, *I* don't have to accept that discipline; I can simply pick up all the plates except the bottom one and then remove that one." So you can—*but then you don't have a stack.* In the everyday use of the term perhaps you do, but you do not have the ADT stack as defined. In terms of the operations listed above, the only stack item you can access is the top one.

You may reasonably ask why anyone would wish to impose such a restriction on themselves. The examples that make up the bulk of the chapter are intended to answer that question.

The way we visualize stacks or draw pictures of them is only a matter of personal taste. For our purposes, we shall draw them with the accessible item at the top, but they are often pictured horizontally or, sometimes, what we call the "top" is shown at the bottom.

The terms "push" and "pop" originated with the kind of "stack" that, in some cafeterias, is supported by a spring. Placing a plate (or tray or saucer) on this type of stack causes the entire stack to move down, so that the top remains at a convenient hand level. Thus, placing a plate on the stack "pushes" it down, and removing one causes it to "pop up." This usage is firmly embedded in the terminology of the field and will be followed here. The image, however, is unfortunate in that it suggests that when we push an item onto a stack all the items below it physically move in storage. Without getting ahead of the story, we may say that such a method is never used to implement a stack.

The defining characteristic of a stack is that all insertions and deletions are made at one end of the collection of items. This can be expressed by saying that the last one in is the first one out. "Last In, First Out" leads to the acronym "LIFO."

4.3 A FIRST STACK EXAMPLE: TESTING FOR PALINDROMES

We can see a simple illustration of the use of a stack and get some practice with its operations by considering a program to determine whether lines of input are palindromes.

A *palindrome* is a sequence of characters that reads the same backward and forward. ABCDCBA is a palindrome. Palindromes are familiar to crossword puzzle addicts; ''Madam, I'm Adam,'' said to Eve, and ''Able was I ere I saw Elba,'' attributed to Napoleon, are familiar examples. Except, of course, that these last two are palindromes only if we ignore spaces and punctuation and if we consider lowercase and uppercase letters equivalent. For the first version of the program we will ignore this detail.

A program to test lines of text to see whether they are palindromes is shown in Figure 4.1. Two comment lines indicate where the stack declarations and procedures will appear in the final program (after we have an implementation). In many compilers it is possible to use a *compiler directive* to specify that the declarations and procedures should be brought in from a library. If such a facility is not available, you can probably accomplish the same result by using your text editor to bring them in from a library. Such a library might be provided by your instructor or by your computer installation manager.

As we now turn to the processing of palindromes, you may simply assume that procedures to carry out the five stack operations listed earlier are available to our program. This should make you no more uncomfortable than it does to write Sqrt or Cos without knowing how those functions are computed.

```
program Palindrome1 (input, output);

{ Determine whether lines read as input are palindromes, i.e.,
  read the same left-to-right as right-to-left. }

{ The stack declarations go here. }

{ The procedures to carry out the stack operations go here. }
procedure LoadTwoStacks (var A, B: Stack);
var
    Ch: char;
begin
    while not EOLN do
    begin
        Read (Ch);
        Write (Ch);
        Push (A, Ch);
        Push (B, Ch)
    end;
    ReadLn;
    WriteLn
end;

procedure StackTransfer (var B, C: Stack);
var
    Ch: char;
begin
    while not StackIsEmpty (B) do
    begin
        Pop (B, Ch);
        Push (C, Ch)
    end
end;
```

(Continued)

(Continued)

```
procedure TestStackIdentity (var A, C: Stack;
                             var StacksAreSame: boolean);
var
   ATop, CTop: char;
begin
   StacksAreSame := true;
   while StacksAreSame and (not StackIsEmpty (A)) do
   begin
      Pop (A, Atop);
      Pop (C, CTop);
      StacksAreSame := ATop = CTop
   end
end;


procedure CheckForPalindromes;
var
   A, B, C: Stack;
   StacksAreSame: boolean;
begin
   CreateStack (A);
   CreateStack (B);
   CreateStack (C);

   while not EOF do
   begin
      LoadTwoStacks (A, B);

      StackTransfer (B, C);

      TestStackIdentity (A, C, StacksAreSame);

      if StacksAreSame then
         WriteLn ('   is a palindrome')
      else
         WriteLn ('   is not a palindrome');
      WriteLn;

      MakeStackEmpty (A);
      MakeStackEmpty (C)
   end
end;


begin
   CheckForPalindromes
end.
```

FIGURE 4.1

A program to check lines of input to determine if they are palindromes.

`CheckForPalindromes` is a procedure that invokes three other procedures (as well as the stack operations). Reading this procedure, therefore, provides a top-level view of the processing.

The method that we shall use to test for palindromes requires three stacks, which we create with `CreateStack`. The processing is done in three basic steps. First, we load the input line into two stacks, which, as we shall see, reverses the line. Second, we transfer the contents of the second stack to a third; this process again reverses the contents, putting the line back into original sequence. Finally, we compare the first and third stacks, character-for-character. If they are the same, then the line reads the same left-to-right as right-to-left.

`LoadTwoStacks` is straightforward. After reading and echoing a character, it pushes the character onto the two stacks that are its parameters. Let us look at it in operation. Suppose the input line contains just the characters `STACK`. Then these are the contents of the stacks and the characters that are written, after reading each of the input characters.

1. After reading the `S`:
Characters written: S

Stack A: Stack B:

| S | | S |

2. After reading the `T`:
Characters written: ST

Stack A: Stack B:

| T | | T |
| S | | S |

3. After reading the `A`:
Characters written: STA

Stack A: Stack B:

A		A
T		T
S		S

4. After reading the C:
Characters written: STAC

Stack A:
```
C
A
T
S
```

Stack B:
```
C
A
T
S
```

5. After reading the K:
Characters written: STACK

Stack A:
```
K
C
A
T
S
```

Stack B:
```
K
C
A
T
S
```

Observe that the last character read is at the top of the stacks, in keeping with the last-in-first-out operation.

What we want to know now is whether the line in these stacks reads the same forward and backward. You can *see* that it doesn't, of course, but a computer cannot "see" such a thing until we tell it how to recognize the fact—by a process of looking at the characters one at a time. A simple way to make the test is to transfer the contents of the B stack to the C stack and then compare A and C. Let us examine the transfer.

Without requiring any knowledge of how many characters there are on the B stack, the following simple loop in `StackTransfer` moves all of them to the C stack:

```
while not StackIsEmpty (B) do
begin
   Pop (B, Ch);
   Push (C, Ch)
end
```

Here are the contents of the two stacks after each iteration of the loop.

1. After the first iteration

    Stack B: Stack C:

    ```
    | C |
    | A |
    | T |
    |_S_|                   |_K_|
    ```

2. After the second iteration

    Stack B: Stack C:

    ```
    | A |
    | T |                   | C |
    |_S_|                   |_K_|
    ```

3. After the third iteration

    Stack B: Stack C:

    ```
                            | A |
    | T |                   | C |
    |_S_|                   |_K_|
    ```

4. After the fourth iteration

    Stack B: Stack C:

    ```
                            | T |
                            | A |
                            | C |
    |_S_|                   |_K_|
    ```

5. After the fifth iteration

    Stack B: Stack C:

    ```
                            | S |
                            | T |
                            | A |
                            | C |
    (empty)                 |_K_|
    ```

At this point the A stack has the line in reverse order, the B stack is empty, and the C stack has the line in the original order. Thus, if the top item of A is the same as the top item of C, then the last and first characters of the input are the same. After popping both stacks, if the new top of A is the same as the new top of C, then the next-to-last and the second characters are the same, and so on. This code in TestStackIdentity checks for that correspondence:

```
StacksAreSame := true;
while StacksAreSame and (not StackIsEmpty (A)) do
begin
    Pop (A, Atop);
    Pop (C, CTop);
    StacksAreSame := ATop = CTop
end;
```

If this loop runs until the A stack is empty, then StacksAreSame was never set to false, meaning that there was never a case where the two characters from the A stack and the C stack were different. In other words, the two stacks contain the same thing. This means that the input line reads the same from left-to-right as from right-to-left, and that the input line is a palindrome.

You are perhaps more accustomed to writing the assignment of a value to StacksAreSame as:

```
if ATop = CTop then
    StacksAreSame := true
else
    StacksAreSame := false;
```

The effect of the two ways is identical; we shall use the shorter.

Here is the output when this program was run with a few lines of text.

```
able was I ere I saw elba
    is a palindrome

Able was I ere I saw Elba.
    is not a palindrome

Madam, I'm Adam.
    is not a palindrome

Vedrai, carino, se sei buonino, che bel remedio ti voglio dar!
    is not a palindrome

123454321
    is a palindrome

12345
    is not a palindrome
```

Before proceeding with more important things, let us see how easily this program could be modified to process text lines according to the everyday definition of a palindrome, in which blanks and punctuation are ignored and uppercase and lowercase letters are not distinguished. Only a few extra lines are necessary to convert lowercase letters to uppercase, and to place a character on the stacks only if it is an uppercase letter. Here is a modified version of `LoadTwoStacks` that carries out these operations.

```pascal
procedure LoadTwoStacks (var A, B: Stack);
const
    ASCIICaseConvert = -32;    { Make this +64 for EBCDIC. }
var
    Ch: char;
begin
    while not EOLN do
    begin
        Read (Ch);
        Write (Ch);
        if Ch in ['a'..'z'] then
            Ch := Chr(Ord(Ch) + ASCIICaseConvert);
        if Ch in ['A'..'Z'] then
        begin
            Push (A, Ch);
            Push (B, Ch)
        end
    end;
    ReadLn;
    WriteLn
end;
```

This is nothing more than an application of the techniques used in the analysis of letter-sequence frequencies in Chapter 2. Here is the output when the program of Figure 4.1 was run with the modified procedure and some different data.

```
Able was I ere I saw Elba.
    is a palindrome

"Madam, I'm Adam."
    is a palindrome

"Eve."
    is a palindrome

Vedrai, carino, se sei buonino, che bel remedio ti voglio dar!
    is not a palindrome

123454321
    is a palindrome

12345
    is a palindrome
```

What happened with the last case? The answer is that there was a subtle and unannounced change in the specifications along the way. The original definition of a palindrome spoke of *characters,* but now our program considers only *letters.* The last line of input contains no letters, and the program, with no instructions to the contrary, reported that a sequence of zero characters reads the same from left to right as from right to left. Exercise 3 at the end of this chapter asks you to make the simple change that will make the program operate in what would presumably be the intended manner.[1]

4.4 AN ARRAY IMPLEMENTATION OF STACKS

Our implementation of a stack for this chapter is to use a record containing an array for the stack, together with an index that tells which item of the array is currently the top item. Here are the `const` and `type` declarations that will be needed:

```
const
    MaxStackHeight = 80;    { or whatever }
type
    ItemType = char;    { or whatever }

    Stack = record
            Item: array [1..MaxStackHeight] of ItemType;
            Top: 0..MaxStackHeight
        end;
```

With this implementation we must first decide about the maximum size stack. In the current application the maximum is the numbers of characters that can be entered in a line of input. (This is why we picked 80 for illustrative purposes.) Any attempt by a user of our procedures to exceed the maximum stack size must be reported, however, because it is an error from which we cannot recover.

We could omit the declaration of `ItemType` and simply declare `Item` to be an array of `char`, but because we will be using stacks in other examples where the items are integers or other types of data, it is cleaner to define explicitly what a stack contains.

The first item pushed onto an empty stack becomes item number 1; if another is pushed without an intervening pop, it becomes item number 2, and so on. So why do we permit the index to the top item of the stack (`Top`) to have the value zero? Because that value is used to indicate that the stack is empty.[2]

---

[1] An earlier version of this program, run with data that did not reveal this behavior, was seen by several dozen reviewers and about three hundred students. *One* reviewer pointed out what would happen with data containing no letters. This is said to add a caution about the inadequacy of testing a program by making up sample data: the special cases that don't occur to you can be big trouble.

[2] Read this carefully. For the index that points at the top of the stack to be zero *does not mean* that the top item *itself* is zero. Indeed, if the index is zero, there isn't any top item. The stack is empty.

Our first stack operation was `CreateStack`. Exactly what is involved in "creating" an ADT depends heavily on implementation and operating system details. We will provide the operation with all ADTs from now on, for generality, although *in this particular case* `CreateStack` and `MakeStackEmpty` both require the same action on the stack record. That action is simply to set the `Top` field to zero.

```
procedure CreateStack (var S: Stack);
begin
    S.Top := 0
end;
```

This gives a value to the `Top` field, making retrieval of it legal. The value given, zero, also happens to be the signal that that stack is empty, so `CreateStack` acts to initialize a stack to empty.

`CreateStack` brings a stack into existence and initializes it to empty. `MakeStackEmpty` takes an existing stack and discards any contents. In this array implementation, the action required in each case is the same. However, when we see the implementation with pointer variables, in Chapter 6, not only will the concepts be different—as they are here—but the implementations will be different and not interchangeable.

```
procedure MakeStackEmpty (var S: Stack);
begin
    S.Top := 0
end;
```

`Push` begins by checking for the error condition of a full stack, which in this implementation is signaled by an array index that has the value `MaxStack-Height`. If the stack is not full, we add one to the index that points to the top of the stack and place the new item in that position.

```
procedure Push (var S: Stack;
                NewItem: ItemType);

{ Assert: Stack array not full. }

begin
   if S.Top = MaxStackHeight then
      StackError (1)
   else
   begin
      S.Top := S.Top + 1;
      S.Item[S.Top] := NewItem
   end
end;
```

`StackError` is a simple procedure to report errors. As with the string procedures of the previous chapter, if you wanted a different way to handle errors you could start by modifying this procedure.

```
procedure StackError (ErrorNumber: integer);
begin
   case ErrorNumber of
      1: WriteLn ('Stack overflow');
      2: WriteLn ('Attempt to pop an empty stack')
   end
end;
```

The error condition for `Pop` is an empty stack. An empty stack in itself is not always an error. A stack often—indeed, usually—becomes empty during the execution of the program that processes it. But an empty stack should be detected with the `StackIsEmpty` operation. An attempt to pop an empty stack is an error for which no remedial action is possible.

```
procedure Pop (var S: Stack;
               var StackValue: ItemType);

{ Assert: stack is not empty. }

begin
   if S.Top = 0 then
      StackError (2)
   else
   begin
      StackValue := S.Item[S.Top];
      S.Top := S.Top - 1
   end
end;
```

The actual "popping" of the stack consists of assigning the value of the top item to `StackValue` and decreasing `Top` by one.

Let us pause at this point. When we pop a stack, all that actually happens in computer storage (in this implementation) is that a pointer to the top of the stack is decremented. Isn't the item that was popped still in the array, at a position one beyond the new value of `Top`? Yes, of course. *But there is no way you can ever retrieve that value* using only the stack operations. Under the ADT point of view, we would say that the value simply does not exist as an item in the stack even though, in this implementation, it happens still to be in the underlying array.

Now we have the test to determine if the stack is empty.

```
function StackIsEmpty (var S: Stack): boolean;
begin
   StackIsEmpty := S.Top = 0
end;
```

We use a `var`, as usual, to save the time of making a copy of the entire record just to test one value in it.

4.5 A SECOND STACK EXAMPLE: EVALUATING AN EXPRESSION IN POSTFIX FORM

With this example we introduce a topic of fundamental importance: postfix notation[3] for arithmetic expressions. This is the way many hand-held calculators operate, and is the form into which a language processor converts a conventional arithmetic expression before generating code to evaluate it. In this section, we shall see what this notation is and explore a program to evaluate a postfix expression. In the next section we shall see one way to convert a conventional expression to postfix form.

First, some terminology. The usual way of writing arithmetic expressions, with an operator between its two operands, is called *infix* form. With *postfix* form, we write an operator after its operands. Finally, *prefix* form places an operand before its operands. Here are some examples:

Prefix	Infix	Postfix
$+AB$	$A+B$	$AB+$
$+*ABC$	$A*B+C$	$AB*C+$
$+A*BC$	$A+B*C$	$ABC*+$
$-/AB/CD$	$A/B-C/D$	$AB/CD/-$
$*+AB-CD$	$(A+B)*(C-D)$	$AB+CD-*$
$-/+A*BCDE$	$(A+B*C)/D-E$	$ABC*+D/E-$

Prefix and postfix forms may seem strange at first contact, but there are languages in which they are the normal form. In LISP, for example, to add 3.14 and 2.72 we would write (PLUS 3.14 2.72).

To get an idea of the way we evaluate a postfix expression, reconsider the previous examples. We scan an expression from left to right. When we encounter an operator, where are its two operands? Answer: they are the two immediately preceding operands. This is true whether the two preceding operands are two variables, or whether one or both is the result of a previous operation. For example, in AB*C+, the operands for * are A and B, but for the + the operands are A*B (the result of the multiplication) and C.

Here is the basic strategy to evaluate a postfix expression using a stack. We process the characters of the expression from left to right. Each operand is pushed onto a stack called OperandStack. When an operator is encountered, it is applied to the top item of the stack (its second operand) and the one below that (its first operand). This result, which is placed back on the stack, becomes an operand for any succeeding operator. Assuming that the postfix expression is correctly formed, i.e., has no syntactic errors, then when the end of the expression is reached the stack will contain just one item—the value of the expression.

[3]Also called *reverse Polish notation*, in honor of the Polish logician Jan Lukasiewicz, who invented it.

Consider an example. Suppose we wish to evaluate the postfix expression

2 3 * 4 5 * + 1 −

which is the equivalent of the infix expression

2 * 3 + 4 * 5 − 1

Here are the successive contents of the operand stack after reading and processing the characters of the postfix form according to the informal algorithm stated in the last paragraph. (Blanks are ignored.)

After 2:

| 2 |

After 3:

| 3 |
| 2 |

After *:

| 6 |

After 4:

| 4 |
| 6 |

After 5:

| 5 |
| 4 |
| 6 |

After *:

| 20 |
| 6 |

After +:

| 26 |

After 1:

| 1 |
| 26 |

After −:

| 25 |

And 25 is, of course, the value of the expression.

Before proceeding to look at a program to do all this, let us pause to note the very attractive advantage of the postfix form of an expression over its equivalent infix form: the postfix form requires no parentheses. All questions about the hierarchy of operators, together with the effect of parentheses, are handled in the conversion from infix to postfix. (This is also true of prefix form.) Consider a few examples.

Infix	Postfix
(A + B)∗C	AB + C∗
A∗(B + C)	ABC + ∗
(A + B)/(C − D)	AB + CD − /
A∗(B + C/(D − E))	ABCDE − / + ∗

Let us now turn to a program to evaluate an expression in postfix form. As noted above, we shall assume that the expression is correctly formed. To further minimize distractions, we shall also assume that all operands are one-digit integers.

Recognizing an operand is simple—it is any member of the set ['0'..'9']. Quotes are needed here because the input consists of *characters;* we need to be able to read both digits and operators and to let the program distinguish between them. What we place on the stack, however, will be *values,* so we must convert from the character representation of a digit to its value. This is easily done with the Pascal function Ord, as we see when we turn to the program of Figure 4.2.

```
program PostfixEvaluate (input, output);

{ A program to evaluate arithmetic expressions in postfix form. }

const
   MaxStackHeight = 80;

type
   ItemType = real;

   Stack = record
              Item: array [1..MaxStackHeight] of ItemType;
              Top: 0..MaxStackHeight
           end;


{ The procedures to carry out the stack operations go here. }
```

(Continued)

(Continued)

```
procedure EvaluatePostfixExpressions;
const
    Blank = ' ';
var
    Ch: char;
    OperandStack: Stack;
    Operand1, Operand2, Result: real;
begin
    CreateStack (OperandStack);
    while not EOF do
    begin
        while not EOLN do
        begin
            Read (Ch);
            Write (Ch);
            if Ch <> Blank then
                if Ch in ['0'..'9'] then
                    Push (OperandStack, Ord(Ch) - Ord('0'))
                else
                begin
                    Pop (OperandStack, Operand2);
                    Pop (OperandStack, Operand1);
                    case Ch of
                        '+' : Push (OperandStack, Operand1 + Operand2);
                        '-' : Push (OperandStack, Operand1 - Operand2);
                        '*' : Push (OperandStack, Operand1 * Operand2);
                        '/' : Push (OperandStack, Operand1 / Operand2)
                    end
                end
        end;    { while not EOLN }

        ReadLn;
        Pop (OperandStack, Result);
        WriteLn (' =   ', Result:5:2);
        WriteLn

    end    { while not EOF }
end;


begin
    EvaluatePostfixExpressions
end.
```

FIGURE 4.2
A program using a stack to evaluate arithmetic expressions written in postfix form.

In the declarations we specify that `ItemType` is `real`, where before it was `char`.

The heart of the program is the `if` statement that is encountered after reading and echoing a character. The first test is used to ignore blanks. The second `if` tests for an operand, which we recognize by asking if the character is a digit. If it is, we convert it to its value and push that value onto the operand stack. If the character isn't a blank or an operand it must be an operator (always assuming no errors.) We get its two operands from the operand stack, after which a `case` statement decides what arithmetic operation to perform on them. The result is pushed back onto the stack. When the end of the expression has been reached, there is one value left on the stack, and that is the value of the expression, which we print.

Here is the output when this program was run with some sample data.

```
73/    =     2.33

345*+  =    23.00

345+*  =    27.00

34*5+  =    17.00

34+5*  =    35.00

4321++*  =    24.00

4321+*+  =    13.00

4321*++  =     9.00

3 4 -   1 2 +   /   =    -0.33

9 3 2 4 + 5 - * / 7 +  =    10.00
```

4.6 A FINAL STACK EXAMPLE: CONVERTING INFIX EXPRESSIONS TO POSTFIX

The task in this application is to read a correctly-formed infix expression in which the operands are one-character variable names, and print a corresponding postfix expression.

In broad outline, the strategy is this. We send each operand directly to the output because operands appear in the same order in postfix form as in infix. Operators, on the other hand, must always be stacked because an infix operator appears before its second operand, whereas in postfix it must follow it.

That much is simple. The complication is that we need a way to decide *when* to send an operator to the output, since operators do not always appear in the postfix form in the same order as in infix form. In other words, we must set up a means to handle the hierarchy of operators and the effect of parentheses. For example, with `A+B*C`, our program must "know" that multiplication has precedence over addition, and construct the postfix expression so that the multiplication is done first. On the other hand, the program must also know that for the same expression with parentheses inserted, `(A+B)*C`, the parentheses force the addition to be done first.

Let us seek an intuitive basis for the conversion algorithm before looking at a program.

The central issue is what happens when we encounter an operator in the input. We know that it goes on the stack, because its second operand has not yet been read. But do we need to send one or more operators from the stack to the output before stacking the new operator?

Consider first only the precedence of operators (in the absence of parentheses). Suppose the infix expression is A*B+C and that we have already processed the first three characters. A and B are therefore already in the output string, the * is on the stack, and the current character from the input string is +. Should we send the * to the output before stacking the +? The answer is "yes," because multiplication has higher precedence than addition. The generalization is clear: an * or / on the stack has higher precedence than a + or − from the input string. In such a case the stack operator is sent to the output before the input character is stacked. (Remember, all this is in the absence of parentheses.)

Now consider the infix expression A−B+C, and again suppose we have reached the second operator. Does the − on the stack take precedence over the + from the input? Again the answer is "yes," because the expression means (A−B)+C, not A−(B+C). Generalization: a + or a − on the stack has precedence over a + or a − from the input and, similarly, an * or a / on the stack has precedence over an * or a / from the input.

Finally, what about parentheses? The answer is simpler than it might seem. A left parenthesis from the input is always placed on the stack because we do not know at that point what its effect will be. This means that an operator on the top of the stack never takes precedence over a left parenthesis from the input, regardless of what the stack operator is. When a right parenthesis is encountered in the input, it causes all operators on the stack, down to but not including the matching left parenthesis, to be sent to the output. Both parentheses are then discarded.

You might be asking, when we see a right parenthesis in the input, how do we know *which* left parenthesis on the stack it matches? The answer is that the matching left parenthesis is always the "nearest" one, looking back toward the left in the expression. In other words, "Last In First Out," which is how a stack operates.

The surprise about all this, if there is one, is that everything in the last several paragraphs can be summarized in one small table that lets us compare the precedence of an operator on the stack with that of an operator from the input.

Operator	Precedence When on Stack	Precedence When in Input
)		0
(	0	5
+ ,−	2	1
*, /	4	3

The right parenthesis has no precedence value on the stack because it is never stacked.

This table is the heart of the algorithm. The time spent satisfying yourself that it actually does capture all the operator and precedence rules will be well repaid. In a compiler for a language with an exponentiation operator, relational operators, and so on, the table would be expanded and we might need to stack operands at some stages. However, this table-driven approach would still be the heart of a complete expression parser. Exercises 12–15 give you an opportunity to explore some extensions to what we are doing here.

A program that does all this is shown in Figure 4.3. Let us look at its general organization before studying the few lines that are the core of the algorithm.

```pascal
program InfixToPostfix (input, output);

{ A program to convert arithmetic expressions from infix to postfix.
  Operands are single letters; operators are +, - , *, and /.    }

const
   MaxStackHeight = 80;
   MaxLineLength = 80;

type
   ItemType = char;
   Stack = record
               Item: array [1..MaxStackHeight] of ItemType;
               Top: 0..MaxStackHeight
           end;

   IndexType = 0..MaxLineLength;

   ExpType = array [1..MaxLineLength] of char;


{ The stack procedures go here. }


function StackTop (S: Stack): ItemType;
{ Return the value of the top element of the stack.
  The stack is not changed. }

begin
   StackTop := S.Item[S.Top]
end;


function StackPrec (Operator: char): integer;
{ Return the precedence of an operator on OpStack. }
begin
   case Operator of
      '('      : StackPrec := 0;
      '+', '-' : StackPrec := 2;
      '*', '/' : StackPrec := 4
   end
end;
```

(Continued)

(Continued)

```
function InPrec (Operator: char): integer;
{ Return the precedence of an operator from the input. }
begin
    case Operator of
        ')'       : InPrec := 0;
        '+', '-' : InPrec := 1;
        '*', '/' : InPrec := 3;
        '('       : InPrec := 5
    end
end;


procedure PutChar (Ch: char;
                   var PostExp: ExpType;
                   var PostIndex: IndexType);
begin
    PostIndex := PostIndex + 1;
    PostExp[PostIndex] := Ch
end;


procedure ConvertInToPost (InExp: ExpType;
                           InLength: IndexType;
                           var PostExp: ExpType;
                           var PostLength: IndexType);
var
    OpStack: Stack;
    InIndex, PostIndex: IndexType;
    InCh, Operator, WasteBasket: char;
begin
    CreateStack (OpStack);
    Push (OpStack, '(');
    InExp[InLength + 1] := ')';
    PostIndex := 0;

    for InIndex := 1 to InLength + 1 do
    begin
        InCh := InExp[InIndex];
        if InCh in ['A'..'Z'] then
            PutChar (InCh, PostExp, PostIndex)
        else
        begin
            while StackPrec(StackTop(OpStack)) > InPrec(InCh) do
            begin
                Pop(OpStack, Operator);
                PutChar (Operator, PostExp, PostIndex)
            end;
            if InCh = ')' then
                Pop(OpStack, WasteBasket)
            else
                Push(OpStack, InCh)
        end
    end;

    PostLength := PostIndex
end;
```

```
procedure ConvertExpressions;
var
    Index, InLength, PostLength: IndexType;
    InExp, PostExp: ExpType;
begin
    while not EOF do
    begin
        InLength := 0;
        while not EOLN do
        begin
            InLength := InLength + 1;
            Read (InExp[InLength])
        end;
        ReadLn;

        Write ('Infix expression:    ');
        for Index := 1 to InLength do
            Write (InExp[Index]);
        WriteLn;

        ConvertInToPost (InExp, InLength, PostExp, PostLength);

        Write ('Postfix equivalent:  ');
        for Index := 1 to PostLength do
            Write (PostExp[Index]);
        WriteLn;
        WriteLn
    end
end;


begin
    ConvertExpressions
end.
```
(handwritten annotation: NOT PASS 80)

FIGURE 4.3
A program using a stack to convert arithmetic expressions written in infix form to postfix.

The package of stack procedures is the same as in the last program, but one more stack operator has been provided as part of this program. This algorithm requires us to examine the top item of the stack, and then, in many cases, *not* remove it. We could, of course, use a combination of a Pop and a Push, with a temporary variable holding the top item while we are deciding what to do with it. But there is no reason not to set up additional operators if they simplify and clarify a program; we have merely extended the definition of our ADT. (Under the rules of Pascal, of course, we cannot return a structured type as the value of a function, so for greater generality this could be a procedure.)

The functions StackPrec and InPrec accept a character that is an operator, and return the precedence of that operator when found on the stack or when found in the input. Extending this program to handle other operators would, up to a point, involve nothing more than adding more lines to these functions. We emphasize ''up to a point,'' however, because eventually we would need two-character operators and, about that time, we would decide to let variables be normal Pascal names. Then we would need a *lexical analyzer* to *tokenize* the input stream, that is, identify a group of characters as an identifier, or a number, or an operator, or whatever else is legal in the language. In other words, here we have the foundations of an expression evaluator, but we are missing big parts of the complete structure.

`PutChar` is a procedure to place a character in the output string; it unclutters the conversion for easier understanding. The real work of the program is done by `ConvertInToPost` and we shall return to that shortly. `Convert-Expressions` does the housekeeping chores: it gets the infix expression, determines its length, calls the conversion routine, and does the printing.

Back to `ConvertInToPost`. After initializing the stack that holds the operators (`OpStack`), we push a left parenthesis onto it. This is one reasonable way to handle the problem of getting the algorithm started. When we encounter the first operator from the input string, we will immediately want to compare its precedence with the precedence of the operator on the top of the stack. We must either put something there in advance, or arrange to handle the first operator differently from all others. The way chosen here appears simplest.

We choose to initialize the stack with a left parenthesis because its stack precedence is lower than that of any other operator. Nothing will force this parenthesis off the stack—and therefore the stack will never be empty—until a matching right parenthesis is encountered. And, you might ask, when will that be? Never, if the expression is correctly formed. So, simply to force the algorithm to terminate correctly, we place a matching right parenthesis after the end of the input. This guarantees that, when the end of the input is reached, any operators left in the stack will be popped to the output.

An operand is recognized, in this simple language, as any uppercase letter; it always goes directly to the output. So the real work of the conversion algorithm lies in the following few lines:

```
while StackPrec(StackTop(OpStack)) > InPrec(InCh) do
begin
    Pop(OpStack, Operator);
    PutChar (Operator, PostExp, PostIndex)
end;
if InCh = ')' then
    Pop(OpStack, WasteBasket)
else
    Push(OpStack, InCh)
```

The `while` statement pops operators as long as the one on the top of the stack has higher precedence than the one from the input; that may be zero, one, or many operators. After the `while` loop terminates, the operator from the input must be stacked, to wait for what comes later—except in the case where the operator from the input is a right parenthesis. In that case, always assuming a well-formed infix expression, there *must* be a matching left parenthesis on the top of the stack. So we discard it, and simply never do anything with the right parenthesis. And that is the algorithm.

Needless to say, things get rather more complex when we incorporate error checking. Exercises 10 and 11 at the end of this chapter ask you to explore this issue.

Now let us watch the algorithm in action on the sample expression $A*(B-C+D)-E/F$.

1. We put a left parenthesis on the stack and get the first input character. It is an operand, so it is sent to the output. At the end of processing this character, we have this situation:

Stack	Output
(	A

2. The left parenthesis on the top of the stack does not have higher precedence than the asterisk from the input, so the asterisk is stacked:

Stack	Output
*	A
(	

3. The asterisk on the top of the stack does not have higher precedence than the left parenthesis from the input, so the left parenthesis from the input is stacked:

Stack	Output
(	
*	A
(	

4. The B goes to the output:

Stack	Output
(	
*	AB
(	

5. The left parenthesis on the top of the stack does not have higher precedence than the minus sign, so the minus sign is stacked:

Stack	Output
−	
(	
*	
(	AB

6. The C goes to the output:

7. The minus sign on the top of the stack has higher precedence (because it is on the stack) than the plus sign from the input, so the minus sign is popped to the output. That leaves a left parenthesis on top of the stack. It does not have precedence over the plus sign, so the plus sign is stacked:

8. The D goes to the output:

9. The plus sign on the top of the stack has higher precedence than the right parenthesis from the input, so the plus sign is popped to the output. The left parenthesis that is now at the top of the stack does not have precedence over the right parenthesis from the input, so the popping of operators stops. The right parenthesis now forces the popping of the stack, and its matching left parenthesis has been discarded:

```
Stack               Output

  *
  (                 ABC − D +
```

10. The asterisk on the top of the stack has precedence over the minus sign from the input, so the asterisk is popped to the output. The only thing left on the stack is the left parenthesis that we put there at the beginning, which

we see is still needed. We test its precedence against that of the minus sign and stack the minus sign:

11. The E goes to the output:

12. The minus sign on the top of the stack does not have precedence over the slash from the input, so the slash is stacked:

13. The F is sent to the output:

14. Now we find the right parenthesis that was placed at the end of the infix expression to match the one that we placed on the stack at the beginning. All remaining arithmetic operators on the stack have precedence over this right parenthesis, so they are all popped to the output. As a final action, meaningless to us, the initial left parenthesis is discarded, leaving this situation:

Stack   Output

(Empty)   ABC − D + *EF/ −

Here is the output when this program converted a number of infix expressions:

```
Infix expression:    A*B+C
Postfix equivalent:  AB*C+

Infix expression:    A*(B+C)
Postfix equivalent:  ABC+*

Infix expression:    A+B*C
Postfix equivalent:  ABC*+

Infix expression:    (A+B)*C
Postfix equivalent:  AB+C*

Infix expression:    A
Postfix equivalent:  A

Infix expression:    ((((A)+B)))
Postfix equivalent:  AB+

Infix expression:    (A+B/C-D)/(E*F*G*H+I*(J/(K+L)))
Postfix equivalent:  ABC/+D-EF*G*H*IJKL+/*+/
```

4.7 THE ADT QUEUE

We now take up an ADT that is closely related to the stack in concept, but harder to implement. We consider its definition and a brief example in this section, study its implementation in the next section, and examine an application study in Section 4.10.

Definition: *A* `queue` *is a collection of data items organized in a linear sequence, together with the following five operations:*

1. `CreateQueue` brings a queue into existence.
2. `MakeQueueEmpty` empties an existing queue.
3. `EnQueue` adds an item at one end, called the *rear,* of a queue.
4. `DeQueue` removes an item from the other end, called the *front,* of the queue, and makes it available for use.
5. `QueueIsEmpty` tests whether a queue is empty.

As with stacks, other operations may be added for convenience. The items that comprise a queue may be simple or structured, just as with a stack.

With a stack, the item we retrieve (with a `Pop`) is the one most recently placed on the stack, leading to the condensed description "Last-In-First-Out," or LIFO. With a queue, the item we retrieve (with a `DeQueue`) is the one first placed on the queue, leading to the condensed description "First-In-First-Out," or FIFO.

Since we encounter queues in everyday life—waiting lines in banks and supermarkets—the queue is the most intuitively obvious data structure that we deal with. It is from these origins, of course, that the terms front and rear derive. Just as with stacks, there is no significance to the way we draw our pictures but, because of the everyday analogies, it is conventional to draw them horizontally.

4.8 AN EXAMPLE: THE PALINDROME PROBLEM AGAIN

The way we tested sentences earlier to see if they are palindromes was somewhat artificial. What we want to know is whether the character string reads the same from front to back as from back to front. Now that we know about queues, we can place the candidate sentence (minus blanks and punctuation) into both a stack and a queue. Because a stack is a LIFO data structure, we retrieve the characters from the stack in a sequence that is right-to-left in terms of the original sentence. But because a queue is a FIFO data structure, we retrieve the characters from it in a sequence that is left-to-right in terms of the original sentence. Thus, the sentence is a palindrome if and only if the character popped from the stack matches the character dequeued from the queue, for all pairs of characters.

A program is shown in Figure 4.4. It assumes the existence of the package of stack procedures shown earlier, and a package of queue procedures that is developed in the next section.

```
program Palindrome3 (input, output);

{ A program using a stack and a queue to check whether lines
  of input are palindromes. This version is case-insensitive,
  and ignores blanks and punctuation. }

{ The program declarations go here. }

{ The stack and queue procedures go here. }


procedure LoadStackAndQ (var S: Stack; var Q: Queue);
const
    ASCIICaseConvert = -32;   { make this +64 for EBCDIC }
var
    Ch: ItemType;
begin
    while not EOLN do
    begin
        Read (Ch);
        Write (Ch);
        if Ch in ['a'..'z'] then
            Ch := Chr(Ord(Ch) + ASCIICaseConvert);
        if Ch in ['A'..'Z'] then
        begin
            Push (S, Ch);
            EnQueue (Q, Ch)
        end
    end;
    ReadLn;
    WriteLn
end;
```

(Continued)

(Continued)

```
procedure TestStackAndQForIdentity (var S: Stack; var Q: Queue;
                                    var StackAndQAreSame: boolean);
var
    StackChar, QChar: ItemType;
begin
    StackAndQAreSame := true;
    while StackAndQAreSame and not QueueIsEmpty (Q) do
    begin
        Pop (S, StackChar);
        DeQueue (Q, QChar);
        StackAndQAreSame := StackChar = QChar
    end
end;


procedure CheckForPalindromes;
var
    S: Stack;
    Q: Queue;
    StackAndQAreSame: boolean;
begin
    CreateStack (S);
    CreateQueue (Q);

    while not EOF do
    begin
        LoadStackAndQ (S, Q);

        TestStackAndQForIdentity (S, Q, StackAndQAreSame);

        if StackAndQAreSame then
            WriteLn ('    is a palindrome')
        else
            WriteLn ('    is not a palindrome');
        WriteLn;

        MakeStackEmpty (S);
        MakeQueueEmpty (Q)
    end
end;


begin
    CheckForPalindromes
end.
```

FIGURE 4.4

A program to check whether lines of input are palindromes. This version uses a stack and a queue.

The procedure `CheckForPalindromes` is quite similar to the one of the same name in Figure 4.1 except, of course, that here we have a stack and a queue instead of two stacks. After the stack and the queue have been loaded, say with the word QUEUE, we have this picture:

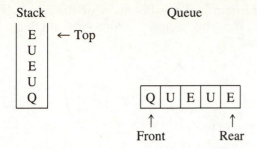

In this case, the top of the stack contains E and the front of the queue contains Q, so the procedure `TestStackAndQForIdentity` can determine in one iteration of the `while` loop that the input is not a palindrome. To determine that the input is indeed a palindrome requires running that loop to completion.

As with the two-stack version, the loop could actually be stopped after it has gone half way. If we were making a career of checking for palindromes, it would be a simple matter to count the characters and add an appropriate test to the `while` loop. On the other hand, if most sentences are not expected to be palindromes, the savings might not be worthwhile. But enough for palindromes.

4.9 AN ARRAY IMPLEMENTATION OF QUEUES

Our first implementation of the queue ADT will be with an array, using a scheme similar to that for stacks in the previous chapter. The main difference is that, because a queue can be accessed at both ends (although for different purposes), we must have fields that point to each. There is another problem as well, but before looking into it let us see this much of the idea in operation.

Suppose we have a queue named Q that holds characters, implemented as an array of six elements numbered zero to five as follows:

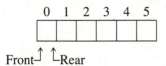

The initialization operation will be to set `Front` and `Rear` so that they both identify element zero, as shown.

Now suppose we wish to enqueue the letters `TOM`. The process would run as follows. We enqueue an item by adding 1 to `Rear` and placing the item in the array element that `Rear` now points to.

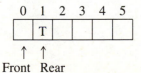

The letter T is now both the front item and the last item of the queue. Our convention is that Front points to the array element *before* the front item. We shall see later why this is necessary.

Next we enqueue the letter O.

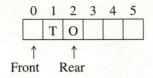

Next, the M.

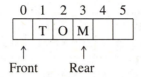

Suppose we now dequeue everything in the queue. To dequeue the item at the front of the queue we increment Front and return the value that Front now identifies. Suppose we have a simple loop to print the contents of the queue, like this:

```
while not QueueIsEmpty (Q) do begin
   DeQueue (Q, Ch);
   Write (Ch)
end;
WriteLn;
```

After the first iteration we would have this picture:

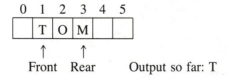

The T is still in the array, but, remembering that Front always points to the array element *before* the front item, we have no way accessing the T—not with queue operations.

Now we dequeue the O.

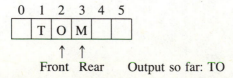

Next we dequeue the M.

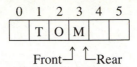

Front⌐ ⌐Rear

Output so far: TOM

The queue is now empty (regardless of what is in the underlying array) and we note that Front and Rear both point to the same array element. Does this mean that we could implement the test for an empty queue as a check to see if Front = Rear? No, for reasons that will become clear shortly.

Let us now enqueue the letters BUCK in this same queue, starting from where we now are. Enqueueing the B means to increment Rear and place the item in the array element that Rear now points to.

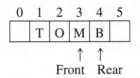

Front Rear

Again.

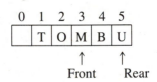

Front Rear

And what happens when we try to enqueue the C? We are at the end of the array, so incrementing Rear would lead to a non-existent array location. Here we see the second big difference between the implementation of stacks and queues. Pushing a stack makes it grow toward one end, and popping it makes it shrink back toward that same end. With a queue, on the contrary, nothing shrinks: Front and Rear always move to the right or, stated otherwise, they move toward larger indices.

It is no solution simply to set up a huge array and hope for the best. Even in perfectly normal operation, during which the queue never approached overflow, we would run "off the end" of the array. It is, however, a solution to set up the array to operate in a circular fashion, in which the element after the last one is zero. (This is usually called *wrapping around* the end of the array, a term that also applies to storage addresses at the hardware level.)

Implementing this solution is a simple matter of doing the addition of 1 to Front and Rear modulo the array size. Assuming that this has been done (we shall see the procedures shortly), we continue with the example.

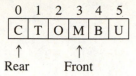

Recalling that Rear always points to the actual rear item but that Front points to the element *before* the front item, we see the earlier pattern is still being followed, but now with the wraparound feature.

Now enqueueing K we have:

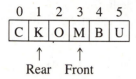

The T left in element 1 from the earlier usage of the underlying array has finally been overwritten.

This could now be dequeued, if we chose, but instead let us examine the final issue in this method of queue implementation by trying to enqueue DAN. We first increment the pointer to Rear and store the D.

```
 0  1  2  3  4  5
 C  K  D  M  B  U
       ↑  ↑
    Rear Front
```

Now we increment the pointer to Rear and store the A.

```
 0  1  2  3  4  5
 C  K  D  A  B  U
 Rear─┘  └─Front
```

Up to this point, we have no problem. Front and Rear point to the same array location, but that is not a problem because we have set up the Front pointer so that it always points to the element before the actual front item. But now there is no room to enqueue anything else.

Thus we see that when Front and Rear point to the same array element, it means either that the queue is empty or that it is full. We need something else to distinguish between the two cases. We shall do that with a boolean field named AnyItem.

The array implementations of the queue operations require the following declarations:

```
const
   MaxQLength = 80;    { or whatever }
   MaxQIndex = 79;     { 1 less }

type
   ItemType = char;    { or whatever }

   QIndex = 0..MaxQIndex;
   Queue = record
                Item: array [QIndex] of ItemType;
                Front, Rear: QIndex;
                AnyItem: boolean
           end;
```

Here are the queue procedures.

```
procedure CreateQueue (var Q: Queue);
begin
   Q.Front := 0;
   Q.Rear := 0;
   Q.AnyItem := false
end;


procedure MakeQueueEmpty (var Q: Queue);
begin
   Q.Front := Q.Rear;
   Q.AnyItem := false
end;


procedure EnQueue (var Q: Queue;
                   NewItem: ItemType);
begin
   if (Q.Front = Q.Rear) and Q.AnyItem then
      QError (1)
   else begin
      Q.Rear := (Q.Rear + 1) mod MaxQLength;
      Q.Item[Q.Rear] := NewItem;
      Q.AnyItem := true
   end
end;
```

(Continued)

(Continued)

CHANGE TO
DEQUE

```
procedure DeQueue (var Q: Queue;
                         var QItem: ItemType);
begin
   if not Q.AnyItem then
      QError (2)
   else begin
      Q.Front := (Q.Front + 1) mod MaxQLength;
      QItem := Q.Item[Q.Front];
      if Q.Front = Q.Rear then
         Q.AnyItem := false
   end
end;


function QueueIsEmpty (var Q: Queue): boolean;
begin
   QueueIsEmpty := not Q.AnyItem
end;


function QueueIsFull (var Q: Queue): boolean;
begin
   QueueIsFull := (Q.Front = Q.Rear) and Q.AnyItem
end;
```

These procedures involve no new concepts, and should be understandable in terms of the example we just presented. We have added a function to test for a full queue, mostly to show how simply it can be done. Note that in `MakeQueueEmpty` we do not bother to set `Front` and `Rear` back to zero; all that is needed is that they point to the same array element.

4.10 AN APPLICATION: QUEUES IN A WAITING LINE SIMULATION

Queues occur frequently in everyday life, so it should not be surprising that they are integral parts of many computer applications. A common example is the study of waiting lines, such as customers in a bank, factory workers at a parts window, or, as in our next example, airline passengers waiting for a ticket agent.

We *simulate* such a situation by setting up a queue ADT and using it to imitate how an actual waiting line would function—except that we will accelerate the times involved. Typical questions of interest are: How long, on average, does a passenger have to wait to get service? What is the average length of the waiting line? What is the variability in these numbers? (If the average is two minutes, but 5 percent of the time the wait is more than 20 minutes, the arrangement is probably unacceptable.)

We will study the simplest of waiting line situations. There is one waiting line, with arrivals on a random basis, and one *server* (ticket agent) with a fixed serving time. The inputs to the simulation, as we shall set it up, are the probability that a passenger arrives within one minute, the (fixed) time to serve a passenger, and the length of (simulated) time the simulation is to run.

An outline of the method is as follows. We establish a queue to hold the waiting passengers; what we actually place in the queue item for a passenger is the time at which the passenger arrives. This is called *time-stamping* the passenger. There is a variable named `Time` that holds the "clock," which is started at zero and is incremented by one at each step of the simulation. When the passenger reaches the front of the queue, the difference between the time at that point and the time stamp showing when the passenger arrived is the number of minutes the passenger waited. This can be zero, if the queue was empty when the passenger arrived and the ticket agent was free. We sum these waits, and at the end of the run divide by the number of passengers to get the average wait. Note that waiting time, as we are using the term, does not include the service time.

We said that passengers arrive "on a random basis." That innocent-sounding phrase covers a great deal of ground, which will not be explored further here. We assume the existence of a function that returns a number between zero and one, with any sub-range as likely as any other sub-range of the same size. To decide whether a passenger arrives during a given one-minute period, we ask whether a random number is less than the value of the probability (read as input) of the arrival of a passenger in any one minute.

A program that carries out the simulation is shown in Figure 4.5. After routine declarations and uncomplicated input, output, and setup operations, the work of the simulation is all in a `while` loop that implements the logic we just described.

```
program Airline (input, output);

{ Waiting-line simulation: single queue, single server. }

const
    MaxQLength = 1000;
    MaxQIndex = 999;

type
    NonNegInt = 0..MaxInt;

    ItemType = NonNegInt;

    QIndex = 0..MaxQIndex;
    Queue = record
                Item: array [QIndex] of ItemType;
                Front, Rear: QIndex;
                AnyItem: boolean
            end;

var
    I: integer;

{ The queue operations go here. }                        (Continued)
```

(Continued)

```pascal
procedure SimulatePassengerService;
var
    PassQueue: Queue;
    ArrivalProbability: real;
    TimeToServeOnePass: NonNegInt;
    LengthOfSimulation: NonNegInt;
    Time: NonNegInt;                    { the "clock" }
    ServiceTimeLeft: NonNegInt;    { to finish with Pass at desk }
    NumberServed:NonNegInt;
    SumOfWaits: NonNegInt;
    PassEntryTime: NonNegInt;
    AverageWait: real;

begin
    ReadLn (ArrivalProbability,
            TimeToServeOnePass,
            LengthOfSimulation);
    WriteLn ('Probability that passenger arrives in 1 minute = ',
             ArrivalProbability:4:2);
    WriteLn ('The time required to service one passenger = ',
             TimeToServeOnePass, ' minutes');
    WriteLn ('The length of the simulation = ',
             LengthOfSimulation, ' minutes');

    CreateQueue (PassQueue);
    Time := 0;
    ServiceTimeLeft := 0;
    NumberServed := 0;
    SumOfWaits := 0;

    while Time <= LengthOfSimulation do
    begin
        { "Random" is a TurboPascal function call }
        if Random < ArrivalProbability then
            EnQueue (PassQueue, Time);         { time-stamp the pass. }

        if ServiceTimeLeft = 0 then             { is the agent free? }
            if not QueueIsEmpty (PassQueue) then    { anybody in Q? }
            begin
                DeQueue (PassQueue, PassEntryTime);
                SumOfWaits := SumOfWaits + (Time - PassEntryTime);
                NumberServed := NumberServed + 1;
                ServiceTimeLeft := TimeToServeOnePass
            end;

        Time := Time + 1;

        if ServiceTimeLeft > 0 then
            ServiceTimeLeft := ServiceTimeLeft - 1
    end;

    if NumberServed = 0 then
        AverageWait := 0.0
    else
        AverageWait := SumOfWaits/NumberServed;
```

```
WriteLn (NumberServed:1,
            ' passengers were served, with an average wait of ',
            AverageWait:4:2, ' minutes');
    WriteLn
end;
```

FUNCTION RANDOM : REAL; EXTEARNAL

```
begin
    SimulatePassengerService
end.
```

FIGURE 4.5
A program using the ADT queue to simulate a waiting line at an airport ticket counter.

Here is the output when this program was run three times.

```
Probability that passenger arrives in 1 minute = 0.10
The time required to service one passenger = 5 minutes
The length of the simulation = 200 minutes
16 passengers were served, with an average wait of 0.25 minutes


Probability that passenger arrives in 1 minute = 0.10
The time required to service one passenger = 5 minutes
The length of the simulation = 200 minutes
29 passengers were served, with an average wait of 3.93 minutes


Probability that passenger arrives in 1 minute = 0.10
The time required to service one passenger = 5 minutes
The length of the simulation = 200 minutes
19 passengers were served, with an average wait of 0.68 minutes
```

Observe that the input data is the same in each case. One passenger arrives on the average of every ten minutes and it takes only five minutes to serve a passenger. What is perhaps most interesting about the results is the variability. With the given passenger frequency and the simulation run set for 200 minutes, we would expect the average number of passengers to be about 20, with variation around that mean. But the amount of variation in the average waiting time might not have been expected. Just for fun, let's pursue this question a bit further.

A modified version of the program, not shown, was set up to run each simulation 200 times, for 200 minutes each, for the same average arrival rate but for several service times. It was also modified to produce the maximum wait (in any of the 200 runs), the average wait for all 200 runs, and the minimum and maximum averages. The first line of the following table, for example, says that when the service time was 3 minutes, the maximum wait in any of the 200 runs was 6 minutes and the average wait was 0.40 minutes. However, in (at least) one run the average wait was zero, and in one it was 1.29 minutes.

Service time	Maximum wait	Average wait	Minimum average	Maximum average
3	6	0.40	0.00	1.29
4	11	0.90	0.00	3.35
5	23	1.69	0.00	5.96
6	38	2.81	0.27	16.82
7	48	5.55	0.20	24.00
8	70	7.80	0.28	34.48

As the service time approaches the average time between passenger arrivals, the system approaches *saturation*. Once passengers are arriving at a faster rate than they can be served, then obviously the line can grow to any length. What might not have been intuitively clear, except that we have all stood in lines and seen it happen, is that a system that is far from saturation—utilized only half the time, say, *on average*—can still have tremendous variability. When the service time is 5 minutes, for example, and passengers are arriving on the average only every 10 minutes, a least one passenger in these simulation runs had to wait 23 minutes, and in one run the *average* wait was longer than the service time! (This is not impossible: it results when passengers arrive in "bunches.")

This the simplest possible simulation, and in fact there are analytic formulas that will tell us all of the above without any computation at all. Exercise 27 at the end of this chapter asks you to investigate a few other situations, closer to reality, that do not have easy formulas describing them.

4.11 CONCLUSION

Stacks and queues are among the fundamental structures of computer science. Whether used explicitly in an application or invoked by a compiler or operating system in a way that is transparent to the programmer working in a high-level language, they are there. We have studied them both so that you can use them as tools in such areas as parsing expressions or simulation, and so that you can understand how various other aspects of programming system operate.

In the next chapter we turn to such an area—recursion—a powerful tool that is implemented using stacks.

EXERCISES

P. 104 × 105

PROCEDURES PUSH AND POP

EMPTY?

1. Write a procedure named `AtLeastTwoInStack` that returns `true` if the stack named as its argument has at least two items in it, and `false` otherwise. Your procedure should use only the primitive stack operators listed at the beginning of the chapter, should never cause an error indication, and should leave the stack unchanged.

2. Write a procedure to pop the top two items in a stack. (This would be useful in evaluating postfix expressions, for example.) The procedure header might be:

```
procedure PopTopTwo (S: Stack;
                   var Top, Second: ItemType);
```

Include appropriate error checking, possibly using the procedure from Exercise 1.

3. Modify the second `LoadTwoStacks` procedure to accommodate numbers as well as letters. That is, we would like `Palindrome1 (12345)` to return `false` and `Palindrome1 (123454321)` to return `true`.

4. ·ASCII characters are not limited to digits and the 26 letters of the alphabet. Modify `LoadTwoStacks` so that `Palindrome (***USA***)` returns `false`, whereas `Palindrome (***AAA***)` returns `true`.

5. Modify the `Push` procedure to `Pop` the top element of a full stack and `Push` the `NewItem` on. Do you need any error messages in this situation? Can you suggest a better name for this operation than using `Push` in a quite different sense than before?

6. Modify the `Pop` procedure to return a "dummy" element, instead of an error message, from an empty stack. Discuss the merits of this and the other error-avoiding procedure suggested in Exercise 5.

7. Rewrite the following expressions in both postfix and prefix form.
   (a) $(A + B) * (C - D/E)/F$
   (b) $((A + B) - (C + D)) * E$
   (c) $A / B + C / D$
   (d) $A * B * (D + E) - F$

8. Use the expressions of Exercise 7 to trace (by hand) the operation of `ConvertInToPost`.

9. Write the following prefix expressions in fully parenthesized infix form.
   (a) $+ * + A B - C D E$
   (b) $A B + C D - * E +$
   (c) $A B D + / B D + A / -$
   (d) $- / A + B D / + B D A$

10. The procedure `EvaluatePostfixExpressions` assumed no errors in input. As written, input is from the terminal, so it seems reasonable that if a typo occurs, we could save the supposedly good data and request the user to reenter the erroneous entry. Modify `Evaluate-PostfixExpressions` to accommodate this error recovery. You may need to check the details of your Pascal system; some of them *buffer* the input, making it difficult or impossible to examine a character before the entire line has been entered.

11. Certain errors do not allow for recovery. In what circumstances should `EvaluatePostfixExpressions` be aborted? Modify the procedure to return appropriate error messages in these circumstances.

12. Extend the precedence table for infix operators to include exponentiation.

13. Using your expanded table from Exercise 12, trace the stacking and unstacking of the following expressions when translating from infix to postfix form.
    (a) $A - B^2 * (C / D)$
    (b) $(X - Y) / (X^2 + Y^2)^{1/2}$
    (c) $X - Y / X^2 + (Y^2)^{1/2}$
    (d) $X - Y / X^2 + Y^{2\ 1/2}$

14. Pascal has no exponentiation operator. Write two Pascal functions, `RealExp` and `IntExp`, of two parameters, which return the first parameter exponentiated by the second. For example, `IntExp (2, 5) = 32`.

15. Real number arithmetic has a unary operator other than exponentiation—the unary minus, which has precedence below exponentiation, but above the binary operators, $*, /, +, -$. Thus $-5 + -2^4 = -5 + -16 = -21$.
    (a) Add the unary minus to the precedence table used to convert infix to postfix notation.
    (b) How can you recognize that a "$-$" is unary rather than binary?
    (c) Modify the program `InfixToPostfix` to include the unary minus.

16. To evaluate a prefix expression using a stack, operators as well as values must be stacked. If we define the variant record in this manner,

```
ItemType = record
            Case Tag: 1..2 of
            1: (R: real);
            2: (Ch: char)
          end;
```

we can stack both values and operators using the array stack implementation. Write a Pascal procedure named `PrefixEvaluate` that returns the value of an arithmetic expression in prefix form. (Hint: Evaluate an operator followed by two numbers before stacking them.)

17. Write a Pascal procedure to translate an infix expression to prefix form. Notice that the order of prefix operators is the same as infix. Does this simplify the procedure?

18. The C programming language allows bit-level as well as arithmetic operations on integers. The *bit-wise and (&)* operator is often used to turn bits off, whereas *bit-wise or (|)* turns bits on. *Bit-wise exclusive or ($^\wedge$)* turns a bit on if only one of the corresponding bits in its two arguments is on, (i.e., N | N = N & N = N, while N $^\wedge$ N = 0). If N is an integer in octal (base 8) notation, then N = N & 0177 turns off all but the low-order seven bits of N, and N = N | 0177 turns on those same seven bits. N = N $^\wedge$ 0177 complements each of the seven low-order bits in N, and leaves the high-order bits unchanged. (Note that "=" is the assignment operator in C.) The bit-wise operators have lower precedence than arithmetic operators, with & before $^\wedge$ before |.

 (a) Add these operators to the precedence table used for conversion from infix to postfix.

 (b) Evaluate the following infix expressions. You will need to rewrite integers in octal form when bit-wise operations are present.

   (i)   5 + 3 & 27
   (ii) 1 | 2
   (iii) 1 & 2 | 16 − 1
   (iv) 15 ^ 5 * 64
   (v)   6 / 3 + 5 | 2 ^ 19 − 3

19. Trace `CheckForPalindromes`, assuming an input string of "Tis Ivan on a visit." (This palindrome appeared in the *New York Times* crossword puzzle of August 12, 1986. Others from the same puzzle were, "Was it a rat I saw?" and "Live not on evil.")

20. A *deque* (double-ended queue, pronounced "deck") is an ADT in which insertions and deletions can be made at either the front or the rear. Thus it combines features of both stacks and queues. Write an ADT definition for a deque.

21. In practice, the deque has two variations. The first is the input-restricted deque, where insertions are restricted to one end only, and the second is the output-restricted deque, where deletions are restricted to a single end. What restrictions would turn a deque into a queue? into a stack?

22. (a) Modify your ADT deque to specify an input-restricted deque.
 (b) Modify the ADT deque to specify an output-restricted deque.

23. Palindromes can be recognized by using a single deque if input is restricted and output is not.

 (a) Implement a deque as an array in a manner similar to the circular queue of this chapter.

 (b) Modify the six queue operations to accommodate a deque. You can either write `DeDequeFromFront` and `DeDequeFromRear` procedures, or write a single `DeDeque` procedure with a parameter indicating front or rear deletion.

 (c) Write a `Palindrome4` program to test palindromes using a deque.

24. Operating systems are responsible for scheduling jobs. The simplest method is first-come-first-serve, which is implemented with a *job queue*. In many installations, not all jobs are equally urgent, and a *priority queue* is used. A priority queue behaves like any other queue except that the item with highest priority gets dequeued first. Suppose priorities are 0, 1, 2, in that order, with 0 being the highest priority.

    (a) How could you schedule prioritized jobs if there are three queues available?

    (b) Suppose the pair (2,5) represents job 5, with a priority of 2. Make a series of queue diagrams to represent the scheduling of jobs arriving in the following order: (1,1), (2,2), (2,3), (0,4), (2,5), (2,6), (0,7), (1,8), (2,9), (0,10), (0,11), (2,12), (1,13), (2,14).

    (c) In real operating systems, jobs leave the job queues as others arrive. Suppose the jobs listed in (b) arrive regularly at one-second intervals and each takes two seconds to complete. That is, by the time the first job has completed, two more have arrived. Redo (b), keeping track of the times.

25. If only one queue is available, we can enqueue jobs in the order they arrive and then suspend operation, every so often, to sort the queue according to priority by using an auxiliary stack. The idea is to push queue elements onto the stack as long as they are in the order of ascending priority. If `FirstItem` is dequeued with lower priority than `StackTop`, the stack is popped and `EnQueued` until `StackTop` has lower priority than `FirstItem`. This process continues until the queue is empty. Items are then on the stack, with those of lowest priority at the bottom, and those of highest priority at the top. They can then be returned to the queue, which will operate in priority order.

    (a) Write an algorithm in pseudo-Pascal to sort a queue using an auxiliary stack.

    (b) Test your algorithm on the job pairs above.

    (c) Compute the worst-case performance of your algorithm if there are N items on the queue to be sorted.

26. Run the simulation program with a service time of one minute. Can you explain the waiting times that you get?

27. Modify the simulation program to handle the following three variations:

    (a) For the first five minutes out of every 100 simulated minutes, a passenger arrives every minute, in "burst mode." See if you can determine how long it takes for the system to recover from such a burst. (Warning: The extreme variability of results must be taken into account.)

    (b) There are two ticket agents, each with a separate queue. An arriving passenger joins the shorter queue, but may then *not* switch queues. Average all waits for both queues.

    (c) There are two ticket agents but a single queue. Whenever either agent becomes free, the passenger at the head of the queue moves to that agent's position. Average all waits, and compare with the results of (b).

SUGGESTIONS FOR FURTHER STUDY

A pleasant tutorial to both the C language and the UNIX™ operating system can be found in Kernighan and Ritchie (1978). The lack of confining rules in C leads to some correct, but fairly arcane expressions. Feuer (1982) leads the novice C programmer through some of the pleasures and pitfalls of this evolving language.

Sorting a priority queue using a stack was suggested in Reingold, Nievergelt, and Deo (1977). A variety of methods for implementing priority queues are discussed in Brinch-Hansen (1973).

The interested student might wish to pursue more realistic queueing systems, where a computer system provides a variety of services such as printers, tape readers, CPUs, and so forth, all of which use job queues. A queueing network is a collection of such services in which customers (jobs) proceed from one stage to another until finished. Tutorials on queueing networks can be found in Volume 9, Number 3 (1977) and in Volume 10, Number 3 (1978) of *ACM Computing Surveys*.

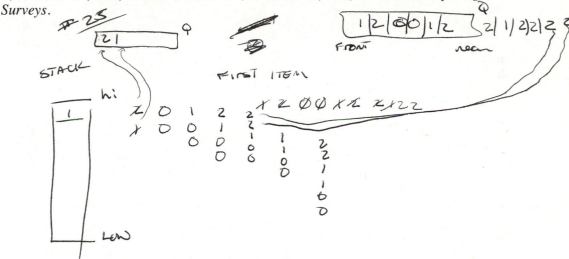

CHAPTER 5

RECURSION

5.1 INTRODUCTION

Recursion is a fundamental concept in mathematics and computer science. Perhaps the simplest example is the recursive definition of the factorial:

$$0! = 1$$
$$N! = N * (N-1)! \, , \quad N > 0$$

This definition is recursive because the factorial is defined in terms of itself—except for one case that is defined non-recursively. The mathematical use of recursion starts this simply, and continues through to active research in recursive function theory, an advanced topic.

In computer science, recursion is used as a tool to define data structures and algorithms, as an algorithm design method, and as a programming technique. Most modern programming languages provide recursion, but it can be simulated in any language. As a programming technique, recursion comes into play any time a procedure calls itself, directly or indirectly. Recursion makes many algorithms easier to analyze (as to time and space requirements) than their non-recursive counterparts. Program verification is also often simpler for recursive algorithms.

As an example of the use of recursion in defining objects in computer science, consider this definition of an unsigned integer:

A *digit* is one of the symbols 0 through 9.

An *unsigned integer* is either a digit, or an unsigned integer followed by a digit.

This definition looks circular at first glance, but it is not, because the definition of a digit provides a non-circular case.

We study recursion mostly because it provides a powerful tool for designing and describing algorithms. If your total prior experience with recursion is an introductory programming course where you saw one or two examples of recursion, you may find that statement difficult to believe. But it's true. Any effort invested in becoming comfortable with this concept is well worth it.

We will begin our presentation with a fairly common example, printing a number in reverse order, and study how the procedure can be implemented using a stack. Next we will look at a number of simple examples of recursive functions to gain familiarity with the concept. Section 5.8 will present a problem that is difficult to approach any way except recursively. Section 5.9 will show recursion in the solution of a standard illustration, the Eight Queens problem, using a technique called backtracking. In Section 5.10 we will consider the removal of recursion, i.e., ways to convert a recursive procedure to an equivalent non-recursive version. Finally, the chapter will close with an application study, in which we can see how recursion can be used to provide a more general solution to an application we studied in Chapter 4, conversion of an infix expression to postfix, which is one part of the general topic of *parsing* text.

All following chapters, especially chapters 6 and 7, draw heavily on recursion.

5.2 A FIRST EXAMPLE: PRINTING A NUMBER IN REVERSE

Here is a recursive procedure that reads a sequence of N characters and prints them in reverse order.

```
procedure PrintInReverse (N: integer);
var
  Ch: char;
begin
  if N = 1 then
  begin
     Read (Ch);
     Write (Ch)
  end
  else
  begin
     Read (Ch);
     PrintInReverse (N - 1);
     Write (Ch);
  end
end;
```

If we call this procedure with `PrintInReverse (3)` and enter `ABC`, the procedure will print `CBA`.

Any recursive procedure must contain a test for the non-recursive *stopping case,* which here is a call to print one character. When there is only one character, the "sequence of characters" is the same whether printed forward or backward, so we know how to handle that case: read the character and print it. Otherwise, we read a character and then invoke `PrintInReverse` again, but this time with the argument being `N-1`. This is the recursive step. In this case, the character that has just been read is *not* printed now; it will be printed later. This is because the `Write` cannot be executed until after the return from the recursive call.

We can see how this procedure operates by following the execution sequence shown in Figure 5.1. Each of the boxes is related to what is called an *activation frame* for the procedure. (The source of this terminology will become clear in the next section.) In each case, at the start we show the values for the procedure's parameter (`N`) and its local variable (`Ch`). Then we show the sequence of actions including, of course, the recursive calls. We assume that the characters read are `ABC`.

The frame at the left shows the status of the variables and the actions for the first call of `PrintInReverse`. Because `N` is not equal to 1, we have a recursive call. The character `A` is read into `Ch` and `PrintInReverse` is called again, this time with `N = 2`.

This takes us to the second frame, where we see statements that `N = 2` and that `Ch` is undefined. How can that be, when we just read `A` into `Ch`? Answer: This is a *new* copy of the variable `Ch`, fresh for this activation frame. Every activation frame has its own copies of the parameters and the local variables.

`N` is still not equal to 1, so we read the `B` into this activation frame's copy of `Ch` and call `PrintInReverse` once again, this time with `N = 1`.

In the final frame we have reached the non-recursive stopping case, so `C` is read and immediately printed. That completes the action of this activation of the procedure, so control returns to the statement following the one that invoked the procedure, in the second activation. This statement is a `Write` of the value in that activation's `Ch`, which, we recall, is still holding the `B`. Now control returns to the first activation, where `A` is printed, and we are finished.

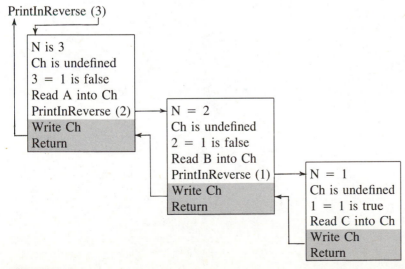

FIGURE 5.1.

Execution sequence of a recursive procedure to print a sequence of characters in reverse.

5.3 HOW RECURSION IS IMPLEMENTED

Printing the three characters in reverse sequence involves three calls of `PrintInReverse`, each time with a different parameter value. The procedure returns occur in the reverse order of the procedure calls, that is, we return from the last call first, then we return from the next-to-last call, and so forth.

This sounds like the LIFO behavior of a stack and, indeed, a stack is used to implement recursion. Let us follow the operation, using a stack of records, each record containing one character field and one integer field. Such a stack record contains the data fields of an activation frame for the procedure, so we identify the stack items accordingly.

After the first call of `PrintInReverse`, before the execution of the procedure body, the stack looks like this:

Frame 1:

Ch:	?
N	3

The "?" means that the field exists, but that nothing has been placed there yet. When the `Read` is executed, we get this stack picture:

Frame 1:

Ch:	A
N	3

Now comes the second call of `PrintInReverse`, leading to a second activation frame.

Frame 2:

Ch:	?
N:	2

Frame 1:

Ch:	A
N	3

Now the `Read` is executed, and we have:

Frame 2:

Ch	B
N:	2

Frame 1:

Ch:	A
N	3

Now we have the third call of `PrintInReverse`:

Frame 3:

Ch:	?
N:	1

Frame 2:

Ch:	B
N:	2

Frame1:

Ch:	A
N	3

After the `Read` we have:

Frame 3:

Ch:	C
N:	1

Frame 2:

Ch:	B
N:	2

Frame 1:

Ch:	A
N	3

This is the stopping case, and we immediately print the value of `Ch`. Which value of `Ch`? The value for this activation frame is simply the `Ch` field of the top item of the stack. The `C` is printed.

Observe that we are using the variables in the activation frame stack from their position at the top of the stack, without popping the stack to access them. This is similar to the way the `StackTop` operation used in Section 4.6 works. "Popping the stack" now means essentially to discard the top frame when the variables in it are no longer needed.

After printing, the work of this invocation of `PrintInReverse` has been completed, and the stack is popped.

Frame 2:

Ch:	B
N:	2

Frame 1:

Ch:	A
N	3

The return is to the `Write` in the second activation of `PrintIn-Reverse`. This `Write` prints what it finds in the `Ch` field at the top of the stack—the `B`. The stack is popped.

Frame 1:

Ch:	A
N	3

The next return is to the `Write` in the first activation. It writes what it finds in the `Ch` field at the top of the stack (the `A`), pops the stack (leaving it empty) and returns to whatever called `PrintInReverse` in the first place. The three characters have been printed in reverse sequence.

This presentation of the implementation of recursion glosses over a number of issues in the interest of simplicity in a first encounter. When and if you study compiler construction you will learn that, in the more general situation, things other than arguments and local variables are placed in an activation frame. But the central idea of a stack of activation frames will always be valid.

This demonstration of how recursion works points up an important aspect of the performance of recursive programs: the stack of activation records takes memory space. In extreme cases this space penalty can make a recursive approach unworkable. Even if things don't get that bad, the space required for the activation records and the time required to move items to them are factors to weigh in using recursion. Sometimes it is possible to recast recursive procedures in such a way as to minimize these penalties.

5.4 A RECURSIVE FUNCTION: THE FACTORIAL

`PrintInReverse` is a recursive procedure. We also frequently use recursive functions. Here is the factorial:

```
function Fact (N: integer): integer;
begin
   if N = 0 then
      Fact := 1
   else
      Fact := N * Fact(N - 1)
end;
```

The execution sequence is similar to that of `PrintInReverse`, except that here the recursive call occurs within an assignment statement. The multiplication in `N * Fact(N - 1)` cannot be carried out until `Fact` has been called with `N = 0`, returning 1. At that point, the multiplications are carried out from 1 up to the value of N. This process is depicted in Figure 5.2, where the numbers on the upward arrows show the values being returned by the function.

Factorial := Fact (3);

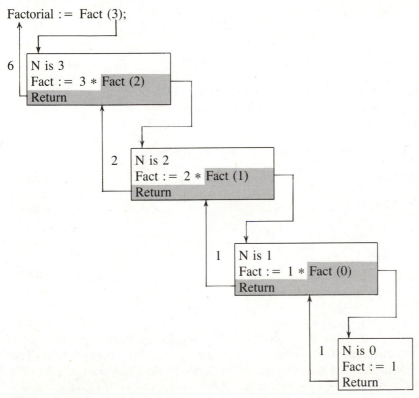

FIGURE 5.2.
Execution sequence of a recursive function to compute the factorial.

5.5 A HIGHEST COMMON FACTOR FUNCTION

The highest common factor (HCF) of two integers, also called the greatest common divisor (GCD), is the largest integer that divides both. An algorithm by Euclid tells us how to find the HCF of two positive (i.e., non-zero and non-negative) integers p and q:

"Divide p by q to give a remainder r. If $r = 0$ then q is the HCF. Otherwise repeat the process with q and r taking the place of p and q."

This translates directly into a recursive function.

```
function HCF (P, Q: PosInt): PosInt;
var
    R: integer;
begin
    R := P mod Q;
    if R = 0 then
        HCF := Q
    else
        HCF := HCF(Q, R)
end;
```

`PosInt` is declared in

```
type
    PosInt = 1..MaxInt;
```

The intent is to exclude zero and negative values. The HCF can be defined for these cases, but this function does not handle them.

A non-recursive version of the algorithm is as follows:

```
function HCF (P, Q: PosInt): PosInt;
var
    R: integer;
begin
    R := P mod Q;
    while R <> 0 do
    begin
        P := Q;
        Q := R;
        R := P mod Q
    end;
    HCF := Q
end;
```

We claim that, once one is comfortable with recursion, the recursive version will be simpler to understand because it is a more "natural" formulation. This claim is based on the fact that the recursive version computes $p\ mod\ q$ in only one place, as in the description, whereas in the non-recursive version it is computed twice. Of course, what seems natural to one person may not seem so to another; we only hope that as you work more with recursion you will join the group that finds it a normal way of expressing algorithms.

5.6 RECURSIVE ADDITION FUNCTIONS

Given two non-negative integers, *a* and *b,* we can find their sum by adding 1 to *b*, *a* times as follows:

```
function Sum (A, B: NonNegInt): NonNegInt;
begin
   if A = 0 then
      Sum := B
   else
      Sum := 1 + Sum (A-1, B)
end;
```

This can be written another way:

```
function Sum (A, B: NonNegInt): NonNegInt;
begin
   if A = 0 then
      Sum := B
   else
      Sum := Sum (A-1, B+1)
end;
```

The second way translates readily into the following iterative version:

```
function Sum (A, B: NonNegInt): NonNegInt;
begin
   while A <> 0 do
   begin
      A := A - 1;
      B := B + 1
   end;
   Sum := B
end;
```

5.7 THREE VERSIONS OF A RECURSIVE FIBONACCI NUMBER FUNCTION

Fibonacci numbers arise in many branches of natural and computer science. They are defined by

$$F_0 = 0$$
$$F_1 = 1$$
$$F_n = F_{n-1} + F_{n-2}, \qquad n > 1$$

This says that the first two Fibonacci numbers are zero and one, and that after that, each Fibonacci number is equal to the sum of the previous two. The first ten Fibonacci numbers are therefore 0, 1, 1, 2, 3, 5, 8, 13, 21, and 34.

This definition leads immediately to a recursive function.

```
function Fib (N: NonNegInt): NonNegInt;
begin
    if N = 0 then
        Fib := 0
    else if N = 1 then
        Fib := 1
    else
        Fib := Fib (N - 1) + Fib (N - 2)
end;
```

It is instructive to run this program. If you do so, you will find that it is exceedingly slow for even moderate values of N. To see why, consider the tree of the execution sequence for, say, $N = 5$:

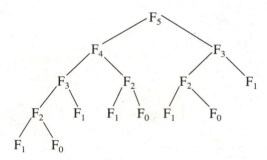

Looking at this diagram and the program together, we see that the meaning is as follows: to compute F_5 we need to compute F_4 which requires F_3 which requires F_2 which requires F_1—which is a non-recursive stopping case. But F_2 also requires F_0, another stopping case. The process continues through the tree. It is not too difficult to show that in evaluating F_k, this procedure will evaluate F_0 and F_1 a total of F_{k+1} times.

It is also possible to find a closed form formula for the Fibonacci numbers.

$$F_k = \frac{1}{\sqrt{5}} \left[\left(\frac{1 + \sqrt{5}}{2} \right)^k - \left(\frac{1 - \sqrt{5}}{2} \right)^k \right]$$

The second term in parentheses is a number less than 1, raised to a power, which becomes negligible for large k. We thus get the remarkable result that we can compute F_k exactly, by rounding this expression to the nearest integer:

$$F_k = \frac{1}{\sqrt{5}} \left(\frac{1 + \sqrt{5}}{2} \right)^k$$

$\dfrac{1 + \sqrt{5}}{2}$ is about 1.618—*larger* than unity, of course. Putting this result together with the number of evaluations of F_0 and F_1 required to compute F_k, we see that the running time of this algorithm is *exponential* in k. An exponential-time algorithm represents a dead end in most investigations.

This version is therefore *outstandingly* slow, and you may hear a remark like, "A recursive function for finding Fibonacci numbers *must* be slow, inherently."

Now, let's see if that is really true. Suppose we modify the function so that along with N there are two parameters A and B, which are two earlier Fibonacci numbers. To get F_n, we call the following modified function with A = 1 and B = 0.

```
function FastFib (A, B, N: NonNegInt): NonNegInt;
begin
   if N = 0 then
      FastFib := B
   else if N = 1 then
      FastFib := A
   else
      FastFib := FastFib (A + B, A, N - 1)
end;
```

If we call this function with FastFib (1, 0, 6), the successive recursive calls will be: FastFib (1, 1, 5), FastFib (2, 1, 4), FastFib (3, 2, 3), FastFib (5, 3, 2), and FastFib (8, 5, 1). This last is the second non-recursive exit case, and the function returns 8, which is indeed F_6.

The execution time of this version is linear in N.

You may be inclined to object: "You have used a recursive *procedure,* but you haven't used a recursive *algorithm:* All you have done is to use a recursive call to implement iteration." And, of course, you would be correct. The function can be rewritten to make the iteration explicit. And, while we are at it, let us embed the three-argument version in a function with the usual one argument, to conceal the inner workings from the user.

```
function FastFib2 (N: NonNegInt): NonNegInt;

   function IterFib (A, B, N: NonNegInt): NonNegInt;
   var
      AOld: NonNegInt;
   begin
      while N <> 0 do
      begin
         AOld := A;
         A := A + B;
         B := AOld;
         N := N - 1
      end;
      IterFib := B
   end;   { of function IterFib }

begin
   FastFib2 := IterFib (1, 0, N)
end;   { of function FastFib2 }
```

If this version is called with `FastFib2 (6)`, the successive values of A and B within `IterFib` will be (1, 0), (1, 1), (2, 1), (3, 2), (5, 3), (8, 5) and (13, 8). At this point the value of B, 8, is assigned as the value of the function.

If you really need to find Fibonacci numbers, then an iterative approach is strongly recommended! We have gone through this exercise in an attempt to demonstrate the difference between a recursive *algorithm* and a recursive *procedure*. We have also seen how a recursive algorithm can be implemented with an iterative procedure, although it will not always be as simple as in this case.

5.8 AN APPLICATION: COUNTING CELLS IN A BLOB

All the examples so far have involved recursive procedures for doing things we know how to do without recursion. Let us now consider an application that it is not obvious how to do at all *except* recursively.

We have a two-dimensional grid of cells, each of which may be empty or filled. Any group of cells that are connected (horizontally, vertically, or diagonally) constitutes a "blob." You might imagine that the cells have been created by scanning a microscope slide of a bacterial culture, and that the purpose is to estimate the degree of infection.

For example, in the grid below the blob that includes the cell in row 2 and column 4 has five cells. The function we seek accepts the coordinates of a cell, and returns the number of cells in the blob that contains the cell. The result is zero if the designated cell is empty.

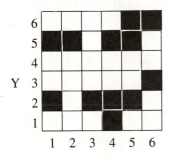

You might wish to stop at this point and see if you can solve the problem yourself. If you can do it without using recursion (other than by writing a recursive program first and then mechanically removing recursion), please send me your program!

A procedure to do the job, together with the necessary program declaratives, follows. The parameters of the procedure are the name of a blob array, together with two integers specifying a cell. The body of the procedure does nothing except invoke an included function. Why do that? The problem is that we shall be invoking the function recursively, eight times, and for a reason that will become apparent shortly, we need to mark each filled cell as being empty. Because of the latter fact, we wish to make the blob array parameter a *value* parameter, so that the caller's array is not destroyed. But remember how a value parameter is passed: an actual copy of it is made and placed in the activation record, and the procedure uses that copy. With eight recursive calls, and with a depth of recursion that could be considerable for blobs with many cells, that could result in a tremendous amount of wasted storage. Furthermore, the time required to make the copy of the array each time would be a severe penalty even if we didn't run out of storage. And, worst of all, the multiple copies would defeat the algorithm: we want each invocation of the function to see the same blob array, not a new one each time.

One simple way to accomplish what is needed is to embed the actual recursive procedure within the one that the caller of the routine sees. The embedded procedure (function, in this case) must, of course, have a different name; for clarity its name should be closely related to that of the including procedure. However it may be short because it isn't used anywhere else.

The procedure that follows assumes these declarations in the main program:

```
const
    MaxX = 100;
    MaxY = 100;

type
    Status = (Empty, Filled);
    BlobArray = array [1..MaxX, 1..MaxY] of Status;
```

Here is the procedure:

```
function CellCount (Grid: BlobArray; X, Y: integer): integer;

    function CC (X, Y: integer): integer;
    begin
        if (X < 1) or (X > MaxX) or (Y < 1) or (Y > MaxY) then
            CC := 0
        else if Grid[X, Y] = Empty then
            CC := 0
        else begin
            Grid[X, Y] := Empty;
            CC := 1 + CC(X+1, Y-1)
                    + CC(X+1, Y  )
                    + CC(X+1, Y+1)
                    + CC(X,   Y+1)
                    + CC(X-1, Y+1)
                    + CC(X-1, Y  )
                    + CC(X-1, Y-1)
                    + CC(X,   Y-1)
        end
    end;    { function CC }

begin   { body of function CellCount }
    CellCount := CC (X, Y)
end;      { function CellCount }
```

In the included function named `CC`, we first check if the cell is in the array. Failure to make this check would lead to out-of-bounds array references in the recursive calls for cells on the edge of the grid. Next, if the cell is empty we return a count of zero. Now, the only remaining case is that the cell is filled. We mark it as empty so that it will not be seen on later recursive calls, and then check its eight neighbors. If we did not mark each filled cell as empty, the recursion would be infinite; any two adjacent cells would ''see'' each other, in an endless recursive chain.

The running time of this algorithm is linear in the number of cells in a blob. For each filled cell, it will call itself eight times. Given the definition of a blob, it would be very difficult—perhaps impossible—to reduce the constant of proportionality below eight. Doing so would require knowing the history of which cells in the area had already been checked. Furthermore, the operations involved in that process could take as long as simply testing all adjacent cells.

Many students arrive at this course with a terror of recursion, regarding it as some combination of the general theory of relativity and medieval alchemy—hopelessly difficult, probably based on witchcraft, and incredibly inefficient. Such students should stop to ponder this example. In a dozen lines of quite clear code, we have solved a problem that this author would have no idea how to do otherwise, and we did it in a way that is probably about as efficient as we could hope to achieve.

5.9 BACKTRACKING VIA RECURSION: THE EIGHT QUEENS PROBLEM

Recursion can be used as a problem-solving technique in situations where there is no way to seek a solution except to try various possibilities, knowing full well that in some cases we will find ourselves at a dead end. At such points we have to go back to an earlier stage in the search and try a different path. Recursion, in such a case, is used to handle the ''going back'' part, which is usually called *backtracking*. We will now turn to a standard illustration of this method, The Eight Queens problem.

The goal of this puzzle is to place eight queens on a chessboard in such a way that no queen attacks any other queen. Two of the many solutions are shown at the top of the next page. In each case, no queen is in the same row, same column, or same diagonal as any other queen.

How could we start to find solutions to this problem? Exhaustive search is prohibitive. Even if we immediately take advantage of the fact that there can be only one queen in each row and only one in each column, there are still 8! = 40,320 possible arrangements to test for attacks along diagonals. No systematic way of placing queens so as to preclude attacks by future placements is obvious.

We are left with the need to generate possible solutions in such a way that if we find we have reached a dead end, we can remove one or more queens, go back to a previous position, move one queen to a different square, and continue the search. In short, we must allow for backtracking.

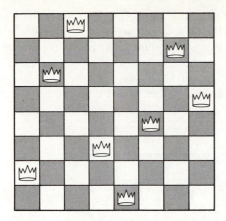 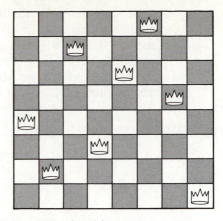

We can describe the algorithm in terms of an ADT we create for this purpose, which we may as well call `Board`. `Board` is a two-dimensional structure with eight rows and eight columns, numbered as in the following diagram, together with the following operations:

1. Place a queen in a square specified by its row and column number. Call this operation `PlaceQueen`.

2. Remove a queen from a square specified by its row and column number. Call this operation `RemoveQueen`.

3. Determine whether a queen in a specified square attacks any other queen already on the board. This may be called `NoAttack`. It returns a `boolean` value.

The implementation of this ADT need not concern us at this stage. Various ways of representing a chessboard are possible; we can delay that decision. The details of implementing the operations must also be postponed, since they are dependent on the representation of the chessboard.

We visualize the (horizontal) rows and (vertical) columns numbered as in the following picture, which contains a third solution.

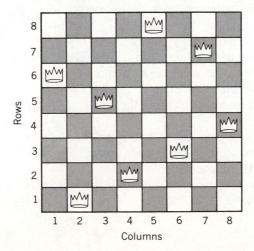

We shall designate the location of a queen by giving its coordinates on this board. For example, (5, 3) would refer to a queen in row 5, column 3. (Note carefully that the rows are numbered from the bottom up, following usual chess notation.)

To get a feel for the search strategy we shall use and the way it employs backtracking, suppose that we have arrived at this board configuration:

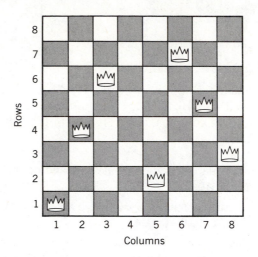

The position is legal, so far: no queen attacks any other. Now we attempt to place a queen in row 8, and cannot do it. All columns have queens except 4, and a queen in that square would attack a queen in row 5, column 7. In short, there is no solution to the eight queens problem that includes the seven queens shown.

So, we backtrack. By the way the search algorithm works (see below) we know that all *earlier* columns in row 7 already have been tried, so let's try moving the queen at (7, 6) to (7, 7) or (7, 8). However, both are obviously illegal, assuming everything stays the same in rows 1 to 6. We cannot place a queen in row 7, given the configuration of rows 1 to 6, so we remove the queen from row 7 and look to see what might be done with row 6.

But, no other position to the right of (6, 3) is legal, so we remove the queen from row 6, too. How about moving the queen in (5, 7) to (5, 8)? No good; remove her.

Rows 5 through 8 are now queenless, and we backtrack to see what we might do with row 4. The queen at (4, 2) must move. Squares (4, 3), (4, 4), and (4, 5) are illegal, but (4, 6) is acceptable.

Now we try row 5 again, and discover that (5, 3) is legal. The first five columns in row 6 are not good, but (6, 7) works. (7, 2) is found to be acceptable, and finally (8, 4). We finally have the following solution:

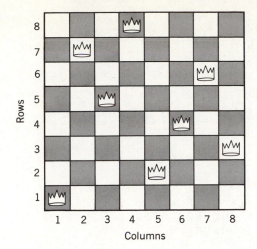

Let us state the strategy in words, then see a procedure.

We have a recursive boolean function named `AddQueen`, which takes a row number as its parameter. It attempts to add a queen in that row, starting its search in column 1. If it can do so, it calls itself for the next row. If it cannot, it "backtracks" by removing the queen from the square just tried. Then it either tries another column in the same row, if there are any more, or it backtracks to the previous level of recursion and moves the queen there. When the function calls itself with the row number being 9, a solution has been found.

The `AddQueen` procedure that follows could be invoked by a statement like

```
if AddQueen (1) then
   WriteBoard
else
   WriteLn ('Didn''t find a solution');
```

Once invoked this way, `AddQueen` calls itself recursively until encountering the `Row > 8` non-recursive exit. Actually, we have no proof of termination for the method, except the after-the-fact confirmation that it does find solutions.

This is the procedure:

```
function AddQueen (Row: integer): boolean;

{ Can we add a queen in this row that does not attack any queen
  elsewhere on the board? }

var
   Col: integer;
   GoodSquare: boolean;
```

(Continued)

```
(Continued)
begin
   if Row > 8 then
      AddQueen := true
   else

   begin
      Col := 1;
      GoodSquare := false;  { haven't placed a queen yet }

      while (Col <= 8) and (not GoodSquare) do
      begin
         PlaceQueen (Row, Col);

         if NoAttack (Row, Col) then
            if (AddQueen (Row + 1)) then
               GoodSquare := true;

         if not GoodSquare then    { backtrack }
         begin
            RemoveQueen (Row, Col);
            Col := Col + 1
         end
      end;

      { what caused exit from while loop? }
      AddQueen := GoodSquare
   end

end;
```

To make this procedure a part of a program, we need to implement the ADT
`Board`. If we were working on a program to handle the game of chess, we
would probably use an array of integers, with positive integers denoting the
various white pieces, negative integers denoting the black, and zero showing an
unoccupied square. If such an implementation were already in place, we could
certainly use it. Because we have nothing in place and want to work only with
queens, a boolean array is simpler.

`WriteBoard` prints a picture of the board configuration, and can be as
simple or as elaborate as you might wish.

With the boolean array as the underlying structure, `PlaceQueen` has only
to set the array element `Board [Row, Col]` to `true`, and `RemoveQueen`
sets it to `false`.

`NoAttack` is a boolean function that determines whether a queen in a given
row and given column attacks any queen already on the board. Because we are
generating boards from the bottom up, so to speak, there can never be a queen
in a higher-numbered row than the one the queen being tested is in. We accordingly need check only the squares below the specified row, in the same column,
and in both diagonals. This is the procedure:

```
function NoAttack (Row, Col: integer): boolean;

{ Does a queen in this position attack a queen already on board?
  Rows are added from 1 up, so need check only below this row. }

var
   R, C: integer;
   SoFarSoGood: boolean;
begin
   SoFarSogood := true;

   { Check same column, all rows below Row }
   R := Row - 1;
   while (R >= 1) and SoFarSoGood do
   begin
      SoFarSoGood := not Board [R, Col];
      R := R - 1
   end;

   { Check diagonal down and to right }
   R := Row - 1;
   C := Col + 1;
   while (R >= 1) and (C <= 8) and SoFarSoGood do
   begin
      SoFarSoGood := not Board [R, C];
      R := R - 1;
      C := C + 1
   end;

   { Check diagonal down and to left }
   R := Row - 1;
   C := Col - 1;
   while (R >= 1) and (C >= 1) and SoFarSoGood do
   begin
      SoFarSoGood := not Board [R, C];
      R := R - 1;
      C := C - 1
   end;

   NoAttack := SoFarSoGood

end;
```

We may note, before passing on, that starting the search with a queen in the corner will require the most backtracking, because such a queen attacks a long diagonal. A slight modification of AddQueen so that it puts the first queen in (1, 5), finds a solution with about five percent as much effort as for a starting position of (1, 1).

How does backtracking contribute to the solution of this problem? Our situation is that we have no algorithm that will tell us where to place a queen, with a guarantee that we will never have to remove it. If such an algorithm exists, it has not been discovered yet. Consequently, we are forced to do some kind of systematic experimentation, backing up when something we try turns out not to be feasible. Backtracking, in effect, handles the bookkeeping of backing up and trying something else. Furthermore, once an early guess has been shown infeasible, backtracking guarantees that we will not pursue hopeless paths any longer than needed to prove that they are hopeless.

Out of the 40,320 possible ways of placing eight queens so that there is only one queen in each row and one in each column, this algorithm checks possible attacks only 877 times for the worst case of starting with the first queen in the corner, and only 41 for the optimal (for the way this algorithm is written) of starting in column 5.

The Eight Queens Problem has a distinguished history, going back some centuries, during which time it has resisted analytical solution by such intellects as the mathematician Carl Friedrich Gauss. As an example of backtracking, it is a permanent part of computer science folklore. Its practical value is, of course, somewhat limited. But problems of an equivalent nature arise in many ordinary computer applications. In these areas an iterative approach tends to be very much more difficult to conceptualize except, of course, by using a stack in what amounts to programming one's own recursion.

5.10 RECURSION REMOVAL

Under certain conditions that cover many applications, there are systematic methods for removing recursion, i.e., converting to an iterative procedure that gives the same results. We shall show an example of the simplest case and state a general method of modest complexity. More complex cases will require investigation of the references or, in some instances, the completion of research still in progress.

The assumptions need to be clear.

First, we shall deal only with recursive procedures, not functions.

Second, we deal only with *direct* recursion, that is, procedures that call themselves. *Indirect recursion,* where, for example, A calls B which calls C, which calls A, is not covered here. Indirect recursion is also called *mutual recursion.*

Third, we assume that all parameters are called by value, which means that a new copy of each parameter is placed in a new activation frame each time the procedure calls itself. (It is possible to relax this restriction, but we want to keep the discussion reasonably simple.)

With these assumptions, let us consider the simplest kind of recursion to remove. This is the case where the last action in the body of the recursive procedure is a direct call of the procedure, which is generally called *tail recursion.* In this case we can replace the recursive call with statements to reassign the parameters of the call, and jump to the first statement of the procedure body.

For example, here is a simple procedure that prints a *natural number* (non-negative integer) with its decimal digits in reverse order:

```
procedure PrintNaturalReverse (N: NonNegInt);
begin
   Write (N mod 10);
   if (N div 10) <> 0 then
      PrintNaturalReverse (N div 10)
end;
```

Because the last statement is a direct recursive call of the procedure, we have an instance of tail recursion. This can be removed, as in this version:

```
procedure IterativePrintNaturalReverse (N: NonNegInt);
begin
   Write (N mod 10);
   N := N div 10;

   while N <> 0 do
   begin
      Write (N mod 10);
      N := N div 10
   end
end;
```

Procedures or functions that use tail recursion are particularly easy to convert to an iterative equivalent. Some compilers are smart enough to recognize tail recursion and remove it automatically, which, of course, is not what we assume here.

We want to emphasize that we spoke of the last *action* in the body of the procedure being a recursive call, not the last *statement*. In a recursive factorial function, for example, we have this body:

```
   if N = 0 then
      Fact := 1
   else
      Fact := N * Fact(N - 1)
```

The last object, in the sense of reading through the text of the procedure, is indeed a recursive call—but the last *action* is the multiplication, which cannot be done until reaching the non-recursive case. This function is not tail-recursive.

Next let us consider a general form for direct *linear* recursion, meaning that there is just one call of the procedure from within itself. The general form of the procedure, with the names we shall use for its various parts, are shown in this schema:

```
procedure LinearRecursiveProc (N: integer);
begin
   if Predicate (N) then
      NonRecursiveCase (N)
   else
   begin
      PreOps (N);
      LinearRecursiveProc (F(N));
      PostOps (N)
   end
end;
```

Most of the names are clear; `PreOps` is a group of zero or more statements prior to the recursive call, and `PostOps` is a group of one or more statements after it. (If the number of statements in `PostOps` is zero, we have tail recursion.) All the actions are indicated as being functions of the parameter. However, this may not always be the case. `F(N)` might be something as simple as subtracting 1 from `N`, or many other things, as we have already seen.

A procedure of this form can be replaced by one of the following form:

```
procedure IterativeProc (N: integer);
var
   S: Stack;
begin
   MakeStackEmpty (S);

   while not Predicate (N) do
   begin
      PreOps (N);
      Push (S, N);
      N := F(N)
   end;

   NonRecursiveCase (N);

   while not StackIsEmpty (S) do
   begin
      Pop (S, N);
      PostOps (N)
   end

end;
```

For an example, consider this procedure, which could be used to print integers if Pascal could print only characters. What we want to do is print the digits of a decimal representation of the (non-negative) integer in normal order, without leading zeros. `N mod 10` gets the rightmost digit, but we want to print that last, not first. This attack leads to something quite similar to `PrintIn-Reverse`, with which we began the chapter.

```
procedure WriteNatural (N: NonNegInt);
begin
    if N < 10 then
        Write (Chr(N + Ord('0')))
    else
    begin
        WriteNatural (N div 10);
        Write (Chr(N mod 10 + Ord('0')))
    end
end;
```

In terms of the general schema above, `Predicate` is `N < 10`, the non-recursive case is printing the character corresponding to a single–digit number, there are no statements before the recursive call (zero statements in `PreOps`), `F(N) = N div 10`, and the one statement in `PostOps` writes the character equivalent of the last decimal digit of the number.

Removal of recursion in this case is achieved by stacking the argument of the procedure, as modified by `F(N)`, doing the non-recursive case, and then popping the stack and applying the `PostOps` to the popped values. In the present example we get the following:

```
procedure IterativeWriteNatural (N: NonNegInt);
var
    S: Stack;
begin
    MakeStackEmpty (S);
    while N >= 10 do
    begin
        Push (S, N);
        N := N div 10
    end;

    Write (Chr(N + Ord('0')));

    while not StackIsEmpty (S) do
    begin
        Pop (S, N);
        Write (Chr(N mod 10 + Ord('0')))
    end
end;
```

Up to this point in the story, recursion removal is quite similar to what a running Pascal program actually does. All arguments (and local variables, if any) are placed on a stack at the time of activation of a procedure in any case. If the procedure calls itself, then a new activation frame contains a new set of arguments. Any reference to an argument within the procedure body is taken to refer to that argument's value in the activation frame at the top of the stack. With this kind of storage management, recursion is not very difficult to implement, and there is no inherent reason why it should be any more inefficient (time−consuming) than any other procedure call.

But now the story does get a bit more complex, and we shall have to be content to sketch the situation before leaving the subject.

With binary recursion, where a procedure calls itself twice (as the first Fibonacci function did), the program must be able to tell where to return to after it completes execution. This is handled by stacking a return address along with the argument(s) and local variables, if any. In general, *n*-ary recursion is possible, as we saw with the blob program, where $n = 8$. Return addresses must be stacked accordingly.

With binary (or *n*-ary) recursion, if one of the recursive calls is the last action in the body of the procedure, tail-recursion removal may be used for that one call, if desired, but the rest would still require a stack.

And here we leave the story of recursion removal, which is an active area of research. Investigators are constantly seeking methods that are simultaneously general, efficient, and easy to understand. With such conflicting goals, much interesting work remains.

5.11 APPLICATION: RECURSION IN CONVERTING AN EXPRESSION FROM INFIX TO POSTFIX

In this application study we shall take another look at the subject of converting an expression in infix form to postfix form. The technique we shall use can be generalized to deal with much more than just arithmetic expressions. For a suitably designed programming language, it is the basis of one major section of a compiler, and provides a foundation for the study of processing *natural language* text, such as English.

We will begin with a definition of the syntax of a legal expression, that is, the components of which it is constructed and the relations between them. To represent the syntax we turn to a system of notation called *BNF,* for Backus-Naur Form.[1] BNF is a *metalanguage:* that is, it is a language for describing a language. The BNF metalanguage is composed of the following elements.

1. *Terminals,* which are objects in the language (a subset of Pascal in this case) that is being described. In our example the terminals will be the letters A through Z, the four arithmetic operators, and the left and right parentheses. Terminals are also called *tokens,* which is the term we shall use in discussing the program that follows. When a terminal appears in a syntax description, it stands for itself.

2. *Non-terminals,* which denote sets of strings that may be reduced to terminals. Non-terminals are enclosed in angle brackets. We shall use <expression>, <term>, <factor>, <adding-operator>, <multiplying-operator>, and <variable-name>. The definitions of these non-terminals are given below.

---

[1]Named for John Backus and Peter Naur, who developed it for describing the syntax of Algol-60, an early programming language that had strong influence on subsequent languages including Pascal.

3. The *metalinguistic symbols* :: = , | , and curly braces: { }. The :: = may be read "is a" or "is produced by." The | means "or." Curly braces mean "zero or more repetitions of."

4. A set of *production rules,* or simply *productions,* which define the ways in which non-terminals may be built up from one another and from the terminals.

The curly braces to designate zero or more repetitions are not part of "pure" BNF, but are used in one common extension of it.

With these definitions, here is the description of an arithmetic expression of the form considered in Chapter 4, which is a subset of what is permitted in Pascal.

<expression> :: = <term> { <adding-operator> <term> }

<term> :: = <factor> { <multiplying-operator> <factor> }

<factor> :: = (<expression>) | <variable-name>

<adding-operator> :: = + | −

<multiplying-operator> :: = * | /

<variable-name> :: = A | B | C | · · · | Z

Reading the first production, we would say "An expression is a term, followed by zero or more repetitions of the combination of an adding operator and a term." For the third we have, "A factor is either an expression in parentheses or a variable name." And a variable name, for our purposes here (as in Chapter 4), is an uppercase letter.

These productions are clearly recursive, because the first three refer to each other in a cycle. As in any use of recursion there has to be a non-recursive exit, and there is: variable names are terminals. Because every non-empty expression must have at least one variable, this assures that as we apply these productions we will eventually "get out."

This is an example of a *context-free grammar,* meaning that each production may be applied at any point in an expression where the non-terminal on the left appears, without regard for what surrounds the non-terminal. A grammar in which we have to know what is on either side of a non-terminal to apply a production is called *context-sensitive.* Most programming languages are largely, but not entirely, context-free.

Given a context-free grammar for an arithmetic expression, writing a program to process an expression is a very simple matter. The program is almost a direct copy of the grammar. This, of course, is part of the attraction of a formal language description, a subject that has received intensive study and is a major branch of computer science. Let us see how this works out for our small application.

The program shown in the following two parts below implements the BNF grammar almost directly.[2] The overall program organization is shown first. We

---

[2]The assistance of Charles Engelke, University of Florida, in writing this program is gratefully acknowledged.

have a main program that contains a loop to get expressions and to invoke the conversion procedure. The procedure `ReadAndEchoInput` does what its name says and places the expression in the array `InputExpression`. A `$` for a sentinel is placed after the end of the expression; we shall see its purpose shortly. `GetToken` obtains the next token from the input array. The `repeat-until` loop is our simple method for skipping over blanks (and any other extraneous characters).

```
program ConvertInfixToPostfix (input, output);

{ Convert infix expressions to postfix,
  using the recursive descent method. }

type
    Index = 0..80;
    TokenType = char;


var
    InputExpression: array [1..80] of TokenType;
    J: Index;
    Token: TokenType;


procedure ReadAndEchoInput;
begin
    J := 0;
    while not EOLN do
    begin
       J := J + 1;
       Read (InputExpression[J]);
       Write (InputExpression[J])
    end;
    InputExpression[J + 1] := '$';    { Sentinel }
    ReadLn;
    WriteLn
end;


procedure GetToken;
begin
    repeat
       J := J + 1
    until InputExpression[J] in ['A'..'Z', '+', '-',
                                 '*', '/', '(', ')', '$'];
    Token := InputExpression[J]
end;


{ The conversion procedures, shown below, go here. }
```

```
begin
    while not EOF do begin
        WriteLn ('The infix expression:');
        ReadAndEchoInput;
        WriteLn ('Has the postfix form:');
        J := 0;
        GetToken;
        ConvertExpression;
        WriteLn;
        WriteLn
    end
end.
```

This program, which is intended solely to illustrate recursion in an important application area, makes use of global variables in a way that we would normally avoid. The reason is that writing the conversion routines with parameters would confuse the situation with respect to recursive calls, and that the alternative of making one giant procedure of almost everything in this program would merely make it harder to understand.

With the overall program organization understood, let us now look at the three procedures that do the work.

```
procedure ConvertExpression; forward;


procedure ConvertFactor;
begin
    if Token = '(' then
    begin
        GetToken;          { move past the '(' }
        ConvertExpression;
        GetToken           { move past the ')' }
    end
    else                   { the token is an identifier }
    begin
        Write (Token);
        GetToken
    end
end;


procedure ConvertTerm;
var
    Operator: TokenType;
begin
    ConvertFactor;

    while Token in ['*', '/'] do
    begin
        Operator := Token;
        GetToken;
        ConvertFactor;
        Write (Operator)
    end
end;
```

(Continued)

(Continued)

```
procedure ConvertExpression;
var
    Operator: TokenType;
begin
    ConvertTerm;

    while Token in ['+', '-'] do
    begin
        Operator := Token;
        GetToken;
        ConvertTerm;
        Write (Operator)
    end
end;
```

These procedures must be positioned to take into account Pascal's requirement that a procedure must be declared before it is invoked. And, because the three procedures invoke each other in a cycle, one of them must have a `forward` declaration. The net result is that the procedures are positioned in reverse order from the way they were described above.

Let us study these procedures with some care, first noting that the main program obtains the first token before invoking `ConvertExpression`.

`ConvertExpression` starts by invoking `ConvertTerm`, since, according to the grammar, the first thing in any expression is always a term, regardless of whatever else there may be. Then, to handle the possibility that the term is followed by an adding operator and another term, the procedure has a `while` loop that tests for the presence of + or −. (You will see shortly that another token will have been obtained, through execution of `ConvertTerm` or `ConvertFactor`, before the test in the `while` is made the first time.) If there is a + or −, that sign is assigned to `Operator`. Then we get another token and, once again we invoke `ConvertTerm`. When that has been completed we write out the operator. This means that the operator is written *after* its operands, as required by postfix form.

`ConvertTerm` follows a similar pattern.

`ConvertFactor` is a little different because it has to deal with the possibility of a parenthesized expression. When a left parenthesis is encountered, we know that we have an expression to evaluate and that a right parenthesis should follow it. To do all this, we need only move past the left parenthesis, invoke `ConvertExpression`, then move past the matching right parenthesis. Naturally, there is no way to reach `ConvertFactor` without first invoking `ConvertExpression`, so we have now carried out a recursive procedure call. Indeed, `ConvertExpression` has invoked itself through a chain of two other procedures. If `ConvertFactor` finds that there is no left parenthesis, then the only other possibility (assuming an error-free expression) is that the expression consists of a variable name. In that case we simply write the variable name and get another token.

What guarantees that the process will terminate? Let us analyze the cases. First, we may reasonably assume that the input string has at least one character and that, if there is only one, it is a variable name. In practice all of this would be built into a single procedure that would be invoked only when another part of the compiler had established that what should come next is an expression (and a correctly-formed expression would not be empty). Now suppose the expression is, in fact, just a single variable name. Then `ConvertExpression` invokes `ConvertTerm`, which invokes `ConvertFactor`. `ConvertFactor`, finding no left parenthesis, writes the variable name and gets another token. This turns out to be the $ sentinel. When control returns to `ConvertTerm`, it will not find either ∗ or /, so its `while` test fails and control returns to `ConvertExpression`. This does not find + or −, so its `while` test also fails and control returns to the main program. For more complex expressions the argument is simply that eventually the $ will be encountered, which will also cause the `while` statements to stop repeating, and the recursive chain will be exited. In any case, termination is guaranteed.

Here is the output when this program was run with a few illustrative expressions.

```
The infix expression:
A
Has the postfix form:
A

The infix expression:
A+B
Has the postfix form:
AB+

The infix expression:
A ∗ B
Has the postfix form:
AB∗

The infix expression:
C + D∗E
Has the postfix form:
CDE∗+

The infix expression:
(C + D)∗E
Has the postfix form:
CD+E∗

The infix expression:
((Q))
Has the postfix form:
Q
```

More interesting, for purposes of understanding how this program works, is the following output of a modified version (not shown) that has a `WriteLn` statement at the start of each of the three procedures. The output shows the procedure name and the value of `Token`. Additionally the writing of tokens was changed to use `WriteLn` instead of `Write`.

```
The infix expression:
A * B
Has the postfix form:
ConvertExpression A
ConvertTerm A
ConvertFactor A
A
ConvertFactor B
B
*


The infix expression:
A + B
Has the postfix form:
ConvertExpression A
ConvertTerm A
ConvertFactor A
A
ConvertTerm B
ConvertFactor B
B
+


The infix expression:
C + D*E
Has the postfix form:
ConvertExpression C
ConvertTerm C
ConvertFactor C
C
ConvertTerm D
ConvertFactor D
D
ConvertFactor E
E
*
+


The infix expression:
(C + D)*E
Has the postfix form:
ConvertExpression (
ConvertTerm (
ConvertFactor (
ConvertExpression C
ConvertTerm C
ConvertFactor C
C
ConvertTerm D
ConvertFactor D
D
+
ConvertFactor E
E
*
```

Let us see how this program works by pretending to be each procedure, as the first infix expression above is processed.

`ConvertExpression` says: "Let's see here. I'm supposed to convert an expression, and I've been given the character `A`. Well, I don't know much about expressions, except that the first thing in one is a term. Let's give `ConvertTerm` the problem."

`ConvertTerm` says: "Let's see here. I'm supposed to convert a term, and I've been given the character `A`. Unfortunately, I don't know much about terms, except that the first thing in one is a factor. Let's give `ConvertFactor` the problem."

`ConvertFactor` says: "Well, all I know about factors is that one either begins with a left parenthesis or is a variable. Did they give me a left parenthesis? No? Well, then it must be a variable name so I'll write that, get another token, and return control to my caller."

`ConvertTerm` is back in control, starting with the statement after the invocation of `ConvertFactor,` i.e., the `while` statement: "Well, the only other thing I know about a term is that it could be followed by a multiplying operator and another term. What am I looking at? Oh! An asterisk. Then I'll call that the `Operator,` get another token, and pass the problem back to `ConvertFactor.`"

`ConvertFactor`: "OK, I'm looking at a character that is a variable name again. I'll write it, get another token, and give the problem back to my caller."

`ConvertTerm` gets control with the statement after the invocation of `ConvertFactor`: "Whatever `ConvertFactor` did, which is none of my business, I'm now supposed to write the `Operator` that got me into this loop, and then see if I should go around the loop again. Well, a dollar sign certainly isn't an asterisk or a slash, so I'm done. Back to you, `ConvertExpression.`"

`ConvertExpression`: "I'm supposed to go through this `while` loop so long as `Token` is a plus sign or a minus sign, but it's neither, so I'm giving control back to whoever called me."

And the program has converted the expression to postfix.

We see that by implementing the defining grammar with a program, we have automatically handled all questions of precedence, without resorting to precedence tables. This is one of the attractions of the method. In fact, for someone who is comfortable with recursion it can be argued that this program is simpler to understand than the table-driven method implemented in Chapter 4.

The process that we have seen here, whereby a string of characters in a language is associated with the defining grammar, is called *parsing*. It is the heart of compiling a program written in a higher-level language like Pascal because the methods that we have seen illustrated with a subset of the arithmetic expression capabilities can be extended to handle an entire program. Needless to say, there are many subtleties and complexities in the complete process that are not even hinted at here, but you have now had a sketch of what is involved.

5.12 CONCLUSION

Recursion is one of the fundamental tools of computer science. In this chapter we have seen a sampling of some of its applications, looked rather briefly at the time and space penalties that sometimes attend its use, and taken an all-too-short look at systematic ways of converting a recursive program to an iterative equivalent.

Once you are comfortable with the concept and workings of recursion, you will use it where it is appropriate, and use iteration otherwise. "Appropriate" uses include situations where an algorithm is inherently recursive, as with recursive descent parsing, and any other case where the recursive formulation is easier to understand and whatever penalties in time and space there may be are acceptable.

We will be making heavy use of recursion in the rest of the book, so you will get many more opportunities to see its usefulness and get practice using it.

As we leave the topic for now, you should be aware that one of the most active areas of current research in computer science is in *functional* and *applicative* languages, each of which, in their pure forms, provide recursion as the only control structure for looping. Another good reason to become comfortable with the concept!

EXERCISES

1. The function *HCF* in Section 5.5 uses four variables, *P, Q, R,* and *HCF.* Draw stack diagrams like those shown in Section 5.3 to trace the operation of *HCF* (28, 12).

2. A number related to the *HCF* is the *LCM,* or least common multiple, of two numbers. The *LCM* of two natural numbers, *N* and *M,* is the smallest integer, *P,* such that *N* divides *P* and *M* divides *P.* For example, the *LCM* of 6 and 9 is 18, the *LCM* of 3 and 6 is 6, and that of 3 and 4 is 12.
   (a) Write a recursive function that returns the *LCM* of two natural numbers.
   (b) Write a non-recursive version of your function.

3. Modify the recursive version of the Sum function to accept negative as well as positive arguments.

4. Draw diagrams for Fib (5) and FastFib (5), tracing the action of the recursive stacks.

5. Fibonacci presented his sequence around the year 1200 with a puzzle that goes as follows: "How many pairs of rabbits will be produced in a year, beginning with a single pair, if in every month each pair bears a new pair that becomes productive from the second month on?"
   If the number of rabbit pairs at month *N* is *Pairs* (*N*), show that *Pairs* (*N*) = *Fib* (*N*). You may assume *Pairs* (1) = *Pairs* (2) = 1, because the first baby rabbits will be born just after the month is up.

6. Trace the operation of `CellCount (A, 4, 2)`, where A is the six-by-six `BlobArray` diagramed in Section 5.8. Now remove the statement `Grid[X, Y] := Empty` from the function `CellCount`, and try the tracing again.

7. Extend the program of Section 5.8 in the following ways.
   (a) Write a function that returns a count of the number of blobs in the grid. (There is a small trap here, which would lead to wrong answers of an obvious sort, but if you understand `CellCount` you will not fall into it.)
   (b) Write a function that returns, as a real number, the ratio of the numbers of cells in the largest blob to the total number of cells in the grid.
   (c) Extend the program, writing whatever functions or procedures you need, so that it returns the average number of cells in a blob if there are at least three blobs, but prints a message if asked to do this computation when there are fewer than three blobs.
   (d) The bacteriology department has modified the definition of a blob to see whether they can obtain a better correlation between computer analysis and analysis done by technicians. The newer definition is that two cells are part of the same blob only if they share an edge. Modify the program so that it asks the user which definition is desired, then proceeds accordingly.
   (Before you start to do all of this piecemeal, surely you will go back to the design stage. Rethink the human interface, the program organization, and the impact of further changes before you start coding.)

8. To reinforce your understanding of backtracking, make the few trivial changes necessary in the `EightQueens` procedures to solve the Four Queens problem. The rules are the same, except that we now have a four-by-four board and four queens.
   (a) Work through this smaller problem by hand, counting the number of times `RemoveQueen` is invoked.
   (b) Suppose that instead of placing the first queen in column 1 of row 1, she is placed in column 2 of row 1. Redo (a) with this change.
   (c) What is the worst-case running time for solving the problem?

9. The solution you found to the Four Queens problem in the previous exercise is only one possibility. There is another arrangement that also solves the problem.
   (a) What is it?
   (b) Write an algorithm to find all solutions to the Four Queens problem.
   (c) Can you extend this algorithm to find all solutions for the Eight Queens problem?

10. Write a Pascal program to find all solutions to the Four Queens problem. If you feel very self-confident, you might do this for the Eight Queens instead.

11. Even rats use backtracking when trying to traverse a maze. We can simulate a maze with a grid. Squares will be marked O (Occupied) or U (Unoccupied), with one square identified as `Start`, and another as `Finish`.

A path is a sequence of adjacent, unoccupied squares beginning at Start and ending at Finish. (Two squares are considered adjacent if they share a common side.) For example, one path through the five-by-five maze below, beginning at the lower left corner (5, 1), and finishing at the upper right corner (1, 5), is drawn in:

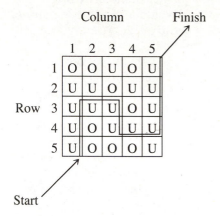

(a) Are there other paths from (5, 1) to (1, 5)?

(b) Write an ADT Maze, describing operations to:
    (i)   Recognize whether two squares are adjacent;
    (ii) Add a square to a path;
    (iii) Remove a square from a path;
    (iv) Recognize a dead end;
    (v) Recognize that you've already tried that direction and ended up at a dead end (this is by far the hardest);
    (vi) Recognize a complete path from Start to Finish.

12. Write a Pascal program using backtracking to find a path through a five-by-five maze. Input should be Start, Finish, and Maze, and output should be a path, or the announcement that there is no path through the given Maze from Start to Finish.

13. The procedure LinearRecursiveProc identified four parts (any of which might be empty) in a recursive procedure containing a single recursive call. Identify these four parts in the procedures PrintIn-Reverse, Fact, HCF, Sum, and FastFib.

14. Using the procedure IterativeProc, construct iterative versions, using a stack, for PrintInReverse, Fact and FastFib. (You will need to recast Fact and FastFib as procedures.)

15. Trace the procedure ConvertInfixToPostfix using some valid expression, such as (A + B) / (C − D + E). (Choosing one with parentheses will show how that portion of the procedure works.) Next try tracing ((A + B) − C, which is not a correct infix expression. Where does the procedure break down? Discuss possible ways to detect errors in infix expressions.

16. It is usually considered poor programming practice to use global variables, and yet the procedures `GetToken`, `ConvertExpression`, `ConvertFactor`, `ConvertTerm`, and `ReadAndEchoInput` in `ConvertInfixToPostfix` have no formal parameters at all. Why was this choice made? Do you think it defensible? If not, suggest which variables might have been passed explicitly to the procedures and why. Rewrite the program accordingly, and discuss the tradeoffs involved.

17. What are the valid sentences described by this BNF grammar?

   <sentence> ::= <subject> <predicate>
   <subject> ::= <noun phrase>
   <predicate> ::= <verb> | <verb><noun phrase>
   <noun phrase> ::= <noun> | <adjective><noun>
   <noun> ::= Cat | Dog | Man
   <adjective> ::= big | little | mean | nice | <descriptor><adjective>
   <descriptor> ::= the | a
   <verb> ::= meeowed | barked | bit | scratched

18. Outline the characteristics of a program that would accept a string of words and determine whether it is a sentence in the grammar defined in Exercise 17. The output of such a program would be simply something like ''is a sentence'' or ''is not a sentence.''

   Do you think you could turn this process around, that is, start with this grammar and *generate* valid sentences in it?

19. Extend the BNF and the program of Section 5.11 to include the relational operators <, >, and =. These have equal precedence with each other, and any of them has lower precedence than any arithmetic operator.

20. Extend the BNF and program of Section 5.11 to include an exponentiation operator, which has higher precedence than any other operator. This gets a bit tricky, because exponentiation in most programming languages is *right associative,* that is, if ^ is the exponentiation operator, `A ^ B ^ C` means `A ^ (B ^ C)`, not `(A ^ B) ^ C`. (The four arithmetic operators, as defined in the BNF of the text and in most programming languages, are *left associative.*)

SUGGESTIONS FOR FURTHER STUDY

Koffman (1985) is an excellent resource for an introductory-level review of recursion in Pascal, and indeed of any other topic in a first computer science course. The `PrintInReverse` and `CellCount` illustrations are modified from this text, although they have appeared elsewhere as well.

The original rabbit story explaining the Fibonacci sequence was reported in his *Liber abaci,* first published in 1202, and for which there is no modern translation. The version cited here comes from Boyer (1968). Reingold, Nievergelt, and Deo (1977) provide combinatorial uses for the sequence as well as closed form approximations for individual terms.

The presentations here and in Chapters 6 and 7 have been heavily influenced by Rohl (1984). This short book is an outstanding tutorial on the value of recursion in Pascal, and how to use it. The concepts are readily adapted to other languages.

Roberts (1986) motivates the concepts of recursion through many simple examples.

Recent material on functional programming, its applications, and the novel architectures devised for its implementation, can be found in the proceedings of a 1985 conference held in Nancy, France (Jouannaud, 1985). Papers in this volume also deal with the class of theoretical functional (FP) languages first defined by Backus (1978). Turner (1981) discusses the future of applicative languages.

The student who is interested in recursion, its applications to artificial intelligence, and the Lisp language in particular, might enjoy McCarthy (1960, 1978), Lisp's inventor, for a history and justification of that language.

Formal grammars, parsers, and recognizers are discussed in any book on compiler construction. A standard treatment is the so-called ''dragon book,'' Aho and Ullman (1977). (The dragon in question is the ''dragon of complexity,'' depicted on the cover as being slain by the tools of compiler construction.) More theoretical aspects of grammars, including their relationship to theoretical machines, can be found in Lewis and Papadimitriou (1981). The original notion of a context-free grammar is due to Chomsky (1957). A readable introduction to the subject from the viewpoint of computer theory is Cohen (1986).

Methods for removing recursion can be found in many data structures or algorithms texts. Kruse (1987) assembles some of the methods in a readable appendix. Knuth (1974) discusses the judicious use of `gotos` as an iterative method well worth considering. Bird (1977) is one of the earlier formal treatments.

CHAPTER 6

LINKED LISTS

Many of the ADTs we study in this book can be viewed as special cases of a more general ADT, the *linked list*. A stack, for example, is readily described (and implemented) as a linked list, as are strings and sets. In this chapter we shall study the linked list ADT and see how it can be applied to these and other situations, together with two common implementations.

The most obvious implementation of linked lists, in any language that provides the capability, is with pointer variables and dynamic storage allocation. This will be the first implementation of linked lists that we study, and will be accompanied with thorough explanations because pointer variables are not always fully covered in a first course based on Pascal. The other implementation, with arrays, is available in any language. The linked list ADT is thus universally available as a tool.

The linked list is *the* basic ADT in some languages. The primary example would be LISP, which stands for List Processing. LISP was one of the earliest high-level languages, introduced in the late 1950s, roughly ten years before Pascal. It now has many variations and intellectual descendants and a wide and loyal user community. If you continue your study in computer science you will almost certainly learn LISP or one of its relatives. All this is said simply to emphasize the fundamental nature of the linked list concept. We will see its usefulness in our work in this book, and what you learn here will provide a good start for further study.

6.2 THE ADT LINKED LIST

> **Definition:** *A linked list is a sequence of zero or more nodes, together with a set of operations. Each node contains two fields, an* Item *field that holds information and a* Next *field that holds a pointer to the next node in the list.*

Before showing one possible set of operations, let us pause briefly to emphasize the ideas of *sequence* and *link* in the definition. The name of a linked list tells us only where the first node is. We find the next node by looking at the Next field of the first node, and so on through the list.

The conventional way to picture a linked list is with a *box-and-arrow* diagram. Each node is shown as a box with an Item part on the left and a Next part on the right. An arrow leads from the Next part to the next node and the last node in the list is shown as a box in which a diagonal line is drawn through the Next part to indicate that there isn't any next node. Here, for example, is a box-and-arrow diagram for a linked list named List1 in which each node holds one character, and which contains the letters of the word LIST.

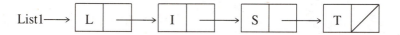

The linked list concept is so broad and general that it is difficult to specify a set that is both minimal, in some sense, and powerful. The operations that follow are representative of what might be provided.

1. CreateList is a procedure that brings a linked list into existence, in a way that depends in part on language and operating system details.

2. Inserting an item into a linked list increases the size of the list. We shall implement procedures for four variations: InsertAtFront, InsertAtEnd, InsertAfterKth, and InsertAfter-Content. The last two differ in whether the insertion is based on position in the list, or on finding a specified item in the list and inserting the new item after it.

3. Deleting an item from a linked list reduces its size. Similar variations can be provided as with insertion.

4. InList is a function that returns true if the item specified as its second parameter is in the named linked list.

5. ListIsEmpty is a function that tests for an empty linked list.

6. ListLength is a function that returns the number of items in a linked list.

7. MakeListEmpty is a procedure that makes an existing linked list empty.

8. Item is a function that returns the information stored in the node currently referenced by the linked list pointer or index. Many variations are possible, such as one that returns the Item portion in the Kth node. This particular example is easily composed from Advance and Item in a simple loop.

9. Advance is a procedure that changes its argument so that it points to the next item in a linked list.

10. CopyList does what its name says. The linked list that holds the copy must already have been created.

11. ConcatList concatenates one linked list to the end of another.

12. As a convenience for study, and at a somewhat less abstract level, we also provide an operation called WriteList that does what you would expect.

The items in a linked list may be any simple or structured type. In our examples we shall deal with single characters or integers, but in many applications the linked list would be composed of records containing a variety of diverse types of data fields.

The fact that items can be inserted in and deleted from a linked list, thus changing its size, is what differentiates a linked list from an array. The fact that the insertions and deletions can be anywhere in the linked list is what distinguishes a linked list from a stack or a queue.

Stacks and queues are both special cases of linked lists. With a stack, all accesses are at one end, called the top. With queues all additions are at one end we call the rear and all removals are at the other end, which we call the front. The general ADT linked list has no such *access restrictions*. We can insert and delete anywhere.

6.3 A NOTE ON TERMINOLOGY

The fundamental idea of a list is the sequence relation, by which we can move from one item in a list to its successor. This concept is broad enough to cover an array implementation in which there are no explicit links, but the successor location is implicit in the sequential allocation under which arrays are usually implemented. But a list implemented in this fashion makes any insertions and deletions in the middle of the list so awkward and slow that it is rarely done. In the literature, therefore, ''List'' usually turns out to mean *linked* list. As a consequence, in an attempt to keep our usage clean while waiting for terminology in computer science to stabilize, we shall use the term linked list. Additionally, because the approach of the entire presentation is based on ''linked'' lists, the word ''list'' will occasionally be used without the ''linked.''

The treatment here deals with *linear* linked lists, meaning that each node has a pointer to its one successor in the list. In Section 6.11 there is an overview of linked lists in which there are pointers to both the successor and the predecessor of each node, which is a *doubly–linked* list. But we do not deal here with what some authors refer to as non-linear linked lists, such as sparse matrices or trees.

6.4 LINKED LIST IMPLEMENTATIONS OF STACKS AND QUEUES

Considering that they are simply special cases of linked lists, it should come as no surprise that the implementation of stacks and queues in terms of list operations is particularly easy. To implement stacks we use `InsertAtFront` for `Push`, and the combination of `Item` and `DeleteKth` for `Pop`. The type declaration in the following would have to be at the program level, of course, in Pascal.

```
type
   Stack = List;


procedure CreateStack (var S: Stack);
begin
   CreateList (S)
end;


procedure Push (var S: Stack;
                NewItem: ItemType);
begin
   InsertAtFront (S, NewItem)
end;


procedure Pop (var S: Stack;
               var StackValue: ItemType);
begin
   if ListIsEmpty (S) then
      StackError (1)
   else begin
      StackValue := Item (S);
      DeleteKth (S, 1)
   end
end;


function StackIsEmpty (S: Stack): boolean;
begin
   StackisEmpty := ListIsEmpty (S)
end;


procedure MakeStackEmpty (var S: Stack);
begin
   MakeListEmpty (S)
end;
```

This set of procedures works correctly with either of the implementations of linked lists—with pointer variables or arrays—that we shall study later. In other words, the ADT linked list is usable as an abstraction in implementing another ADT. This kind of generality is precisely why we emphasize the abstract data type approach.

The implementation of queues in terms of linked lists is similar. We use `InsertAtEnd` for `EnQueue`, and use the same combination of `Item` and `DeleteKth` for `DeQueue`.

```
type
   Queue = List;


procedure CreateQueue (var Q: Queue);
begin
   CreateList (Q)
end;


procedure MakeQueueEmpty (var Q: Queue);
begin
   MakeListEmpty (Q)
end;


procedure EnQueue (var Q: Queue;
                   NewItem: ItemType);
begin
   InsertAtEnd (Q, NewItem)
end;


procedure DeQueue (var Q: Queue;
                   var QItem: ItemType);
begin
   if ListIsEmpty (Q) then
      QError (1)
   else
   begin
      QItem := Item (Q);
      DeleteKth (Q, 1)
   end
end;


function QueueIsEmpty (Q: Queue): boolean;
begin
   QueueIsEmpty := ListIsEmpty (Q)
end;
```

6.5 INFINITE PRECISION ARITHMETIC WITH LINKED LISTS

Applications arise in which it is useful to be able to deal with numbers of arbitrary size, without having to consider the limits of the sizes of numbers in the usual machine representations. A linked list, implemented with pointer variables and dynamic storage allocation, is a natural solution: we obtain storage for digits only as needed. Such an approach is often called *infinite precision* arithmetic, suggesting that numbers may be as large as we please. However, we realize that nothing in a computer is really infinite, and that we are still limited by the size of storage.

We shall illustrate the rudiments of the approach by showing decimal addition of integers represented in decimal form, one digit per node.

We begin with a design decision. Does the first node of the list contain the most significant digit or the least significant digit? It turns out, that to handle carries, we need to be able to work with the numbers starting at the least significant digit, so we will build linked lists holding numbers in that form.

Here is a procedure that reads a decimal number of indefinite length, starting as usual with the most significant digit, but placing each successive digit at the head of the list. Following the nodes through the completed list, therefore, we will traverse the number from least significant digit to most significant or, if you prefer, from right to left.

```
procedure ReadNumberAndMakeList (var L: List);
{ Creates list holding decimal number, with least significant
  digit at head of list to simplify carry in addition. }
var
    DigitChar: char;
    DigitValue: integer;
begin
    CreateList (L);

    while not EOLN do
    begin
        Read (DigitChar);
        DigitValue := Ord(DigitChar) - Ord('0');
        InsertAtFront (L, DigitValue)
    end;

    ReadLn
end;
```

We see that the digits of the number are read one at a time, as characters, and are converted to their integer equivalents for storage. Here are the box-and-arrow diagrams for the numbers 123 and 98765.

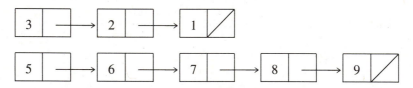

Now when we add two such numbers, we can deal with the digits in order, from the *head* (first node) of a linked list to its *tail* (last node), which corresponds to a right-to-left sequence as the numbers were originally read. The digits of the sum will be created in the same sequence mathematically, i.e., from least significant to most significant. This means that the head node of the sum will be created first. In reading the numbers, we created the head node last.

In the addition routine we shall build the linked list for the sum as we go, adding each new node to the tail of the list. The addition routine must, of course, take into account that the two numbers may be of different lengths. The main loop, therefore, is a while that keeps going as long as at least one list is not empty. Within this loop we must supply a zero corresponding to a non-existent digit position in the shorter of the two numbers.

The carry digit starts at zero and after that is one or zero depending on whether or not the sum of two digits is greater than nine. The logic must account for the fact that because of carries, the sum list can be longer than either of the lists for the numbers being added.

The addition procedure is shown in Figure 6.1.

```
procedure AddInfinite (A, B: List; var C: List);
var
    ADigit, BDigit, CDigit, Carry: integer;
begin
    CreateList (C);
    Carry := 0;

    while (not ListIsEmpty (A)) or (not ListIsEmpty (B))
    begin
        if ListIsEmpty (A) then
            ADigit := 0
        else
        begin
            ADigit := Item (A);
            Advance (A)
        end;

        if ListIsEmpty (B) then
            BDigit := 0
        else
        begin
            BDigit := Item (B);
            Advance (B)
        end;

        CDigit := ADigit + BDigit + Carry;
        if CDigit > 9 then
        begin
            InsertAtEnd (C, CDigit - 10);
            Carry := 1
        end
        else
        begin
            InsertAtEnd (C, CDigit);
            Carry := 0
        end

    end;   { while not both empty }

    if Carry = 1 then
        InsertAtEnd (C, 1);

end;   { procedure AddInfinite }
```

FIGURE 6.1.
A procedure to do infinite precision decimal arithmetic, using lists.

Printing one of our numbers can be done most simply with a recursive approach.

```
procedure WriteInfinite (L: List);
var
   Ch: integer;
begin
   if ListIsEmpty (L) then    { nothing to do }

   else
   begin
      Ch := Item (L);
      Advance (L);
      WriteInfinite (L);
      Write (Ch)
   end
end;
```

A complete program using these routines requires the usual declarations that we have already seen, with an `ItemType` of `integer`, plus the list package and a simple main program. Here is some output when such a program was run with some sample data.

```
123
98765
98888

12345
65
12410

999999999999999999999
1
1000000000000000000000

18321760437682173787832614003
17345495060983200
18321760437699519282893597203

00000103
1
00000104
```

The last example suggests an improvement that makes for a simple exercise: delete leading zeros as numbers are read.

For serious work, we would probably want to make more efficient use of storage than to put a single-decimal digit in a space that could hold a large integer. One way to approach the change would be to view each digit as being in base 10,000, or something of the sort, with appropriate changes in the routines for reading and printing.

6.6 A POINTER VARIABLE
IMPLEMENTATION OF LINKED LISTS

The first thing we need to do to implement a linked list with pointer variables is to provide the declarations that define the nodes, as follows:

```
type
   ItemType = char;    { or whatever }

   NodePtr = ^Node;
   Node = record
             Item: ItemType;
             Next: NodePtr
          end;

   List = NodePtr;
```

We maintain our flexibility, just as we did with stacks and queues, as to the type of information in the `Item` portion of a node. In principle, this could be any simple or structured type, although we shall see that the implementation of some operations would not permit structured types to be used.

`NodePtr` (node pointer) is declared to a pointer as a `Node`, which is defined immediately. This is a forward reference, and is explicitly permitted in the language definition. It is necessary because the definition of the record `Node` contains a reference to `NodePtr.` A forward reference would be required one way or the other. A `Node` record consists of two fields: `Item`, which contains the information stored in the node and `Next`, a pointer to the next node in the list.

We see that the name of a linked list is just a pointer to the first node. This is the simplest way to do it but other approaches will be sketched in Section 6.10.

With this approach, all `CreateList` needs to do is give the value `Nil` to the pointer variable sent to it as follows:

```
procedure CreateList (var L: List);
begin
   L := Nil
end;
```

Basically, a pointer variable holds an address in computer memory. Assigning the value `Nil` to a pointer variable gives it a special value that says it points to nothing at all. This operation allows us to test the value of the pointer variable to see if it is, in fact, pointing at data.

We shall now show the operations of the linked list ADT in a sequence that emphasizes the more primitive nature of some of them. That is, we really must have `CreateList, Item,` and several of the others, to do much of anything with a linked list as an ADT. Here are some that will be used heavily in implementing the others.

`ListIsEmpty` requires only a test of whether the value of the pointer variable is `Nil`, as it will be if the linked list has just been created and is empty, or if all list nodes have been deleted.

```
function ListIsEmpty (L: List): boolean;
begin
    ListIsEmpty := L = Nil
end;
```

This does require some discipline of the user, however. If L has not been initialized (with CreateList) to Nil, the operation will be unreliable, at least. Some implementations will give a run-time error indication if an attempt is made to use an uninitialized pointer variable. Others will operate in totally unpredictable ways, ranging from merely wrong to disastrous. There is no mechanism, using only standard Pascal features, to enforce discipline in the use of pointer variables. Unfortunately, programming errors based on such problems are all too common, and sometimes very difficult to track down. Great care in initializing pointer variables is required.

The function Item returns as its value the Item portion of the node pointed to by its parameter. This is another place where the rules of Pascal would restrict this implementation to item fields consisting of simple types, i.e., no records or arrays.

```
function Item (L: List): ItemType;
begin
    Item := L^.Item
end;
```

The procedure Advance changes its linked list parameter so that it points to the next node in the linked list. Used in conjunction with Item, it permits us to retrieve the information in a linked list.

```
procedure Advance (var L: List);
begin
    L := L^.Next
end;
```

ADDNODE (L^.NEXT, 'R')

The various insertion operations draw on a procedure called AddNode, which makes it possible to insert a new node at the beginning or the end of a list, or between two nodes. This procedure does much of the pointer variable manipulation for our implementation. It creates a node *before* the one pointed to by its first (List) argument, makes that argument point to the new node, gives the Item portion of the new node the value specified by the second (ItemType) argument, and makes the Next portion of the new node point to what the argument originally pointed to. Here is the procedure:

```
procedure AddNode (var L: List;
                   NewItem: ItemType);
var
    Save: NodePtr;
begin
    Save := L;
    New (L);
    L^.Item := NewItem;
    L^.Next := Save
end;
```

ADDS TO LIST JUST BEFORE where you tell it to

For a good understanding of linked lists and their pointer variable implementation, it will be useful to follow through the construction of a small list, using `AddNode`.

Suppose we create a linked list named `LL` with `CreateList,` which gives the value `Nil` to the pointer variable `LL`. Now let us execute the statement:

```
AddNode (LL, 'I');
```

The result should be to create a new node containing the letter `I` in its `Info` field and a `Nil` value in its `Next` field, with the pointer variable `LL` pointing to it.

In terms of a diagram, we start with `LL` having the value `Nil,` which we may show this way:

LL⟶ Nil

The first action of `AddNode` is to carry out an assignment of the pointer variable LL to the pointer variable `Save`. So, the value of `Save` is now `Nil`. We have this picture:

Save⟶
LL⟶ Nil

The next action is to execute the Pascal procedure `New` with LL as argument. This allocates storage for a record of the type `List,` and the compiler determines how much storage is required from the declarations. It also makes the pointer variable LL point to this newly allocated storage, instead of to `Nil` as it did to start. We show this as a new box for a node, with LL pointing to it and with the old arrow to `Nil` crossed out.

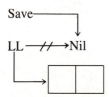

Nothing has been shown in either the `Item` or `Next` fields, because nothing has been assigned to them yet.

The next statement in `AddNode` gives the value of `NewItem, I` to the `Item` field.

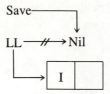

The final action is to assign the value held by `Save,` (which is `Nil`) to the `Next` field of the new node.

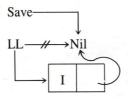

We can now show all the work of `AddNode` in a single diagram, with circled numbers to show the sequence of actions.

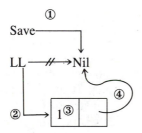

The result is displayed in box-and-arrow notation.

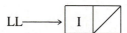

The slash, we recall, is the graphical indication of the value `Nil,` which marks the end of the linked list. Nothing is now shown for `Save,` because once the procedure is exited, that local variable ceases to exist.

Now suppose we add a node after this one. This is equivalent to placing a new node at the end of an existing list.

```
AddNode (LL^.Next, 'T');
```

Here is the graphical representation of what happens.

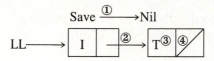

Next consider this statement, which amounts to inserting a new node at a place that is neither the beginning nor the end of the list.

```
AddNode (LL^.Next, 'S');
```

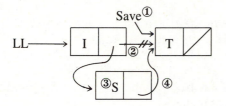

Finally, let us insert a new node at the head of the list.

```
AddNode (LL, 'L');
```

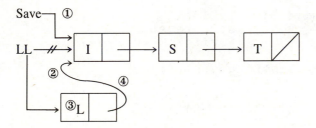

It is important to realize that once allocated, the nodes of a linked list do not move in storage. When we say we "insert" a new node in a list, what actually happens is that storage is allocated wherever the system chooses (which we can't even determine), *and then pointers are adjusted*. This is one of the major incentives for using linked lists: insertions and deletions do not require, as they do with arrays, that existing data be moved.

With `AddNode` as a tool procedure, the insertion operations are readily implemented. Here is `InsertAtFront`.

```
procedure InsertAtFront (var L: List;
                             NewItem: ItemType);
begin
   AddNode (L, NewItem)
end;
```

`InsertAtEnd` is readily implemented with `AddNode`, using a recursive approach that proceeds through the list until finding a `Nil` value.

```
procedure InsertAtEnd (var L: List;
                           NewItem: ItemType);
begin
   if ListIsEmpty (L) then
      AddNode (L, NewItem)

   else
      InsertAtEnd (L^.Next, NewItem)
end;
```

If, in fact, there is at least one node in the list, a `Nil` pointer variable value will occur when the end of the list has been reached. Additionally, the `Next` field of the last node is modified to reflect the addition of a new node. But the operation generalizes to the case of an empty list, where the "end" is also the beginning. In this case, the pointer to the head of the list has to be modified, which is why the list name is a `var` parameter.

The variation called `InsertAfterKth` approaches the linked list in terms of the fact that the nodes are *sequenced,* i.e., there is a first node, from which we can proceed to the second node, and so forth. The design decision is that we shall report an error if the list does not have a *Kth* node, that is, if the value supplied for K is less than 1 or greater than the length of the list.

```
procedure InsertAfterKth (L: List;
                              K: integer;
                              NewItem: ItemType);

{ Assert: 0 < K <= ListLength(L). }

begin
   if (K < 1) or ListIsEmpty (L) then
      ListError (L)

   else if K = 1 then
      AddNode (L^.Next, NewItem)

   else
      InsertAfterKth (L^.Next, K - 1, NewItem)
end;
```

We see that computing the length of the list to determine whether K is too large is not necessary. Although it could be done, it would be wasteful. Instead, we have the procedure call itself recursively, reducing the value of K each time until it reaches 1. If this can be done, the list indeed has at least K nodes. (We shall not show the `ListError` procedure, which merely prints an error message.)

Why is the name of the linked list in `InsertAfterKth` not a `var` parameter? The answer is that the argument supplied for that parameter is never changed by the procedure. The only thing that ever changes in the existing list is the `Next` portion of some node. And, changing the value of a field in a record pointed to by a pointer variable does not change the value of the pointer variable itself.

Another way to approach a linked list is through the contents of the nodes. `InsertAfterContent` seeks a node containing the value sent as its second parameter and, if it finds such a node, inserts a new one immediately after it. Failure to find such a node is reported as an error.

```
procedure InsertAfterContent (L: List;
                              Content: ItemType;
                              NewItem: ItemType);

{ Assert: Content is in List. }

begin
   if ListIsEmpty (L) then
      ListError (2)

   else if Item (L) = Content then
      AddNode (L^.Next, NewItem)

   else
      InsertAfterContent (L^.Next, Content, NewItem)
end;
```

The assertion here is essentially a promise to check that the statement is true and to report an error if it is not.

This is one case where the ''or whatever'' in the definition of `ItemType` is not really correct. Pascal does not permit the comparison of structured variables. This implementation works with any simple `ItemType`; for structured types it must be regarded as pseudocode, describing actions that would take some doing to be programmed in Pascal.

A user of this approach would presumably want to be able to test whether a node containing a given item is already in the list, which is what `InList` does.

```
function InList (L: List;
                 SearchItem: ItemType): boolean;
begin
   if ListIsEmpty (L) then
      InList := false

   else if Item (L) = SearchItem then
      InList := true

   else
      InList := InList (L^.Next, SearchItem)
end;
```

This procedure works as intended, but its use of recursion carries an avoidable penalty. Every time a recursive procedure is invoked, the activation frame contains another copy of all the parameters—including, in this case, the parameter `SearchItem,` which never changes. A simple solution is to make a two-level procedure. The user's procedure invokes a contained procedure (invisible to the user), that has only the linked list as a parameter.

```
function InListImproved (L: List;
                             SearchItem: ItemType): boolean;

   function IL (L: List): boolean;
   begin
      if ListIsEmpty (L) then
         IL := false

      else if Item (L) = SearchItem then
         IL := true

      else
         IL := IL(L^.Next)
   end;   { of function IL }

begin
   InListImproved := IL(L)
end;   { of function InListImproved }
```

In any serious use of this kind of implementation, where the performance penalty of the extra variable in the activation frame (and the time needed to load it) would be a consideration, we would apply this technique wherever it would help. This would assist in about half our procedures. On the other hand, if this penalty is a problem, we most likely have an even bigger problem with the linear-time performance of any linked list approach. We leave further consideration of this issue to the chapter exercises, Chapter 9, and your further study.

Now we take up deletion of a node, and for this we have a tool procedure, `DeleteNode,` which is akin to `AddNode. DeleteNode` disposes of the node pointed to by its argument and then makes that argument point to whatever the `Next` field of the disposed node originally pointed to. (See the examples that follow.) The procedure follows.

```
procedure DeleteNode (var L: List);
var
   Save: NodePtr;
begin
   Save := L;
   L := L^.Next;
   Dispose (Save)
end;
```

Again, `DeleteNode` deletes the node to which its one argument points. That one node may be anywhere in a linked list; if the pointer to it is the link portion of a node, that link is adjusted so that it points to the node after the one that was just deleted.

Let us follow the operation of `DeleteNode` as the nodes are removed from the linked list that was created above with `AddNode`.

We may start by deleting the first node.

```
DeleteNode (LL);
```

In the condensed box-and-arrow depiction of the operation of this procedure, the symbolism for the third action suggests that the storage for the node is returned to availability for reallocation.

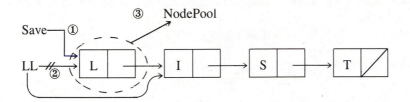

Now we would like to see how `DeleteNode` performs when asked to delete a node that is between two other nodes, so we execute:

```
DeleteNode (LL^.Next);
```

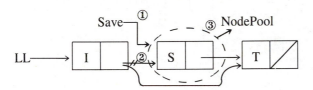

Now we watch the deletion of a node at the end of the list.

```
DeleteNode (LL^.Next):
```

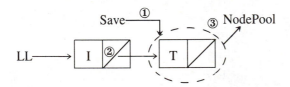

Finally, here are the actions to delete the only node in a list.

We want to emphasize that in designing and testing procedures to operate on linked lists we must consider all the various special cases. For `AddNode` the special cases were an initially empty list, addition of a node before the head of the list, addition of a node after the last node, and addition of a node at a position that is neither before the first node nor after the last node. For `DeleteNode` the situation is similar, except that instead of deleting a node from an empty list, which should not happen if the procedures that use these tools are correct, we have the case of deleting the only node in a list.

Whenever we can identify all the special cases and then satisfy ourselves that we have handled all of them correctly, we add considerable assurance that an implementation is correct. The real challenge, often, is to be sure we have enumerated all the cases.

Now we can implement our list deletion operations. Here is `DeleteKth`:

```
procedure DeleteKth (var L: List;
                         K: integer);

{ Assert: 0 < K <= ListLength(L). }

begin
   if ListIsEmpty (L) then
      ListError (3)

   else if K = 1 then
      DeleteNode (L)

   else
      DeleteKth (L^.Next, K - 1)
end;
```

We shall not show all the variations this time because they are readily written as exercises. Note that `DeleteFront` is an easy special case, with K = 1.

`ListLength` has a simple recursive implementation, as follows:

```
function ListLength (L: List): integer;
begin
   if ListIsEmpty (L) then
      ListLength := 0
   else
      ListLength := 1 + ListLength (L^.Next)
end;
```

An iterative method would work just as well in this case.

`MakeListEmpty` walks through a list, deleting nodes until it finds that it has reached the end of the list.

```
procedure MakeListEmpty (var L: List);
{ NOTE: probable infinite loop if L not already created. }
begin
   while L <> Nil do
      DeleteNode (L)
end;
```

Our warning here again relates to the fact that an uninitialized pointer variable can lead to big trouble. In this case, the procedure would go into an infinite loop unless it just happened to come across a place in memory holding whatever special contents the Pascal implementer uses to indicate a `Nil` value. While looking for this unlikely possibility, the procedure would create havoc with the storage management system. Whatever else happened, further execution of the offending program would be impossible and, in an extreme case, it might have mangled the storage management system so badly that the whole operating system would have to be re-initialized to run any other program. Pointer variables do have hazards, and require intelligent and cautious use.

`CopyList` is interesting in that the operation is quite simple to implement with recursion and considerably more difficult without it.

```
procedure CopyList (OldList: List;
                    var NewList: List);
begin
   if ListIsEmpty (OldList) then
      NewList := Nil
   else
   begin
      AddNode (NewList, OldList^.Item);
      CopyList (OldList^.Next, NewList^.Next)
   end
end;
```

Here is a non-recursive version.

```
procedure NonRecursiveCopyList (OldList: List;
                                var NewList: List);
var
   P: NodePtr;
begin
   if ListIsEmpty (OldList) then
      NewList := Nil
   else
   begin
      New (NewList);
      NewList^.Item := OldList^.Item;
      P := NewList;
      OldList := OldList^.Next;
      while not ListIsEmpty (OldList) do
      begin
         New (P^.Next);
         P^.Next^.Item := OldList^.Item;
         P := P^.Next;
         OldList := OldList^.Next
      end;
      P^.Next := Nil
   end
end;
```

The reason this non-recursive version is so much more complex is that we have to maintain a pointer (the P) to the node *before* the one we are creating. The link portion of this previous node cannot be established until after the new node has been created. This "trailer node" is routinely required in non-recursive list processing.

ConcatList takes two linked lists as arguments, and concatenates the second one to the end of the first. We call the parameters Left and Right because of the positions they have in the result.

```
procedure ConcatList (var Left: List;
                          Right: List);
var
   P: NodePtr;
begin
   if ListIsEmpty (Right) then    { nothing to do }

      else if ListIsEmpty (Left) then
         Left := Right

      else
      begin
         P := Left;
         while P^.Next <> Nil do   { find tail of Left }
            Advance (P);
         P^.Next := Right
      end
end;
```

WriteList is a tool procedure used to study list operations and work with examples. An iterative approach is natural.

```
procedure WriteList (L: List);
begin
   while not ListIsEmpty (L) do
   begin
      Write (Item (L));
      Advance (L)
   end
end;
```

6.7 ANALYSIS OF LINKED LIST OPERATIONS

The linked list operations are relatively easy to analyze, although if we need to be as precise as possible it is necessary to know something about the probabilities in the application.

Most of the "really" primitive operations in our selection execute in constant time: CreateList, ListIsEmpty, Item, and Advance. The InsertAtFront is also a constant-time operation as implemented here.

Most of the the other operations execute in time that is proportional to the length of the list, since some action has to be done for every node in the linked list. In this category are InsertAtEnd, ListLength, MakeListEmpty, CopyList, and WriteList. (Some of these can be reduced to constant-time operations by using some form of a header node, as sketched in Section 6.11.) ConcatList runs in time proportional to the length of the Left list. The running time of InsertAfterKth is clearly proportional to K.

The two operations remaining from those enumerated in Section 6.2 are a little more interesting. `InsertAfterContent` has to go half-way through the list, on the average, if all node contents are equally likely and if the `Content` is present. To determine that the `Content` is *not* present, it must traverse the entire list. Both operations are *O(ListLength)*, in other words, but if we wish a more precise estimate we can make it—assuming we know something about the probability of finding the Content. Similar comments apply to `InList`.

6.8 AN ARRAY IMPLEMENTATION OF LINKED LISTS

Not all languages provide pointer variables and dynamic storage allocation. Does this mean that in such languages linked lists are unavailable? Hardly. It does reduce flexibility in one regard, but the ADT can still be used.

The approach is to set up an array of records, each record holding one node. The link portions of these nodes are now array indices rather than pointer variables. With this one change, together with a few syntactic differences in the way fields are designated, we have a linked list implementation that is almost equivalent—at the ADT level—to the pointer variable implementation with dynamic storage allocation.

There is one exception. In Pascal we must decide the size of an array at the time we write the program, so we must decide in advance how many nodes there can be in all lists in a program. With pointer variables, we have considerably more flexibility because the system will keep giving us dynamically-allocated storage so long as there is storage to allocate. This is less of a difference than might first appear, though, because memory is not infinite.

Usually, pointer variables and dynamic storage allocation are preferred, when available. However, the array implementation is not difficult, as we now see.

Here are the declarations we shall use:

```
const
   NumberOfNodes = 1000;   { or whatever }
   Zilch = 0;

type
   ItemType = char;   { or whatever }

   NodeIndex = 0..NumberOfNodes;
   Node = record
             Item: ItemType;
             Next: NodeIndex
          end;

   AvailableStorage = array [1..NumberOfNodes] of Node;

   List = NodeIndex;

var
   AS: AvailableStorage;
   Avail: List;
```

The parallels with the pointer variable implementation are close enough that we choose to emphasize them. The signal for the end of a list will be called `Zilch`, American slang for zero; we cannot redefine the reserved word `Nil`. `NumberOfNodes` sets the limit on the total number of nodes in all lists. `ItemType` is as usual. However, instead of `NodePtr` we have `NodeIndex`, which runs from zero to the number of nodes. The array that holds the nodes will be indexed from one, but we need the index value zero to stand for the end of a list; this is the `Zilch`. Furthermore, `AvailableStorage` is a type declaration for the storage our procedures will allocate when lists are created. Finally, a `List`, which before was a `NodePtr`, is now a `NodeIndex`.

As a global variable at the main program level, we establish `AS` to be the array that holds all the nodes. `Avail` is the index of this array.

A key feature of this implementation is that the available storage will itself be a linked list, so that nodes may be obtained from it and returned to it. To establish this condition with our array, we need to establish the links. `InitializeAvail`, which deals with the global variables `AS` and `Avail` and has no parameters, does the job. The simplest way to set up the links is for the link of each node record in the array to point to the next record, except the link of the last, which is set to `Zilch`. Then, `Avail` is initialized to one, the index of the first node. This procedure must be executed before any linked list operations are carried out.

```
procedure InitializeAvail;
var
   I: NodeIndex;
begin
   for I := 1 to NumberOfNodes - 1 do
      AS[I].Next := I + 1;
   AS[NumberOfNodes].Next := Zilch;
   Avail := 1
end;
```

Now we need an equivalent of `New`, which we shall call `NewNode`. Like `New`, it is a procedure, which makes its `var` argument point to the storage for a new node. After checking that storage is still available, the argument is set equal to `Avail`, and `Avail` is advanced to the index of the next record in the list. The first time `NewNode` is invoked, it gives its argument the index value 1 and `Avail` is set to 2.

```
procedure NewNode (var Node: NodeIndex);
begin
   if ListIsEmpty (Avail) then
      ListError (0)
   else
   begin
      Node := Avail;
      Avail := AS[Avail].Next
   end
end;
```

`DisposeNode` is analogous to `Dispose`. The link field of the node being returned is made equal to the current value of `Avail`. Then, `Avail` is points to the disposed node.

```
procedure DisposeNode (P: NodeIndex);
begin
   AS[P].Next := Avail;
   Avail := P
end;
```

The nodes do not move as these operations take place; only the links change. The actual storage for all nodes in all linked lists is always just the array `AS`. The manipulation of the `Next` fields of these records does the work.

`CreateList` gives the value `Zilch` (zero) to the list variable sent to it.

```
procedure CreateList (var L: List);
begin
   L := Zilch
end;
```

Given these implementation preliminaries, the procedures that do most of the work are now simple translations of their pointer variable equivalents. Here is `AddNode`:

```
procedure AddNode (var L: List;
                   NewItem: ItemType);
var
   Save: NodeIndex;
begin
   Save := L;
   NewNode (L);
   AS[L].Item := NewItem;
   AS[L].Next := Save
end;
```

To the user of a package based on the array implementation, nothing appears to have changed. The procedure name is the same, it has the same parameter list, and the types of those parameters appear to be the same. We say "appears," because we know that back in the declarations things are different and, of course, in Pascal we cannot completely hide that kind of detail from the user.

`DeleteNode` is a similar story.

```
procedure DeleteNode (var L: List);
var
   Save: NodeIndex;
begin
   Save := L;
   L := AS[L].Next;
   DisposeNode (Save)
end;
```

We may pause, now that we have the facilities to follow an example, to see the array implementation in operation. Let us follow the same operations we used to illustrate the pointer variable implementation.

After the `InitializeAvail` has been executed, we have this picture of the array `AS` assuming, for simplicity of illustrative purposes, that `Number-OfNodes = 6`.

Element number	Item	Next
Avail → 1	—	2
2	—	3
3	—	4
4	—	5
5	—	6
6	—	0

The hyphens for the `Info` fields are intended to indicate that they are empty.

After `AddNode (LL, 'I')`, which adds a node to an empty list, the picture looks like this:

Element number	Item	Next
LL → 1	I	0
Avail → 2	—	3
3	—	4
4	—	5
5	—	6
6	—	0

After `AddNode (AS[LL].Next, 'T')`, which adds a node at the end of a non-empty list, we have the following picture:

Element number	Item	Next
LL → 1	I	2
2	T	0
Avail → 3	—	4
4	—	5
5	—	6
6	—	0

After `AddNode (AS[LL].Next, 'S')`, which adds a node between two nodes, the array looks like this:

	Element number	Item	Next
LL →	1	I	3
	2	T	0
	3	S	2
Avail →	4	—	5
	5	—	6
	6	—	0

After `AddNode (LL, 'L')`, which adds a node at the front of a non-empty list, the array is in the following form:

	Element number	Item	Next
	1	I	3
	2	T	0
	3	S	2
LL →	4	L	1
Avail →	5	—	6
	6	—	0

Now we can watch nodes being deleted for each of the four cases, which we shall do in a different sequence than with the pointer variable implementation. After `DeleteNode (AS[LL].Next)`, which deletes a node between two other nodes, we have the following structure:

	Element number	Item	Next
Avail →	1	I	5
	2	T	0
	3	S	2
LL →	4	L	3
	5	—	6
	6	—	0

After `DeleteNode (LL)`, which deletes the front node of a list having more than one node, the array looks like this:

Element number	Item	Next
1	I	5
2	T	0
3	S	2
4	L	1
5	—	6
6	—	0

LL → 3
Avail → 4

After `DeleteNode (AS[LL].Next)`, which deletes the last node of a list, the picture is as follows:

Element number	Item	Next
1	I	5
2	T	4
3	S	0
4	L	1
5	—	6
6	—	0

Avail → 2
LL → 3

After `DeleteNode (LL)`, which deletes the only node in a list, we have an array in the following format:

Element number	Item	Next
1	I	5
2	T	4
3	S	2
4	L	1
5	—	6
6	—	0

Avail → 3

We can plainly see that only the links change. `Avail` has indexed various nodes during the execution of the program, but the available storage is always a linked list. After the program has returned nodes to the available space list, the `Item` fields contain information. However, under the ADT discipline there is no possible way we could access them, any more than we can get at the storage for items after they had been popped off a stack.

Note that after adding nodes and then deleting them in a different order, the links in the `Avail` list are quite different from their starting values. Note, too, that while LL had any nodes, the underlying array held two lists: LL and `Avail`. Each was marked by a zero value in its last node.

The various other list procedures are direct translations of what we saw before. Here are six of them.

```
procedure Advance (var L: List);
begin
   L := AS[L].Next
end;


function ListLength (L: List): integer;
begin
   if ListIsEmpty (L) then
      ListLength := 0
   else
      ListLength := 1 + ListLength (AS[L].Next)
end;


procedure InsertAtEnd (var L: List;
                       NewItem: ItemType);
begin
   if ListIsEmpty (L) then
      AddNode (L, NewItem)
   else
      InsertAtEnd (AS[L].Next, NewItem)
end;


procedure DeleteKth (var L: List;
                     K: integer);

{ Assert: 0 < K <= ListLength (L). }

begin
   if ListIsEmpty (L) then
      ListError (3)
   else if K = 1 then
      DeleteNode (L)
   else
      DeleteKth (AS[L].Next, K - 1)
end;
```

(Continued)

(Continued)

```
procedure CopyList (OldList: List;
                      var NewList: List);
begin
   if ListIsEmpty (OldList) then
      NewList := Zilch
   else
   begin
      AddNode (NewList, AS[OldList].Item);
      CopyList (AS[OldList].Next, AS[NewList].Next)
   end
end;


procedure WriteList (L: List);
begin
   while not ListIsEmpty (L) do
   begin
      Write (Item (L));
      Advance (L)
   end;
   WriteLn
end;
```

Some older languages, such as Fortran, do not have pointer variables or records. A linked list facility can still be implemented with them although any resulting program would be a little hard to read. To do so, we simply set up as many arrays, of size `NumberOfNodes`, as there are fields. Each array would be of an appropriate type (real, integer, character, and so forth); all of the these arrays could be indexed by variables of type `NodeIndex`, including `Avail`. These *parallel arrays,* as they are sometimes called, could then be accessed as though they were the fields of a record, albeit with different syntax.

As a final note on this alternative implementation of linked lists, note that with suitable modifications (to take account of many hardware-dependent factors), we have a technique here that applies to storage on magnetic disk. The full story belongs in another course, but if you wish to experiment with linked records on disk in Pascal, the closer parallel is with the array implementation.

6.9 STRINGS IMPLEMENTED AS LINKED LISTS

As we saw in Chapter 3, a string is most useful if it is of variable length. Such is not the case with Pascal strings. In Chapter 3 we also saw that implementing a variable-length string in a fixed-length array is a waste of storage.

The obvious solution is to use a linked list implemented with pointer variables. Only as much storage is allocated as is needed for the actual length of the string, and when a string is no longer needed the storage can be reclaimed. Most of the string operations are simpler to implement as well.

Offsetting these advantages is the space required for the links, which is not a trivial consideration. In one machine architecture that comes to mind (the IBM 370 family), a link would take four times as much storage as a character. In other machine architectures it could be more or less.

It would serve no useful purpose to present a complete set of procedures equivalent to those already developed in Chapter 3. We shall, instead, select a subset to implement, focusing on the usefulness of the ADT linked list and of recursion.

The global declarations are just those for linked lists, with an `ItemType` of `char`, plus a type declaration stating that a string is a list.

```
type
   ItemType = char;

   NodePtr = ^Node;
   Node = record
              Item: ItemType;
              Next: NodePtr
          end;

   List = NodePtr;

   StrType = List;
```

Many of the simpler string procedures can be implemented merely by invoking the corresponding linked list actions. Here, for example, is all that is required to implement `CreateString`, `MakeStrEmpty`, `StrLength`, `AppendChar` and `ConcatStr`:

```
procedure CreateString (var S: StrType);
begin
   CreateList (S)
end;


procedure MakeStrEmpty (var S: StrType);
begin
   MakeListEmpty (S)
end;


function StrLength (S: StrType): integer;
begin
   StrLength := ListLength (S)
end;


procedure AppendChar (var S: StrType;
                          Ch: char);
begin
   InsertAtEnd (S, Ch)
end;


procedure ConcatStr (var Left: StrType;
                         Right: StrType);
begin
   ConcatList (Left, Right)
end;
```

ReadLnStr operates slightly differently here than in the Chapter 3 version. There, working with an array implementation, we could read the characters into the array starting in position 1, thus destroying any previous contents. This gave the effect of an implicit MakeStrEmpty at the beginning of the procedure. Here, working with pointer variables, we might like to do something similar, but should we use CreateString or MakeStrEmpty? If we use CreateString on a string that already exists, we destroy accessibility to the storage for the nodes of the string. If we use MakeStrEmpty on a string that has not previously been created, we risk an infinite loop as the procedure looks for a Nil pointer. (These are the Scylla and Charybdis of working with pointer variables.) The upshot is that we must ask the user to deal with this problem. If we are in a mood to make a virtue of necessity, we can also point out that this permits the user to append input characters to an existing string!

```
procedure ReadLnStr (var S: StrType);

{ Read from position of file pointer to EOLN, then ReadLn.
  Characters are appended to S--this procedure cannot
  know whether to execute CreateString or MakeStrEmpty. }

var
    P: NodePtr;
    Ch: char;
begin
    while not EOLN do
    begin
        Read (Ch);
        InsertAtEnd (S, Ch)
    end;

    ReadLn
end;
```

Invoking InsertAtEnd for every character is not an efficient way to work. Every time it is executed it starts at the head of the list and searches to the end. In a string package intended for heavy use this method should be replaced by a simple loop to follow the list, to add nodes as characters are read, and finally to insert a Nil pointer in the Next field of the last node.

CompareStr shows lists and recursion to fine advantage. The implementation in Chapter 3 works, but it is hardly intuitive; in fact, it is a rather "dense" code. Now, with a clear definition of what we mean by string comparison, we can write simple, straightforward code.

Recall that the design decision was to return one of the characters =, <, or >, depending on whether the first string is equal to, less than, or greater than the second. Two strings are considered equal if, and only if, they match on a character-by-character basis and are of the same length. If two strings are identical up to the length of the shorter, the shorter is considered to be less than the longer. The only remaining possibility is that the strings are equal up to some character position in which they differ. In that case the one differing character determines the result. In shorthand form, let us look at a few examples: SMITH = SMITH, SMITH < SMITHSON, SMITH > JONES, GEWISSEN > GESELLSCHAFT. The function is shorter than the English description.

```
function CompareStr (S1, S2: StrType): char;
begin
   if ListIsEmpty (S1) and ListIsEmpty (S2)  then
      CompareStr := '='

   else if (Item (S1) < Item (S2)) or ListIsEmpty (S1) then
      CompareStr := '<'

   else if (Item (S1) > Item (S2)) or ListIsEmpty (S2) then
      CompareStr := '>'

   else
   begin
      Advance (S1);
      Advance (S2);
      CompareStr := CompareStr (S1, S2)
   end
end;
```

There is a subtle problem in this procedure. If the strings are of unequal length but match through all the characters of the shorter string, then when the `Item` function tries to get the next character of the shorter string it will be trying to dereference the `Nil` pointer. That is illegal. The good news is that some Pascal implementations flag the error; the bad news is that others will give no error indication, but produce monumentally meaningless—*at best*—results. A simple solution, for this case, is to note that the `or` test will stop the recursion upon detecting the `Nil` value. Consequently, we don't really care about the other part of the `or`. Therefore, we also don't care what value `Item` returns. The `Item` function can be modified to send back any character at all for a `Nil` argument.

So far we have been able to implement all the string operations without "breaking," or "going under" the ADT linked list. For the remaining operations from Chapter 3 (`InsertStr`, `DeleteStr`, `SearchStr`, and `CopyStr`), it becomes awkward and/or highly inefficient to stay entirely within the ADT list. Simpler and faster code results if we make direct use of pointer variable operations.

Our goal in this chapter is to explain the concept of the linked list and to show its usefulness, not to claim that it is wise design to stay at the ADT list level for *every* possible application. We therefore leave this topic, with the implementation of the other string operations left to you as an exercise.

6.10 SETS IMPLEMENTED AS ORDERED LINKED LISTS

A linked list provides another way to implement sets, besides the array and bit-vector methods that we have already seen.

The advantages of a linked list over the methods of Chapter 3 are that we don't have to decide in advance about the maximum cardinality of the set being represented, and that there is no space penalty if the set elements are widely separated in value. For example, the set {1, 10, 1000} can be held in three nodes, just as the set {1, 2, 3} can.

To achieve acceptable efficiency with a list implementation of sets we must establish an *ordered* list, meaning that the items stored in the nodes are in ascending sequence. This greatly facilitates the set union operation, for example, because we can proceed through each list in sequence, determining quickly whether a given element in one set is in the other. Set union can therefore be carried out in time that is linear in the sum of the lengths of the lists. For sets with a large range of values in their base types but with relatively few elements, like {1, 2, 1000}, this implementation is much faster than the array or bit-vector methods.

To work with this implementation, we need a way to build an ordered list. This is useful knowledge because other applications sometimes benefit from keeping lists of ordered values. Assume the usual declarations, as follows:

```
type
    ItemType = char;    { or whatever }

    NodePtr = ^Node;
    Node = record
                Item: ItemType;
                Next: NodePtr
           end;

    List = NodePtr;

    SetType = List;
```

Here is a procedure for inserting an item in an ordered list:

```
procedure InsertInOrderedList (var L: List;
                                NewItem: ItemType);
begin
   if ListIsEmpty (L) then
      AddNode (L, NewItem)

   else if NewItem = Item (L) then    { NewItem already in list }

   else if NewItem < Item (L) then
      AddNode (L, NewItem)

   else
      InsertInOrderedList (L^.Next, NewItem)
end;
```

Note that we have ''gone under'' the ADT level in using L^.Next to specify the next node for the recursive call. If we try to stay entirely at the level of the ADT linked list, our alternatives are somewhere between complicated and impossible, in part because of Pascal syntax restrictions. But, as noted in connection with strings, we do not deny our faith in the usefulness of the abstract data type concept by declining to do everything with the list primitives stated at the beginning of the chapter.

Here is a procedure for finding the union of two sets represented in this manner:

```
procedure Union (Set1, Set2: SetType;
                 var UnionSet: SetType);
begin
   if ListIsEmpty (Set1) then
      CopyList (Set2, UnionSet)

   else if ListIsEmpty (Set2) then
      CopyList (Set1, UnionSet)

   else if Item (Set1) < Item (Set2) then
   begin
      AddNode (UnionSet, Item (Set1));
      Union (Set1^.Next, Set2, UnionSet^.Next)
   end

   else if Item (Set1) = Item (Set2) then
   begin
      AddNode (UnionSet, Item (Set1));
      Union (Set1^.Next, Set2^.Next, UnionSet^.Next)
   end

   else   { Item (Set1) > Item (Set2) }
   begin
      AddNode (UnionSet, Item (Set2));
      Union (Set1, Set2^.Next, UnionSet^.Next)
   end
end;
```

If either set is empty, then the union of the two sets is just the other set. Next, if the current item from Set1 is less than the current item from Set2, then we want to insert the item from Set1 into the union set. Then we want to move on to the next node in Set1 but stay with the current node in Set2. If the items are equal, we insert that item in the union set and move on to the next nodes in both Set1 and Set2. The only case left is that the item from Set1 is greater than the item from Set2, in which case we insert the item from Set2 into the union set and move on to the next node in Set2, staying all the while with the current node in Set1. This is actually what the code says, except in fewer symbols! Perhaps by now you are beginning to be comfortable enough with reading code that this kind of English translation is becoming less necessary.

In that spirit, here is a procedure to determine whether one set is a subset of another, without the simultaneous translation. (This should work both ways: if you have managed to forget what ''subset'' means, you ought to be able to deduce the definition from the code.)

```
function SubSet (Set1, Set2: SetType): boolean;

{ Returns true if Set1 is a subset of Set2 }

begin
   if ListIsEmpty (Set1) then
      SubSet := true

   else if ListIsEmpty (Set2) then
      SubSet := false

   else if Item (Set1) < Item (Set2) then
      SubSet := false

   else if Item (Set1) = Item (Set2) then
      SubSet := SubSet (Set1^.Next, Set2^.Next)

   else   { Item (Set1) > Item (Set2) }
      SubSet := SubSet (Set1, Set2^.Next)
end;
```

We will leave writing a procedure for set intersection for you as an exercise. You may also wish to write procedures to implement set operations using unordered lists. Even if you do not write these, you should think about how they would work, and compare the running time—as a function of set size—with the procedures we have discussed based on ordered lists.

6.11 OTHER FORMS OF LINKED LISTS

We have based our presentation in this chapter on the simplest form of the implementation of a list so as to focus on fundamental issues. Before leaving the subject we should point out that there are a number of other approaches that have advantages in certain circumstances.

In the body of this chapter, we have presented what is called a *singly-linked list without a header node*. That is, each node contains one link (to its successor in the list) and there is no special node at the beginning of the list. An empty list is represented by a Nil pointer value or the equivalent in an array implementation.

To illustrate the possible variations we shall use a list of records about students in a seminar. Only the student names will be shown. Here, in box-and-arrow form, is the list as implemented earlier:

One common variation is a *singly-linked list with a header node*. A special node is established that does not contain any data. Rather, it contains information about the list. In its simplest form the node might contain only a pointer to the first node in the list, but it could also contain a pointer to the last node in the list, or a field giving the length of the list. These features would provide greater speed in certain operations. A pointer to the last node as well as the first would speed queue operations, and any application that frequently needs the length of the list would be well served by not having to traverse the entire list to get this easily maintained piece of information.

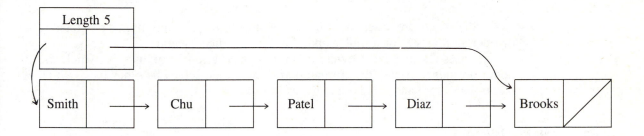

In the infinite-precision arithmetic example we had a case in which a *doubly-linked list* would have been useful. Because of the way carries propagate, it was preferable to arrange the list with the least significant digit in the first node. Yet, for printing we wanted the most significant digit first. Many other applications arise in which it is convenient to be able to move through a list in either direction. The answer is to put two link fields in each node, one pointing to the successor and one to the predecessor of the node.

This convenience is not free. Beside the space for the extra links, we have the added complexity of the `Insert` and `Delete` operations, which now have more links to manipulate. For some applications the benefits clearly outweigh the extra space and effort, and doubly-linked lists are definitely indicated.

Doubly-linked lists can be set up with or without a header node. We diagram a version with a header node.

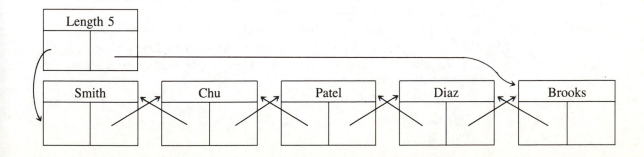

Another variation is that the link in the last node, instead of containing an indication that it is the last node, can point back to the head of the list. This is called a *circularly-linked list*. The diagram shows a header node version.

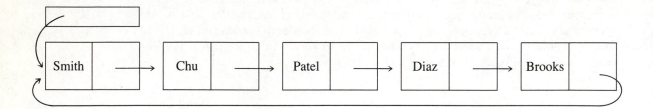

Finally, there are cases in which convenience, or programming, or efficiency of operation argue for a trailer node instead of a header node.

Exercises 21 and 22 provide an introductory glimpse of lists in which the nodes are not restricted to information but may themselves be other lists, which is the way LISP and related languages work.

6.12 CONCLUSION

The linked list is one of the most general and widely used ADTs. Its importance has been recognized since the earliest days of computer science. It has been intensively studied, and great effort has gone into developing implementations to provide various compromises among the conflicting goals of speed, storage efficiency, programming simplicity, and application flexibility.

In our introduction to this subject, we have concentrated on the basics in an attempt to give you a solid grounding in the concept. In your continued study and work you will repeatedly encounter the ADT list and its variations and applications. The exercises at the end of this chapter explore a few of the many issues that we have not covered here.

EXERCISES _____

1. Modify the procedures in the infinite-precision arithmetic package to:
    (a) Delete leading zeros as numbers are read;
    (b) Allow for numbers with decimal points, such as `1234.5` or `12.345`.
2. Write a procedure `WriteInfinite(Addend1, Addend2, Sum)` that aligns all three numbers on the sum, i.e., the first example from the chapter will be printed as

      123

    98765

    98888

3. Write a recursive procedure `AddInfiniteRec` (`N`, `Sum`) that reads `N` infinite-precision numbers and places their sum in `Sum`.

4. To make more efficient use of storage in the infinite-precision arithmetic package, we might store an integer between zero and 9999 in each `Item` field, which gives the effect of base 10,000 numbers. In this implementation the list (5, 6, 7, 8, 9) would represent $9 \times 10^0 + 8 \times 10^4 + 7 \times 10^8 + 6 \times 10^{12} + 5 \times 10^{16} = 5\ 0006\ 0007\ 0008\ 0009 = 50$ trillion, 6 billion, 700 million, 80 thousand and 9.

   (a) Rewrite the procedures `ReadNumberAndMakeList`, `AddInfinite`, and `WriteInfinite` to store base 10,000 numbers.

   (b) Another implementation, along the same lines, would be to store numbers in base `MaxInt` + 1. (In many Pascals, `MaxInt` = 32,767.) Rewrite the procedures of (a) to accommodate this design.

   (c) Include the facility to handle numbers with decimal points in your package.

5. Modify the `Sort` procedure of `LetterPairs3` (Section 2.15) to sort a linked list. You will need a `Swap` procedure to swap two nodes. (A sequence of box-and-arrow drawings will help.)

6. Write and test two Pascal procedures to reverse a list.

   (a) The first procedure should leave the original list unchanged and construct a new reversed list.

   (b) The second procedure should reverse the original list by reversing only the pointers.

7. The performance of `AddInfinite` (Section 6.5, based on the implementation in Section 6.6) is very poor for long numbers. Identify the one statement that totally dominates the running time of this procedure, and analyze the performance of `AddInfinite` as a function of the number of digits in the sum. Suggest (and program if you wish) a solution in terms of either a stack or a linked list approach in which a header node (Section 6.11) contains pointers to both the first and the last nodes of a list.

8. Implement the operations `Item`, `InsertAfterKth`, `InsertAfterContent`, `InList`, and `ConcatList` using the array implementation in Section 6.8.

9. Implement the operation `MakeListEmpty` using the array implementation of Section 6.8. (Do you have to worry about losing addressability of nodes? The array `AS` is never deallocated during program execution, after all, because it is declared at the main program level and allocated on the stack.)

10. Write procedures for the string operations not included in Section 6.9. The most obvious way is to give up on a strict adherence to the ADT approach, using references to the `Item` and `Next` portions of a node. If you want a project instead of an exercise, try to modify the definitions and/or implementations of the linked list operations so that you can implement these string operations without ''going under'' the linked list ADT.

11. Write a Pascal boolean function `IsSublist (List1, List2)` that returns `true` if `L1` is a sublist of `L2`. Note that a sublist and a subset are different. (e, f, g) is a sublist of (a, b, c, d, e, f, g, h), but not of (a, e, c, f, g).

12. Write Pascal procedures, following the style of `Union` and `Subset` in Section 6.10, for `Intersection` and `Difference`.
    (a) Include the declarations and procedures given in the chapter and test your package on `Primary = {red, white, blue, yellow}`, `Orange = {red, yellow}`, `Green = {blue, yellow}`, and `Lavender = {red, blue}`.
    (b) How could you construct the set `Black`, with black being defined as the absence of all color?
    (c) Sets won't work to arrive at a full palette of colors produced by mixing unequal amounts of the primary colors, such as `RedOrange = {red, red, yellow}`. To allow for this, we need an ADT called a *bag* or *multiset*. A bag is just like a set, except that duplicates are allowed. Modify your linked list set package to make a Bag package.

13. Consider an ordered list, as in Section 6.10. As we move through the list, the `Item` values appear in ascending sequence.
    (a) Write a Pascal procedure to remove duplicates from such a list. Consider two list nodes as duplicates if their `Item` fields, not just the keys, are the same. You might want to consider a subprocedure `NodesAreEqual` to test for equality of nodes and make your procedure more general.
    (b) Analyze the run time for your procedure in terms of the length of the list.
    (c) Write a Pascal procedure to insert an item into an ordered list only if its `Item` field is not already present.
    (d) What is the run time for your procedure in (c)?

14. Redo Exercise 13 for an unordered list.

15. Several methods of sorting depend on the ability to merge two shorter ordered lists, such that the merged list is ordered. For example, the two lists (1, 3, 5, 7) and (2, 3, 6) would merge to the list (1, 2, 3, 3, 5, 6, 7).
    (a) Write a procedure, `Merge (L1, L2: List)`, that modifies `L1` to be the merge of `L1` and `L2`.
    (b) Rewrite (a) so that `L1` and `L2` are not modified, and the merged list is returned as the new list `L3`.
    (c) Modify your procedures in (a) and (b) to eliminate duplicates.

16. Several of the string procedures or functions can be implemented more efficiently if a header node is kept for each string, containing the string's length. (A header is sometimes called a *dummy node* because it contains no `Item` information.)
    (a) How could you include this header, using the same `Node` declaration as used for list nodes?
    (b) Rewrite the list procedures to accommodate lists with headers. Be sure to increment the list length when a node is added.

(c) Discuss the advantages and disadvantages of implementing variable length strings as arrays or as linked lists. Consider both storage requirements and running time.

17. Rewrite the list operations of this chapter to handle doubly-linked lists that are with or without headers.

18. In Exercise 20 of Chapter 4, a *deque* was defined to allow insertions and deletions at either end. Implement the ADT deque as a doubly-linked list, using your list operations from Exercise 17.

19. To avoid infinite loops while processing a circular singly-linked list (also called a *ring*), a special *header node* is often included. The empty ring is just the header itself with its `Next` field pointing to itself.
    (a) Write an algorithm to copy a ring.
    (b) Write an algorithm to concatenate two circular rings. (The concatenated rings should have only one header.)
    (c) Write an algorithm to erase (empty) a circular list.

20. The circular array implementation for queues keeps two variables, `Front` and `Rear`, with `Front = Rear` and the status of `Q.AnyInfo` as the test for an empty or full queue. Implement the queue ADT as a ring. (This will involve rewriting the list operations `CreateList`, `MakeListEmpty`, `InsertAtEnd`, `ListIsEmpty`, and `DeleteKth`.)

21. A *generalized list* is one in which each node may be either atomic or another list. If `GenList = (a₁, a₂, ..., aₙ)`, then `Head (GenList)` = a_1, and `Tail (GenList) = (a₂, ..., aₙ)`. (In LISP, `Head` is called `Car`, and `Tail` is called `Cdr`, indicating registers on the machine for which LISP was originally implemented.) The following declaration could be used for a generalized list.

```
GeneralList = ^GeneralListNode

GeneralListNode = record
                    case (Tag: boolean) of
                    true: (A: Atomic);
                    false: (L: GeneralList)
                  end;
```

(a) Draw box-and-arrow diagrams to display the following generalized lists. (Lowercase letters represent atoms, whereas uppercase letters or items contained in parentheses represent lists.)
    (i) A = (a, b, c)
    (ii) B = (a, (b, c))
    (iii) C = ( )
    (iv) D = (a, a, ( ))
    (v) E = (a, E)
(b) Which of these *nodes* are atomic and which are lists?
(c) What is the length of each of the preceding lists?

22. Pascal versions of LISP's atomic types are `char`, `real`, `integer`, and `string` (providing the string begins with a character and has no blanks). Define an `Atomic` type and implement the following LISP-like functions, using the `GeneralList` type of the previous exercise.

(a) `List` (L) returns boolean;

(b) `Atom` (X) returns boolean;

(c) `Car` (L) returns `GeneralListNode`;

(d) `Cdr` (L) returns `GeneralList`;

(e) `Length` (L) returns integer;

(f) `Cons` (X, L1) returns a new list, L2, with `Cdr` (L2) = L1, and `Car` (L2) = X.

(g) `Nconc` (X, L1) behaves the same as `Cons`, but modifies L1.

(h) `Append` (`L1`, `L2`) returns a new list that is the concatenation of `L1` and `L2`. `L1` and `L2` remain unchanged.

23. A *concordance* to a text is a list of its key words and where in the text they are found. A start toward building a concordance was suggested in the letter sequence frequencies program of Chapter 2.

Another way to count word frequencies would be to build a linked list as text is read, keeping track of the pages on which each word occurs. A Pascal declaration is

```
PageList = ^PageNumber;

PageNumber = record
                N: integer;
                Next: PageList
             end;

WordPtr = ^WordRec;

WordRec = record;
             Word:  {Any convenient, simple string type};
             Refs: PageList;
             NextWord: WordPtr;
          end;

Concordance = record
                 Length: integer;
                 Words: WordPtr
              end;
```

Write a Pascal program to build a concordance. Test your program with a text of your choice (at least three pages). Would you want to eliminate infrequently occurring words as was done in `WordFrequencies`? What sort of words should be removed from the concordance?

24. A concordance is built to allow look-ups. Even if your concordance of Exercise 23 is ordered, with the `Word` field as key, it will be very slow if the list is long.

(a) Modify your program to keep the concordance as an ordered list, but split it if it becomes too long. (This is why we kept a header node with a `Length` field.) You will need to keep an array or extra linked list to index the subconcordances.

(b) Another way to speed up searches is to maintain a single unordered list, and use a *self-organizing linear search*. After each record is found, the list is reorganized in some fashion to keep the more frequently accessed records near the front of the list. These methods can also be used when building a list such as a concordance. If a word is read that is not on the list, it is inserted at the end.

    (i) Modify your concordance program of Exercise 23, using `MoveToFront,` which moves an accessed record to the front of the list.

    (ii) Modify your concordance program using `Transpose,` which exchanges the accessed record with the one immediately in front of it.

25. Using the airline queue program of Chapter 4, make any modifications necessary to use the linked-list implementation for a queue.

(a) Make modifications in your linked list version to accommodate random integral service times between one and five minutes. To do this you will need to investigate the random number generator available to you on your computer and modify it to return integers in the appropriate range.

(b) Make further modifications to simulate four servers and one passenger queue.

26. (Adapted from Shortt and Wilson (1979)). Suppose that a five-lane bridge crosses the East River between Manhattan and Queens in New York. A counting bar is embedded in the pavement in each lane, and traffic densities are automatically computed. On the basis of the difference in the two densities, factors from -2 to 2 are assigned and lanes automatically allocated to traffic going west (into Manhattan) and east (into Queens). Allocation is as follows:

(a) If the density factor is 0, representing equally heavy traffic in each direction, three lanes are allocated going east and two going west.

(b) If the factor is ± 1, allocation is 3–2 in favor of the heavier traffic.

(c) If the factor is ± 2, lane allocation is 4–1 in favor of the heavier traffic.

    To avoid frequent switching of lane directions, densities are computed every half hour and are based on the number of cars counted since the last density computations.

(d) Define a function to compute density factors based on the difference in computed east and west traffic densities.

(e) Write a Pascal program using `EastQueue` and `WestQueue` to simulate lane switching on the bridge. Traffic in each direction should be randomly generated. (You may want to modify your function defined in (a) if lane switching occurs either too often or not often enough.)

(f) Modify your random traffic generator to simulate heavier traffic west (into Manhattan) during the 7:30 to 9:30 AM rush hours, and east (out of Manhattan) from 4:00 to 6:00 PM.

SUGGESTIONS FOR FURTHER STUDY _____

Advantages of circular lists are discussed in Tremblay and Sorenson (1984). When processing certain types of data, e.g., memory management schemes in a computer system, checks have shown that there is a much greater chance of referencing a node near that most recently processed rather than near those further away. Thus, search procedures may be more efficient originating at the node last referenced, with the possibility of still traversing the entire list, rather than at the head of the list. As an application, see Knuth's (1973) package for arithmetic on polynomials implemented as circular lists.

A rationale for and description of the LISP environment can be found in Sandenwall (1978). However, LISP dialects have only begun to be standardized with the recent development of Common LISP, Steele (1984). The availability of Common LISP interpreters and compilers (or at least a substantial subset) for small systems and micros makes it attractive.

The *ACM Computing Surveys* contain tutorials on several interesting list applications. Williams (1971) describes the use of list structures in graphics applications requiring quick insertions and deletions. Cohen and Gotlieb (1970) consider grammars for syntactic analysis in compilers. Cohen (1981) surveys garbage collection (the retrieval of free storage) in linked structures. As in most *Computing Surveys* articles, there are extensive bibliographies.

Algorithms for several varieties of self-organizing linear searches can be found in Hester and Hirschberg (1985). Such methods take execution history into account, to move frequently-accessed records so as to improve speed of the algorithm. Cost analyses are also detailed.

An overview of computer simulation is contained in a monograph from the Mathematical Association of America, edited by Seymour Pollack (1982). The Block/CSMP and 360/CSMP simulation languages are discussed for use in modeling continuous systems, in contrast to GPSS/360 and SIMSCRIPT, which are used with discrete probabilistic models.

CHAPTER 7

TREES

7.1 INTRODUCTION

Our topic for this chapter—trees—is one of the most fundamental in computer science, and has many applications, implementations, and variations. Trees are the basis for a number of ways to retrieve information rapidly. They are also useful as the primary data structure for some of the phases of a compiler or other language processor. Other applications abound.

Trees have a slightly more elaborate structure than the ADTs we have studied previously and are not often covered in a first course. Consequently, there is a fair amount of new terminology to introduce to you. Accordingly, we shall first explore the data objects involved in a binary tree. Then we will define an ADT for a particularly useful type of binary tree, the binary search tree, with a set of operations. We will study one useful implementation of binary trees, with pointer variables, in some detail. We will leave array implementation to you as an exercise.

We will then devote considerable attention to expression trees, which are heavily used in processing programs and any other text that involves algebraic expressions. This will be followed by a preview of expression optimization, which can be pursued at any length in exercises and projects. A variation called a threaded tree will then be considered to deal with a potential performance problem. The chapter will close with a brief discussion of general trees.

7.2 BINARY TREES:
GENERAL CONCEPTS

We will begin with a definition of the objects of the ADT tree, so that we can become familiar with the concepts and terminology before dealing with the operations of the ADT. As usual, implementation will be taken up after the operations have been studied.

Definition: *A* binary tree *is a finite set of* nodes *that is either empty, or consists of a* root *and two disjoint binary trees called the* left subtree *and the* right subtree. *A node contains information, the nature of which depends on the application.*

Here are some binary trees, with the items in the nodes being integer values.

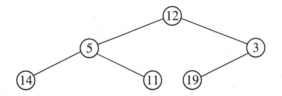

The root of this binary tree is the node containing 12; the left subtree of 12 has a root containing 5 and the right subtree of 12 has a root containing 3. The node at 5 has subtrees with roots containing 14 and 11; both of these latter have empty subtrees. The node at 3 has a left subtree with a root containing 19 and a right subtree that is empty.

We see that the trees of computer science, in contrast to those of the garden variety, have their roots at the top.

Here is a binary tree:

The tree consists of a root node containing 8; this node has right and left subtrees that are both empty.

Here are two binary trees:

These are different binary trees. One has a left subtree with a node containing 6 and an empty right subtree; the other has an empty left subtree and a right subtree with a node containing a 6. At this point the distinction may not seem important; you will see later that it is.

Here is the terminology we shall use in discussing binary trees.

The roots of the subtrees of a node are called its left and right *children*. If node A has node B as a child, then A is the *parent* of B. The root of the entire tree has no parent. The *ancestors* of a node are its parent and all the ancestors of the parent, which may be called *grandparents,* and so forth. The *descendants* of a node are its children and all of their descendants. Two nodes that have the same parent are called *siblings*. A node that has two empty subtrees is called a *leaf*. A node that has one or two non-empty subtrees is termed an *interior node*.

For examples of this terminology, consider this tree:

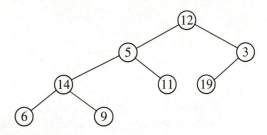

The children of the node containing 12 are the nodes containing 5 and 3. The children of 5 are 14 and 11, and the parent of 5 is 12. The descendants of 5 are 14, 6, 9, and 11. The ancestors of 9 are 14, 5, and 12. The pairs of siblings are 5 and 3, 14 and 11, and 6 and 9. The leaves are 6, 9, 11, and 19. The interior nodes are 12, 5, 3, and 14.

The *level* of a node in a binary tree is equal to one more than the number of its ancestors. Thus, the level of the root of the entire tree is one.[1] In the tree we just showed, the nodes at level 2 are 5 and 3; those at level 3 are 14, 11, and 19; those at level 4 are 6 and 9. Alternatively and equivalently, we can recursively define the level of a node to be one more than the level of its parent, with the level of the root of the entire tree defined as one.

The *height* of a binary tree is equal to the number of different levels of its nodes. Thus a tree with only a root is of height one; the tree shown immediately above is of height four.

There are several special types of binary trees. A *full* binary tree has all its leaves on the same level, and every node has either zero or two children, as in this example:

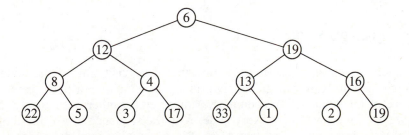

[1]The literature is about evenly divided on whether the level of the root node is defined as zero or one. The choice here seems to lead to a more intuitive definition of the height of a tree.

An alternative definition is that all of the interior nodes of a full binary tree have two non-empty subtrees.

It is not difficult to prove that a full binary tree of height k contains $2^k - 1$ nodes and 2^{k-1} leaves. A full binary tree is also called a *complete* binary tree.

A *skewed* binary tree contains only left or only right children, as in these examples:

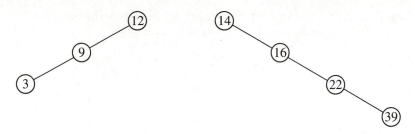

These binary trees have *degenerated* into special cases that are essentially linear lists. Many other shapes of binary trees share this characteristic, such as this one:

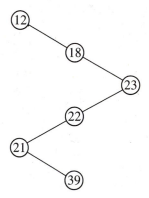

According to our definition, these are definitely binary trees but, as we shall see, they lead to poor performance of search algorithms, and we accordingly seek to avoid them when we have a choice.

7.3 TRAVERSAL OF BINARY TREES

Many applications of binary trees require that we "visit" all of the nodes of a tree. Visiting a node may mean simply printing its contents, or perhaps retrieving one piece of information for a summary, among many other possibilities. Sometimes we need merely to visit every node, with the sequence of visiting the nodes being of no consequence. In other cases, it is essential to visit the nodes in some specific sequence. The conventional terminology is to say that we *traverse* a binary tree when we visit all its nodes in some systematic fashion.

The traversal of a binary tree is approached through the recursive definition, under which we have to do three things: visit a node, traverse the left subtree, and traverse the right subtree. The question is, in what sequence do we carry out these three operations? If we assume that the left subtree will be traversed before the right subtree, we have three possibilities:

Preorder **traversal:**

1. Visit the root;
2. Traverse the left subtree; and,
3. Traverse the right subtree.

Inorder **traversal:**

1. Traverse the left subtree;
2. Visit the root; and
3. Traverse the right subtree.

Postorder **traversal:**

1. Traverse the left subtree;
2. Traverse the right subtree; and
3. Visit the root.

Consider this illustrative tree, where we have single letters in the nodes now, instead of integers.

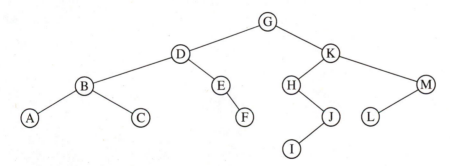

The three traversals are:

Preorder traversal: GDBACEFKHJIML.

Inorder traversal: ABCDEFGHIJKLM.

Postorder traversal: ACBFEDIJHLMKG.

Let us "walk through" the preorder traversal to see how the recursive definition applies.

We visit the root and print G.

We traverse the left subtree of G, which is rooted at D. Visiting the root of this subtree, we print D.

We traverse the left subtree of D; visiting its root, we print B.

We traverse the left subtree of B; visiting its root, we print A. This is a leaf; traversing its subtrees means only recognizing that they are empty. We have completed the traversal of the left subtree of B.

Next, we traverse the right subtree of B; visiting its root, we print C. This is a leaf, so we are finished with the right subtree of B.

The next right subtree not yet visited is that of D; we visit its root and print E. This node has no left subtree.

We traverse the right subtree of E; visiting its root, we print F.

The next right subtree not yet visited is that of G; visiting its root, we print K.

Traversing the left subtree of K, we visit its root and print H.

Since H has no left subtree, we visit its right subtree; visiting its root, we print J.

Traversing the left subtree of J, we visit its root and print I.

The next right subtree not yet traversed is rooted at M; we visit its root and print M.

Traversing the left subtree of M and visiting its root, we print L. This is a leaf, and there are no right subtrees awaiting traversal, so our preorder traversal of the binary tree is complete.

Consider the three traversals of these two trees.

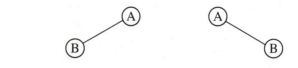

Preorder:	AB	AB
Inorder:	BA	AB
Postorder:	BA	BA

Only the inorder traversals are different, but that is enough. The two really are different binary trees.

7.4 THE ADT BINARY SEARCH TREE

Let us now provide a complete definition—including operations—of a useful special case of a binary tree, the binary search tree.

Definition: *a* binary search tree *is a binary tree in which the values in the left subtree of a node are all less than the value in the node, and in which the values in the right subtree of a node are all greater than the value in the node. The subtrees of a binary search tree must themselves be binary search trees.*

Here is an example.

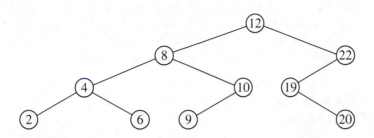

There is no standard set of primitive operations for binary trees; too much depends on the application. Here is one useful set, in which the letters BST in an operation name mean that the operation applies specifically to binary search trees. The absence of these letters means that the operation applies to any binary tree.

CreateTree is a procedure that brings a tree into existence, with the usual proviso that details depend on language, implementation, and operating system.

TreeIsEmpty is a function that returns true if the tree is empty, and false otherwise.

Item is a function that returns the value in the root of the tree to which its argument points. According to the definition, every node in a tree is the root of a tree, even if some of them are seen as subtrees. Consequently, Item can be used to obtain the value in any node as long as we have a pointer to it.

LeftChild is a procedure that takes a tree as its argument, and changes that argument to be its left child (which may be empty).

RightChild is a procedure that takes a tree as its argument, and changes that argument to be its right child (which may also be empty).

InsertBSTNode is a procedure that inserts a new node into a binary search tree in such a way that the enlarged tree is also a binary search tree. That is, in the modified tree, all the values in the left subtree of a node are still less than the value in the node, and all the values in the right subtree are greater than the value in the node. As we shall see, the new node is always a leaf.

`IsInBST` is a function that takes a tree and a value as arguments, and returns `true` if the specified value is in the binary search tree.

`DeleteBSTNode` is a procedure that deletes a specified node in such a way that the modified tree is also a binary search tree.

`NodeCount` is a function that returns the number of nodes in a binary tree.

`Height` is a function that returns the height of a tree. The definition of height, we recall, makes the height of a tree consisting of a single node, one.

`PreOrderTraverse`, `InOrderTraverse`, and `PostOrder-Traverse` carry out the three standard traversals. As they visit each node they can carry out whatever operation the application requires. For illustrative purposes we shall simply print the node contents.

7.5 THE ADT BINARY SEARCH TREE IN A RUDIMENTARY DATABASE APPLICATION

A *database* is a collection of information about some subject—the students in a university, the customers of a telephone company, the information in a person's address book, and so on. As the term is currently used in the commercial data processing world, a *database management system* (DBMS) includes facilities for inserting, deleting, modifying, and retrieving information from a database. A complete system is both extremely powerful and highly complex. The study of the use of database systems is a complete course in an information systems program, and the implementation of database systems is a complete computer science course. Here, we shall present a very simple example of such a system to illustrate binary search trees. Exercises 6 to 8 at the end of this chapter ask you to extend the example to slightly more realistic situations, and you should read them even if you don't do them.

Our DBMS will handle just three kinds of *transactions*. Each transaction, read from input, will consist of a *transaction code* consisting of one of the letters `I`, `Q`, or `D`, together with an *Item* consisting of one integer. A transaction code of `I` signifies an *insertion*. The item value should be inserted into a binary search tree that holds our database. A transaction code of `Q` signifies a *query*, which in this example will simply return a message as to whether such an item is in the database. A transaction code of `D` signifies a *deletion*. The database node holding that value should be removed.

Our program is designed to process as many such transactions as there are inputs, then print the contents of the database together with a node count and the height of the tree. The procedure of Figure 7.1 does this.

```
procedure SimpleDataBase;

var
    DataBase: Tree;
    TransCode: char;
    Item: ItemType;
begin
    CreateTree (DataBase);

    while not EOF do
    begin
        ReadLn (TransCode, Item);
        WriteLn ('Echo: ', TransCode, ' ', Item);

        if not (TransCode in ['I', 'Q', 'D']) then
            WriteLn ('Bad transaction code ', TransCode, ' ignored')

        else
            case TransCode of

            'I': InsertBSTNode (DataBase, Item);

            'Q': if IsInBST (DataBase, Item) then
                    WriteLn (Item, ' is in database')
                 else
                    WriteLn (Item, ' is not in database');

            'D': DeleteBSTNode (DataBase, Item)

            end   { case }

    end;   { while not EOF }

    Write ('The contents of the database: ');
    InOrderTraverse (DataBase);
    WriteLn;
    WriteLn;
    WriteLn ('The height of the tree: ', Height (DataBase));
    WriteLn ('The number of nodes is: ', NodeCount (DataBase))

end;   { procedure }
```

FIGURE 7.1

A procedure using a binary search tree to hold a simple illustration of a database.

Here is the output when a program containing this procedure was run.

```
Echo: I 24
Echo: I 14
Echo: I 12
Echo: I 10
Echo: I 37
Echo: I 13
Echo: Q 13
13 is in database
Echo: D 13
Echo: Q 13
13 is not in database
Echo: I 29
Echo: D 12
Echo: I 44
Echo: I 17
Echo: Q 37
37 is in database
The contents of the database: 10 14 17 24 29 37 44

The height of the tree: 3
The number of nodes is: 7
```

Observe that the inorder traversal of a binary search tree visits the nodes in sequence of the node values. This is a very useful feature. For example, we can sort a set of records into ascending sequence by building a binary search tree from them, then traversing the tree in inorder. This is a sorting method called *Treesort,* which is occasionally useful.

We see that our tree, after insertions and deletions, has seven nodes and a height of three. It is thus a full binary tree, and here is what it looks like:

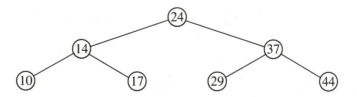

A successful search in this tree cannot require more than three comparisons, and will average two. In general, the number of comparisons required to locate a node that is in a full binary tree is about lg N. As it happens, no search method that depends on key comparisons can be faster.

This makes binary search trees look very attractive for data retrieval, and indeed they are. But this good performance is not assured. Let us see what kind of a tree we get with the same data but presented in a different order.

```
Echo: I 10
Echo: I 44
Echo: I 14
Echo: I 13
Echo: I 37
Echo: I 17
Echo: I 12
Echo: I 24
Echo: D 12
Echo: I 29
Echo: D 13
Echo: Q 17
17 is in database
Echo: Q 28
28 is not in database
The contents of the database: 10 14 17 24 29 37 44

The height of the tree: 7
The number of nodes is: 7
```

The same seven values in the database, but now the height of the tree is seven! The search time will be the same as for a linear list. Here is the tree.

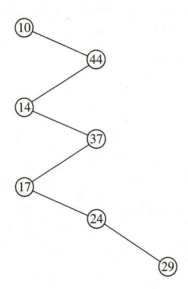

A great many different binary search trees can be formed from permutations of the same data. For fast retrieval, meaning the fewest comparisons, we like the tree to be "bushy," or "spread out," rather than "deep" or "narrow." Various means exist to find an economically attractive compromise, in which we achieve a reasonably bushy tree without excessive extra effort in building the tree. See Section 9.11.

7.6 A POINTER VARIABLE IMPLEMENTATION OF BINARY TREES

The most straightforward way to implement a binary tree is with pointer variables. We define a node to consist of a value and two pointers, with the following declarations:

```
type
    ItemType = . . .  {as needed for the application }

    TreePtr = ^TreeNode;
    TreeNode = record
                    Item: ItemType;
                    Left, Right: TreePtr
                end;

    Tree = TreePtr;
```

With such declarations, the implementation of most of the binary tree operations listed at the beginning of Section 7.4 is fairly simple. Only `Delete-BSTNode` involves much work.

`CreateTree` is the analog of `CreateStack`, `CreateQueue`, and `CreateList`. Its only action, in this pointer variable implementation, is to set to `Nil` the pointer variable sent to it.

```
procedure CreateTree (var T: Tree);
begin
    T := Nil
end;
```

`TreeIsEmpty` needs only to check whether the value of the pointer variable sent to it is `Nil`.

```
Function TreeIsEmpty (T: Tree): boolean;
begin
    TreeIsEmpty := T = Nil
end;
```

`Item`, `LeftChild`, and `RightChild` are simple analogs of similar linear list operations.

```
function Item (T: Tree): ItemType;
begin
    Item := T^.Item
end;
```

```
procedure LeftChild (var T: Tree);
begin
    T := T^.Left
end;
```

```
procedure RightChild (var T: Tree);
begin
   T := T^.Right
end;
```

IsInBST provides a gentle introduction to the use of recursion in working with trees. Because a tree is an inherently recursive structure, starting with the definition, it should come as no surprise that we use a recursive procedure.

```
function IsInBST (T: Tree;
                  ItemValue: ItemType): boolean;
begin
   if TreeIsEmpty (T) then
      IsInBST := false

   else if ItemValue = Item (T) then
      IsInBST := true

   else if ItemValue < Item (T) then
      IsInBST := IsInBST (T^.Left, ItemValue)

   else
      IsInBST := IsInBST (T^.Right, ItemValue)
end;
```

The logic is that if the tree is empty, ItemValue obviously is not in it. Otherwise, if the Item field in the node pointed to by the argument is equal to ItemValue, then obviously the item is in the tree. If neither of these cases is true, we wish to invoke the function recursively, going down the left subtree if ItemValue is less than the Item value in the current node, and going down the right subtree otherwise. Eventually, one of the non-recursive cases will be encountered, either by finding a match or by finding an empty subtree after finding no match anywhere earlier.

InsertBSTNode finds the correct place in a binary search tree in which to insert a node having the value sent to it. As we did with linear lists, we employ a tool procedure—this time called MakeNode—to simplify the presentation.

```
procedure MakeNode (var T: Tree;
                    NewItem: ItemType);
begin
   New (T);
   T^.Item := NewItem;
   T^.Left := Nil;
   T^.Right := Nil
end;
```

The main work of InsertBSTNode is to find the right place in the binary search tree to make the insertion. The logic is quite similar to that in IsInBST.

```
procedure InsertBSTNode (var T: Tree;
                        NewItem: ItemType);

{ Assert: NewItem not already in tree. }

begin
   if TreeIsEmpty (T) then
      MakeNode (T, NewItem)

   else if NewItem < Item (T) then
      InsertBSTNode (T^.Left, NewItem)

   else if NewItem > Item (T) then
      InsertBSTNode (T^.Right, NewItem)

   else
      TreeError (1)
end;
```

If the value of the tree pointer sent to `InsertBSTNode` is `Nil`, we invoke the procedure `MakeNode`, which makes a new node. The value sent to it is its `Item` field and `Nil` values are assigned to its left and right children. If the value of the tree pointer is not `Nil`, `InsertBSTNode` searches the tree recursively until it locates the correct place to insert the new node. We assume that nodes having the same value are not permitted; in some applications duplicates are allowed, and the routines can be modified accordingly. Because the newly inserted node has no children, it is by definition a leaf. The parent of the new node may or may not have been a leaf before the insertion; afterwards, it obviously is not a leaf.

It is instructive to follow the construction of a binary search tree and to see how the recursive procedure locates the correct place in which to insert a new node. Let us build a binary search tree from the following integer data: 12, 22, 8, 19, 10, 9, 20, 4, 2, and 6. The result will be the tree shown as the first example of a binary search tree at the beginning of Section 7.4. (Many other sequences of the same numbers would result in the same tree.)

We begin by creating a tree with `CreateTree`, which sets the pointer to that tree to `Nil`. We next send `InsertBSTNode` the value 12. The tree is empty at this point, so 12 becomes the value in the root node.

When 22 is sent, the tree pointer is no longer `Nil`. `InsertBSTNode` asks whether the 22 is less than the value in the node pointed to by T, which is the 12. The answer is "no," so it asks if the 22 is greater than the 12. The answer is "yes," so `InsertBSTNode` calls itself, with the right subtree specified as the tree for insertion. This pointer is `Nil`, so a new node is created and made the right child of the root.

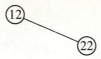

We then send the 8. It is found to be less than the value in the root, so `InsertBSTNode` calls itself with its left subtree as the tree into which to insert. This is `Nil,` so a new node is created and made the left child of the root.

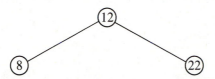

The 19 is next. It is greater than the value in the root, so the recursive call is with the pointer to the right subtree. This is not `Nil,` so `InsertBSTNode` now asks whether the 19 is less than 22, the node now under consideration. The answer is "yes," so `InsertBSTNode` calls itself recursively, with the pointer to the left subtree of the node containing 22. This is `Nil,` leading to the following tree.

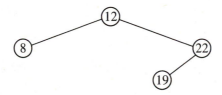

Now the 10 is found to be less than the 12 in the root but greater than the 8 in the left subtree.

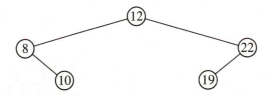

Now, the 9 is less than 12, so we go to the left subtree. The 9 is greater than the 8, so we go to the right subtree of the 8. The 9 is less than the 10, which has an empty left subtree, so the 9 is inserted there.

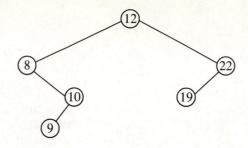

The 20 is now inserted as the right child in the left subtree of the right subtree of the root.

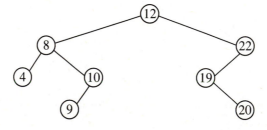

Next the 4:

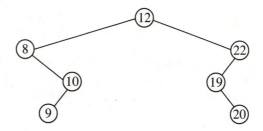

The 2:

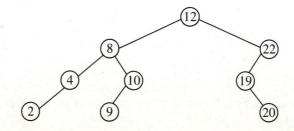

Finally, the 6:

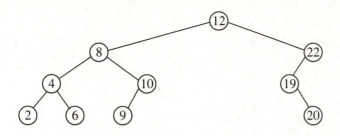

Deleting a node from a binary search tree requires that the tree—after the deletion—still satisfy the binary search tree criterion. There are four cases, three of which are quite simple, and the fourth of which takes a bit of effort. Consider one of the illustrative trees shown earlier.

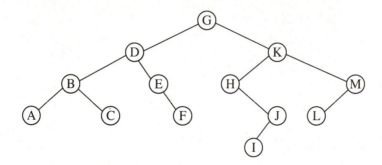

Case 1: The node to be deleted is a leaf, such as nodes A, C, F, I, or L in our diagram. This is almost trivial: set to `Nil` the pointer in its parent that points to it, and dispose of the node.

Case 2: The node to be deleted has an empty left child but a non-empty right child, such as E. This is barely harder than Case 1: replace the deleted node with its right child. Cases 1 and 2 are readily combined: just "promote" the right child, which will be `Nil` if the deleted node happens to be a leaf.

Case 3: The node to be deleted has an empty right child but a non-empty left child, such as J or M. Promote the left child.

Case 4: Neither child is empty, such as B, D, G, or K. Various solutions are possible. The best, in one sense, is the one that keeps the tree as bushy as possible, i.e., minimizes its height. This will minimize search time. To do this, replace the value in the deleted node with its predecessor under inorder traversal, then (recursively) delete the node that holds the predecessor. The predecessor will be the rightmost node in the left subtree of the node to be deleted—C if B or D is deleted, F if G is deleted, and J if K is deleted. Because it is in the left subtree, it must be less than everything in the right subtree, and because it is the inorder predecessor it must be greater than anything else in the left subtree. The recursive deletion will eventually find one of the simpler cases.

Here is the `DeleteBSTNode` procedure, which calls a procedure named `FindPredecessor`. The code for the latter procedure is shown immediately after this code.

```
procedure DeleteBSTNode (var T: Tree;
                              ItemValue: ItemType);

{ Assert: ItemValue is in tree. }

var
   Temp, Predecessor: Tree;
begin
   if T = Nil then
      TreeError (2)

   else if ItemValue = Item (T) then
   begin
      if TreeIsEmpty (T^.Left) then
      begin   { T has an empty left child--may be a leaf }
         Temp := T;
         T := T^.Right;
         Dispose (Temp)
      end

      else if TreeIsEmpty (T^.Right) then
      begin   { T has a empty right child }
         Temp := T;
         T := T^.Left;
         Dispose (Temp)
      end

      else
      begin   { neither child is empty: find inorder predecessor }
         FindPredecessor (T, Predecessor);
         T^.Item := Item (Predecessor);
         DeleteBSTNode (T^.Left, Item (T))
      end
   end

   else if ItemValue < Item (T) then
      DeleteBSTNode (T^.Left, ItemValue)

   else
      DeleteBSTNode (T^.Right, ItemValue)
end;
```

This is `FindPredecessor`.

```
procedure FindPredecessor (T: Tree;
                            var Predecessor: Tree);
begin
   Predecessor := T^.Left;
   while not TreeIsEmpty (Predecessor^.Right) do
      RightChild (Predecessor)
end;
```

Let us watch this procedure in action as it deletes three nodes from the full tree in our database example.

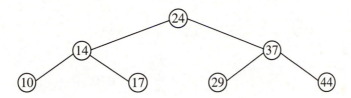

We first delete 29, which is a leaf, so nothing else about the tree has to be changed.

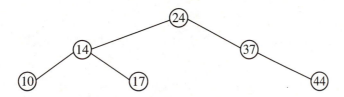

From this we now delete 37, which (now) has an empty left child, so we "promote" its right child.

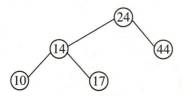

Now let us delete the root of the entire tree. Neither child is empty, so we need to find the inorder predecessor of the 24. This, we recall, is the rightmost node in the left subtree of the node we seek to delete. `FindPredecessor` locates this node, returning a pointer to it. This pointer is used to place the value 17 in place of the 24. The 17 now exists in two different nodes in the tree, but we immediately proceed to remove the ''extra'' one, by, of course, recursively invoking `DeleteBSTNode`. Why not just use `Dispose` to get rid of the node? Because that rightmost node in the left subtree could itself have a left subtree, which, of course, we do not want to lose.

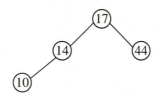

`NodeCount` is a comic relief, by comparison with `DeleteBSTNode`.

```
function NodeCount (T: Tree): integer;
begin
   if T = Nil then
      NodeCount := 0
   else
      NodeCount := 1 + NodeCount (T^.Left) + NodeCount (T^.Right)
end;
```

`Height` is similarly simple, with the help of a function `Max` that returns the larger of its two arguments.

```
function Max (A, B: integer): integer;
begin
   if A > B then
      Max := A
   else
      Max := B
end;
```

```
function Height (T: Tree): integer;
begin
   if TreeIsEmpty (T) then
      Height := 0
   else
      Height := 1 + Max (Height (T^.Left), Height (T^.Right))
end;
```

The three traversals are direct code equivalents of the definitions we have already seen.

```
procedure PreOrderTraverse (T: Tree);
begin
   if not TreeIsEmpty (T) then
   begin
      Write (Item (T), ' ');
      PreOrderTraverse (T^.Left);
      PreOrderTraverse (T^.Right)
   end
end;


procedure InOrderTraverse (T: Tree);
begin
   if not TreeIsEmpty (T) then
   begin
      InOrderTraverse (T^.Left);
      Write (Item (T), ' ');
      InOrderTraverse (T^.Right)
   end
end;


procedure PostOrderTraverse (T: Tree);
begin
   if not TreeIsEmpty (T) then
   begin
      PostOrderTraverse (T^.Left);
      PostOrderTraverse (T^.Right);
      Write (Item (T), ' ');
   end
end;
```

As noted, all we do when we visit a node is print its contents. In an actual application, there might be a variety of work to do, probably done by invoking a procedure.

7.7 EXPRESSION TREES

As another example of the usefulness of binary trees, one that does not require the tree to be a binary search tree, consider the processing of algebraic expressions. The trees are called *expression trees* or *algebra trees*. An expression tree has operators in its interior nodes, and has operands in its leaves. Here, for example, is the expression tree for the expression A * B + C:

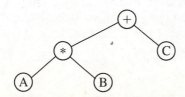

The three traversals are as follows:

1. Preorder traversal: $+ * A B C$
2. Inorder traversal: $A * B + C$
3. Postorder traversal: $A B * C +$

These traversals are precisely the prefix, infix, and postfix forms of the expression, and they reveal an aspect of the attractiveness of binary trees: if we can build the expression tree corresponding to an algebraic expression, then a postorder traversal immediately gives us the postfix form of the expression. Naturally, we already know two ways to convert an expression to postorder form without using trees. But, having an expression in binary tree form makes various other operations possible, as we shall see in Section 7.8.

Consider another expression, $(A + B) * (C - D + E) + F / (G - H)$. Here is the expression tree:

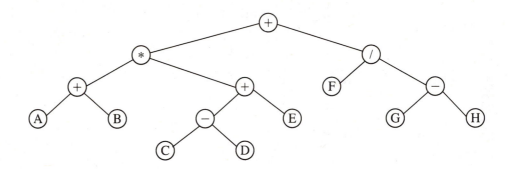

The three traversals are:

1. Preorder traversal: $+ * + A B + - C D E / F - G H$
2. Inorder traversal: $A + B * C - D + E + F / G - H$
3. Postorder traversal: $A B + C D - E + * F G H - / +$

We see that the preorder traversal gives the prefix form of the original expression and the postorder traversal gives the postfix. Inorder traversal seems to have lost the effect of the parentheses, but actually nothing has been lost; to recover an expression from an expression tree turns out to take more effort than just making an inorder traversal, but this is left to you as an exercise.

Before proceeding, note that *unary* operators, such as negation or square root can be represented in an expression tree simply by establishing the convention that such an operator has an empty right subtree. Here, for example, is the expression tree corresponding to $(A - B + C) * (-D)$:

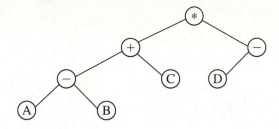

A procedure to build such a tree will be simpler to follow if we build a new node in a separate procedure, as follows:

```
procedure MakeExpTreeNode (var T: TreePtr;
                           Token: char;
                           Left, Right: Tree);
begin
   New (T);
   T^.Item := Token;
   T^.Left := Left;
   T^.Right := Right
end;
```

MakeExpTreeNode is modified from earlier related versions. It accepts pointers to left and right subtrees, as well as a token to place in the node and a pointer to which to give a value. We do this so we can insert both leaves and interior nodes as the tree is built. This is quite different from binary search trees, where new nodes are always leaves.

The work of expression parsing is based on recursive descent logic, which we used in Chapter 5. The procedure of Figure 7.2 uses the same basic logic as that of Section 5.11, but here we choose to nest the procedure for Factor within that for Term, and within that for Expression. This time an operand is either a single letter or a single digit. Also, the body of Expression has a bit of extra work to do because it has to recognize a unary minus (the only unary operator we consider). Finally, this time we build error detection into Factor, which, because it produces leaves, can recognize characters that do not fit the grammar of a valid algebraic expression.

Execution of this procedure begins with the body of Expression. We start by checking for a minus sign as the first character. This is now legal: it is a unary minus. When we create a node containing a unary minus, we must use a different character to prevent erroneous interpretation of the resulting postfix expression. We use the tilde (~). The pointers to the children of this new node are specified as Nil.

If the first token that Expression encounters is not a unary minus, then it invokes Term just as in the recursive descent logic of Section 5.11. When execution resumes in Expression, we enter a loop that looks for plus or

```
procedure Expression (var T: Tree);

    procedure Term (var T: Tree);

        procedure Factor (var T: Tree);
        begin
            if Token in ['A'..'Z', '0'..'9'] then
            begin
                MakeExpTreeNode (T, Token, Nil, Nil);
                GetToken (Token)
            end

            else if Token = '(' then
            begin
                GetToken (Token);   { skip over the left paren }
                Expression (T);
                if Token = ')' then
                    GetToken (Token)   { skip over the right paren }
                else
                    WriteLn ('Right parenthesis expected')
            end

            else
                WriteLn ('Operand or left parenthesis expected')
        end;   { procedure Factor }

    begin   { procedure Term }
        Factor (T);
        while Token in ['*', '/'] do
        begin
            MakeExpTreeNode (T, Token, T, Nil);
            GetToken (Token);   { skip over the * or / }
            Factor (T^.Right)
        end
    end;   { procedure Term }

begin   { body of procedure Expression }
    if Token = '-' then   { unary minus }
    begin
        MakeExpTreeNode (T, '~', Nil, Nil);   { note symbol }
        GetToken (Token);   { skip over the unary minus }
        Term (T^.Left)
    end
    else
        Term (T);
    while Token in ['+', '-'] do
    begin
        MakeExpTreeNode (T, Token, T, Nil);
        GetToken (Token);   { skip over the + or - }
        Term (T^.Right)
    end
end;   { procedure Expression }
```

FIGURE 7.2
A procedure to produce an expression tree from an algebraic expression.

minus signs. (A minus sign encountered at this point is a *binary* operator.) When either a plus or a minus sign is found, a node containing that operator is immediately created. It contains the operator in its `Item` field, its left child becomes the operand to which the old value of `T` pointed, and the new value of `T` points to the node containing the plus or minus. After moving past the operator, the body of `Expression` then invokes `Term` to process the right operand of the plus or minus. By sending a pointer to the right child of the operator to `Term`, the result of `Term`'s action will become the right child of the operator, as it must be.

`Term` is similar, except there is no unary operator to deal with.

`Factor` expects to find either an operand or a left parenthesis. An operand becomes a leaf. If the token that `Factor` is processing is not an operand, a left parenthesis should enclose an expression, according to the grammar. Thus we have mutual recursion, as expected. If `Factor` finds a left parenthesis but, when it regains control after invoking `Expression,` does not find a right parenthesis, it reports the error. And if it encounters neither an operand or a left parenthesis it also reports that error.

Here is the output when this program was run with a program that handled input/output and called for a postorder traversal of the expression tree:

```
The infix expression:
A * B + C
Has the postfix form:
AB*C+

The infix expression:
(A + B) * (C - D + E) + F / (G - H)
Has the postfix form:
AB+CD-E+*FGH-/+

The infix expression:
(A - B + C) * (-D)
Has the postfix form:
AB-C+D~*

The infix expression:
-(A + B/C/D)
Has the postfix form:
ABC/D/+~

The infix expression:
A*-B
Has the postfix form:
Operand or left parenthesis expected
A*B-

The infix expression:
X*
Has the postfix form:
Operand or left parenthesis expected
X*
```

(Continued)

(Continued)

```
The infix expression:
(A + B) * (C + D
Has the postfix form:
Right parenthesis expected
AB+CD+*

The infix expression:
A + BQ) * C
Has the postfix form:
AB+
```

We see that it correctly processed two expressions containing no errors and no unary minus, several expressions with unary minus signs, and several with errors. However, it did not catch all the errors.

Let us follow the building of the expression tree for the third example, (A − B + C) * (−D). First a node is created holding A, which becomes the (temporary) root of the tree.

This is the left operand of the minus sign, so the minus sign becomes the root.

The B is the right operand of the minus.

Everything in the tree so far becomes the left operand of the plus sign, so the latter becomes the new (but still temporary) root.

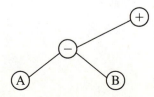

Now C becomes the right operand of the plus.

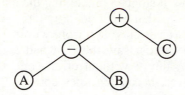

Next the asterisk becomes the new (and, as it happens, final) root.

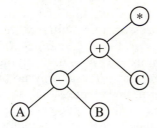

Now the unary minus become the right child of the root.

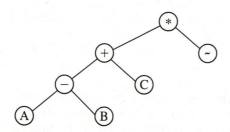

Finally, the unary minus gets its single operand.

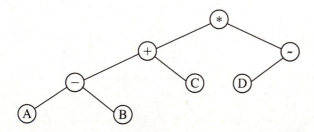

Postorder traversal of this tree produces the expression shown in the output.

Note that the erroneous expression in the final illustrative case was not diagnosed. (We said that it would catch *some* errors.) It is instructive to follow the logic of the program to see why it stopped processing the expression after finding the B. In fact, it did exactly what we told it to do. With no opening left parenthesis, `Expression` was not invoked from within `Factor`, and when the `while` loop in `Expression` saw the Q it had a non-recursive ending case. Some errors "fall out" almost without effort, but to find all of them is somewhat more work. However, because it does not involve tree concepts, we will not pursue the subject.

7.8 DETECTING IDENTICAL SUBTREES IN AN EXPRESSION TREE

Before we leave expression trees let us see one hint of how they may be used, by a compiler or other expression processor, to simplify expressions.

The issue is this. Given an expression like (A + B) + (A + B), we see immediately that it could be rewritten as 2*(A + B), giving the same result with two arithmetic operations instead of three. Presumably no programmer would write an expression like the first form, but expressions do arise that can be rewritten so as to save time, perhaps as the output of some other expression processor. An *optimizing compiler* undertakes, among many other things, to rewrite such expressions. How is that done?

To suggest an answer and to see another use of binary trees, consider the case illustrated above—the addition of identical subexpressions. In expression tree terms, it is clear that such a case is represented by an interior node containing a plus sign, which has identical left and right subtrees. The subtrees in the previous example both involve leaves, but we wish an algorithm that recognizes any identical subtrees, such as in: (A*B/C + A*B/C) * (D/(E−F) + D/(E−F)) + G. Here, A*B/C is a common subexpression in the first term, and D/(E−F) is a common subexpression in the second.

What we need is a procedure that traverses the expression tree and looks for plus signs. Whenever it finds one it checks to see if the left and right subtrees are identical and if so, modifies the subtree rooted at the plus sign. We know how to make a systematic traversal of the tree; preorder turns out to be best, as we shall see. The thing we need, then, is a `boolean` function that determines whether two trees are identical. Here is such a procedure:

```
function SameTree (T1, T2: Tree): boolean;
begin
    if TreeIsEmpty (T1) and TreeIsEmpty (T2) then
        SameTree := true

    else if TreeIsEmpty (T1) or TreeIsEmpty (T2) then
        SameTree := false

    else if Item (T1) <> Item (T2) then
        SameTree := false

    else
        SameTree := SameTree (T1^.Left, T2^.Left) and
                    SameTree (T1^.Right, T2^.Right)
end;
```

Two trees are considered to be the same if they have the same structure and the same contents in corresponding nodes. The procedure will be recursive (of course!), with three terminating conditions:

1. Both trees are empty, in which case they are clearly identical.

2. One tree is empty and the other is not, in which case they are not identical because they do not have the same structure.

3. The values in the roots are not the same, in which case the trees are obviously not identical.

If none of these stop the recursion, we check both subtrees using the same procedure. Note that the tests need to be made in this exact order. If the second and third were reversed, we could be asking for the `Item` value in a node when the tree pointer has the value `Nil,` which is a run-time error.

When we find two identical subtrees of a node containing a plus sign, we first need to dispose of one of the subtrees so that the storage space for that subtree does not become "lost in space." Here is a procedure to dispose of a tree:

```
procedure DisposeTree (var T: Tree);
begin
   if T <> Nil then
   begin
      DisposeTree (T^.Left);
      DisposeTree (T^.Right);
      Dispose (T)
   end
end;
```

With `SameTree` and `DisposeTree` as tools, the procedure to optimize an expression tree is not difficult, as shown in `Optimize.`

```
procedure Optimize (var T: Tree);
{ Simplify sum of identical operands. }
var
   Temp1, Temp2: Tree;
begin
   if    TreeIsEmpty (T^.Left)
      or TreeIsEmpty (T^.Right) then    { non-recursive exit }

   else
   begin
      if (Item (T) = '+') and (SameTree (T^.Left, T^.Right)) then
      begin
         DisposeTree (T^.Left);
         Temp1 := T;    { will need to dispose of this one node }
         MakeExpTreeNode (Temp2, '2', Nil, Nil);
         MakeExpTreeNode (T, '*', Temp2, T^.Right);
         Temp1^.Right := Nil;  { don't dispose of right sub-tree }
         Dispose (Temp1)
      end;
      Optimize (T^.Left);
      Optimize (T^.Right)
   end
end;
```

We choose preorder traversal because that visits the root first. We are thus assured that we will detect the largest identical subtrees first. The non-recursive exit is that either subtree is empty. If neither is empty we ask if the node contains a plus sign and if the subtrees are identical. If so, we dispose of the left subtree. This choice is arbitrary. We could just as well dispose of the right subtree, with corresponding changes later. The difference is whether $((A + B) + (A + B))$ is changed to $2*(A + B)$ or to $(A + B)*2$. Having disposed of the left subtree, we create a new node containing the operand 2. This, in turn, becomes the left child of a new node that has an asterisk in place of the plus sign and the original right subtree. The procedure is completed with the recursive optimization of the left and right subtrees.

The action of this "optimization" procedure is shown in the examples that follow. We place "optimization" in quotes because, in fact, this is no more than a teaser. Many other techniques would be employed in a true optimization, and not all of them would be built on a simple expression tree.[2]

```
The infix expression:
(A + B) * C
Has the postfix form:
AB+C*
The "optimized" form is:
AB+C*

The infix expression:
(A + B) + (A + B)
Has the postfix form:
AB+AB++
The "optimized" form is:
2AB+*

The infix expression:
C * ((A + B) + (A + B)) / (D - E)
Has the postfix form:
CAB+AB++*DE-/
The "optimized" form is:
C2AB+**DE-/

The infix expression:
(A*B/C + A*B/C) * (D/(E-F) + D/(E-F)) + G
Has the postfix form:
AB*C/AB*C/+DEF-/DEF-/+*G+
The "optimized" form is:
2AB*C/*2DEF-/**G+

The infix expression:
((A + B) + (A + B)) + ((A + B) + (A + B))
Has the postfix form:
AB+AB++AB+AB+++
The "optimized" form is:
22AB+**
```

<hr>

[2] "Optimization" should always be in quotes in this context because there is no meaningful definition of "optimum." As used in compiler construction, "optimize" means simply "make it faster and/or smaller."

We see that the "optimized" version is not all it could be because we obviously have not combined `2*2` into `4`. Nevertheless, it is impressive how much the program can do, based on the simple idea of looking for identical subtrees.

7.9 THREADED TREES

There is a performance problem associated with binary tree traversal, one that, happily, we can remove with only a small space penalty.

We saw earlier, in a rather informal way, that if a binary search tree is fairly bushy, the number of comparisons necessary to locate a node (or determine that it is not present) is $O(\lg N)$, but that in the worst case—when the tree degenerates to a linear list—it is $O(N)$. We then have a problem with both the slow linear time performance and the space required for the recursion stack when a recursive traversal algorithm is applied to such a tree. In an extreme case, the stack of activation frames could take more space than the tree.

The best approach to this problem, in most cases, is some kind of tree-balancing algorithm that keeps the search tree reasonably bushy as it is being built. We shall see one such, the AVL tree, in overview fashion in Section 9.11.

There is also another approach, which is interesting in that it removes recursion—and the space penalty for its recursion stack—in a fundamentally different way from the recursion removal methods of Section 5.10. The latter require the space for an explicit stack and are therefore of no help in this situation.

With the threaded tree method we take advantage of the fact that just about half of the links in any binary tree are `Nil`. This is not hard to see. A tree with N nodes has $2N$ links, only $N - 1$ of which can be pointing to non-empty subtrees. These "unused" links are not entirely without a function for they let us determine that a subtree is empty. But that function can be accomplished other ways, as we shall see.

Our solution will be to replace each `Nil` right link, except that of the last node in the tree under inorder traversal, with a special pointer to the inorder successor of the node. This special pointer must be distinguishable from a regular pointer, and we shall call it a *thread*. The resulting tree is called a *right inorder threaded tree*.

Here is an example in which the threads are drawn as dotted lines:

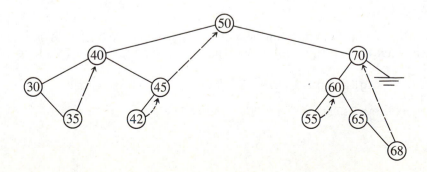

The symbol for the right child of the node containing 70 is that for an electrical ground, which is sometimes used to designate a `Nil` pointer. This node is the last in an inorder traversal, and is recognizable as such by the fact that its right link is a regular link, not a thread.

To implement a threaded tree we need a way to distinguish between a thread and a regular link. With our pointer variable implementation, the most obvious way to make this distinction is to provide a separate field in the definition of a node, with an enumerated type. (With an array implementation, a negative value for the node index would serve the same purpose, with no extra trouble and, in some cases, less space.) Here are the declarations we shall use:

```
type
   ItemType = integer;    { or whatever }
   PtrType = (RegularLink, Thread);

   TreePtr = ^TreeNode;
   TreeNode = record
                 Item: ItemType;
                 Left, Right: TreePtr;
                 RightPtrType: PtrType
              end;

   Tree = TreePtr;
```

We are implementing only right threads, so we need no designation of the type of a left link.

The main work comes in inserting a node into a threaded binary search tree, and in the traversal. It will help clarify the presentation if we have a tool procedure for making a node, which includes setting the link type, as follows:

```
procedure MakeThreadedNode (var T: Tree;
                            NewItem: ItemType;
                            NewRightPtr: Tree;
                            NewRightPtrType: PtrType);
begin
   New (T);
   T^.Item := NewItem;
   T^.Left := Nil;
   T^.Right := NewRightPtr;
   T^.RightPtrType := NewRightPtrType
end;
```

A further slight simplification is provided by having a `boolean` function that tells what kind of right link a node has, as in `RightLinkIsThread`.

```
function RightLinkIsThread (T: Tree): boolean;
begin
   RightLinkIsThread := T^.RightPtrType = Thread
end;
```

The insertion requires that we handle new left leaves slightly differently from new right leaves. The thread of a new left leaf points to its parent, and its parent's left link had to have been `Nil` for the insertion to occur. The thread of a new right leaf, on the other hand, must be made to point to whatever its parent's right link pointed to, and the parent's right link, which used to be a thread, must be redesignated as a regular link. Try these descriptions on the preceding tree, assuming that you have already established which node is the parent of the new node.

That much is actually fairly simple. But now we have a bit more work to do to find the place of insertion because the point of the method is to avoid recursion and the space penalty for its stack. Instead, we use an iterative approach that stops upon finding either a `Nil` pointer or a thread.

The only special case in all this is the very first node of the tree, which must be set up with a `Nil` right link. We recall that a `Nil` right link identifies the last node in the tree under inorder traversal, which holds the largest value, and which will let us recognize the completion of the traversal.[3]

All of this comes together in the procedure of Figure 7.3, which should be readable in conjunction with the preceding description.

In traversing a threaded tree we first travel down the left links as far as possible, using an iterative loop. This positions us at the smallest value in the tree (or subtree), which is the first node under inorder traversal. We use pointers P and Q, with Q being the "trailer." When we reach the leftmost node, Q will point to that node and P will be its left link.

It will turn out, much later, that this process could have positioned us at the right link of the last node under inorder traversal—i.e., we might be finished. If this is not the case, then we are ready to visit node Q.

The next node in inorder succession is now somewhere in whatever Q points to, but that may be either a regular link or a thread. If it is a regular link we are ready to repeat the process, which means to go down the left links of this new subtree. But if it is a thread, there is no right subtree and we want to follow the thread.

---

[3]A common alternative tree implementation uses a header node, which would modify some of the details here, but still require attention to the special cases.

```
        procedure InsertThreadedNode (var T: Tree;
                                          NewItem: ItemType);

        { Assert: NewItem not already in tree. }

        var
            Parent, Child: TreePtr;
            FoundLeaf: boolean;
        begin
            if TreeIsEmpty (T) then    { root of entire tree }
                MakeThreadedNode (T, NewItem, Nil, RegularLink)

            else
            begin
                Child := T;

                FoundLeaf := false;
                while not FoundLeaf do
                begin
                    Parent := Child;
                    if NewItem < Item (Parent) then
                        if TreeIsEmpty (Parent^.Left) then
                            FoundLeaf := true
                        else
                            Child := Parent^.Left
                    else
                        if RightLinkIsThread (Parent)
                            or TreeIsEmpty (Parent^.Right) then
                            FoundLeaf := true
                        else
                            Child := Parent^.Right
                end;

                if NewItem = Item (Parent) then
                    TreeError (1)    { duplicate not allowed }

                else if NewItem < Item (Parent) then
                    MakeThreadedNode (Parent^.Left, NewItem,
                                        Parent, Thread)

                else
                begin
                    MakeThreadedNode (Parent^.Right, NewItem,
                                        Parent^.Right, Thread);
                    Parent^.RightPtrType := RegularLink
                end

            end    { begin -- other than root of entire tree }

        end;   { procedure }
```

FIGURE 7.3
A procedure to insert a node in a right in-threaded binary search tree.

Here is the procedure:

```
procedure ThreadedInOrderTraverse (T: Tree);
var
    P, Q: TreePtr;
begin
    P := T;
    repeat

        { find leftmost node, = smallest item in (sub)tree }
        Q := Nil;
        while not TreeIsEmpty (P) do
        begin
            Q := P;
            P := P^.Left
        end;

        if not TreeIsEmpty (Q) then    { found last node? }
        begin
            Write (Item (Q), ' ');
            P := Q^.Right;
            while (Q^.RightPtrType = Thread) and (P <> Nil) do
            begin
                Write (Item (P), ' ');
                Q := P;
                P := Q^.Right
            end
        end

    until TreeIsEmpty (Q)
end;
```

We can study the action of this procedure in terms of the sample tree shown earlier.

Following the left links takes us to 30, which we print. This node has a regular right link, so we return to the beginning of the `repeat` loop. But 35 has an empty left subtree, so the `while` loop body is not executed and we print the 35. Now we discover that 35 has a thread in its right link, so we use the auxiliary pointer Q to follow it to 35's inorder successor and print it. But now 40 has a regular right link, and we return to the start of the `repeat` loop—but with P having been set to point to 45. The left links from here get us 42, then a thread back to 45, and now yet another thread, back to the root of the entire tree. The 50 is printed, and again P has been set to the right link of the 50.

Following the left links we find 55, then follow a thread to 60. The 65 has an empty left subtree, so we go to 68, then follow a thread to the 70. Now watch closely! After printing the 70, P is set to the right link of 70, which is `Nil`. (It got that way when the 70 was inserted in the tree, and 70's right link was made to be the same as the right link of its parent.) Now back to the beginning of the `repeat` loop. Q is set to `Nil` in an initialization operation as always, the `while` body is not executed because P is `Nil,` and now, finally, the `if` statement that tests to see if Q is an empty tree gives a yes answer, and the `repeat` test is satisfied.

Clearly, threaded trees can have left threads as well as right, making it possible to find the predecessor of a node or facilitating various other operations. This will be left as an exercise for you, as will deletion from a threaded tree.

Are threaded trees worth the trouble? Basically, the answer depends on whether you need the stack space used when non-threaded trees encounter the special cases that degenerate into linear lists, or nearly so. If you are short of space and cannot be sure that the special cases are impossible, then threaded trees offer one solution. Their price, however, is at least one bit in every node, to distinguish between a regular link and a thread.

7.10 A SKETCH OF GENERAL TREES

This chapter has concentrated on binary trees because they are fundamental, have many applications, and can so easily be used to represent general trees. We will close the chapter with an overview of general trees and their representation as binary trees.

A general tree relaxes the requirement that each node have exactly two children, either or both of which may be empty. Instead, the general tree definition says simply that a node has zero or more children. Here, for example, is a general tree.

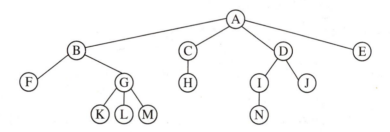

This might be a portion of a genealogical tree, with the children being human children instead of metaphorical ones.

Here is another example, where Σ is a generalized summation operator and Π is a generalized product operator.

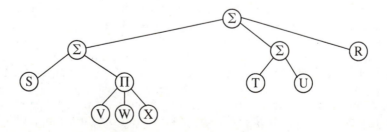

Such a form might be an intermediate step in a compiler that produces a program for a parallel computer, where, with effective organization, a number of computations can proceed simultaneously.

General trees arise in a number of other areas of application, a few of which are sketched in the exercises at the end of the chapter.

It is possible to set up a new ADT for a general tree, with an appropriate definition of the object and a set of operations. There is little point in doing so, however, since the implementation is readily accomplished with binary trees, a number of the operations carry over unchanged, and the rest depend heavily on the particular application.

The basic idea in representing a general tree as a binary tree is to *order* the children of a node, say, from left to right. Now, in the binary tree representation, each node has two link fields, which we may call `First` and `Next,` rather than `Left` and `Right.` The `First` field of a node points to the first (leftmost) child of a general tree node. And, because the children are ordered, we can say that the `Next` field points to the next sibling. This is easier to illustrate than describe. Here is the first tree above, represented as a binary tree:

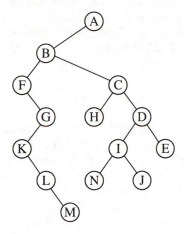

The correspondence between the two trees is more easily seen if we draw the binary tree form in a different orientation.

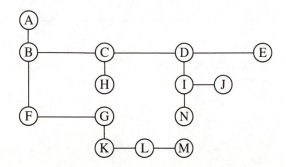

The traversal of a general tree requires us to make a choice about the sequence in which to visit the nodes. Preorder traversal means visiting a node *before* visiting any of its children; postorder traversal means visiting a node *after* visiting all of its children. Inorder traversal of a general tree is less well defined because we would need a decision as to when to visit the parent of a set of children in relation to visiting the children themselves.

Applying the same preorder and postorder traversal algorithms that we have already studied to the binary tree representation of a general tree gives just the traversals of a general tree that we need. The preorder traversal of the binary tree representation of our sample general tree gives: `A, B, F, G, K, L, M, C, H, D, I, N, J,` and `E.` This amounts to traversing the entire subtree of the leftmost child, then the entire subtree of the next child, and so forth. Another way to describe the action is to note that it follows each path from a node as far toward the bottom of the tree as possible before considering the siblings of the node.

The postorder traversal of the binary tree representation of our sample tree gives `M, L, K, G, F, H, N, J, I, E, D, C, B,` and `A.` As stated, every node is visited before its parent. This gives the effect of exploring the tree in a bottom-up fashion, looking at leaves first. Both traversals have applications.

7.11 CONCLUSION

We have now introduced you to some of the most important concepts of trees, binary trees especially, and seen an indication of their usefulness. The exercises for this chapter are fairly extensive so as to give you an idea of some of the wide range of issues that we were not able to cover in this introduction. You should read them even if you don't try to do them all.

We shall see binary search trees again in Chapter 9, and in Chapter 10 we shall see that a tree is an important special case of a more general object, the graph.

EXERCISES

1. Assume, as in Section 7.3, that "visiting" a node in a binary tree means to print its `Item` field. Traverse each of the following trees in preorder, inorder, and postorder.

a.

b.

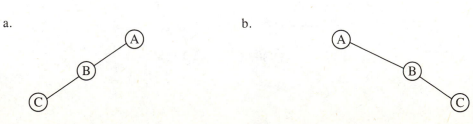

c.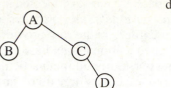

d.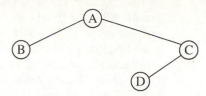

e.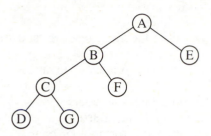

f.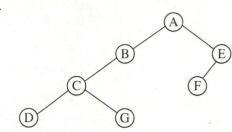

2. We observe that two trees with the same nodes have different shapes if any one of the three traversals returns different lists when applied to each of the two trees.
- **(a)** Draw two different trees that yield the same inorder traversal.
- **(b)** Do the same for postorder traversal.
- **(c)** Do the same for preorder traversal.
- **(d)** Draw two different trees that have the same preorder and the same postorder traversals.
- **(e)** Suppose (a, b, c, d) is the inorder traversal of a tree, and (b, a, d, c) is its postorder.
  - **(i)** Do these two orders define exactly one tree, or more than one?
  - **(ii)** What do you conclude from this? Can you prove it?

3. Develop an algorithm and write a Pascal program to produce a binary tree:
- **(a)** Given the preorder and inorder traversal lists.
- **(b)** Given the postorder and inorder traversal lists.

4. Write a procedure `PrintTree (T: Tree; Spaces: String)` to print out a tree in the "right shape." That is, a left subtree should print to the left and below its root, and a right subtree to the right and below its root. You won't know the size of a tree prior to printing it, so this is easiest to do "sideways," that is, in "reverse inorder."
- **(i)** Print out the right subtree.
- **(ii)** Print out the root.
- **(iii)** Print out the left subtree.

Your tree will then have the "right shape" if you turn the printout. Be careful about the number of `Spaces` needed. Working this out by hand on graph paper with a small sample tree might be helpful.

5. Write a procedure `TreeSort,` which accepts an array and returns the same array in ascending order, by building a binary search tree and then traversing it in inorder. (Note: This isn't very hard, but will give you practice in making tree declarations and tidy recursive calls.)

6. Conceptually, a *hierarchical* data base system is modeled after a *forest* (collection) of binary trees. The *data base definition* provides a description of the trees. Trees are traversed in preorder, so the root provides a category heading for its subtrees. Consider an educational data base, with each tree in the forest representing a different course offered in a particular semester.

   (a) Draw a data base design (forest of binary trees) for an educational data base, including:

   (i) Course offerings;

   (ii) Prerequisites for each course;

   (iii) Section of course, including location, teacher, and students enrolled.

   (b) In what ways could your schema be optimized? Consider such things as:

   (i) A student enrolled in more than one course.

   (ii) A teacher teaching more than one course.

   (iii) One course being a prerequisite for another course offering.

   (Hint: Think about pointers.)

7. Many large data bases, still in use, were established using primitive versions of Fortran or COBOL, and are accessed by coded operations. Assuming two global pointers to a data base, CP = *Current* pointer, and MRA = pointer to the *Most Recently Accessed* node, some of the most common operations are:

   GU: Get Unique, which locates the first occurrence of a root of a tree or subtree satisfying specified conditions. After a GU, CP and MRA both point to the node just located.

   GN: Get Next, which locates the first child if given a parent node, or the next sibling, given a child node. After GN, both CP and MRA point to the node found.

   GNP: Get Next within Parent, which locates the child node next to that pointed to by MRA. CP remains pointing to the parent node, while MRA moves to point to the node just located. GNP can move MRA down several levels in a data base. That is, a parent is thought of as any ancestor, be it parent, or great-grandparent.

   PRINT: Prints information pointed to by MRA.

   Write Pascal algorithms to implement each of the three preceding data base operations. Refer to your schema of the preceding exercise.

8. Use the course schedule of your school for the current semester to implement the educational data base of Exercise 6. Using the operations of Exercise 7, implement them so that a sequence of operations can answer the following queries:

   (a) GU (Course, Course = 'Ceramics I');

   (b) GN (Student);

   (c) GNP (Teacher);

   (d) GNP (Student, Grade = 'A');

   (e) PRINT the entire tree for 'Ceramics I'.

9. The cost of a search in a binary tree can vary from $O(\lg N)$ to $O(N)$, depending on the shape of the tree. It is not always possible to keep a tree perfectly balanced, so compromises must be made. One such compromise is called a *Fibonacci tree*. It is defined recursively as follows:

1. The empty tree is the Fibonacci tree of height 0.
2. A single node is the Fibonacci tree of height 1.
3. If T_{h-1} and T_{h-2} are Fibonacci trees of height $h-1$ and $h-2$, then T_h is the Fibonacci tree of height h, with root X, left subtree T_{h-1}, and right subtree T_{h-2}.
4. There are no other Fibonacci trees.

(a) Show with diagrams that Fibonacci trees are unique in shape.
(b) Write an algorithm to compute the number of nodes in T_h.
(c) Using T_4 and T_5, construct non-Fibonacci trees, such that the heights of the left and right subtrees differ by at most 1.
(d) Prove by induction that the number of nodes in a Fibonacci tree is minimal among all trees where the height of the left and right subtrees differ by at most 1.

10. A *decision tree* is a tree where, at each node, a decision can be made, according to an associated set of rules, about which branch to follow. An example is a sudden-death tennis tournament. Starting at the bottom of the tree we list all the players. The tree can then be built, bottom-up, from the entire roster of players to the single winner (who is at the root). Now suppose we move through such a decision tree, starting at the root, and find the player in the path Win, Win, Win, Lose. We have found the player who lost to the tournament winner three matches before the final.

(a) Gather the details on some tennis tournament and build its decision tree, with the winner at the root.
(b) Given your tree from (a), which player lost to the loser of the finals?
(c) Under what circumstance(s) is the losing finalist not the actual second-best among all the contestants?

11. A sorting method known as *tree selection* or *tournament sort*, proceeds as described by the following pseudocode:

- The items to be sorted are placed in the `Item` fields of the leaves of a binary tree, just as in a sudden-death tennis tournament.
- The following two steps are carried out in a loop, until the item in the root node is `-Infinity`:
- Working up the tree, largest elements (winners) are placed in parent nodes.
- The root `Item` is written out to the sorted list, and `-Infinity` is placed into the leaf location it came from.

(a) Draw the successive trees needed to sort (5, 20, 32, 14, 2, 6, 0) into ascending order using tree selection.
(b) Do you need to perform the second step above for each pair of siblings in the tree at each iteration?
(c) Given your observation in (b), what is the cost of tree selection in terms of the number of elements to be sorted?

12. As we will see in Section 8.11, a tree can be implemented as an array *without links*. For each interior node `TreeArray [i]`, its left child is in `TreeArray [2i]` and its right child is in `TreeArray [2i + 1]`. We start with `TreeArray [1]` = `RootNode`.

   (a) Write a Pascal function, `Parent (I: ChildIndex)`, that returns the `TreeArray` index for the parent of a child node with index `I`.

   (b) Using your function from (a), write a Pascal procedure for `TreeSelection`.

13. In Section 7.5 we said that the number of comparisons required to locate a node in a full binary tree is about lg N, and that no method that depends on key comparisons can be faster.

   (a) Can you prove this? Think about a decision tree where each decision cuts out half of the remaining elements.

   (b) What if we had an N-way tree, where each interior node had N or fewer children, and each decision removed $(N-1)/N$ of the remaining elements. Why is the cost of searching for a single element not less than $O(\lg N)$?

14. Write the following two procedures to copy a binary tree:

   (a) A recursive procedure; (All we need to do here is create a new root, place the `Item` field of the old root into the `Item` field of the new root, and then recursively copy the left and right subtrees.)

   (b) An iterative procedure.
   Do you think (b) is easier to write having already done (a)?

15. What do the following procedures do?

   (a)

```
procedure Mystery1 (T: Tree);

var
PtrQ: Queue;
P: TreePtr;
begin
   CreateQueue (PtrQ);
   EnQueue (PtrQ, T);
   while not QueueIsEmpty (PtrQ) do
   begin
      DeQueue (PtrQ, P):
      if not TreeIsEmpty (P) then
      begin
         Write (P^.Item, ' ');
         EnQueue (PtrQ, P^.Left);
         EnQueue (PtrQ, P^.Right)
      end
   end
end;
```

(b) Mystery2 is the same as Mystery1, with two changes:
- **(i)** A stack is used instead of a queue, with Push and Pop replacing EnQueue and DeQueue.
- **(ii)** P^.Right is pushed onto the stack before P^.Left.

16. Write an iterative Pascal procedure, IterInsertBSTNode, that performs the same function as the recursive InsertBSTNode.

17. Write a Pascal function, NumLeaves (T: Tree), that returns the number of leaves in a binary tree, T. Can you think of an application area where such a function might be useful?

18. Write a boolean function, SearchTree (T: Tree), that returns true if T is a binary search tree, and false otherwise. What is the worst cost, least cost, and average cost of your function in terms of the number of nodes in the tree?

19. Consider the three infix arithmetic expressions, $5 - 2 - 3$, $5 - (2 - 3)$, and $(5 - 2) - 3$.
- **(a)** Write their postfix and prefix expressions.
- **(b)** Draw the expression tree for each expression.

20. We saw in Section 7.7 that inorder traversal of an expression tree does not necessarily produce a correctly parenthesized infix expression. A simple modification to InOrderTraverse would be the following algorithm, adapted from Rohl (1984):

```
AllParenInOrderTraverse (ExT: ExpressionTree);
begin
    if not (EmptyTree (ExT) then
    begin
        Write ('(');
        AllParenInOrderTraverse (ExT^.Left);
        Write (ExT^.Item);
        AllParenInOrderTraverse (ExT^.Right);
        Write (')');
    end;
end;
```

If this algorithm is applied to the following tree,

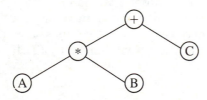

the fully parenthesized result is (((A) * (B)) + (C)).

(a) What would `AllParenInOrderTraverse (T)` produce if applied to this tree?

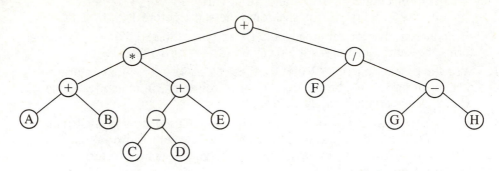

(b) Being careful to include the special consideration for right trees of minus signs (see the examples in the previous exercise), write algorithms to decide:

(i) when parentheses are needed to enclose an expression from a left subtree;

(ii) when parentheses are needed to enclose an expression from a right subtree.

(c) Write a procedure, `MinParenInOrderTraverse`, that produces a correct, but minimally parenthesized, infix expression from an expression tree.

21. Suppose you have a pile of eight coins and one of them is counterfeit. Suppose also that it is lighter than the others. You have a balance scale.

(a) Can you find the bad coin in two weighings? (Hint: Try a three-way decision tree, which reduces the number of candidates for the counterfeit coin at each level.)

(b) How many weighings are needed to identify one counterfeit out of 10 coins? 15? 30? 81? 100?

22. A *game tree* is a tree in which the current status of the game is kept in the `Item` field of each node. Children represent the status subsequent to each possible move.

A game of *nim* starts with *N* piles of tokens. A *move* consists of a player removing one or more tokens from a single pile. Two players, A and B, alternate making moves, with the player removing the last token losing. For example, suppose play begins with two piles, one containing two tokens and the other one, which we will denote by (2, 1). Here is the game tree.

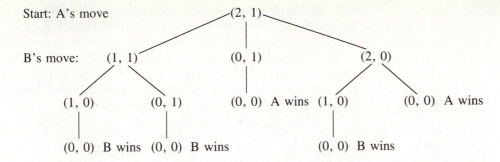

Start: A's move

B's move:

A, moving first, must take one or more tokens from one pile, up to the number of tokens in the pile. There are three choices: one from the first pile, both from the first pile, or one from the second. These possibilities are the children of the starting position. B, moving next, has two choices in the first case, only one in the second, and two in the third. In the second case, because B is forced to take the last token, A wins. This tree shows all the possibilities in the game.

The first thing to note when evaluating winning positions is that symmetric moves may be eliminated from the tree. For this two-pile game, the position (n, m) is essentially the same as (m, n). The tree with symmetric nodes on the same path removed is depicted as follows.

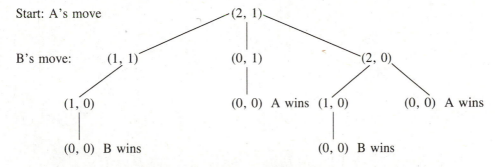

Start: A's move

B's move:

(a) Does the first player have a forced win?

(b) Draw the game tree for a (3, 2) nim game.

(c) Write an algorithm to remove symmetric nodes among siblings for a two-pile nim game.

23. In computer games, in which a human player plays against a computer, the computer can decide which move to make by a *mini-max* process. Suppose, for example, that the computer has the first move in a game of nim. The game tree is constructed, and scores assigned to the leaves of the tree. If A (the computer) wins, a 1 is assigned, and if B (the person) wins, a 0 is assigned. As a result, the mini-max tree may be configured as follows.

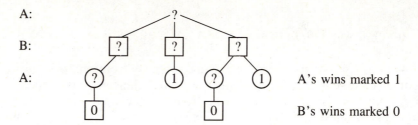

A's wins marked 1

B's wins marked 0

To compute mini-max scores for the interior nodes, now shown as question marks, we compute the *minimum* values of the children on B's moves (nodes drawn as circles), and the *maximum* values of the children on A's moves (squares).

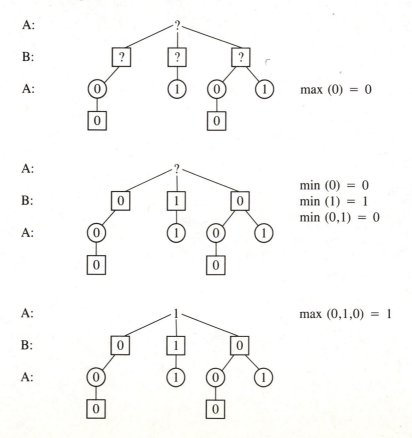

max (0) = 0

min (0) = 0
min (1) = 1
min (0,1) = 0

max (0,1,0) = 1

A winning strategy for the computer, A, would be to choose a move with a *max* score (in this case, 1). For its opponent, B, a winning strategy would be to choose a move with *min* score (in this case, 0).

(a) Draw a mini-max tree for the (3, 2) nim game.
(b) Can the first player force a win in this game?
(c) Write a Pascal procedure to produce an (n, m) nim game tree.
(d) Write a Pascal procedure to compute the mini-max tree for an (n, m) nim game, with your tree of (c) as input. Do you have to construct an entire tree, or will an additional field in the `Item` field of the game tree nodes do?

24. Using your procedures from Exercise 23, write an interactive Pascal program to play an (n, m) nim game. There are several variations:
(a) Computer chooses n and m, human player goes first.
(b) Human player chooses n and m, computer goes first.
(c) Computer chooses n and m, and goes first.
(d) Human player chooses n and m, and goes first.

In any case, after each move, the current status of both piles should be printed for the user's knowledge, plus some prompt as to how to enter the next move.

25. In exercises 6 through 8, we looked at a data base organized as a forest of binary trees. To unify the data into one tree, we could add a new root node, with pointers to each of the roots in the forest.
(a) Add such a root node to your forest of course offerings in the educational data base.
(b) Redraw the general tree of (a) as a binary tree.
(c) Would this representation be good in a data base such as this one, where the number of course offerings might vary from semester to semester?
(d) Suppose a course was canceled. Would deletion from the data base be easier in this schema or in the schema of exercise 6?

26. Write the operations of Section 7.6 using an array implementation instead of pointer variables, along the lines of the array implementation of linked lists in Section 6.8.

27. Extend the program of Section 7.8 to perform other simplifications of expression trees, using identities such as the following:
(a) $A + 0 = 0 + A = A$.
(b) $A * 1 = 1 * A = A$.
(c) $A * 0 = 0 * A = 0$.
(d) $A - A = 0$.

28. Suppose you are working with a microcomputer without a built-in multiply instruction, so that multiplication (using a procedure call) is much more expensive than addition. Modify the program of Section 7.8 so that it recognizes multiplication of any expression by 2, and replaces it with the computation of a temporary variable (unless the expression is a leaf) followed by the addition of the temporary variable to itself.

29. Suppose you have an expression tree in which each operand is either the variable X or a constant, and the operators are just addition and multiplication. Write a procedure that produces another tree that represents the derivative of the first. (Hint: Use recursion, with the non-recursive exits being cases you can handle, such as the derivative of a variable or a constant, or the derivative of a sum or product. The result will have a great many expressions such as $X + 0$ and $X * 1$, so you will want to use the program from Exercise 27 to simplify it.)

30. Describe the action required when a program to evaluate an expression in postfix form encounters a unary minus sign.

31. Extend the threaded tree algorithms of Section 7.9 to include deletion from a threaded tree, and left threads.

SUGGESTIONS FOR FURTHER STUDY

Many undergraduate data base texts use the same data set repeatedly to demonstrate various principles. An educational data base, organized as a forest of students, can be found in Vasta (1985). Ullman (1982) uses the inventory of a health food store, and Date (1981) considers an international hardware firm. Any of these could be used as a framework for programming a rudimentary, tree-structured DBMS. Both are standard texts that go far beyond than the rudiments.

Tree selection is discussed in Knuth Vol. 3 (1973b). He presents, in addition to various sorting methods based on tree selection, an interesting historical and mathematical account of lawn tennis tournaments. In 1883, Lewis Carroll first became interested in the perceived unfairness of second and third prize awards.

Chess continues to be of interest to the theoretical computer science community, with Kenneth Thompson of AT&T Bell Telephone Laboratories recently devising a program to analyze certain complex end games. Gleick (1986) reports that these new results refute some of the common knowledge of chess grandmasters, and could permanently alter the playing of the game in those (admittedly unusual) situations. The algorithm is based on backtracking, similar to that used in the Eight Queens problem in Chapter 5.

As usual, there are outstanding tutorials in *Computing Surveys* that survey both foundations and recent areas of application. Moret (1982) discusses decision tables, based on the definitions and implementations of Metz and Barnes (1977). Applications include data bases, pattern recognition, taxonomy recognition and identification, machine diagnosis, switching theory, analysis of algorithms, and independent models of discrete (particularly boolean) functions.

The *quadtree,* one having up to four children for each internal node, is considered in an article by Samet (1984). It is particularly useful in graphics and image processing, where square regions are partitioned into finer and finer quadrants, with an increased depth of recursive partitioning resulting in better resolution (granularity) of the image. This article, as are most in *Computing Surveys,* is quite accessible to the diligent student.

CHAPTER 8

SORTING

8.1 INTRODUCTION

Sorting is a process by which a collection of items is placed into ascending or descending order on one of the fields in the items; this field is called the *key*.

Sometimes the items are records, in the usual Pascal sense, with one of the fields being the key. Other times, especially for studying sorting algorithms, each item is just an integer, with the collection being an array. In this case we can say that the task of sorting is to produce a permutation of the array elements that places them in ascending order. Allowing for the possibility of duplicates, we can make the statement broader by saying *non-descending* order instead of ascending order.

As an example of sorting records, we might have an accounts-receivable application, in which data is kept about payments due from customers. If the records are arranged so that the first record has the smallest customer number, the second record has the next-to-smallest customer number, and so forth, then the group of records is said to be sorted into ascending order on customer number, which is the key in this illustration. The customer ''number'' might, in fact, have character data. With an appropriate comparison routine, the sorting problem is unchanged.

Sorting is also done to facilitate some other operation, especially searching. Finding a specified item in a table is usually much faster if the items are sorted, because we can then use a method that takes $O(\lg N)$ time instead of $O(N)$. This issue will be explored in the next chapter.

Because of its fundamental importance, sorting has been studied intensively since the beginning of modern computing, starting in the early 1950s. Many methods have been devised. We shall study six in this chapter, exploring the advantages and disadvantages of each. This is necessary because there is no one "best" method. The method that is best in a given circumstance depends on factors such as these:

1. The number of items and, in particular, whether all of them can fit in the primary storage of the computer. If they can, we can use *internal* sorting. If not, we turn to *external* methods, in which the records are maintained on a secondary storage medium such as tape or disk. In this book we will discuss only internal methods.

2. The number of characters in an item in relation to the number of characters in its key. A personnel file, for example, might contain many hundreds of characters of information about salary history, dependents, insurance, and so forth, but have a 10-digit employee number as the key. Some sorting methods require much more movement of the items than others; such a method would be a poor choice in this case.

3. Average versus best-case performance. Some sorting methods have dramatically better performance in the best case—such as input that is already sorted—than for the average. Others take little or no advantage of such cases. Is such a best case likely enough so that a sorting method should be chosen with this factor in mind?

4. Average versus worst-case performance. Some sorting methods have superior performance in the average case, but are dramatically slower in their worst case. How likely is the worst case, and how serious is its degraded performance?

5. A requirement that the sort be *stable,* meaning that items with equal keys are required to remain in the same relative order after the sort as before.

The sorting methods we shall study in this chapter may be categorized by the average time they require as a function of the number of items, N.

1. $O(N^2)$, or quadratic: selection sort, insertion sort.
2. Not completely analyzed but about $O(N^{1.2})$: Shell sort.
3. $O(N \lg N)$: Quicksort and heapsort.
4. $O(N)$: bucket sort, one name for a highly special case of a method called radix sort. (There are heavy restrictions on the use of this method, which is presented mostly for comparison.)

Several other sorting methods are reviewed in the chapter exercises. One that is commonly taught, bubble sort, is left to an exercise because it is slower than any of the others.

8.2 A NOTE ON TERMINOLOGY

In this chapter we shall generally speak of sorting a *table of items,* but because the algorithms are demonstrated with Pascal procedures that sort an *array of elements,* that terminology is also used. In some places, the term *file of records* is used, following standard presentations. (These last terms had been in use long before they were given specialized meanings in Pascal.) Fortunately, the variation in terminology is seldom a real problem because the meaning is generally obvious from the context. And, you may as well be prepared to see an even wider variation in terminology in studying the large body of literature on sorting.

8.3 SELECTION SORT

Selection sort is one of the simplest sorts to understand and implement. As with other quadratic methods, it is applicable only to small tables, meaning at most a few hundred items. It is sometimes an acceptable choice despite its inherent slowness, and it provides a basis for comparison when we consider other methods.

The approach is to select the item having the smallest[1] key and to interchange it with the item that was initially in the first position. This selected item is now in its correct final position and may be ignored in subsequent processing. Now we select—from only those remaining—the item having the smallest key, and interchange it with the item in the second position. This process is repeated for all positions up to the next-to-the-last, at which point the table is in ascending sequence or, as we say, has been sorted.

To see how this works with sample data, let us assume for the moment that the key is the entire item. The first line in the example that follows is the original unsorted table. In the subsequent lines, the items that have been placed in their correct sorted position at the end of that pass through the file are underlined.

```
Original table:    27   80   02   46   16   12   54

After pass 1:      02   80   27   46   16   12   54

After pass 2:      02   12   27   46   16   80   54

After pass 3:      02   12   16   46   27   80   54

After pass 4:      02   12   16   27   46   80   54

After pass 5:      02   12   16   27   46   80   54

After pass 6:      02   12   16   27   46   54   80
```

[1]We shall assume throughout that the file is to be sorted into ascending (non-descending) order (smallest first, largest last). Sorting into descending (non-ascending) order requires changing only the statements that compare keys.

A procedure that implements this method is almost a direct translation into Pascal of the English description in the preceding paragraph. Here are the main program declarations that are assumed:

```
const
   MaxN = 10000;   { or whatever }
type
   KeyType = integer;   { or whatever }

   Index = 0..MaxN;
   SortArray = array [Index] of KeyType;
var
   A: SortArray;
   N: Index;
```

(Index starts at zero for convenience in other methods.)

This is the selection sort procedure:

```
procedure SelectionSort (var A: SortArray;
                             N: Index);
var
   I, J, Small: Index;
begin
   for I := 1 to N - 1 do
   begin
      Small := I;
      for J := I + 1 to N do
         if A[J] < A[Small] then
            Small := J;
      Swap (A[I], A[Small])
   end
end;
```

The procedure Swap, which is used in a number of the methods, is as follows:

```
procedure Swap (var X, Y: KeyType);
var
   Temp: KeyType;
begin
   Temp := X;
   X := Y;
   Y := Temp
end;
```

The analysis of selection sort is simple. For a given size table, the number of comparisons is fixed. The inner loop is executed $N-1$ times on the first execution of the outer loop, $N-2$ times on the second execution of the outer loop, and so forth, until, on the last execution of the outer loop, it is executed once. The number of executions of the inner loop is therefore the sum of the integers from 1 to $N-1$, which is $N(N-1)/2$. The method is therefore of order $O(N^2)$, or quadratic, regardless of how many data items have to be moved.

The comparison in the inner loop is also carried out a fixed number of times, but the number of times the statement `Small := J` is executed depends on the data. If the file is already in sequence, it is not executed at all. Analysis that we shall not reproduce here shows the maximum to be $N^2/4$ and the average about $(N+1)(\ln N + .577) - 2N$. The average is much less than the maximum, so that there is not too much difference between the average and best-case performance of selection sort. This is good news as regards the average, but bad news about the best: it is still quadratic. Most other methods that have quadratic average performance have best-case performance that is much faster than quadratic.

The amount of data movement is completely fixed as this procedure is written: we exchange `A[I]` and `A[Small],` even when `Small = I`. We did this because it turns out that if all orderings of the keys in the input are equally likely, inserting this test would save far fewer than N swaps. On the average, therefore, testing for `I = Small` would take more time than it would save.

Selection sort is an *in-place* method, meaning that sorting is carried out by moving items within the original table. The only additional storage required is the trivial amount needed for swapping items.

Selection sort is so simple and quick to program that it is a reasonable choice for small tables. For large tables it is never the best choice.

To illustrate the differences in sorting methods, we shall run the program for each method on several tables of integers produced by Turbo Pascal's `Random` function, and executed on an IBM Personal Computer AT. The tables are of various sizes, to show the growth of running time as a function of N, and two are already in sequence, one ascending and one descending. The results for all the sorting methods we study are shown in the table in Section 8.13, to which reference should be made. (See page 310.)

We see that the growth of execution time for selection sort is definitely quadratic, to within a second or so. We also see that for larger tables it is so slow as to be of no value. Finally, we see experimental verification of the analysis of the number of executions of the assignment `Small := J.`

This program illustrates a phenomenon that occurs frequently: the running time of the program is almost completely dominated by one small inner loop.

8.4 INFORMAL PROGRAM VERIFICATION OF SELECTION SORT

In Chapter 1 we saw that a "good" computer program has many desirable characteristics: speed, portability, the ability to be modified and understood, and so forth. But the quality at the top of the list is *correctness*. Correctness may not be *sufficient*, for a correct program may be too slow to be useful. But it is assuredly *necessary*. No other combination of good qualities can redeem a program that does not do what the user expects it to do.

Much work has been done in recent years in *formal program verification,* in which the methods of mathematical logic are used to reason about program correctness. In its full-scale version, program verification is beyond the scope of this book, but informal methods can help us nevertheless.

For most programs from now on, we shall show a *loop invariant* for crucial loops, as a comment at the beginning of a loop and sometimes as a sketch. Following Dromey (1982), we define a loop invariant as a property (predicate) that captures the progressive computational role of the loop while, at the same time, remaining true before and after each execution of the loop body. Discovering a useful loop invariant can be a non-trivial task and is beyond the scope of this book. Here we shall simply display the invariant for a loop and use it as a means to improve our confidence that the loop is correct.[2]

Given a loop invariant, we take several steps to *verify* that the loop is correct.

1. Show that the invariant is true before the execution of the loop begins.

2. Show that the invariant remains true after each execution of the loop body.

3. Show that termination of the loop, combined with the truth of the invariant, means that the desired result has been achieved.

4. Prove that the loop terminates.

Consider the following loop, which sums the elements 1 through 10 of an array A:

```
Sum := A[1];
K := 1;

{ Invariant:  1 <= K <= 10 and Sum is the sum of A[1..K]  }
while K < 10 do begin
   K := K + 1;
   Sum := Sum + A[K]
end;
```

The $A[1..K]$ here is shorthand for "$A[1]$ through $A[K]$." The invariant thus expresses the fact that, at each stage of the execution of the loop, we have (at least) partially completed the task we set out to do.

Let us analyze the operation of this program in terms of its invariant assertion.

1. The invariant is true before the execution of the loop begins. At that point, Sum is equal to $A[1]$ and K is 1, so Sum is indeed the sum of $A[1..K]$.

2. After each execution of the loop body, the assertion is still true because K has been increased and one more element of A has been added to Sum.

3. When the `while` test fails, $K = 10$, so Sum is the sum of $A[1..10]$. This is the desired result.

4. The loop will terminate. K is initialized to a value less than 10 and is increased by 1 each time through the loop, so it will reach 10.

---

[2]The qualifier *useful* in the definition is important. The predicate $0 < 1$, for example, is true for any loop but it does not "capture the progressive computational role" of any loop.

We have thus proved, albeit in a quite informal way, that the program does what we want it to do.

The careful reader may have noticed a parallel between program verification and the mathematical method of proof by induction. This is no accident. Formal program verification is, in one way of viewing it, an elaboration in computer science terms of proof by induction.

Let us see how our informal method applies to selection sort. The study will be simpler if we replace the `for` loops with equivalent `while` loops.

```
procedure SelectionSort (var A: SortArray;
                              N: Index);
var
   I, J, Small: Index;
begin
   I := 1;

   { Invariant:  A[1..I-1] sorted and <= A[I..N] }
   while I <= N - 1 do
   begin
      Small := I;
      J := I + 1;

      { Invariant:  A[Small] <= A[I..J-1] }
      while J <= N do
      begin
         if A[J] < A[Small] then
             Small := J;
         J := J + 1
      end;

      Swap (A[I], A[Small]);

      I := I + 1
   end
end;
```

The invariant of the outer loop captures the way the sorting method works, by expanding the portion of the array that is both sorted and smaller than everything in the rest of the array. Applying our checklist, we have the following results:

1. The invariant is true before beginning the execution of the loop, with the understanding that when $I = 1$, the notation `A[1..I-1]` denotes an empty segment of the array. An empty segment is, trivially, sorted.

2. Does each execution of the loop body leave this invariant true? That depends on the inner loop and the `Swap`. We shall see that it does.

3. When the outer loop terminates, as this version of the program is written, $I = N$, so the invariant says that `A[1..N-1]` is sorted and less than or equal to `A[N]`. Therefore, the entire array is sorted.

4. The loop will terminate: `I` starts at 1 and is increased by 1 each time through the loop, so it will eventually reach `N`.

The invariant of the inner loop says that `A[Small]` is the smallest of all the elements examined so far, from `A[I]` to `A[J − 1]`. Checking this, we have the following information:

1. With `Small` initialized to `I` and `J` initialized to `I + 1`, the invariant is true before execution of the loop body. This is because `A[I]` is indeed the smallest of all the elements from `A[I]` to `A[I]`.

2. Each execution of the loop body leaves the invariant true because `Small` is assigned a new value, if necessary, to make it the index of the smallest element in the range of those examined. `J` is incremented in the process, so `A[I..J−1]` is still the correct designation for the range.

3. This loop terminates with `J = N + 1`, so `A[Small]` is the smallest of the elements in `A[I..N]`, according to the invariant, which is the purpose of this loop.

4. The loop will terminate because it counts from `I + 1` to `N`, and the largest value of `I` is `N − 1`.

A useful form in which to present a loop invariant is often a simple sketch, which can succinctly convey the effect of a loop. Here is the "graphical invariant" for the outer loop:

This picture makes it clear that the outer loop systematically expands the set of elements that are in their correct final positions.

Our presentation of program verification has been decidedly informal. We have not derived the invariants, which can require a fairly complex process in which logical inference goes from the preconditions that exist before the loop begins to the postconditions we wish to be true when it ends. Furthermore, we have omitted quite a number of details in invariants when they can safely be assumed, such as the fact that loop indices must fall within the range of the defined elements of the array.

Nevertheless, the use of loop invariants in this manner will add to our confidence that programs are correct. At this stage, we are using them essentially as supplemental documentation, but also as a new kind that can be extended—with further study not to be undertaken here—to mathematical reasoning about programs. You may safely assume that verification will be stressed in your future studies, so this chance to become familiar with the basics of the concept and the terminology should not be missed. We shall show loop invariants on most loops from now on.

8.5 SORTING COMPLETE RECORDS

Sorting methods are usually presented and explained as we shall do here, with the key being the entire record. ("Record" fits here, either in its historical sense or in the sense appropriated by Pascal.) This simplifies exposition and is occasionally what is needed in applications. However, the more common situation is for records to contain a great deal of information other than the key. All that is required to make our illustrative programs work in this more realistic case is to define the record, specify that the sort array consists of these records, and then carry out comparisons based only on the key portion. The Swap procedure is modified to exchange records, and the input and output operations are modified to deal with fields of the records.

To illustrate the technique we show a complete program, including procedures to handle reading data into some of the fields of the records to be sorted, and printing output. The key here is the employee name, which is defined to be a Pascal string type of 20 characters, stored in last-name-first format. Here is the program.

```
program SelectionSortOfRecords (input, output);

const
   MaxN = 100;

type
   Index = 0..MaxN;
   SortRecord = record
                   SocSecNum: string[11];
                   EmployeeName: string[20];
                   Address: array[1..4] of string[20];
                   ZIP: string[10];
                   Sex: char;
                   BirthDate: string[8];
                   HireDate: string[8];
                   PayRate: real;
                   Deductions: 0..15
                end;

   SortArray = array [1..MaxN] of SortRecord;


var
   A: SortArray;
   N: Index;


procedure GetData (var A: SortArray;
                   var N: Index);
var
   I: Index;
begin
   WriteLn ('The data as read:');
   WriteLn;
```

(Continued)

```
(Continued)
     I := 0;
     while not EOF do
     begin
         I := I + 1;

         ReadLn (A[I].EmployeeName, A[I].SocSecNum,
             A[I].BirthDate, A[I].PayRate);

         WriteLn (A[I].EmployeeName, A[I].SocSecNum:13,
             A[I].BirthDate:10, A[I].PayRate:6:2)
     end;

     N := I;

     WriteLn;
     WriteLn
end;


procedure Swap (var X, Y: SortRecord);
var
     Temp: SortRecord;
begin
     Temp := X;
     X := Y;
     Y := Temp
end;


procedure SelectionSortOfRecords (var A: SortArray;
                                      N: Index);
var
     I, J, Small: Index;
begin
     for I := 1 to N - 1 do
     begin
         Small := I;
         for J := I + 1 to N do
             if A[J].EmployeeName < A[Small].EmployeeName then
                 Small := J;
         Swap (A[I], A[Small])
     end
end;


procedure Print (var A: SortArray;
                 N: Index);
var
     I: Index;
begin
     WriteLn ('The sorted file:');
     WriteLn;

     for I := 1 to N do
         WriteLn (A[I].EmployeeName, A[I].SocSecNum:13,
             A[I].BirthDate:10, A[I].PayRate:6:2)
end;
```

```
begin
   GetData (A, N);
   SelectionSortOfRecords (A, N);
   Print (A, N)
end.
```

Here is the output when this program was run with a small set of sample data.

```
The data as read:

Smith,William        121-45-9876    56/02/23    4.50
Edwards,David        220-08-1990    52/03/29    6.00
Davids,Edward        382-09-9011    28/10/29    6.00
Kije,Lt.             000-00-0000    35/11/31    2.34
Winters,Rosamunde    203-66-3214    63/01/06    4.90
Smith,Arlene         733-81-4123    58/02/24    4.50
Greenberg,Morris     987-53-2844    44/06/22    7.25
Vermont,Maurice      987-53-2844    44/06/22    7.25
McHale,Susan         330-09-1243    43/09/30    7.50
Patel,Krishna        209-48-4312    68/11/22    4.92
Onegin,Eugene        091-92-4231    48/06/19    8.00


The sorted file:

Davids,Edward        382-09-9011    28/10/29    6.00
Edwards,David        220-08-1990    52/03/29    6.00
Greenberg,Morris     987-53-2844    44/06/22    7.25
Kije,Lt.             000-00-0000    35/11/31    2.34
McHale,Susan         330-09-1243    43/09/30    7.50
Onegin,Eugene        091-92-4231    48/06/19    8.00
Patel,Krishna        209-48-4312    68/11/22    4.92
Smith,Arlene         733-81-4123    58/02/24    4.50
Smith,William        121-45-9876    56/02/23    4.50
Vermont,Maurice      987-53-2844    44/06/22    7.25
Winters,Rosamunde    203-66-3214    63/01/06    4.90
```

It is important to understand that "the key" is not fixed for all time when the record type is defined. In fact, nothing in the record definition makes any reference to a key. We might wish to sort these same records on social security number for reporting withheld taxes or, perhaps, sort them into decreasing order of wage rate to simplify inspecting the file for possible fraudulent modification. The only change needed in this program would be in the fields specified in the key comparison, and a change from a less-than sign to a greater-than sign to get decreasing sequence.

In short, any field in a record can be used as a key. There is no restriction to numeric fields, no limitation on position within the record, and so forth. There is not even a requirement that sorting be done on a single field. For example, in an accounting application it might be useful to have a report presented in order of date, and within each date have the account information in account number order. This is readily done through a comparison routine in which date is considered as more significant than account number.

8.6 INSERTION SORT

Insertion sort is also quadratic method, but one that has advantages in certain circumstances. However, before looking into it, let us try to understand the limitations of selection sort.

Selection sort follows a rigid pattern, examining all remaining keys in every pass and taking no advantage of any existing order in the original file. An input file that is already in correct order will still take $N(N-1)/2$ comparisons. That is not good, because files that are already sorted are fairly common in some applications.

Insertion sort wastes no time in such a situation. It makes $N-1$ comparisons and no data movement, and is finished. And, even if a table is not already completely sorted, insertion sort takes advantage of whatever order it finds.

Let us see the method in operation with the sample data used before. This time, the numbers underlined are not necessarily in their correct, *final* positions; rather, all those underlined are in correct position *relative to each other*. This is why the 27 is underlined in the line for the original table. A table consisting of one item is sorted by definition.

```
Original table:   27   80   02   46   16   12   54

After pass 1:     27   80   02   46   16   12   54

After pass 2:     02   27   80   46   16   12   54

After pass 3:     02   27   46   80   16   12   54

After pass 4:     02   16   27   46   80   12   54

After pass 5:     02   12   16   27   46   80   54

After pass 6:     02   12   16   27   46   54   80
```

Note that, on the first pass, no item had to be moved. One comparison establishes that 80 is larger than 27, so the 27 and the 80 are in correct position relative to each other although neither is in its correct final position.

Here is the graphical loop invariant for the overall process.

Sorted	?
1	I N

The ? indicates that nothing is known about where these elements belong in the final sorted array. This is different from selection sort, where all elements in the upper part of the array were greater than or equal to the others. The position of the index I relates to the program implementation, which we may now see.

The procedure is as follows:

```
procedure InsertionSort (var A: SortArray;
                              N: Index);

var
   I, J: Index;
   Temp: KeyType;

begin
   A[0] := -MaxInt;     { sentinel }
   I := 2;

   { Invariant:  A[1..I-1] sorted and A[0] = -MaxInt }
   while I <= N do
   begin
      Temp := A[I];
      J := I;

      { Invariant:  Temp <= A[J..I] }
      while A[J - 1] > Temp do
      begin
         A[J] := A[J - 1];
         J := J - 1
      end;

      A[J] := Temp;

      I := I + 1
   end
end;
```

Iteration I of the outer loop inserts A[I] in its ordered position within A[1..I-1]. The insertion is done by placing element I in a temporary location, then comparing it with each of the preceding elements (from right to left) until finding one that is smaller. Each time that the answer is "no, this isn't the place yet," an element is moved to make space. Eventually, the element to be inserted will be larger, at which point the temporary element can be inserted.

And what if the key of the record is the smallest in the file? Then, the proper position to insert it is in the place occupied by the first record, which means that we need an element zero as a sentinel consisting of a larger negative number than is possible for a key.[3] Exercise 7 asks you to recode this procedure to work without a sentinel and to explore the performance tradeoffs involved.

Note that we do not bother to test for the case where an element is being "inserted" into its own record location because it is the largest of the elements

---

[3]This requires that the array sent to InsertionSort have space for the sentinel, which would not be acceptable in a general-purpose sorting routine. We strive here for simplicity of understanding, not for programs that could immediately be put into production.

from 1 to *I*. The test in the following modified statement,

```
if J <> I then
    A[J] := Temp;
```

would almost always be false, and making the test would take more time than would be saved in the few cases where the insertion could be skipped.

Analyzing insertion sort requires much more effort than for selection sort, and we shall not attempt it. The results are as follows.

1. In the *best* case, which is an already-sorted file, the performance is linear: $N-1$ comparisons and no moves.

2. The *average* case is quadratic in both the number of comparisons and the number of moves: about $N^2/4$ of each. This is half as many comparisons as selection sort but far more moves.

3. The *worst* case, in which a file is in reverse sequence, takes about $N^2/2$ comparisons and the same number of moves. This is the same number of comparisons as selection sort and a great many more moves.

Insertion sort's quadratic performance is a serious drawback for large files, but its best-case performance is the best possible and the method is stable. Whether insertion sort is faster or slower than selection sort depends on the details of how the compiler generates code.

If you refer to the table in Section 8.13, you will see that insertion sort takes longer than selection sort, but with a different compiler it might be faster. In the best case of already sorted input, for a table of 8000 elements, insertion sort is finished in six seconds. Only one pass is required and there is no data movement. In the worst case of input in reverse sequence, the method is terribly slow because of a great deal of data movement.

Perhaps you are now ready to believe that quadratic sorting methods should never be used for large tables (meaning more than a few dozen to a few hundred). This is the beginning of wisdom, but not the whole story. There is a critical qualifier on the average performance results. It is based on *randomly ordered* input, meaning that all permutations of the keys are equally likely. In such a table, with *N* distinct keys, the probability of encountering any particular sequence of keys is just $1/N!$, which, for large *N*, is exceedingly small. But in some applications, input that is *almost* in sequence occurs a great deal more often than this. Indeed, sometimes the input can be guaranteed to be almost in sequence because of the way it was generated.

To see how insertion sort responds to such input, consider the following modification of the table of 8000 integers. First, we confess that these integers were created with a special characteristic that is useful here—they are all in the range of 0 to 9999. Now suppose that before being sent to insertion sort they are sorted on just the first (leftmost) digit. Then, assuming that the numbers are evenly distributed over the range of 0 to 9999, as they are, we would expect to have about 800 in the range of 0 to 999, about 800 in the range of 1000 to 1999, and so forth.

Perhaps this will seem like a lot of order to you, or perhaps it will seem like not very much. We will not attempt to quantify the concept of partial ordering beyond the general remarks in the previous paragraph. Be that as it may, does this degree of ordering make much of a difference in the sorting time? Absolutely! With this input, the insertion sort program takes just 10 minutes, instead of nearly two hours. If we use the same file except but sort it on the first *two* digits, the program takes just over one minute. If the input is already in sequence on the first three digits, it takes just 11 seconds. Think about that. This last input could have a thousand sequences like 3608, 3604, 3607, 3600, 3603, 3602, 3606. Not sorted at all, *but close*. With this high degree of ordering, insertion sort is about as fast as any method can be.

If we have some way of knowing that the input is guaranteed to have a high degree of order, or perhaps even if that is only probable, insertion sort is very attractive, especially because it is also stable.

8.7 ADDRESS TABLE SORTING

When the sort key is much smaller than the item, which is often the case in applications, the time required for item movement in a method such as insertion sort can become a significant fraction of the total running time. There is a way out of this problem, which applies to any sorting method at all: don't move the items themselves, but move indices to the items.

Here are the parts of a program for insertion sort that have to be modified for this approach:

```pascal
program InsertionSortWithAddressTable (input, output);

const
    MaxN = 10000;   { or whatever }

type
    KeyType = integer;   { or whatever }
    Index = 0..MaxN;

    SortArray = array [Index] of KeyType;

    PermutationArray = array [Index] of Index;

var
    A: SortArray;
    P: PermutationArray;
    N: Index;


procedure PrintWithAddressTable (var A: SortArray;
                                 N: Index;
                                 P: PermutationArray);
var
    I: Index;
```

(Continued)

(Continued)
```
begin
   WriteLn ('The sorted file:');
   for I := 1 to N do
      WriteLn (A[P[I]])
end;


procedure InsertionSortWithAddressTable (var A: SortArray;
                                         N: Index;
                                         var P: PermutationArray);
var
   I, J: Index;
   TempIndex: Index;    { note change }
begin
   for I := 0 to N do
      P[I] := I;

   A[0] := -MaxInt;    { sentinel }
   I := 2;

 { Invariant:  A[P[1]..P[I-1]] sorted }
   while I <= N do
   begin
      TempIndex := P[I];
      J := I;

      { Invariant:  A[TempIndex] <= A[P[J]..P[I]] }
      while A[P[J - 1]] > A[TempIndex] do
      begin
         P[J] := P[J - 1];
         J := J - 1
      end;

      P[J] := TempIndex;

      I := I + 1
   end
end;
```

Our main new feature here is an array, here called a *permutation array,* that has the same number of elements as there are elements to be sorted, and which is initialized so that `P[I] = I`. `TempIndex` is now the index of an element to be inserted, where before `Temp` was itself the element. The test to determine whether the correct insertion point has been located still compares array elements, but uses array indices that are elements of the permutation array. The critical change is that when an element is to be moved, the permutation array is changed instead.

When the sorting is complete, the input array has not been changed at all. However, the permutation array gives the order in which the items should be accessed to get them in ascending sequence on their keys.

This sounds more complex than it really is. Here is what happens to the permutation array when the sample data is sorted by insertion, with the address table modification. Underlined indices refer to records that are in correct sequence relative to each other.

Original table:	27	80	02	46	16	12	54
Permutation array as initialized:	1	2	3	4	5	6	7
Permutation array after pass 1:	1	2	3	4	5	6	7
Permutation array after pass 2:	3	1	2	4	5	6	7
Permutation array after pass 3:	3	1	4	2	5	6	7
Permutation array after pass 4:	3	5	1	4	2	6	7
Permutation array after pass 5:	3	6	5	1	4	2	7
Permutation array after pass 6:	3	6	5	1	4	7	2

The final arrangement of the permutation means that if we get item 3, then 6, then 5, and so on, we will access the items in the ascending sequence of their keys, which is seen to be the case.

This modification adds overhead, of course. If the key is the entire item, then the program will run more slowly than the simpler version. This modification comes into its own when the key is only a small part of the complete item.

If the requirement is to produce a permutation of the input array, as in the general statement of the task of sorting, then there is an additional penalty in both space and time. A third array will have to be set up to hold the items temporarily as they are first picked up in ascending sequence from the input array, then moved back to it. In many applications this added step would not be necessary, however, because whatever processing comes next could simply pick up the items from the input array.

Address table sorting can be used with any of the sorting methods we study. It is an attractive possibility when the input file exists as a linked list. It places pointers in the permutation array instead of indices, which takes one pass through the linked list. After sorting, if the file is again required to be a linked list, a new one can be built by first picking up the records in the order specified in the permutation array, then discarding the original list. Details depend on the application and the purpose of the sorting.

8.8 SHELL SORT

A straightforward modification of insertion sort leads to a method that is much faster. It is called Shell sort after its developer, Donald L. Shell.[4]

[4]It is a personal pleasure to write about this method because Dr. Shell was my supervisor at the Aircraft Gas Turbine Division of the General Electric Company a few years before he did this work.

The reason insertion sort is relatively slow is that when it finds an item to be out of place, the item is moved by a laborious process of swapping immediate neighbors. Looking back at the sequence of operations with our sample data, for example, remember that the 80 had to be moved five times to get it into the correct final position.

Shell sort deals with this problem by first sorting subfiles, usually several times, in such a way that in the early passes items are moved long distances if needed, with far fewer swaps. The final pass is an ordinary insertion sort, but by then it is guaranteed that no item is very far from its correct position. The size of the subfiles is determined by an increment between items. These increments decrease on successive passes, so the method is more formally called a *decreasing increment sort*.

Let us follow the method with a slightly larger sample than before.

27   80   02   46   16   12   54   64   22   17   66   37   35

We start with an initial increment of five, which is essentially an arbitrary choice for illustrative purposes. This makes a subfile of the first, sixth, and eleventh elements (27, 12, and 66). Taking these three items in isolation, we sort them by any handy method—insertion sort is an obvious choice—leading to the following situation:

12   80   02   46   16   27   54   64   22   17   66   37   35

After switching the 12 and the 27, the subfile is in order.

Now we move on to the subfile consisting of 80, 54, and 37:

12   37   02   46   16   27   54   64   22   17   66   80   35

Note that, by sorting this small subfile, we have moved the 80 from item 2 to almost its final position. Now we attack the subfile consisting of 02, 64, and 35:

12   37   02   46   16   27   54   35   22   17   66   80   64

Next we start at 46 and form another subfile by taking every fifth element. But this time there are only two elements:

12   37   02   22   16   27   54   35   46   17   66   80   64

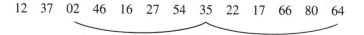

Finally, starting at 16 and taking every fifth item we have a subfile of two that is already in order:

12 37 02 22 16 27 54 35 46 17 66 80 64

This is the last sort of subfiles in the first phase. The file is assuredly not sorted at this point, but with modest effort we have made a giant stride in the right direction.

Now we will go through the same process, but this time use subfiles consisting of every second item—again an arbitrary choice for the increment. (But this increment does have to be smaller than the previous one.) The first subfile has seven items. After sorting them we have this situation:

02 37 12 22 16 27 46 35 54 17 64 80 66

Now we take every second item starting with element two. This gives a subfile of six items. After sorting them we have:

02 17 12 22 16 27 46 35 54 37 64 80 66

Most items are still not in their correct final positions, but no item is more than two positions away from where it belongs. One final pass with an increment of one, which is straight insertion sort, produces the sorted file:

02 12 16 17 22 27 35 37 46 54 64 66 80

Shell sort has not been completely analyzed at the time of writing. Doing so is a formidable challenge, because the performance depends on the sequence of the increments, and no one has ever been able to prove that any particular sequence is optimal. Some sequences are known for theoretical and/or empirical reasons to be better than others, but that is all that can be said for the present time.

However, simple sequences are known to work fairly well, and to give performance that is about $O(N^{1.2})$, which is a great deal better than quadratic. Such a sequence is suggested by Sedgewick (1983): . . . , 1093, 364, 121, 40, 13, 4, 1, which is generated by the following relation:

$$Inc_1 = 1$$
$$Inc_{i+1} = 3\,Inc_i + 1$$

In the procedure that follows we have a program that does all this, although in a different order. The increments are generated by applying the preceding formula until obtaining an increment that is greater than the size of the file. Then, at the beginning of each pass, the old increment is divided by three and the remainder discarded. This means that the first increment used is the largest one in this sequence that is smaller than the number of elements.

```
procedure ShellSort (var A: SortArray;
                         N: Index);

label 99;

var I, J: Index;
    Inc: integer;
    Temp: KeyType;

begin
   Inc := 1;
   repeat
      Inc := 3*Inc + 1
   until Inc > N;

   repeat
      Inc := Inc div 3;
      I := Inc + 1;

      while I <= N do
      begin
         Temp := A[I];
         J := I;

         while A[J - Inc] Temp do
         begin
            A[J] := A[J - Inc];
            J := J - Inc;
            if J <= Inc then goto 99
         end;

         99: A[J] := Temp;

         I := I + 1
      end

   until Inc = 1

end;
```

The difference in the order of operations, compared with the description at the beginning of the section, is that this program does not deal with all the items of a subfile together. Rather, it takes the *second* item of every subfile, places it in position, then moves on to the *third* element of every subfile and places it in position, and so forth. Stopping the search for the right place to insert a record offers a new challenge. If we used the sentinel method, we would need Inc of them for the largest value of Inc used. The solution used here is an ''escape'' from the loop using a `goto`. Readers unalterably opposed to all use of `goto` statements are free to rewrite the procedure. But such readers are requested to review their reasons for proscribing the use of *all* `gotos`, and decide whether the reasons really apply to a situation where the transfer is two lines forward.

We have not shown invariants in this program, for the strictly pragmatic reason that the notation gets very messy. Exercise 9 challenges you to devise an invariant, or to rewrite the procedure so that it is easier to provide one.

The table of comparisons in Section 8.13 shows that Shell sort is much faster than quadratic. Shell sort takes advantage of any existing order in the input, but it cannot do as well as straight insertion sort on a file that is almost or completely in sequence, because of its fixed sequence of decreasing increments. Can you explain why it does better on input that is in reverse sequence than it does on random input?

Additionally, and unfortunately, Shell sort is not stable. To see this, consider the keys 13, 12, 12 and suppose the first increment is 2. Then, on the first pass the 13 and the second 12 will be exchanged, and the relative order of the two 12s has been reversed.

8.9 THE DIVIDE–AND–CONQUER STRATEGY

Let us pause now for some brief mathematical preliminaries that will be helpful for the topic we will describe next, Quicksort.

When faced with a problem to solve, one approach is break it into two (or more) smaller problems and then deal with the parts separately. In many cases the total effort will be less, and sometimes much less. Our goal for this section is to quantify the amount of saving.

Let us denote by $C(N)$ the cost (effort, time) of solving a problem of size N, where N is the number of elements in an array to be searched, the number of nodes in a binary tree, or whatever else determines the size of the problem. Now suppose that by inspecting one element we can cut the size of the problem in half, remove one of the halves from further consideration, and then attack the remaining half by the same strategy. An example would be searching for a specified leaf node value in a full binary tree. In this case, you could think of $C(N)$ as being the number of comparisons required to locate the leaf.

A formula for the cost of solving the complete problem is

$$C(N) = C(N/2) + 1$$

The meaning of the formula is: "The cost of solving a problem of size N is the cost of solving a problem of size $N/2$, plus one operation to determine which half to deal with next."

This is an example of a *recurrence relation*: $C(N)$ is defined in terms of itself. Solving a recurrence relation means finding a formula on the righthand side that involves only N, not the function C. This can be a challenge, in general, but the two we need are not difficult.

Suppose $N = 2^n$. (If this is not the case, our formula will be slightly off, but in practice an approximation is all we seek anyway.) Then we can rewrite the recurrence relation as

$$C(2^n) = C(2^{n-1}) + 1$$

Now if we apply this formula n times to the righthand side, we get just n 1s, so

$$C(2^n) = n$$

But, if $N = 2^n$, then $n = \lg N$ and we have the desired result

$$C(N) = \lg N$$

This is the result we have already seen for the number of comparisons required to locate a node in a full binary tree. In the next chapter we shall see in the next chapter that it is the number of comparisons required in binary search.

Now consider a hypothetical sorting method in which the file is divided into two equal parts, then the same method is applied recursively to each part. (One of the attractions of Quicksort is that it comes fairly close to this, on the average.) Here, we must deal with both parts of the problem, rather than discarding one of them as we did before, and we must eventually inspect every element. So the recurrence relation is

$$C(N) = 2C(N/2) + N$$

Again writing $N = 2^n$, we have

$$C(2^n) = 2C(2^{n-1}) + 2^n$$

Now we introduce a small trick. Divide both sides by 2^n:

$$\frac{C(2^n)}{2_n} = \frac{C(2^{n-1})}{2^{n-1}} + 1$$

Applying this formula repeatedly to its righthand side again gives n, from which we have

$$C(2^n) = n2^n$$

But, because $2^n = N$ and $n = \lg N$ this becomes

$$C(N) = (\lg N)\, N$$

or, as it is usually written,

$$C(N) = N \lg N$$

The divide-and-conquer strategy thus leads to $O(N \lg N)$ performance. In many cases of interest this is not only far better than other alternatives, but is demonstrably the best possible.

We turn now to a sorting method that is built on this strategy, Quicksort. It is not possible to assure that at each stage the problem is divided into two subproblems of equal size. However, the method comes close enough to this that its average performance is $O(N \lg N)$, which can be proven to be the best possible for a method that involves comparison of keys.

8.10 QUICKSORT

The sorting method with the best average-case performance yet discovered was named Quicksort by its developer, C. A. R. Hoare. In one of its several variations, it is probably the most widely used method for internal sorting files of significant size.

Quicksort is a recursive method of sorting an array `A[1..N]`. The first step is to *partition* the array so that the following is true:

1. Some value P is in its final position in the array. In the notation and algorithm to follow, this will be `A[J]`.

2. All elements to the left of `A[J]` are less than or equal to it. These are called the *left subfile*.

3. All elements to the right of `A[J]` are greater than or equal to it, and they constitute the *right subfile*.

After partitioning, the picture looks like this:

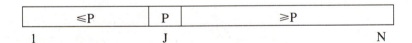

The original sorting problem has been reduced to the problem of sorting the two subfiles separately. The ideal case of equal size subfiles is not attainable, but the average performance is close enough to make the method extremely fast.

As a top-level pseudocode, the method is as follows:

```
procedure QuickSort (A, Left, Right);
if Right > Left then
begin
    Partition file, moving partitioning value P to position J
    QuickSort (A, Left, J-1);
    QuickSort (A, J+1, Right)
end;
```

To sort an array, we invoke a procedure based on this pseudocode with `QuickSort (A, 1, N)`.

Now let us return to partitioning, which is the heart of the method. There are many methods available, mostly intended to improve performance. We use one suggested by Sedgewick that is very fast, and which handles duplicate keys correctly and rapidly. A few of the many other possible variations and refinements are discussed after the presentation of the basic method. For simplicity's sake, our description assumes that all of the keys are distinct. However, the same algorithm will work for duplicate keys.

Given an array `A` of `N` elements to be sorted, we place in `A[N+1]` a sentinel that is as least as large as any element in the array. We choose the leftmost element, `A[1]`, as the partitioning element, and initialize two pointers so that `I` designates the leftmost element as `Left`, and so that `J` designates the sentinel element just to the right of the rightmost element, `Right`. When Quicksort is first invoked, we have this picture:

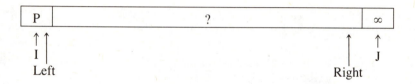

The ? in the middle of the picture means that we know nothing about these elements' relation to each other or to `P`; ∞ stands for the sentinel.

Now, we adjust the two pointers. A loop that increments `I` stops upon finding that `A[I] > P,` and a loop that decrements `J` stops when `A[J] < P`. This results in the following picture:

We now interchange `A[I]` and `A[J],` giving this picture:

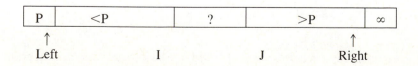

Now we go back and move the pointers again until A[I] > P and A[J] < P. Eventually the pointers must cross, with I = J + 1, at which point we want out of the loop. The picture is then as follows:

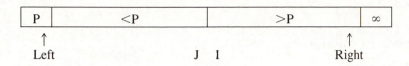

Where are we now? We know that A[Left+1..J] are less than P; the left-to-right movement of I assures us of that, remembering that J = I − 1. Likewise, we know that A[I..Right] are greater than P because of the position of the J pointer. We now exchange A[Left] and A[J], which completes the partitioning with A[J] the partitioning element. This is the resulting picture of those actions:

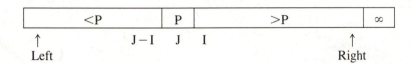

Quicksort can now be called recursively for the two partitions.

If there are equal keys the process still works, but in a slightly different manner. If some key equal to P is in its correct position, then the pointer scans could stop with I = J; after one more time through the loop, iteration stops with I = J + 2. At this point we know not only that A[Left+1..J] ≤ P and A[J+2..Right] ≥ P, but also that A[J+1] = P. Now, after the exchange of A[Left] and A[J], we have two elements in their final positions in the subfile, (A[J] and A[J+1]).

To sort an array, A, we invoke the following procedure with Quicksort (A, 1, N):

```
procedure QuickSort (var A: SortArray;
                     Left, Right: Index);
var
   I, J: Index;
   P: KeyType;
   Finished: boolean;
```
(Continued)

(Continued)

```
   begin
      if Right > Left then
         begin
            I := Left;
            J := Right + 1;     { gets sentinel when Right = N }
            P := A[Left];
            Finished := false;

            { Invariant:  A[Left+1..I] <= P  and  A[J..Right] >= P }
            while not Finished do
            begin
               repeat
                  I := I + 1
               until A[I] >= P;

               repeat
                  J := J - 1
               until A[J] <= P;

               if J < I then
                  Finished := true
               else
                  Swap (A[I], A[J])
            end;

            Swap (A[Left], A[J]);

            QuickSort (A, Left, J - 1);
            QuickSort (A, I, Right)
         end
end;
```

The following diagram shows the first partitioning step for an array consisting of the keys shown on the first line. Elements marked by arrows are those pointed to by I and J, and each line is the result of a pointer increment or an exchange.

```
19   80   02   46   16   12   54   64   22   17   66   37   35
     80
     ->
                                                            35
                                                            <-
                                                       37
                                                       <-
                                                  66
                                                  <-
                                             17
                                             <-
19   17                                      80   66   37   35
          02
          ->
               46
               ->
```

```
                                        22
                                        <-
                                  64
                                  <-
                            54
                            <-
                      12
                      <-
19   17   02   12     46   54   64   22   80   66   37   35
                16
                ->
                      46
                      ->
                16
                <-
16   17   02   12   19   46   54   64   22   80   66   37   35
```

The next diagram shows the successive partitioning stages for this input. Each underlined partitioning element has been placed in its final position. The subfiles are shown as they appear after the partitioning.

```
19   80   02   46   16   12   54   64   22   17   66   37   35

16   17   02   12   19   46   54   64   22   80   66   37   35

02   12   16   17

02

     12

          17

                    22   35   37   46   80   66   64   54

                    22   35   37

                         35

                              37

                                   54   66   64   80

                                   54

                                        64   66

                                        64
```

For a thorough understanding of the algorithm, we strongly recommend working through this example.

One of the drawbacks of Quicksort is that its worst case is a file that is either correctly sorted or that is in descending sequence. Then, every partitioning step produces one subfile of length zero, and requires as many comparisons as the length of the subfile to do it. The method thus degenerates to a selection sort which, of course, is $O(N^2)$. Furthermore, in such a situation, the implicit stack required for recursion grows to a depth of N, wasting storage, and this limits the size of the file that can be sorted. Because a completely sorted input file is fairly likely in practice, this is an unacceptable situation.

The table in Section 8.13 demonstrates all of this. For random input Quicksort is very fast indeed, but our Turbo Pascal program crashed because it ran out of space for the runtime stack needed for the extreme depth of recursion. The largest already-sequenced input that this program could handle was only about 2500 elements. Naturally, with a different compiler or computer, this particular problem could be sidestepped, but the point is still valid: the size of the runtime stack can limit the size of the input that we can process.[5]

Separate runs, not summarized in the table, demonstrated that Quicksort degenerates to quadratic performance on input that is in either ascending or descending sequence.

Many of the variations of Quicksort are designed to make it handle special cases gracefully, meaning that its performance does not degrade seriously from the $O(N \lg N)$ average behavior.

One such special case for some implementations is a subfile of equal (duplicated) elements. Depending on the details of pointer movement and exchanges, the algorithm can again degenerate to $O(N^2)$, because the subfile is reduced to two partitions of highly unequal size—zero and one less than the number of elements. Achieving this unhappily pessimal (worst possible) partition takes one less exchange than the number of elements in a partition. Sedgewick's implementation does much better. In such a case, each pointer moves one position, after which there would be a "useless" exchange of equal keys. "Useless" is placed in quotes because of what is gained: after $N/2$ iterations of the partitioning loop, the subfile has been divided exactly in half, which we have already seen is optimal.

The best solution to the depth-of-recursion problem seems to be not to invoke Quicksort recursively at all unless the subfile is larger than some threshold, such as a dozen elements. Cranking up the mechanism of Quicksort is hardly efficient when there are simpler methods to sort short files quickly. Even better, according to careful studies[6], is just not to sort the small subfiles at all, then follow Quicksort with an insertion sort. Since no element will be very far from its correct position, this last step will go very quickly.

---

[5]There are algorithmic approaches to this problem, which lead to an assured maximum depth of recursion that is $O(lg N)$. See the references on sorting at the end of the chapter.

[6]See Robert Sedgewick, *Quicksort*, Ph. D. thesis, Stanford University. Stanford Computer Science Report STAN-CS-75-492, May 1975.

There is also a simple solution to the problem of poor performance with sorted input. Instead of using the first element of the array as the partitioning element, generate a random number, *r,* where *r* is in the range of 1 to the number of elements in the partition. Now, although the worst case is still $O(N^2)$, it is extremely unlikely that we will encounter it. (The probability of encountering this worst case is $1/N!$, where N is the number of elements in the file. For tables of realistic size, meaning at least hundreds, this number is negligible.)

A better method, which does not require a random number generator, is called the *median-of-three* method. Here, we choose the median of the Left element, the Right element, and the one halfway between them. Unless this median is already the Left element, we exchange it with Left. Perhaps needless to say, the median-of-three method must be used in conjunction with provision for a minimum-size partition, to assure that there are at least three elements of which to find the median.

We put these improvements together in the following program. It is somewhat faster, in the average case, than the previous version because it handles small subfiles with the final insertion sort. For the special cases of many equal keys and of files in sequence, the median-of-three modification makes it run much faster than the average.

```
procedure QuickSortWithMinPartition (var A: SortArray;
                                     Left, Right: Index);
var
    I, J: Index;
    P: KeyType;
    Finished: boolean;
begin
    if Right-Left + 1 >= MinPartition then begin
        I := Left;
        J := Right + 1;            { gets sentinel when Right = N }

        { Get median of 3 for partitioning element }
        Swap (A[(Left+Right) div 2], A[Left+1]);

        if A[Left+1] > A[Right] then
            Swap (A[Left+1], A[Right]);

        if A[Left] > A[Right] then
            Swap (A[Left], A[Right]);

        if A[Left+1] > A[Left] then
            Swap (A[Left+1], A[Left]);

        P := A[Left];

        Finished := false;
        { Invariant:  A[Left+1..I] <= P  and  A[J..Right] >= P }
```

(Continued)

(Continued)

```
      while not Finished do begin
         repeat
            I := I + 1
         until A[I] >= P;

         repeat
            J := J - 1
         until A[J] <= P;

         if J < I then
            Finished := true
         else
            Swap (A[I], A[J])
      end;

      Swap (A[Left], A[J]);

      QuickSortWithMinPartition (A, Left, J - 1);
      QuickSortWithMinPartition (A, I, Right)
   end
end;
```

A program designated `Quicker` in the table of Section 8.13 uses a minimum partition of 12 elements, and follows the partial sorting by this procedure with a straight insertion sort. We see that it is around ten percent faster for random input than the earlier version. For already sorted input the program rapidly determines that nothing is required. For input in reverse sequence, however, a great deal of data movement results, with poor performance.

It turns out, perhaps surprisingly, that the speed is not sensitive to the choice of minimum partition size. On randomly-sequenced input, values between about 6 and 20 give roughly the same total time for the speeded-up Quicksort followed by insertion sort.

The final problem we shall consider is that Quicksort is not stable. A rather simple solution is to attach to each record its sequence number in the original file. This number is made a part of the key in such a way that it is the least significant part. This keeps records with the same keys in the same relative sequence as they have in the input. The sequence numbers must, of course, be stripped off at the end, if they were actually placed in the records. This technique can be applied to any unstable sorting method, which is one reason we devote little attention to stability.

In summary, Quicksort is the fastest general-purpose method known, and is eminently suitable for sorting large internal files. If the records are large in relation to the keys, the address table modification can be used. The method is not stable, but a simple modification can achieve stability if needed. The worst-case behavior is unacceptable, but it can be made negligibly unlikely.

No sorting method that depends on comparison of keys can be faster than $O(N \lg N)$, and since the inner loops of Quicksort are about as fast as one can imagine, it is unlikely that anything significantly faster will be developed. Much can be done in the way of fine tuning, however.

8.11 HEAPSORT

Heapsort is an $O(N \lg N)$ method that is not as fast as Quicksort, on the average, but which has a worst-case performance that is not much slower than its average performance. It is an in-place method without recursion, so it requires no extra storage. These characteristics make it an interesting sorting method in its own right. A heap is also the natural implementation of a priority queue, noted in Exercise 24 of Chapter 4.

A *heap* is both a special kind of binary tree and a special way of representing it, without links.[7] To describe a heap, let us introduce the idea of an *almost full binary tree,* which is the same as a full binary tree if the number of nodes is of the the form $2^n - 1$. Otherwise, all the leaves are on two levels, with all the leaves on the bottom level as far to the left as possible. Such a tree has the following characteristic shape:

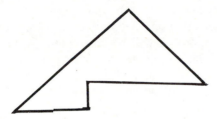

Then a heap is defined to be an almost full binary tree in which the value in each node is greater than, or equal to, the values of both of its children, if any. Clearly, the largest value in such a tree must be in the root. Here, for example, is the heap that will result from the first part of the heapsort algorithm with the sample data we shall use:

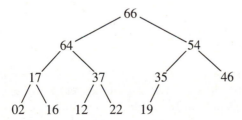

Observe that there is no assured ordering between the left and right children of a node. Note too, that a node may have zero, one, or two children but, if there is only one, it must be the left child.

Part of the reason for imposing these restrictions on the placement of nodes is that we may now store the binary tree in an array, without links to children or wasted space.[8] To see how this is possible, suppose the nodes of the preceding

---

[7]Unfortunately, the word heap is also used in computer science in an entirely unrelated way to mean the part of storage available for dynamic allocation with pointer variables, as distinguished from the part allocated on the runtime stack.

[8]*Any* binary tree can be stored in an array, actually, but in the general case there will be much wasted storage.

tree are numbered starting with 1 for the root, then continuing in a left-to-right scan of each successive lower level. Now imagine that the numbers of the nodes are array indices, as follows:

I:	1	2	3	4	5	6	7	8	9	10	11	12
A[I]:	66	64	54	17	37	35	46	02	16	12	22	19

Now for the key fact. The children of node *I* are to be found in node *2I* and node *2I* + 1. The relationship between a node and its (zero, one, or two) children is now implicit in the array locations assigned to the nodes.

Heapsort is a two-stage process. In the first, we make a heap of the elements of the array to be sorted, and in the second we convert the heap into a sorted array. The procedures to carry out the steps are called `SiftUp` and `SiftDown,` for reasons that will become apparent shortly. In discussing these operations and our assertions, it will be convenient to have a shorthand way to state which elements of the array constitute a heap or are sorted. "Heap(1, K)" will be an assertion that "the elements from 1 to K satisfy the heap condition." Likewise, "Sorted(1, K)" will be an assertion that the first K elements of the array are sorted.

Let us now see how `SiftUp` works, in terms of the following initial array values: 19 02 46 16 12 54 64 22 17 66 37 35. We will first show how we build the heap, in graphical form. However, bear in mind that all data storage is in an array, as we shall show in discussing the program.

A single element automatically has the heap property, so we begin with the following picture:

19

This is element 1, the root of the tree (heap). It will not be the root of the complete heap, because it is not the largest element in the array. But at this stage of the heap building it is the only node in the tree, so of course it is the root.

Now we pick up the second element. Think of elements 1 and 2 as an almost full binary tree represented implicitly, giving this picture:

We ask: "Is this a heap?" Well, yes it is. The value in every node is larger than or equal to its children. Nothing else needs be done at this stage.

Now we "pick up" the third element, the 46, and think of that and the other three elements as a tree. ("Picking up" the element only means incrementing an index, because the element is in array location three.) The picture now looks like this:

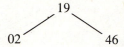

Is this a heap? Well, no: 19 is not larger than 46. But restoring the heap property requires, in this case, only exchanging the larger child with its parent, as follows:

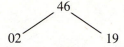

The 46 has "sifted up" to its proper level.
    Next the 16 is added.

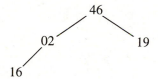

This is not a heap because 16 is greater than 02, so we exchange 16 with its parent.

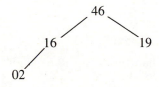

This tree satisfies the heap property.
    Then, we add the 12.

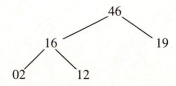

This is a heap.

Now we condense the presentation, showing just the heap that results from adding each new item, with arrows to indicate the exchanges that were necessary to reestablish the heap property.

We add the 54.

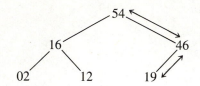

Next comes the 64.

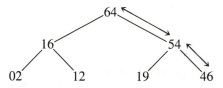

Next, we add the 22.

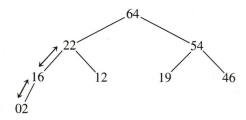

In this case, the new element had to sift up two levels, which was not all the way to the root.

Now the 17 is added.

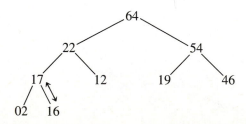

The 66 must sift up to the root, and does so in three steps.

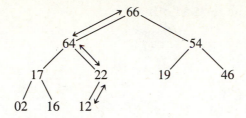

The 37 goes up only one level.

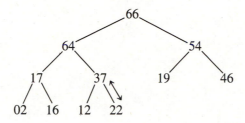

Finally, sifting the 35 up one level gives us our final heap.

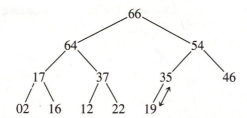

If our 12 numbers are presented in the order shown, then the heap building process must lead to the heap we have obtained. But with the same numbers in other sequences, other heaps could result. There are many almost full binary trees formed from these 12 numbers, in which each node is greater than either of its children. (The process is easier to study if there are no duplicated keys, but everything works routinely when there are.)

How long does it take to build a heap of N elements? We have seen that when we add a new node, it may stay where it is, or move all the way to the root, or settle anywhere in between. Moving it all the way to the root is the worst case, which takes lg N steps, so for N items the effort is $O(N \lg N)$.

Recalling that all data storage for the array being sorted is in the array itself, we get the following graphical loop invariant for the heap-building stage:

Heap	?
1 I	N

Here is a procedure for `SiftUp`.

```
procedure SiftUp (var A: SortArray;
                  K: Index);

var
   P: Index;    { parent node }
   C: Index;    { child node }
begin
   C := K;
   P := C div 2;

   { Invariant:  Heap(1, K) except perhaps, at start, between
     C and its parent. }
   while (A[P] < A[C]) and (C > 1) do
   begin
      Swap (A[P], A[C]);
      C := P;
      if C > 1 then
         P := C div 2;
   end
end;
```

To help you study the program, the following display shows the array as it develops into a heap. The assertion on the first line simply means that element 1, considered by itself, is a heap. The assertions on the remaining lines apply to the array *after* adding one more node to the heap and sifting it up as necessary. The jagged diagonal line traces the growth of the heap.

Element:	1	2	3	4	5	6	7	8	9	10	11	12
Heap(1, 1):	19	02	46	16	12	54	64	22	17	66	37	35
Heap(1, 2):	19	02	46	16	12	54	64	22	17	66	37	35
Heap(1, 3):	46	02	19	16	12	54	64	22	17	66	37	35
Heap(1, 4):	46	16	19	02	12	54	64	22	17	66	37	35
Heap(1, 5):	46	16	19	02	12	54	64	22	17	66	37	35
Heap(1, 6):	54	16	46	02	12	19	64	22	17	66	37	35
Heap(1, 7):	64	16	54	02	12	19	46	22	17	66	37	35
Heap(1, 8):	64	22	54	16	12	19	46	02	17	66	37	35
Heap(1, 9):	64	22	54	17	12	19	46	02	16	66	37	35
Heap(1, 10):	66	64	54	17	22	19	46	02	16	12	37	35
Heap(1, 11):	66	64	54	17	37	19	46	02	16	12	22	35
Heap(1, 12):	66	64	54	17	37	35	46	02	16	12	22	19

Now that we have a heap, we can proceed with the second half of the sorting process, which may be summarized as follows. Exchange the root (element 1) with the last element in the heap portion of the array. Because the root is always the largest node value in a heap, after the exchange that element is in its correct final position in the sorted array. At that point, remove it from further consideration. The heap is now one element smaller, except that it isn't a heap anymore because the exchange broke the heap property. But fixing up the heap is simple: one needs only to exchange the root node with its larger child repeatedly, "sifting it down" the tree until it is larger than either of its children. We now have a heap again, and the process repeats. The graphical invariant is as follows:

Heap	Sorted

1   I   N

All elements in the heap portion are less than or equal to the elements in the sorted portion.

This process can also be demonstrated graphically. We start with the heap.

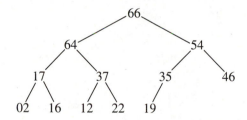

The root is exchanged with the rightmost leaf on the bottom level. This puts the 66 in its correct final position, so we drop it from further consideration as we work with the elements that are still part of the heap.

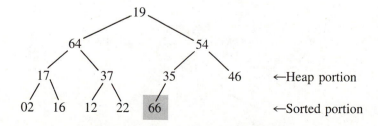

←Heap portion

←Sorted portion

This is not a heap. We begin to fix it by exchanging the root with its larger child.

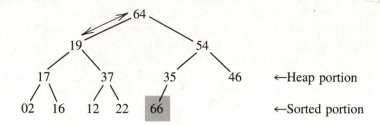

The 19 is still not right. Again we exchange it with its larger child.

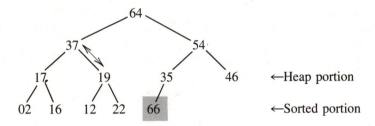

We exchange once more.

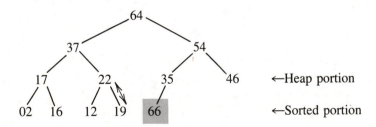

This is now a heap.

Now we exchange the root with the last leaf of the heap portion, which puts the 64 in its final position.

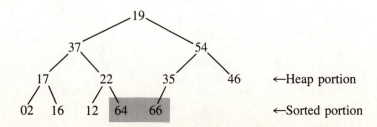

Next, we exchange the root with its larger child.

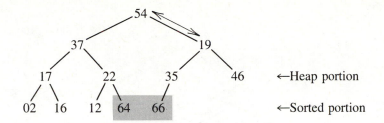

We're not finished yet. We shall have to exchange the 19 with its larger child.

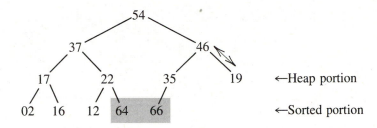

The last element in the heap portion is now the 12. Exchanging it with the root, we arrive at the following situation:

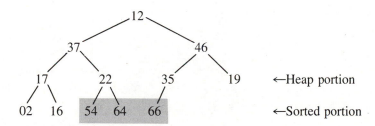

Let us now speed the explanation by showing just the successive reestablished heaps, omitting the diagrams of the intermediate trees while sifting the root down to its correct position. The results are as follows:

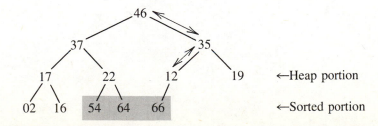

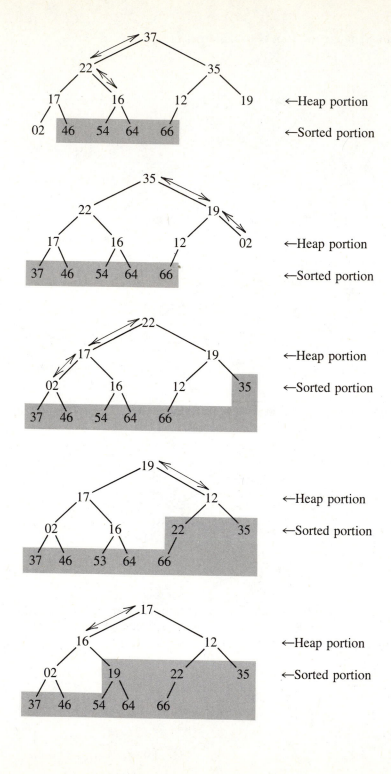

←Heap portion

←Sorted portion

←Heap portion

←Sorted portion

←Heap portion

←Sorted portion

←Heap portion

←Sorted portion

←Heap portion

←Sorted portion

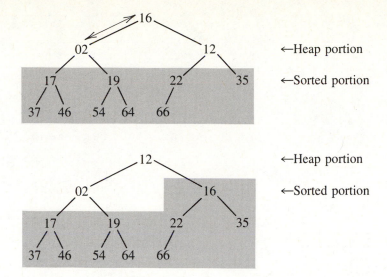

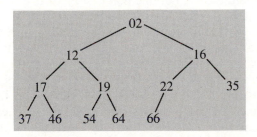

No exchanges were needed in this last, because the 12 was larger than its larger child, which was its only child.

Finally, we exchange the rightmost leaf of the heap portion with the root, reduce the size of the heap by one, and have the following structure:

←Sorted

All of the elements of the array are now in their correct sorted positions.

The `SiftDown` procedure is as follows:

```
procedure SiftDown (var A: SortArray;
                    K: Index);

label 99;
var
    P: Index;    { parent node }
    C: Index;    { child node }
```

(Continued)

(Continued)

```
begin
   P := 1;

   { Invariant: Heap(1, K) except perhaps, at start, between
     P and its children, of which there may be 0, 1 or 2. }
   while true do
   begin
      if 2 * P > K then
         goto 99                        { P has no children--heap OK }
      else
         C := 2 * P;

      if C + 1 <= K then                { does right child exist? }
         if A[C + 1] > A[C] then
            C := C + 1;                  { C is the larger child }

      if A[P] > A[C] then goto 99;      { heap OK }

      Swap (A[P], A[C]);

      P := C
   end;

99:   { null statement for exit }
end;
```

The loop invariant is that elements 1 through K form a heap, except that node P may be out of place with its child(ren) (the value of this element changes during the execution of the loop).

We have a slightly unusual feature here, but one that is sometimes the clearest way to express the purpose. We have what appears to be an infinite loop. It is *not* infinite, of course, because we terminate it either upon finding that the root node has been sifted down to a leaf, or when it has been sifted down to where it is larger than its child(ren). You might ask why we do the multiplication 2 * P twice, instead of just writing C := 2 * P? We do this because if the child does not exist, this would lead to an array index out of the range of the array, resulting in a runtime error in a system that does range checking.[9] Note that, in comparing a parent with its larger child, we must be sure that the right child exists.

Here is the progression of the array as this procedure executes, starting with the heap that was created by SiftUp. The assertions at the left of each line, after the first, are for the array *after* the execution of SiftDown.

---

[9]This would not happen if the maximum array size specified in the program declaratives is at least twice as large as the actual array size. The program could then work just fine on small sample data, and blow up with larger files. The astute reader will perhaps be able to guess how this fact was established.

Element:	1	2	3	4	5	6	7	8	9	10	11	12
Heap(1, 12):	66	64	54	17	37	35	46	02	16	12	22	19
Heap(1, 11), Sorted(12, 12)	64	37	54	17	22	35	46	02	16	12	19	66
Heap(1, 10), Sorted(11, 12)	54	37	46	17	22	35	19	02	16	12	64	66
Heap(1, 9), Sorted(10, 12)	46	37	35	17	22	12	19	02	16	54	64	66
Heap(1, 8), Sorted(9, 12)	37	22	35	17	16	12	19	02	46	54	64	66
Heap(1, 7), Sorted(8, 12)	35	22	19	17	16	12	02	37	46	54	64	66
Heap(1, 6), Sorted(7, 12)	22	17	19	02	16	12	35	37	46	54	64	66
Heap(1, 5), Sorted(6, 12)	19	17	12	02	16	22	35	37	46	54	64	66
Heap(1, 4), Sorted(5, 12)	17	16	12	02	19	22	35	37	46	54	64	66
Heap(1, 3), Sorted(4, 12)	16	02	12	17	19	22	35	37	46	54	64	66
Heap(1, 2), Sorted(3, 12)	12	02	16	17	19	22	35	37	46	54	64	66
Heap(1, 1), Sorted(2, 12)	02	12	16	17	19	22	35	37	46	54	64	66

Now we are finished.

The entire process can be neatly summarized in the following picture, as suggested by Bentley (1985).

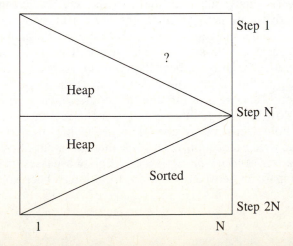

Imagine that the array is drawn horizontally, as usual, and that time moves from the top of the picture to the bottom.

The complete heapsort process would be invoked by the following procedure:

```
procedure HeapSort (var A: SortArray;
                         N: Index);
var
   I: Index;
begin

   { Invariant:  Heap(1, I-1) }
   for I := 2 to N do
      SiftUp (A, I);

   { Inv: Heap(1, I) and Sorted(I+1, N) and A[1..I] <= A[I+1..N] }
   for I := N downto 2 do
   begin
      Swap(A[1], A[I]);
      SiftDown (A, I - 1)
   end

end;
```

The table in Section 8.13 shows that heapsort is somewhat slower than Quicksort, but that its worst-case performance is not too much worse than for random input. This is because heapsort is *guaranteed* to run in $O(N \lg N)$ time, regardless of the order of the input, which may sometimes justify its use even though its average-case time is considerably slower than Quicksort.

8.12 BUCKET SORT

The last method we shall study applies only in restricted conditions, but when it can be used nothing is faster. The running time is linear in the number of records. How can that be, you might ask; didn't we say earlier that no sorting method could be faster than $O(N \lg N)$? The answer is that there was a crucial qualification on the earlier statement: *No method that depends on key comparisons* can be faster than $O(N \lg N)$. Bucket sort involves no comparison of keys whatever.

To see how the method works, let us take the most restrictive conditions: the keys are a dense (no gaps) subset of the integers, say in the range of 0 to 99, and there are no duplicate keys. That is, there are 100 records, and their keys are a permutation of the integers from 0 to 99. We set up another array of the same size as the array to be sorted, which we call a *bucket array*. We now *distribute* the input records to the buckets (elements) of this second array, each input record going to the bucket with index equal to the key of the record.

The distribution takes one pass through the input, which is obviously a linear-time operation. Now we also go through the bucket array once, in sequence from the first (which holds zero, the smallest key in the file) to the last (the key of which is 99). Each record is simply put back into the input array. This is also a linear-time operation. *And we are finished.* After two passes over the N items, with never a comparison between two keys, the file has been sorted.

Let us relax one of the restrictions before showing a procedure. If the keys are not a dense subset of the integers, we may still use the method if the range of possible values is not too much greater than the number of items to be sorted. We set up the bucket array to have space for every possible key value and somehow mark every item as empty, then distribute the items. Finally we go through the bucket array, picking up the non-empties. The method is still linear, but the proportionality constant is larger for the dual reasons that we have to initialize the bucket array and that the bucket array is larger than the file to be sorted.

Here is a procedure based on these assumptions. The value for the constant `Range` is based on the sample data we have been using.

```
procedure BucketSort (var A: SortArray;
                          N: integer);

{ Assert (not checked): elements are integers in the range
  of zero to Range, and there are no duplicates. }

const
   Range = 9999;

var
   Bucket: array [0..Range] of integer;
   I, J: integer;

begin
   { Mark all buckets as empty }
   for I := 1 to Range do
      Bucket[I] := -1;

   { Distribute records to buckets }
   for I := 1 to N do
      Bucket[A[I]] := A[I];

   { Pick up the non-empties }
   J := 0;
   for I := 1 to Range do
      if Bucket[I] > 0 then
      begin
         J := J + 1;
         A[J] := Bucket[I]
      end
end;
```

The table on the next page shows that this method is very fast indeed. (We must also confess that there are no duplicates in the data.) Its performance is hardly a function of table size, for a fixed size of the bucket array, because of the overhead involved in initializing the bucket array and picking up the items from it. Stated otherwise, this demonstrates that bucket sort works best when the keys are fairly close to a dense subset of the integers. With 100 integers and 10,000 buckets, we are rather far from that condition.

The restrictions are serious, of course. The method cannot be used with keys that are strings or real numbers, or even—as shown—with negative integers. However, sometimes the keys can be mapped into a subset of the positive integers so as to make the method usable. Likewise, the restriction of no duplicates can sometimes be handled with linked list techniques.

We demonstrate this method because it is useful occasionally, and, when it does work, it is blindingly fast. We also show it to make the point that the $O(N \lg N)$ barrier on sorting methods applies only when key comparisons are used.

Bucket sort is a limiting special case of a more general method called *digit sort* or *radix sort*. This method was the basis of sorting decks of punched cards long before the computer era. This is of historical interest, since punched card technology was one of the strands of development that led to modern computers. But since some students today may never have seen a punched card, we move on.

8.13 COMPARING THE METHODS

A table that shows the time required to sort data of various sizes and characteristics by each of the methods we have discussed follows. All data was generated by a program written in Turbo Pascal, using its `Random` function and rejecting duplicates.

Comparison of Sorting Times for Different Table Sizes

	Number of items							
	100	500	1000	2000	4000	8000	8000 sorted asc.	8000 sorted desc.
Selection	1	18	1:12	4:46	18:58	1:15:23	1:15:16	1:45:22
Insertion	1	23	1:33	6:21	25:15	1:41:15	6	3:20:34
Shell	1	3	8	19	42	1:40	40	59
Quick	<1	2	5	10	22	45	runtime crash	runtime crash
Quicker	<1	2	4	9	18	40	19	14:28
Heapsort	1	6	13	29	1:04	2:19	3:31	2:09
Bucket	3	3	3	3	5	6	6	6

These times are in seconds (x), or minutes and seconds (xx:xx), or hours and minutes and seconds (x:xx:xx) for running the programs in the text on an IBM Personal Computer AT. The details of time comparisons should be taken with a grain of salt; programs written in a different version of Pascal running on another machine might show considerable variations. Used only for comparative purposes, however, these times provide a basis for obtaining a good deal of insight.

We see that for small tables it really doesn't matter much what method you use. If you know your table can never have more than a few dozen items, you may as well use any method you are sure you can write quickly without error. Your time will be a more important issue than the computer's running time.

We also see that selection sort and insertion sort really do have quadratic behavior, to within a few seconds: doubling the table size quadruples the running time almost exactly. Theory is vindicated by the clock. We see, too, that selection sort is quadratic even in its best case.

Insertion sort, on the other hand, takes full advantage of whatever order it finds. If the input is already sorted, it detects that fact and quits. It is as fast, in this case, as any method we used. But its worst-case behavior is truly terrible.

Shell sort is much faster than insertion sort, on the average. Presented with sorted input, Shell sort takes longer to detect the fact because it still goes through its fixed sequence of diminishing increments.

Heap sort is rather slower than Quicksort, on average, but its worst-case performance is not much worse than its average performance.

Bucket sort is very fast indeed, if its severe restrictions permit it to be used. It also has a fixed overhead, as our program is written, initializing the bucket array and collecting the items after distribution.

Which is best? By now, you know that the answer has to be: "It depends."

- For small tables, use anything simple that you understand fully.
- If you are positive that the input is almost sorted, insertion sort is fast and relatively simple.
- For tables of modest size (up to around a thousand, say), Shell sort is about as fast as Quicksort and is simpler to write. Completion of research currently under way may improve its attractiveness, as better sequences of diminishing increments are found.
- If you need to sort tables of thousands of items, then by all means use some improved version of Quicksort. Nothing is faster except bucket sort (which is too limited to be of general applicability).
- If you absolutely cannot tolerate the degraded worst-case performance of Quicksort, even if it should happen only once every ten years, then a well-tuned version of Shell sort or heapsort may be the right choice. Their average performance is not too much slower than Quicksort, and never gets really bad regardless of the initial ordering.

8.14 CONCLUSION

We close this discussion with a warning. Sorting is so important a part of computer science, and of the application of computers, that you need to know *much* more about it than we offer in this chapter. Such a remark applies to everything in the book, of course, but there seems to be a seductiveness about the apparent simplicity of writing a better sort routine. What this presentation has not emphasized, and could not have stressed, within the pedagogical constraints of introducing the subject, are the complications involved in *generalizing* a sort routine. People don't just want to sort integers, they want to sort complete records, with multiple-part keys that are not necessarily Pascal primitive types, and so on and so on. And, we have dealt only with *internal* sorting, which restricts the size of files below what is needed for many applications.

This book is intended for, among others, precisely the kind of people who will be writing sorting programs and other tools for use by others. These tools include database systems, graphics packages, word processing systems, and so on ad infinitum. Consequently, we have introduced the central topic of sorting in an attempt to clarify the issues involved. But, before you set out to write a general-purpose sorting system you need to know much more about analysis of algorithms, which, in turn, requires understanding of combinatorics. You also need to know about external storage devices such as tapes and disks, and the very different considerations that apply with them. Finally, you need to know what people do with sorting, that is, the applications of computers.

EXERCISES

1. Is `SelectionSort` stable? Can you prove your answer?

2. (For the mathematically inclined.) We stated in the analysis of `SelectionSort` that "we exchange `A[I]` with `A[Small]` even when `Small = I`. It turns out that if all orderings of the keys in the input are equally likely, inserting this test would save far fewer than N swaps."

    (a) Suppose you use the Pascal function `Random (N)`, to generate `N` random integers, `A[1]` to `A[N]`, between 0 and $N-1$. What is the probability that `A[1] < A[I]` for all `I > 1`? Assume that each value is equally likely to be generated by `Random`.

    (b) How can we be reasonably sure that we don't generate any duplicates among our N integers using Pascal's `Random` function?

    (c) Find the expected number of times `I = Small`, when sorting a random `SortArray` of length N if `Prob(A[I] = A[J]) = 0 (I ≠ J)`.

    (d) Test your answer to (c) by adding a counter to the `Selection-Sort` program to count the number of times `Swap (A[I], A[Small])` was called, with `I = Small`.

3. Bubble sort is an $O(N^2)$ method that is slower than selection sort in its average performance, but which takes better advantage of initial ordering than selection sort. In its usual form it is based on comparing, and exchanging if necessary, pairs of adjacent elements in the table. This is done N times, or until a pass through the table requires no exchanges.

    A variation of bubble sort, due to Knuth (1973), is the *odd-even transposition sort*. The algorithm is summarized in this pseudocode:

```
OddEvenSort (SortArray, ArrayLength);
    Phase = 0;
    while Phase < ArrayLength do
      CompareAndSwitchOdds;
      Phase = Phase + 1;
      if Phase < ArrayLength then
      begin
          CompareAndSwitchEvens;
          Phase = Phase + 1
      end
    end
end;
```

CompareAndSwitchOdds goes through a SortArray, A, comparing A[1] with A[2], A[3] with A[4], A[5] with A[6], and so on, switching if necessary, so that A[i] < A[i+1]. CompareAndSwitchEvens behaves similarly for A[2] and A[3], A[4] and A[5], and so forth.

(a) Show that a SortArray of length ≥ 3 can be sorted in N phases, alternating between odd and even.

(b) Show that the number of comparisons is $O(N^2/2)$.

(c) Program and test an OddEvenSort.

(d) Describe how you could sort a SortArray of length N, if you had N CPUs running simultaneously, with communication between CPU_i and CPU_{i+1}, and between CPU_i and CPU_{i-1}. Show that the sort time is now $O(N)$.

4. Write loop invariants, draw the "graphical invariants," and verify them (using the four-step process of Section 8.4) for the following loops:

(a) Find an element, Target, in an unsorted array.

```
I := 0;
Found := false;
while (I < RowMax) and (not Found) do
begin
    I := I+1;
    if A[I] = Target then
        Found := true
end;
```

(b) Find Target in an unsorted matrix.

```
I:= 0;
J:= 0;
Found := false;
while I < RowMax do
begin
    I := I+1;
    while (J < ColMax) and (not Found) do
    begin
        J := J+1;
        if A[I,J] = Target then
            Found := true
    end
end;
```

(c) The `for` loop in the procedure `ConcatStr` of Section 3.10.

(d) The `while` loop of `DeleteStr` of Section 3.10.

(e) The `repeat` loop of `SearchStr` of Section 3.10.

5. In the `OddEvenSort` of Exercise 3, define:

```
Misplaced [I] = number of array elements, A[J],
for which A[J] < A[I], and J > I
```

Then an invariant for the `while` loop of `OddEvenSort` is:

```
{Invariant: Misplaced [I] <= ArrayLength - Phase,
  and 0 <= Phase <= ArrayLength.}
```

(a) Draw the "graphical invariant" corresponding to this invariant.

(b) Follow the four steps of Section 8.4 to verify that the loop is correct.

6. `SelectionSortOfRecords` swapped entire records when their keys were out of order. Modify the program to sort a table of pointers to the records.

(a) Assume the records are stored in an array, and the pointers are indices into the array.

(b) Assume the records were dynamically created as a linked list and the pointers are memory addresses, stored in `PermutationArray`.

7. Recode `InsertionSort` so that it does not use a sentinel to detect the case where an element must be inserted into the first position of the table, but instead makes an explicit test. Be sure your program will not cause a reference to a non-existent array location, or create an array index that is out of bounds.

   The argument for this modification is that it removes the need for an extra position in the array as well as the need for modification of the array to be sorted. The argument against it is performance. A test is made a great many times (how many?) to detect a condition that occurs only rarely. Discuss the tradeoffs.

8. We demonstrated the procedure `ShellSort` using the increments (5, 2, 1). The program shown would use a different set of increments. What is it? In terms of the program,

(a) What is the value of `Inc` prior to entering the `repeat` loop?

(b) Trace the procedure `ShellSort` (by hand) on the same 13-element file.

(c) Rewrite the `repeat` loop, eliminating the `goto`.

(d) Which loop do you find easier to read? Which would you describe as "better programming practice"? Why?

9. Write an invariant for the `repeat` loop of Shell sort. You will find this task easier if you work from the inside out. That is, write an invariant for the inner `while`, then the outer `while`, and finally the `repeat`. You may use your `goto`-less loop of the preceding exercise if you wish. You might also consider replacing the `repeat` loop with a `while` loop, the latter being easier to verify.

10. The Towers of Hanoi is a puzzle consisting of N graduated disks with holes in their centers, and a board with three pegs to hold the disks. Initially, all N disks are on `Peg1`, with the larger disks beneath the smaller. The challenge is to move all N disks to `Peg3`, using all three pegs but never allowing a disk to rest on one that is smaller than it is. A recurrence relation representing the number of disk movements needed is

$$M_n = 2M_{n-1} + 1.$$

   (a) Explain why the recurrence counts the minimal number of moves needed correctly.
   (b) Solve the recurrence, if $M_1 = 1$.

11. Trace (by hand) both versions of `QuickSort` (i.e., with and without the median-of-three modification, using a minimum partition of three elements for the latter). Use the following three files:
   (a) 1 2 3 4 5 6
   (b) 6 5 4 3 2 1
   (c) 3 5 1 6 2 4.

12. We suggested that `QuickSort` could be made more efficient if small files were sorted using the procedure `InsertionSort`. Add this feature to the second `QuickSort` procedure, and try it out with different threshold values. Keep track of run times. (The most efficient threshold value depends on your hardware and operating system as well as `QuickSort` itself.) Start with a threshold value of 9 or so, and increase it until performance appears to deteriorate. Do you see the value of declaring the threshold in the `const` statement?

13. As reported in this chapter, running `QuickSort` produced a program crash when the recursive stack overflowed. A direct attack on this problem would be to eliminate some or all of the recursion.
   (a) The second recursive call can be eliminated with a loop, as was done in Chapter 5, because it is an example of tail recursion. Rewrite `QuickSortWithMinPartition,` replacing the statement `QuickSortWithMinPartition (A, I, Right)` with a loop.
   (b) Eliminate the recursive calls entirely by stacking the bounds of the larger subfile and processing the smaller subfile with a loop that replaces the tail recursion. Manage an explicit stack in the program rather than use recursive calls.

14. `QuickSort` is not practical for files on external media such as magnetic disks, as the time for swaps is excessive. One method that can be used with tables too large to be stored internally is `MergeSort`. The internal `BinaryMergeSort` recursively splits an array into two parts, and merges sorted subfiles of half the length. A `Merge` procedure creates a sorted list from two shorter, sorted lists, as shown with this box-and-arrow diagram.

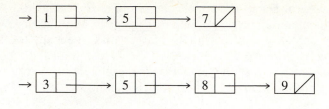

becomes:

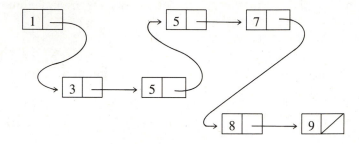

(a) Write an algorithm Merge (List1, List2, Length1, Length2) to merge two sorted linked lists. Be especially careful about what happens when one of the lists is exhausted but the other is not.

(b) Program your procedure and test it on several pairs of short ordered lists.

(c) What is the cost of your merge in terms of the number of comparisons made? If this cost is greater than $O(Length \ (List1) + Length \ (List2))$, try to improve your algorithm.

15. BinaryMergeSort proceeds by merging sorted sublists, called *runs*, of length 1, into runs of length ≤ 2, runs of length ≤ 2 into runs of length ≤ 4, runs of length ≤ 4 into runs of length ≤ 8, and so on until the entire file is sorted. In the following example, underlines denote the ends of runs.

run length:	1	<=2	<= 4	<=8
	5	4	3	2
	4	5	4	3
	6	3	5	4
	3	6	6	5
	11	2	2	6
	2	11	6	6
	6	6	11	11

One algorithm to accomplish `BinaryMergeSort` follows:

```
BalancedMergeSort (List[0], List[1], List[2], List[3]);

{ List[0] initially contains an unsorted file.
  After completion of BalancedMerge it contains the sorted file. }

MakeEmpty (List[1]);
Transfer half of List[0] to List[1];
I = 0;
MaxNumRuns = Round (Length (List[0]) / 2);

while MaxNumRuns > 1 do
begin
   J = (I + 1) mod 3;
   MakeEmpty (List[J]);
   MakeEmpty (List[J + 1]);
   Merge runs from List[I] with List[I+1], placing the new
      longer runs alternately onto List[J]] and List[J + 1];
   MaxNumRuns = Round (MaxNumRuns / 2);
   I = J;
end;

Merge last runs into List[0]
```

(a) Test this algorithm using the 13-element test data from Section 8.8.

(b) Program `BalancedMergeSort`. Some of the details were left out of the algorithm, such as how to recognize the end of a run and how to deal with merging two lists where one has fewer than `MaxNumRuns`.

(c) What is the cost of `MergeSort` in terms of the number of comparisons made?

16. Suppose the starting array values of Section 8.11 were reversed. That is, the original list to be sorted is: 35 37 66 17 22 64 54 12 16 46 02 19. Use the procedure `SiftUp` to create a heap from this list. Is it the same or a different heap than that constructed from the original list, beginning with 19 and ending with 35?

17. The procedures `SiftUp` and `SiftDown` both use swapping to move an element into a desired position. This process can be speeded up by using a technique like that in `InsertionSort`, where the element to be moved is placed in a temporary location. Then, elements are moved one place as needed until the final location is determined. And, finally, the temporary variable is placed in the final location. Modify `HeapSort` to use this method.

18. The procedure `SiftDown` contains a test to determine a if right child exists. If the heap has an odd number of elements, the answer will always be "yes," and the test is pointless. (Prove this.) If the number of elements is odd, the question is required only when the process of sifting down has to go to the bottom of the heap, which will not be often. As a function of *N,* how many times is this test made? Run a modified version of `HeapSort` to provide experimental evidence of how many times the test is needed.

The test can be removed entirely if `A[N+1]` is given the value `MaxInt` in case *N* is even, with `MaxInt` serving as a sentinel. Discuss the merits of this approach, comparing the advantage of time savings with the disadvantages of requiring array modification and the reservation of space for the sentinel.

19. If the amount of data is too great to be held in internal memory, some kind of external sorting procedure must be used where only portions of the data are brought into internal memory for sorting and then they are written out to disk or tape for later merging. `BalancedMergeSort` can be used as an external sort, with the four lists playing the roles of four external disk areas or tapes. However, the first few merges, with runs of small size, should be handled otherwise to minimize the number of external accesses.

A first step in many external sorting routines is to create runs as long as possible. A variation of `HeapSort`, called `Replacement-Selection`, has been shown to produce runs about twice as long as the size of the heap. The idea is as follows:

1. Bring in as many items from the unsorted `List[0]` as a `Sort-Array [1..Max]` can hold.

2. Invoke `HeapSort`, with the following modifications:
   a) After `SortArray` has been transformed into a heap using `SiftUp,` write `LastOut = A[1]`, to external memory.
   b) Replace `A[1]` with a `NewItem` from `List[0]` if `NewItem <= LastOut`.
   c) Repeat (a) and (b) until `SortArray` is empty.

3. Step 2 created a single run. It is invoked repeatedly until `List[0]` is empty, and the runs have been written out alternately to `List[2]` and `List[3]`.

4. `BalancedMergeSort` then proceeds with the initial runs on `List[2]` and `List[3]`, instead of on `List[0]` and `List[1]`.

(a) Using an array size of 1..8 and a list of random integers created using Pascal's `Random (N)`, test `CreateRuns`, as outlined above, on a list of something over 100 items. What is the average run length?

(b) As a project, you might program a simulation of an external `BalancedMergeSort`, using a file type to simulate external files. The declarations would be as follows:

```
type
   ExternalFile = File of integer;
var
   ExternalFiles: array [0..3] of ExternalFile;
```

(c) Add performance checks to your program in (b) to tally the lengths of initial runs, the number of external accesses, and the number of file rewinds (resets).

20. External accesses can be reduced further by buffering the runs and writing them out to the external files only when the buffer is full.

(a) Add this feature to your simulation program.

(b) Double-buffering can speed things up even more if reading from and writing to different buffers can occur simultaneously. Add a second buffer to your program to hold the next items to be read into central memory. Your buffer from (a) will now hold items read out from central memory after a merge pass, as well as initial runs, until an external file is ready to receive them. It is reasonable to make the following assumptions:

- Either buffer can receive data from or send data to central memory.

- Buffers are managed by the CPU, but data need not flow through central memory to be transferred from an external device to a buffer.

- A buffer may not be written to until it is cleared of prior data.

- Both buffers plus the CPU may be active simultaneously, where an active buffer is being either read to or written from, but not both.

(c) Comment on any scheduling difficulties you see in the coordination of the four external devices, the CPU, and the two buffers.

21. Bucket sort was described as one example of a *radix sort*. In general, radix sort can be applied to items of the form $R_n R_{n-1} \ldots R_2 R_1 R_0$. The simplest example is the decimal integers. (The radix of the decimal integers is 10.) For example, the integer 52,304, can be thought of as $R_4 R_3 R_2 R_1 R_0$, where $R_4 = 5$, $R_3 = 2$, $R_2 = 3$, $R_1 = 0$, and $R_0 = 4$. The idea behind radix sort is that if a set of numbers is in order on the rightmost k digits, applying BucketSort to the $k+1$st digit puts them into order on their rightmost $k+1$ digits.

To implement this method we need two sets of buckets, one holding numbers already sorted on the kth digit, and an empty set into which to transfer them (based on the $k+1$st digit). For example, suppose we have the two-digit numbers, 02 57 63 94 17 22 63. We first place them in ten buckets based on the 0th digit, as follows:

```
            22    63              17
            02    63    94        57

bucket:  0    1    2    3    4    5    6    7    8    9
```

The next (and, in this case, final) sort proceeds from 9 down to 0, emptying these buckets into the second set of buckets, according to the first digit.

```
                                63
         02    17    22         57    63              94

bucket:  0    1    2    3    4    5    6    7    8    9
```

(a) What happens if you empty the first buckets from bucket 0 up to bucket 9, rather than as stated?

(b) Still using two sets of 10 buckets, follow radix sort through by hand for the following three-digit numbers:

157 362 004 056 943 999 821 643 234 225 042 320 961 558

(c) If each bucket is implemented as a linked list, is a queue or a stack more appropriate? Does it matter?

(d) How would you link the final set of buckets to provide a sorted linked list?

(e) What is the cost of radix sort?

(f) How many buckets would be needed to sort a dictionary list that has words up to 25 characters long? How many passes would the sort require?

(g) Program radix sort and test it on a randomly generated list of 1000, four-digit integers.

22. We have considered several sorting methods in this chapter and these exercises. Complete a table for data on these methods, with the following column headings:

Sort **Cost** **Memory Requirements** **Overhead** **When to Use**

Overhead includes program complexity, extra storage for pointers, counters, procedure calls, and any other factors not included in the cost computations.

SUGGESTIONS FOR FURTHER STUDY

Knuth Vol. 3 (1973b) is the standard reference on sorting and searching methods. It is an almost encyclopedic treatment, although Knuth says that he treats "only about 25" of the "many different sorting algorithms" invented. The mathematical level of the text in the volume makes some demands far beyond anything reasonably to be expected of undergraduates, but one of the beauties of Knuth's superb exposition is that you don't have to read it all to get the parts you need at a particular point in your study. Any serious student of computer science should own all three volumes of Knuth, as well as the planned later volumes when they appear.

Martin (1971) is a short and readable survey of sorting methods, including a bibliography that was complete at the time of publication.

Amsterdam (1985) provides a good overview of sorting methods, focussing on the comparison of methods.

Shell sort was introduced in Shell (1959).

Quicksort was introduced in Hoare (1961), where it occupied less than half of one page. It was more fully described in Hoare (1962), which still makes for interesting reading.

Sedgewick (1983) contains a highly readable presentation on sorting methods, as well as of algorithms in many other areas. The presentation of Quicksort in this chapter was influenced by Sedgewick (1978).

Heapsort is described in Floyd (1964). The presentation here was influenced by Bentley (1985). Bentley (1984) is an intuitive approach to Quicksort, with graphical invariants. (Both of the Bentley papers are from the "Programming Pearls" column of the *Communications of the ACM;* Bentley (1986) is a collection of the columns.)

Since the development of sorting methods began in the 1950s and most of the corresponding theoretical work was completed during the late 1960s, it might seem that sorting methods would not be a current area of research. However, the increasing practicality of *concurrent* or *parallel* processing calls for the adaptation of old single-processor algorithms and the creation of new ones. Even bubble sort, usually belittled as having nothing to be said for it except a catchy name, has useful parallel versions, as suggested in Exercise 3. Bitton (1984) describes parallel methods, with or without ancillary disks or tapes. Included are parallel versions of bubble sort, tree sort, bucket sort, and merge sort. The goal is to develop sorting methods that achieve the lower bound of $O(\lg N)$ performance, using many $O(N)$ machines running in parallel. Open questions involve the interplay of new VLSI (Very Large Scale Integration) chips with well-understood sorting methods.

Shneiderman (1984) considers the question of just how fast people want or need programs to run. An old rule of thumb that states that the human toleration of computer response delays has a break point at two seconds, seems to vary with the application. Research into human-computer interaction indicates that errors and frustration vary with both response times and the task at hand.

Gries (1981) presents loop invariants as part of the process of simultaneously developing a program and formally proving its correctness. The presentation assumes some mathematical maturity on the part of the reader, and is directed to upper-level undergraduate or beginning graduate students. Other works that deal with program verification are Dromey (1983), Hehner (1984), and Mili (1985).

Lueker (1980) contains a tutorial on solving recurrence relations. As usual with *Computing Surveys* tutorials, an extensive bibliography is included.

Knuth (1973b) includes extensive material on external sorting methods. Elementary treatments are included in Garland (1986), Tenenbaum and Augenstein (1986) and Graham (1982).

CHAPTER 9

SEARCHING

9.1 INTRODUCTION

Searching is a process in which we look for, locate, and retrieve one item from a table of items. It is one of the most common uses of a computer, either as the primary purpose of an application or as a tool in doing something else.

For example, when I need computer supplies such as paper, ribbons, or diskettes, I locate what I need in the catalog for a company named Inmac and then place a phone call. I then give the telephone order clerk a short description of what I want, together with the Inmac stock number. In little more time than it takes to type the stock number, the clerk is reading me the current price, availability, and a precise description so we can both be sure we are talking about the same thing. Inmac has many thousands of stock numbers; all the information associated with any stock number is available to the clerk within a few seconds. This is an example in which searching is a major purpose of the entire application.

For the case in which searching is a tool, consider the symbol table in a compiler. For each of the identifiers in a Pascal program, for example, there is a considerable amount of associated information: what kind of object is it; if a variable, what kind; if an array, how many dimensions, and so on. The collection of all the identifiers in a program and the information associated with each is called the *symbol table*. Every time an identifier occurs in a declaration, an entry must be added to the symbol table; every time an identifier occurs other than in a declaration, the symbol table must be searched.

These two examples introduce some terminology and survey some design issues. Let us now turn to the specifics.

The collection in which we search is called either a *file of records* or a *table of items*. The former is more common in data processing, the latter in computer science. As in the treatment of sorting, we will generally speak of a table of items.

Each entry in a table has, at least, one *key* field by which it is identified; it also usually has at least one non-key field, and may have many. In both of the earlier examples, there are many non-key fields (price, quantity on hand, and so forth). The number of non-key fields varies in some applications, although not in this chapter. An example of a table containing only keys would be a spelling checker: all we want to know is whether the word is in the table or not. If it is, there is nothing about the word to look up.

To concentrate on the algorithms and the design tradeoffs, we shall only work with a key field and one non-key field. We shall call the latter the `Info` field.

The search process is entered with a *search argument:* we seek the table item having that value as its key. If there is such an item, the search process may return the non-key information or, alternatively, just the address of the item. If the table does not contain such an item, we return information stating that fact, either with a `boolean` variable or perhaps by returning a non-existent address that signals the absence.

In some circumstances it is useful to distinguish between search and *retrieval,* the latter being the process of obtaining the non-key information.

There are many search techniques. No one is "best," and none that we shall study is so bad that there would never be a use for it. As usual, "it depends." On what? The following list highlights the issues you should consider when choosing a technique.

Speed versus space. As so often, we have a choice between fast methods that waste some storage, and slower methods that economize it.

Static versus dynamic tables. Some tables are built in a preliminary operation, before any searching is done; after that, there are only occasional updates to the table. Our mail order example is a case in point. Naturally, for a mail order catalog new products are inserted, old products are deleted, and existing entries are updated with prices changes, and so forth. But, once the system has been set up, there are far fewer changes than there are retrievals, and it may be possible to make all the modifications at night when the system is not on-line. In other cases, insertions, searches, and deletions may be randomly mixed, and modifications may be as frequent as retrievals. An example would be an airline reservation system, where inserting new information quickly is a primary design requirement.

Table size. In a very small table (a few dozen items) it may be best to examine each entry in sequence, with no ordering imposed on the entries. Techniques that save time over this approach, for larger tables, could have overhead that would cost more time than they would save. In a table that is larger (hundreds of items to tens of thousands), the primary consideration is usually minimizing the average time to find an item (or determine that it is not present). If the entire table can be kept in primary storage while it is being searched, this criterion reduces to minimizing the number of comparisons.

There are several choices for this approach, as we shall see later in the chapter. If the table must be kept on secondary storage (disk, usually) then an entirely different consideration comes into play—the time to make one disk access is roughly ten thousand times as long as the time to make a comparison in primary storage. In this case all emphasis switches to minimizing the number of disk accesses. We shall explore this issue in an overview fashion in Section 9.11.

Are duplicates permitted? In some applications the presence of two entries with the same key would be a clear-cut error, one that the program must detect. Duplicate declarations of a program variable would be an example. In other cases duplicates are a normal part of the application, with nothing to be done when they occur. An example would be from the same application: a list of duplicate symbols to be reported with the diagnostic messages.

There are other issues, as we will see as we go along, but these are the dominant ones.

9.2 SEARCHING IN ADT TERMS

In ADT terms, we can think of a table in abstract terms, independent of implementation (array, linked list, tree, indexed external storage). In practice, no one would set up an all-purpose searching program intended to work well regardless of whether there are seven items or seven million. But we can do almost that while we are exploring the various standard algorithms and their various tradeoffs.

We need define only three operations:

1. `Insert` places a new item, with values for its `Key` and `Info` fields, in a table. Depending on the implementation, this may require actions involving items that are already in the table, but at the ADT level we ignore that.

2. `Search` either returns the `Info` information or the address of the entry. Depending on implementation, this might be an actual primary storage address, an index value for an array, a pointer to a node in a linked list, or a hardware-dependent disk location.

3. `Delete` removes an item from a table, acting on the remaining items in any way that the implementation may require.

We shall introduce a compromise to this completely abstract approach by not defining an ADT *table*. Defining one would nicely conceal the implementation details from the user of a package, but we are not really developing a search package. Rather, we are trying to learn algorithms and tradeoffs. Because the algorithms will be presented as Pascal procedures, having an ADT *table* would complicate things more than it would be worth. All procedure bodies would be cluttered up with extra field qualifiers, for example. Not an ideal solution, perhaps, but book design and program design have certain similarities—and intelligent compromise between conflicting goals is an essential part of each.

A second compromise is that we shall not provide for deletion from hash tables. The considerable extra complexity would not teach you enough to be worth the effort. Adding this capability makes a good exercise.

9.3 SEQUENTIAL APPROACHES

In a sequential search we compare the search argument with the keys of the table items until we either find the desired entry or discover that it is not present. The number of comparisons may be as small as one if the key of the first entry we examine matches the search key. It may be as large as N, the number of entries, if we do not find a match until examining the last entry. And, it may be $N+1$, depending on the implementation, if it is necessary to examine all entries to determine that the search argument does not match the key of any entry.

The table in a sequential search is essentially a list in the broader sense that includes both linked lists and arrays accessed sequentially.

Sequential search is something akin to quadratic sorting methods: just fine for small tables, hopeless for large. No matter what we do, sequential search is going to run in linear time, i.e., $O(N)$, where N is the table size. If N is 10,000, you are simply *not* going to be using sequential search. Binary search and searching in an AVL tree both run in $O(\lg N)$ time, with various differences in their limitations. Hashing runs in constant time if you can afford to waste some storage to buy the speed. Furthermore, the coding aspects of sequential search are essentially exercises for you at this stage of your study. We would gain little by laboriously showing procedures to search for a specified item in an array or a linked list.

We shall therefore be content simply to describe the variations in the major approaches, and summarize the times for the various operations as functions of table size.

Sequential search in an unordered array is a matter of setting up a loop to compare the search argument with the successive array items until either finding a match or reaching the end of the table. If all items are equally likely to match the search argument and the search argument is present in the table, then it clearly takes $N/2$ comparisons, on the average, to locate an item. If the search argument is not present in the table, the loop must examine every item to determine that fact, which requires N comparisons.

Insertion in an unordered array is simplicity itself. We place the new item at the end of the table and increment N, which takes no time to locate the correct position and one array operation for the insertion.

Deletion in an unordered array requires an average of $N/2$ comparisons to find the item, then one array operation to move the Nth item to the location of the deleted item, followed by decrementing N.

These results are summarized in a table in Section 9.10. The quantities shown are intended to be counts of array operations—comparisons or stores. Depending on coding details, it may not always be literally true that an insertion or deletion takes exactly as long as a comparison. Just remember that, for a large table, insertion takes vastly less time than searching.

Searching in an ordered array is appropriate when the application is such that there are many unsuccessful searches. A successful search still takes an average of $N/2$ array operations, but searching can stop once a value larger than the search argument has been encountered. Consequently, an unsuccessful search now also takes an average of $N/2$ array operations.

Insertion in an ordered array pays a price for the improved search performance: a new item must be inserted in its correct location in the table, which requires an average of $N/2$ array operations to locate. Then, everything after that position in the array must be moved one position to make room.

Deletion in an ordered array pays the same price: finding the correct location takes an average of $N/2$ array operations, and when the place has been found everything beyond it must be moved.

Sequential search in an unordered linked list has the same performance as the unordered array method, but takes more space (for the links). It is a little hard to see where it would be the best choice because for small tables arrays are simpler, and for large tables the sequential approach is hopeless anyway.

Sequential search in an ordered linked list is a different story. The fact that the list is ordered gains the same advantage of faster performance on an unsuccessful search that an ordered array does, but insertion and deletion are much faster because no movement of entries is required.

In those cases where the sequential approach is indicated, there are a number of variations, coding stratagems, and application considerations to think about. Some of these are explored in Exercises 1 and 2, where you are asked to code the approaches and offer your evaluation of some of the tradeoffs. Since the sequential approach basically makes sense only on small tables (dozens to at most hundreds of items), and because fine-tuning doesn't buy much in such a case anyway, we shall devote no more time to the subject.

9.4 BINARY SEARCH

If our application is such that we can do all the insertions first, before any searches, and if there are no deletions, then the divide-and-conquer strategy gives us a great reduction in search time, from $O(N)$ to $O(\lg N)$. For a table of, say, 10,000 items, this means that the *maximum* number of comparisons is 14, as compared to an *average* of 5000 for the sequential search.

To gain this vast improvement in speed, we pay the price of having to sort the table in a preliminary operation. Furthermore, we cannot process intermixed insertions, searches, and deletions, i.e., the method is limited to static applications.

Here is the problem. We wish to determine whether the sorted array A contains the element `SearchArg`. More precisely, we know that $N > 0$ and that `A[1] < A[2] < ... < A[N]`. The "answer" is a value for the variable `Pos` (for "position"). If `Pos = 0` then `SearchArg` is not in `A[1..N]`. Otherwise $1 \leq Pos \leq N$ and `SearchArg = A[Pos]`.

Binary search responds to this problem by keeping track of a range within the array which must contain `SearchArg`, if it is anywhere in the array. Initially, the range of possibility is the entire array. The range is continually decreased by comparing its middle element with `SearchArg` and discarding half the range. This process is continued until `SearchArg` is found in the array or until the range in which it "must be" is known to be empty, meaning that `SearchArg` is not present. The process takes about lg *N* comparisons.

To translate this statement to code, we need a way to represent the "range of possibility" in terms of the array *A*. If we visualize the array horizontally, then `Left` and `Right` make sense. We start with the initialization `Left = 1` and `Right = N,` which simply says that we will search the entire table for `SearchArg`.

The method of binary search is to cut the possible range in half repeatedly. We do this by computing a value of `Mid`, the midpoint of the range between `Left` and `Right,` and then asking whether `SearchArg < A[Mid]`. If the answer is yes, then `SearchArg` cannot possibly lie in the range `A[Mid..Right]`. It may turn out not to be *anywhere* in the array, but it *positively* cannot be in the right half. In that case we can, therefore, set `Right` equal to `Mid − 1,` thus eliminating half of the range from further consideration.

If the answer to the question whether `SearchArg < A[Mid]` is no, then `SearchArg` cannot possibly lie anywhere in the range `A[1..Mid−1]`. `SearchArg` might be equal to `A[Mid]`, if we are lucky, or it may still not be anywhere in the table. But, it positively is not in the half of the table to the left of `Mid`. One way to proceed is to set `Left` equal to `Mid + 1,` then immediately check whether `SearchArg = A[Mid]`. If we have hit on it, then we are finished. If we have not hit it, we go back around the loop, again reducing the possible range by half. That should be *approximately* half, of course, because the range will not always have an even number of elements.

And what if `SearchArg` is not in the table at all? That fact will be signaled by the condition `Left > Right,` meaning that, in the process of continually eliminating half of the possible range from further consideration, we have eliminated everything. When the possible range is down to one element and that isn't it, then the next cutting-in-half step results in a range having no elements at all.

The termination condition on the loop, therefore, is either that we have located the position of `SearchArg` in the table, or that `Left > Right,` meaning that it isn't there. After the loop stops, we can make a simple test to determine what stopped it and either set `Pos` equal to `Mid` or to zero.

The translation to code is now immediate. We assume the following declarations:

```
const
   MaxN = 10000;          { or whatever }

type
   KeyType = integer;     { or whatever }
   InfoType = integer;    { or whatever }
```

```
            Item = record
                       Key: KeyType;
                       Info: InfoType
                   end;

            Index = 0..MaxN;

            SearchTable = array [1..MaxN] of Item;
```

Here is a procedure based on the algorithm as we described it, with pre- and post-conditions and a loop invariant.

```
procedure BinarySearch (var A: SearchTable;      { var for speed }
                        N: Index;
                        SearchArg: KeyType;
                        var Pos: Index);
{ Pre: A[1] < A[2] < ... < A[N] and N > 0 }
{ Post: if  1 <= Pos <= N, then A[Pos].Key = SearchArg
         if Pos = 0, then SearchArg not in A[1..N]. }

var
    Left, Right, Mid: Index;

begin
    Left := 1;
    Right := N;

    { Invariant: A[Left].Key <= SearchArg <= A[Right].Key,
                 or SearchArg not in table. }
    repeat
        Mid := (Left + Right) div 2;

        if SearchArg < A[Mid].Key then
            Right := Mid - 1
        else
            Left := Mid + 1

    until (SearchArg = A[Mid].Key) or (Left > Right);

    if SearchArg = A[Mid].Key then
        Pos := Mid
    else
        Pos := 0
end;
```

Note the use of the `var` parameter for the table. It would be small comfort to know that we had held the maximum number of comparisons to 14, if an entire 10,000-item table had to moved to the run-time stack every time the procedure was invoked.

This program will fail, unfortunately, in a Pascal system that does run-time checking, when the search value falls outside the table. `Mid` will then be zero or `N + 1,` and the array reference `A[Mid]` will be illegal. The *result* would be correct, but there will be a meaningless error message and a run-time crash. Exercise 3 asks you to consider this issue.

We have already seen, in Section 8.9, that a divide-and-conquer strategy in which we repeatedly discard half the problem leads to a running time of $O(\lg N)$. Binary search is an optimal search strategy in the sense that no method than depends on comparison of keys can take fewer than $O(\lg N)$ comparisons.

So, why would anyone ever use any other search method? Two reasons. First, the array must be sorted. This essentially eliminates binary search from consideration in dynamic search situations, where searches are intermixed with insertions and/or deletions. Second, in some cases it is possible to eliminate key comparisons entirely, leading to a search time that is $O(1)$, i.e., it is constant—independent of the size of N. Such methods are the subject of the next section.

9.5 HASHING

The searching methods we have considered so far have depended on comparisons of keys. Our next approach dispenses with key comparisons as the fundamental search tactic and, instead, applies a transformation to the keys, attempting to arrive at an address where the associated item may be found. The ideal case would be for each possible key value to transform to a unique storage location. The item could be inserted in this location in an array and then retrieved by applying the same transformation to a search key and getting the item from that same location.

Nothing can be quite that good, but this general idea is the basis of the search method based on *hashing*.

Let us see how this would work in terms of a simple example. Suppose we have about 10 items to store and retrieve, based on unique keys that are in the range of 0000 to 9999. If we can afford the wasted storage, the fastest possible way to handle this search problem is to set up an array with 10,000 items and an index range of 0000..9999. Now the key can be used directly to store and retrieve items. Nothing can be faster.

On the assumption that this kind of wasted storage is not acceptable, or that the keys are not directly translatable to array indices, we look for some way to do nearly the same thing. Suppose we transform the keys by dividing by 13, and then use the remainder as the index with which to access an array of 13 items that are numbered from 0 to 12. Here are some sample keys and the array indices to which they are transformed by this method:

Key	Transformed Key
1234	12
5021	3
7423	0
2000	11
9043	8
6296	4

If we could be assured that every key would transform to a unique array location, we would have an outstanding search method! But this is clearly not possible. At the very least, we know we cannot handle more than 13 keys this way. And, in fact, we must accept the fact that even when the table is not full, there can be two or more keys that transform to the same table location.

The transformation is called *hashing,* a term that comes from slang usage under which we say that the (meaningful) key has been converted into "hash," i.e., something so different that it has no visible relation to the key. The image is that when a sufficient number of leftovers are chopped up and put into one dish, the resulting hash does not permit accurate identification of the ingredients.

This image is accurate in the sense that when we have only the hashed key we cannot reconstruct the original key, because the hash transformation is many-to-one. Indeed, if we now hash the key 6620 by dividing by 13 and use the remainder as the hashed address, we get 3, which was also the hashed address for 5021. This is called a *collision*.

As a search method, hashing reduces to two problems; finding a hashing method that minimizes collisions, and *resolving* collisions when they do, inevitably, occur. The basic goal in looking for a good hash function is to spread the hashed keys evenly over the entire hash table. Stated otherwise, we seek to minimize *clustering,* which is the tendency for many keys to hash to the same location.

This is a classical computer science problem. Hashing has been used since the earliest days of computing, and the attributes of various hashing methods have been studied intensively. However, a thorough study of this area is beyond our scope. We shall be content to say a little about the choice of the divisor in the remainder method already illustrated, and leave the rest to your further study.

Let us begin our study with a more precise statement of the remainder method. We compute

$$H(K) = K \bmod M$$

where K is the key, $H(K)$ is the hash function, and M is the divisor under discussion. Clearly,

$$0 \le H(K) < M$$

If the key is alphabetic, it must, of course, be converted to numeric form before hashing. In Pascal this requires a bit of coding effort and considerable wasted machine time. At the machine-language level the effort is usually much less.

Some choices of M are better than others. We do not choose M to be an even number, because then $H(K)$ is odd when K is odd and $H(K)$ is even when K is even. In any table in which there are many more odd numbers than even, or vice versa, the result would be a bias in the hash addresses, leading to clustering. We would definitely not choose M to be a power of the radix of the computer, because then $K \bmod M$ would be just the least significant digits of K: the leading digits would be ignored. For example, with a poor choice of $M,$ the identifiers `APtr`, `BPtr,` and `CPtr` might all hash to the same location. This is not a total catastrophe, because the collision resolution scheme still permits retrieval of each identifier, but it is an undesirable inefficiency.

We must leave the details to a later course or later study, but until then here is a primitive approach that will keep you out of some trouble: always use a prime number for M, and pick it to be about twice as large as the largest possible number of table items.

Now we turn to the of primary focus in our treatment—ways to handle collisions.

First of all, recall that a collision occurs when two or more keys hash to the same table index. How do we know this has happened? Part of the answer is that when an item is inserted in a hash table, the key must be placed in the table, so that that table location can be recognized as occupied if another key later hashes to the same location. This means, in turn, that to detect collisions reliably the entire table must be initialized to a value that *cannot* occur as a key. Now, when we have computed a hash table index for an insertion, we first inspect the key portion of that item (which may be the *entire* item, of course) to see whether that location is still available. If it is, we insert the new item there; if not, we must resolve the collision.

Sometimes it may be preferable to establish a field (one bit will do) that signals whether anything has been placed in a given hash table location, rather than initializing the key fields to some illegal value.

There are two major classes of collision resolution schemes: *open addressing* and *chained addressing*. In open addressing, when a collision is detected we simply look, in some systematic way, for an unoccupied location in the table. Clearly, this means that the maximum number of items that can be stored in a hash table under open addressing is equal to the table size. In chained hashing we make a linked list of all the items that hash to the same location, which, up to a point, permits the number of items to exceed the hash table size.

Let us take up each of these in order, with two variations of the open addressing approach.

9.6 LINEAR PROBING HASHING

The simplest open addressing scheme is called *linear probing hashing:* we simply look at the next table location, modulo M. That is, we probe sequentially through the table starting at the initial hash index returned by the hash function. If we reach the end of the table in this process, we *wrap around* from the end of the table to the beginning, which is what the ''modulo M'' means.

And what guarantees termination? Well, nothing, actually, unless we have some way to know that the table is not full. A table that has no open locations when we try to insert a new key is said to *overflow*. It is not difficult to add a test for this condition, but we shall not do so, because anything approaching overflow would so badly degrade performance that the user of hash searching must take other precautions to assure that it does not happen. The problem is that as the table approaches overflow, most accesses will lead to long collision resolution paths. In practice, it would be essential to test for overflow for we cannot simply say that it shouldn't happen and let it go at that.

Our program that implements linear probing hashing will use the following declarations:

```
const
   M = 100;    { hash table size; normally prime; see text }
   MMinus1 = 99;

type
   KeyType = integer;     { or whatever }
   InfoType = integer;    { or whatever }

   Item = record
               Key: KeyType;
               Info: InfoType
           end;

   Index = 0..MMinus1;

   HashTable = array [Index] of Item;
```

The divisor *M* in the hashing function is set up as a constant. We use 100, which would be an exceedingly poor choice in practice, for the pragmatic reason that it facilitates study of how the algorithm operates.

```
function Hash (Key: KeyType): Index;
begin
   Hash := Key mod M
end;
```

Initialization of the hash table consists of setting each entry to `MaxInt,` which is assumed not to be a legitimate key.

```
procedure LinearHashInitialize (var A: HashTable);
var
   I: Index;
begin
   for I := 0 to MMinus1 do
      A[I].Key := MaxInt
end;
```

The procedures `LinearHashInsert` and `LinearHashSearch` operate as described above.

```
procedure LinearHashInsert (var A: HashTable;
                            NewKey: KeyType;
                            NewInfo: InfoType;
                            var InsertionIndex: Index);
var
   H: Index;
begin
   H := Hash (NewKey);
   while A[H].Key <> MaxInt do
      H := (H + 1) mod M;

   A[H].Key := NewKey;
   A[H].Info := NewInfo;
   InsertionIndex := H
end;
```

(Continued)

(Continued)

```
procedure LinearHashSearch (var A: HashTable;
                            SearchArg: KeyType;
                            var Successful: boolean;
                            var SearchIndex: Index);
var
   H: Index;
begin
   H := Hash (SearchArg);

   while (A[H].Key <> SearchArg) and (A[H].Key <> MaxInt) do
      H := (H + 1) mod M;

   Successful := A[H].Key <> MaxInt;
   SearchIndex := H   { meaningless if not Successful }
end;
```

The comment on the last line of the procedure perhaps requires some defense. It may seem questionable to send back a meaningless value for the `SearchIndex` when the item was found not to be in the table. But we are depending on the user of this procedure to inspect the value of `Successful` before doing anything with the result. If that degree of responsibility cannot be relied upon, then there is also no way to assure that the user will not simply use an old value for `SearchIndex`, which is what would still be there if we inserted a test so as not to store the meaningless value.

We shall not implement a `Delete` operation, which is considerable additional effort. The problem is that the deleted entry might be part of a collision resolution chain. In that case, we must either reorganize the chain, which is a lot of trouble, or mark the location as unused. In the latter case there must be a mechanism to recognize when too many locations have been so marked and to reorganize the whole table periodically. This can certainly be done, and in a hash table application where deletions are possible it must be done. However, the extra work would not be adequately repaid in increased understanding of hashing or searching.

Here is the output of this program for a few illustrative operations.

```
Insertion;    Key:   123    inserted into bucket:    23    Info: 1234
Insertion;    Key:     8    inserted into bucket:     8    Info: 8888
Insertion;    Key:   108    inserted into bucket:     9    Info: 1088
Insertion;    Key:   208    inserted into bucket:    10    Info: 2088
Insertion;    Key:   308    inserted into bucket:    11    Info: 3088
Search:       Key:     8    Info: 8888
Search:       Key:   208    Info: 2088
Search;       Key:    63    not in the table
Search;       Key:    11    not in the table
Search;       Key:   408    not in the table
Insertion;    Key:    10    inserted into bucket:    12    Info: 1000
Insertion;    Key:     9    inserted into bucket:    13    Info: 9999
Insertion;    Key:     7    inserted into bucket:     7    Info: 7777
Insertion;    Key:   408    inserted into bucket:    14    Info: 4088
Insertion;    Key:    13    inserted into bucket:    15    Info: 1333
Search:       Key:    13    Info: 1333
Search:       Key:   408    Info: 4088
```

Keys 8, 108, 208, and 308 all hash to 8, with the divisor of 100 chosen to simplify studying the operation of the program. They are placed in locations 8, 9, 10, and 11, as the late-comers make linear probes upon finding that location 8 is occupied. When 10 hashes to 10, the linear probe has to go to 12 to find an empty location. (We would say that the collision resolution paths *overlap* in this case.) Key 9 hashes to 9, but the next available location by then is 13. Key 7 finds bucket 7 available, but 408 has to go to 14, and 13 has to go to 15.

We see here the effect of clustering: with several keys hashing to the same location, we find a collision resolution path as long as six, when key 408 had to go to bucket 14.

9.7 QUADRATIC HASHING

One way to attack the clustering problem is to probe in some way other than in successive table locations. The method, called *quadratic hashing,* probes the table in increasing increments, modulo the table size: $h(k)$, $H(K) + 1$, $H(K) + 4$, $H(K) + 9$, $H(K) + 16$, and so forth. Developing the squares of the integers as required here can be done without multiplication, as shown in the program.[1]

Here is the modified procedure for insertion, using quadratic hashing.

```
procedure QuadHashInsert (var A: HashTable;
                          NewKey: KeyType;
                          NewInfo: InfoType;
                          var InsertionIndex: Index);
var
   H: Index;
   Inc: integer;
begin
   H := Hash (NewKey);
   Inc := 0;

   while (A[H].Key <> MaxInt) and (A[H].Key <> NewKey) do
   begin
      H := (H + Inc + 1) mod M;
      Inc := Inc + 2
   end;

   A[H].Key := NewKey;
   A[H].Info := NewInfo;
   InsertionIndex := H
end;
```

---

[1] The method works because $d/dx\ x^2 = 2x$. Actually, a table of any polynomial may be constructed using variations of this method, and functions can be approximated from their Taylor Series. In the precomputer era, with computational tools that were vastly slower than today's simplest home computers, these *finite difference methods* were heavily used. By "slow" we mean that a fraction of a minute was required to do a single addition, multiplication was so awkward that people went to great lengths to avoid it, and division was almost impossible.

A few minutes spent tracing through the loop to find an empty hash table location will convince you that it really does generate the squares of the integers.

The modification to the `Search` procedure is simply to make the same change in the probing loop, and we shall not show it.

Here is the output for the same data as before.

```
Insertion;    Key:    123    inserted into bucket:    23    Info: 1234
Insertion;    Key:      8    inserted into bucket:     8    Info: 8888
Insertion;    Key:    108    inserted into bucket:     9    Info: 1088
Insertion;    Key:    208    inserted into bucket:    12    Info: 2088
Insertion;    Key:    308    inserted into bucket:    17    Info: 3088
Search:       Key:      8    Info: 8888
Search:       Key:    208    Info: 2088
Search;       Key:     63    not in the table
Search;       Key:     11    not in the table
Search;       Key:    408    not in the table
Insertion;    Key:     10    inserted into bucket:    10    Info: 1000
Insertion;    Key:      9    inserted into bucket:    13    Info: 9999
Insertion;    Key:      7    inserted into bucket:     7    Info: 7777
Insertion;    Key:    408    inserted into bucket:    24    Info: 4088
Insertion;    Key:     13    inserted into bucket:    14    Info: 1333
Search:       Key:     13    Info: 1333
Search:       Key:    408    Info: 4088
```

The four keys ending in 8 still hash to 8, but now the probe sequences for collision resolution are different. Key 108 goes to 9, but 208 jumps ahead by four, to 12, and 308 leaps ahead by 9, to 17. (Thus we see the squares of the integers begin generated without multiplication.) The 10 now finds bucket 10 free. Key 9 goes to 13, and 7 to 7. Key 408 jumps ahead by 16 to 24, and 13 goes to 14.

With this data, we see that quadratic hashing uses five fewer probes as linear hashing. The data was chosen to demonstrate this point, to be sure, but the only real ''tampering'' with the data was to make this happen long before the table approached overflow.

In using any open addressing hashing method, we must decide the table size in advance, which is awkward in some applications. The safe way is to guess high, but this wastes storage, and in many cases, still doesn't provide any real assurance that overflow won't occur. Naturally, any hashing system wastes some storage in a deliberate tradeoff to gain speed. But, it is painful to allocate, say, 500 locations to a hash table that will usually contain only a few dozen entries. A way out, in some cases, is *adaptive hashing,* in which the hash table is automatically enlarged and reorganized when is gets too close to being full, without coming to a full halt to rebuild the whole structure.

9.8 CHAINED HASHING

Chained hashing is one way to solve this problem. With this method, we compute an index to a hashing table in the same way as before. But now a table location does not hold an actual item, but rather holds a pointer to a linked list of all items that hash to that location.

We need the following declarations:

```
const
   M = 100;    { hash table size; normally prime; see text }
   MMinus1 = 99;

type
   KeyType = integer;      { or whatever }
   InfoType = integer;     { or whatever }

   ItemPtr = ^Item;
   Item = record
             Key: KeyType;
             Info: InfoType;
             Next: ItemPtr
          end;

   Index = 0..MMinus1;

   HashTable = array [Index] of ItemPtr;
```

Initialization now means setting all hash table entries to `Nil`, because all linked lists are empty.

```
procedure ChainHashInitialize (var A: HashTable);
var
   I: Index;
begin
   for I := 0 to MMinus1 do
      A[I] := Nil
end;
```

Insertion is a matter of placing a new node at the front of the linked list pointed to by the pointer variable found at the hash table location.

```
procedure ChainHashInsert (var A: HashTable;
                           NewKey: KeyType;
                           NewInfo: Infotype);
var
   H: Index;
   P: ItemPtr;
begin
   H := Hash(NewKey);
   New (P);
   P^.Key := NewKey;
   P^.Info := NewInfo;
   P^.Next := A[H];
   A[H] := P
end;
```

Searching is straightforward linked list processing.

```
procedure ChainHashSearch (var A: HashTable;
                           SearchArg: KeyType;
                           var SearchInfo: InfoType;
                           var Successful: boolean);
var
   P: ItemPtr;
begin
   P := A[Hash(SearchArg)];
   Successful := false;

   while (P <> Nil) and (not Successful) do
      if P^.Key = SearchArg
      then
         Successful := true
      else
         P := P^.Next;

   if Successful then
      SearchInfo := P^.Info
end;
```

Chained hashing has several advantages over open addressing methods. The major one, for many purposes, is that the *load factor* can be greater than 1.0, i.e., there can be more items stored in the lists than there are table locations. This makes it very attractive in cases where the maximum number of entries is difficult to predict. But, one must not press this advantage too far. If the number of items greatly exceeds the number of table locations, then, of course, the lists become long and performance falls off toward that for sequential methods.

Because collision resolution paths cannot overlap, chained hashing requires fewer storage accesses, both for successful and unsuccessful operations. There is also no question of contamination of the table by deletions. We simply change one link and return the item storage to the memory management system.

There are many other approaches to the basic issues in hashing, as you may discover in the sources listed in the bibliography.

The major points about hashing are as follows:

1. Hashing obtains search times that are independent of the number of items by deliberately wasting some storage.

2. This high speed, which no other method can match, can be compromised by clustering and by excessive collision resolution operations in a table that is approaching overflow.

3. Chaining reduces the severity of these problems, but at the expense of extra storage for the links.

4. Hashing is dynamic. Mixtures of insertions, searches, and deletions are handled smoothly, with only minor problems in some variations.

5. Hashing is an attractive way to implement sets. Knowledge of the universal set permits making a good choice of table size; insertion need only involve avoiding inserting the same item twice, because that has no meaning for sets; all operations times are independent of how many of the possible set elements are present. With simple changes it is also a good way to implement a *bag,* which is like a set except that duplicates are permitted.

9.9 AN OVERVIEW OF AVL TREES

We have seen that hashing has a number of advantages, which lead to its widespread use in a variety of applications. But the way hashing deals with the space-time tradeoff forces us to waste some storage and, in a situation where it is difficult to predict how much storage is needed, we must waste a *lot* of storage and/or go to the extra time and trouble of adaptive hashing. Furthermore, although hashing is spectacularly fast on the average, its worst-case behavior, when heavy clustering occurs, is poor.

An AVL tree is a specialized binary search tree developed by two Russian mathematicians, G. M. Adel'son-Vel'skii and E. M. Landis, in 1962.[2] The major advantage of AVL trees is that they permit insertion, retrieval, and deletion to be done in a dynamic application, all with a worst-case performance of $O(\lg N)$. Furthermore, no additional storage is needed beyond that for links in the binary tree representation.

An AVL tree is a *height-balanced tree:* we require that, at every node in the tree, the height of the left and right subtrees differ by no more than one. As we saw in Chapter 7, we can by no means assume that a binary search tree will grow in such a way as to satisfy this condition, and the heart of the method is a technique for *rebalancing* the tree when an insertion has unbalanced it.

Here are some height-balanced trees:

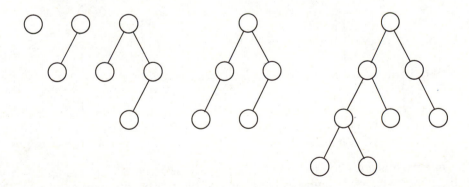

[2]*Doklady Akademia Nauk SSSR* **146** (1962); English translation in Soviet Math. **3,** 1259-1263.

These three trees are not height-balanced:

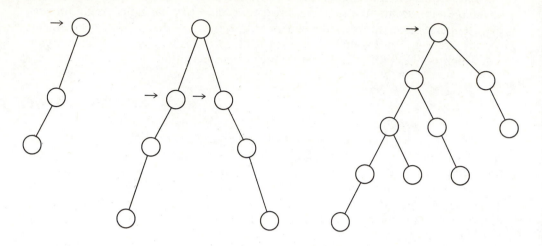

The balance requirement is violated at each of the nodes marked with arrows. The addition of a node (which always occurs at a leaf, of course) can cause the tree to become unbalanced anywhere between the grandparent of the new node and the root of the tree.

Adding a new node to a height-balanced tree may or may not cause it to become unbalanced. If it does, rebalancing the tree requires either a single or a double *rotation,* as they are called, depending on which of two cases we have encountered. A case requiring a single rotation is shown in the following sketch, where the balance factors are for the tree after addition of the new node.

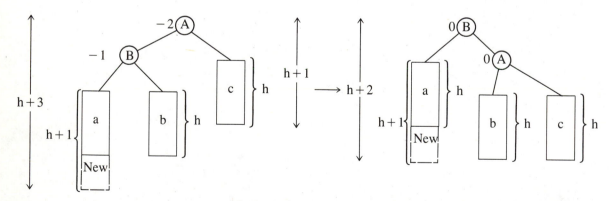

The number outside the circle representing a node is called the *balance factor* of the node, which we define as the height of the right subtree minus the height of the left subtree. The rectangles represent subtrees of equal height, possibly zero. We see in the diagram on the left that a tree that was balanced—the height of its left and right subtrees differed by one—has become unbalanced because after the addition of a new node, its left subtree is two higher than its right. The problem has been corrected in the diagram on the right, by what we shall call a *right-rotation* of the subtree rooted at A.

It is crucial, of course, that this rotation not destroy the lexicographic ordering of the nodes under an inorder traversal. We still need for the transformed tree to be a binary search tree. A simple demonstration that a rotation does preserve lexicographic order follows; the addition of the 4 has unbalanced the tree at its root:

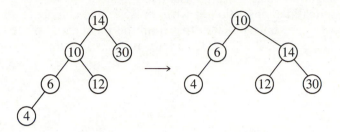

This is a right rotation; there is a symmetrical left rotation.

Rebalancing the tree is a simple matter of adjusting three links. Here is the code for a procedure that does a right rotation:

```
procedure RotateRight (var T: Tree);
var
    Temp: Tree;
begin
    Temp := T;
    T := T^.Left;
    Temp^.Left:= T^.Right;
    T^.Right:= Temp
end;
```

This is just a cyclic reassignment of three pointers.

A tree can become unbalanced in a way that requires two rotations to correct. Here is the general picture of one of the two symmetric cases:

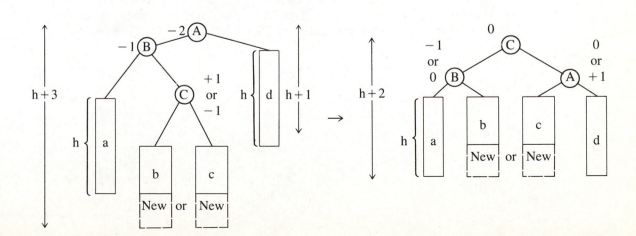

As before, the rectangles represent subtrees of arbitrary height, possibly zero. If the subtrees are of non-zero height, then subtrees b and c can either be of the same height or differ by one. To cause imbalance in the latter case, the new node must be added to the higher subtree.

To correct this situation, we first do a *left* rotation around B , followed by a *right* rotation around A . In coding terms, we can either do two separate rotations, or set up a single procedure that adjusts five links.

For a numerical demonstration of what an AVL tree can accomplish, suppose we build an ordinary binary search tree from the input: 50, 45, 15, 10, 75, 55, 70, 80, 60, 32, 20, 40, 25, 22, 31, and 30. It looks like this:

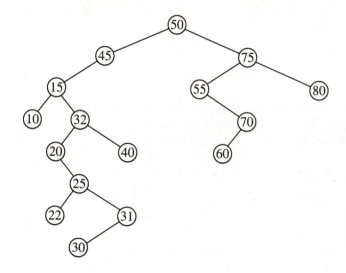

We see that we have one node at level 1, two at level 2, three each at levels 3, 4, and 5, one at level 6, two at level 7, and one at level 8. Summing level numbers for all nodes and dividing by the number of nodes gives the average node height, a rough but serviceable measure of the effort to retrieve a node from this tree. The result for this tree is about 4.3.

Because this is only an overview, we shall not go through the details of rebalancing this tree as it is built. It turns out, however, that rebalancing is required five times, when the nodes for 15, 55, 60, 25, and 30 are inserted. The result is as follows:

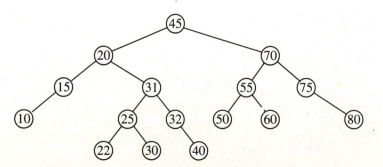

What we have accomplished by the trouble of making these five rotations? Going through the same counting of levels as before, we find that the average node height is 3.5. This is only a little worse than an optimum binary search tree, which would have only one node on the bottom level instead of three, with a resultant average search path length of about 3.2.

Naturally, one set of sample data doesn't make a theorem. In general, an AVL tree turns out to require about 40 percent fewer comparisons to retrieve a node than a random binary search tree. If there are sufficiently more retrievals than insertions in an application, then the AVL tree makes great sense. Plus, it buys a guarantee that the search time will never degenerate too much below the average. In comparison, a random binary search tree can degenerate badly.

In summary:

1. In the average number of comparisons required to retrieve a node value or to establish that it is not in the tree, AVL trees save about 40 percent over random binary trees. Better yet, the worst-case behavior is still $O(\lg N)$.

2. AVL trees waste no storage, at least not the way hash tables do. However, they require space for the links and the balance factors.

3. The tree rebalancing needed to provide these benefits happens less than half of the time when a new node is inserted. The process requires an algorithm that can locate the correct place to do the rebalancing; the rebalancing itself requires only the adjustment of a few pointers.

4. Performance of AVL algorithms is independent of the order in which insertions and searches is carried out. In particular, they can be mixed, i.e., searches in a dynamically changing search tree incur no time penalty.

5. Whether there is a net benefit depends on the relative number of insertions and searches. If there are few searches relative to insertions and there is no serious penalty for longer-than-average searches, then AVL trees are not worth the trouble. If there are many more searches than insertions, and especially if they are intermixed, an AVL tree can be a good choice. This assumes, of course, our ground rule for the chapter: the table must fit in main storage.

9.10 COMPARISON OF THE METHODS

The search methods we have considered can be compared, in an approximate kind of way, by the average number operations they take to carry out searches, insertions, and deletions, as a function of the number of table items. The table on the next page shows this comparison.

This table can help you see the major differences between methods, but it should not be taken too literally. For example, when we say that the cost of an insertion in an unordered array is 1, we mean that the time is constant. The cost of insertion in a hash table is also constant if the table is much less than full. But, naturally this does not mean that computing the hash function is free. With these provisos, the table does provide a basis for some generalizations about the usefulness of the various approaches to searching.

	Succ. Search	Unsucc. Search	Locate insert position	Insert	Locate delete position	Delete
Unordered Array	$N/2$	N	0	1	$N/2$	1
Ordered Array	$N/2$	$N/2$	$N/2$	$N/2$	$N/2$	$N/2$
Unordered linked list	$N/2$	N	0	1	$N/2$	1
Ordered Linked list	$N/2$	$N/2$	$N/2$	1	$N/2$	1
Binary search	lg N	lg N	Does not apply			
Hashing*	1	1	0	1	0	1
AVL tree	lg N	lg N	lg N	lg N	lg N	lg N

*Assumes load factor $\ll 1$.

Arrays and linked lists are simple to program, just fine for small tables, useless for large ones, and sometimes a reasonable choice for medium-sized ones. As crude and slow as it is, an unordered array does have the advantage that it applies to dynamic situations, meaning that there is a mixture or insertions, deletions, and searches. The code is simple, with few traps. When tables get so large as to slow down the linked list approach, a self-organizing approach may redeem them.

For static applications—no insertions or deletions once the table is built— binary search is a leading contender. Even when there is a mixture of insertions and searches, the details of the application may still permit binary search to be used, as when a new item can be inserted while waiting for the completion of a buffered input operation.

When speed is critical and there is adequate memory space, hashing usually wins. There are various ways to get in trouble (clustering, badly degraded performance of an open addressing system as the table fills), so the method has to be adjusted to the specifics of the application. That having been said, hashing still has wide applicability.

AVL trees are attractive when $O(\lg N)$ performance is needed in a dynamic situation and when it is difficult to predict table size so as to design an appropriate hash table.

9.11 AN OVERVIEW OF THE ISSUES IN EXTERNAL SEARCHING

The purpose of many, if not most, computer applications is rapid storage and retrieval of amounts of data that are much larger than can be retained in the main memory of any computer, but which must be stored on magnetic disk. Examples range from airline reservations systems to college registrar's data bases, from insurance policyholder files to telephone directory assistance, from a list of all authorized users of a time-shared computer to mail-order catalogs. Any member of modern society could expand this list many times over.

In all such applications the primary characteristics are a *vast amount* of data, and the need to be able to find the data about any one passenger/student/

policyholder/subscriber/user/product in a time scale of a few seconds. "A vast amount" of data means at least thousands of items, with hundreds of thousands not uncommon and millions not rare. A few seconds might mean that 10 to 20 seconds would be acceptable in some cases, but in others a small fraction of a second would be more realistic.

The techniques you have learned in this chapter, and indeed the rest of the book, are useful tools in these kinds of applications. But we must consider yet another factor that comes into play, one that completely dominates other issues. It is that the time needed to get one item from a disk is roughly 10,000 times as long as the time to do an internal operation such as comparing two keys. Once you have found one item on a disk, the rest of the group it is part of may be obtained very quickly. But, finding that first one means waiting for a physical device to turn, and that means a time scale vastly longer than the times involved with transistors.

What this all boils down to is that in searching for data on disks, the primary consideration is to minimize the number of *disk accesses,* the number of times we go to disk for data. Let us build up the argument for the basic approach to disk searching in a few steps.

The absolute minimum number of accesses is, of course, one. Suppose (unrealistically) that the data base (collection of items) were small enough that, having invested the time waiting to find locate the first item, we could then read in all the others. Once in internal storage, the techniques studied in this chapter would come into play: binary search, hashing, AVL trees, or whatever might best fit the application characteristics.

Next, suppose that there is more data in the data base than we can obtain with one disk read. What shall we do? Read the first group, then the second, and so forth, until finding the one that contains the item we want? It is obvious that this won't do get the job done.

Instead, we need to obtain, on the first access, some type of *index* that will, if possible, tell us exactly where to go to get our first item of interest. If the amount of data is larger, so that one access cannot get an index to everything, then perhaps on one access we can get a partial index. This would let us pick the right piece of the rest of the index, and in turn, let us find the data. The total would be three accesses.

This is the motivation behind a special kind of tree known as a *B-tree.*[3] A B-tree of order m is a general tree in which the following conditions exist:

1. All leaves are at the same level.

2. All internal nodes except the root have at least $\lceil m/2 \rceil$ children and, at most, m children.

3. The root has at least two children and may have as many as m.

4. The number of values in each internal node is one less than the number of children it has, and these values partition the values in the children of the node.

[3]The origin of the name has been lost in the mists of history. The "B" definitely does *not* stand for "binary," but whether it stands for "Bayer," "Boeing," or any of several other possibilities, is not clear. See the discussion in Comer (1979).

Here, for example, is a B-tree of order 5:

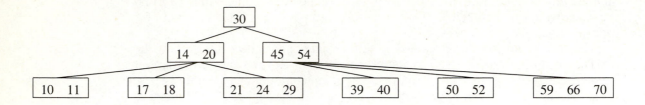

The maximum search path length is always three in this tree.

Let us watch this B-tree grow as values are inserted into it in the following sequence: 10, 21, 20, 11, 39, 17, 24, 45, 30, 18, 59, 29, 54, 70, 14, 40, 50, 60, 66, 52.

The first four can be placed in the root, and they are arranged in increasing order.

$$\boxed{10 \quad 11 \quad 20 \quad 21}$$

Insertion of the 39 requires this node to be split, with the median of the five values becoming the new root.

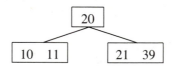

We thus see that, in contrast with a binary search tree, a B-tree grows new levels at the root instead of at the leaves.

Now 17, 24, and 45 can be inserted into the leaves.

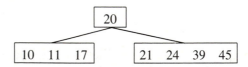

Insertion of the 30 forces splitting a leaf. The median of the values, which happens to be the new value, goes to the node above it.

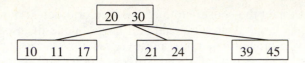

The 18, 59, 29, and 54 can be inserted into leaves.

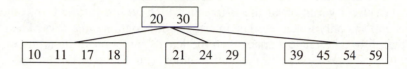

Insertion of the 70 forces splitting the rightmost leaf. The median of the values, which is not the inserted item this time, goes to the node above:

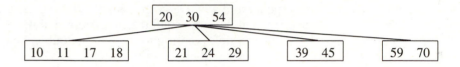

As we insert the 14, the leftmost leaf splits. The 40, 50, 60, and 66 can then go into leaves.

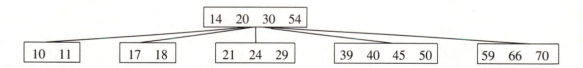

Finally, we insert the 52. Its insertion into a leaf forces the leaf to split, with the median of the five values (45) going to the node above. But now that node has to be split, with its median (30) becoming a new root of the final B-tree.

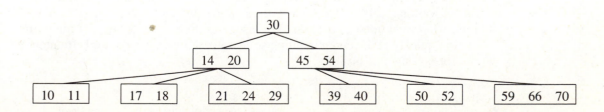

We have illustrated the construction of a B-tree of order 5, but in practice the order would be as large as possible and still have a node fit in one disk storage unit. The units of storage (the amount retrieved with one access) are in the range of 512 to 4096 characters typically, and B-trees of order 200 are not uncommon.[4]

We close this overview of external searching with a sketch of one popular disk storage management system that is founded on the B-tree idea.

Suppose we make two changes to the schema we just sketched. First, we assume that the records contain much information (dozens to hundreds or thousands of characters) but that the keys are much shorter (dozens of characters). Now we devise a variation of the B-tree in which record information other than the keys appears only in leaves. The interior nodes contain only keys. The interior nodes therefore take far less space than the leaves, and constitute an index to the information in the leaves. If the entire index (all the interior nodes) can be retrieved with one disk access, then any record can be obtained in a total of two accesses. If there are too many records for this to work, then perhaps it can be done with three—one to the top level of the index, followed by a second to the appropriate part of the rest of the index, then the record itself. In practice, very large files can be managed in this way, with a maximum of three or four disk accesses.

As a second change, we introduce links between the leaves. Having located any one record, it is not necessary to go back through the index retrieval process to find its successor, because there is a link pointing to it. With a doubly-linked list the records can be retrieved in either sequence.

As a result, we thus have a combination of a hierarchical index that permits rapid location of any one record in a data base (that may be massive), and the advantage of rapid processing of records in sequence. The method is according called an *indexed-sequential access method,* with the acronym ISAM. In any of a number of variations, it is widely used in the commercial data processing world.

9.12 APPLICATION: LETTER-SEQUENCE FREQUENCIES REVISITED

The letter-sequence frequency application that we studied in Chapter 2 was essentially a searching problem, which we solved there with an array. Suppose we broaden the requirement to *word* frequencies, and see how the methods of this chapter might be applied.

Once we need to report the frequencies of entire words, the method used in Chapter 2 becomes completely impractical. Now we need some way to store words of varying length, together with their frequency counts, in such a way that insertions and updates are fast. We also need to be able to inspect the entire collection quickly at the end of reading so that we can pick out the high-frequency words for sorting and printing.

---

[4]Searching in these indexes would draw on the techniques for internal searching that we have already considered.

This description translates into the need for a dynamic technique. By the nature of the task, insertions and retrievals are intermixed in a random way that cannot be avoided. With hundreds of words, sequential methods would be much too slow on both insertions and retrievals. The intermixture of insertions and retrievals rules out binary search, which would require linear-time effort on each insertion to keep the table sorted.

That leaves hashing, which is the only dynamic method we have studied in enough detail to see programs. (AVL trees might also be a reasonable approach, but because hashing has much wider applicability we would prefer to illustrate it anyway.)

The overall program design from Section 2.10 requires little change. A hierarchy chart can now be sketched as follows:

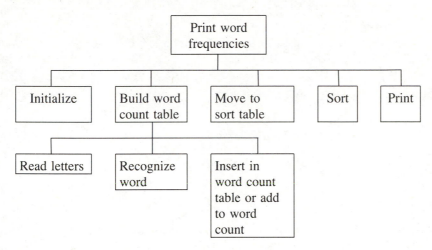

The program will make heavy use of packages of procedures developed in previous chapters, with some necessary modifications as noted. The overall work of building the word frequency table will be a single procedure, with six sets of programs brought in by a compiler directive. (Your compiler directives might be different, or you might have to bring the programs in with an editor.) All the interesting parameters, such as the minimum word length to be reported, are shown as constants at the beginning of the program, to make them easy to find and (safely) modify.

The program of Figure 9.1 consists mostly of the procedure `Report-WordFrequencies,` which is embedded in a main program.

The string package brought in under the name `StrPak` is borrowed from Chapter 3 and based on an array implementation. The code brought under the names `GetWdPak` and `HashPak` are described in the following pages. `MovePak, SortPak,` and `PrintPak` are service routines, changed only slightly from their Chapter 2 versions, and will not be shown.

The work of the procedure is neatly summarized in the rather brief code in its body, which closely parallels the hierarchy chart. The only detail in the code not shown on the chart is the test for a minimum length word. You might wish to set this threshold at four, for example, to exclude "the" and "and," etc., which might not be of interest.

```
program WordFrequency (input, output);
{ Produce a word frequency report. }

procedure ReportWordFrequencies;

const
   MaxStrLength = 80;
   SortTableSize = 500;
   MinWordLength = 5;
   MinWordFreq = 5;
   HashTableSize = 1009;
   HashTableSizeMinus1 = 1008;

type
   StrIndex = 0..MaxStrLength;

   StrType = record
                Ch: array [1..MaxStrLength] of char;
                Length: StrIndex
             end;

   HashTablePtr = ^WordCountRecord;

   WordCountRecord = record
                        Word: StrType;
                        Count: integer;
                        Next: HashTablePtr
                     end;

   HashIndex = 0..HashTableSizeMinus1;

   HashTableType = array [HashIndex] of HashTablePtr;

   SortTableType = array [1..SortTableSize] of WordCountRecord;

var
   Word: StrType;
   HashTable: HashTableType;
   SortTable: SortTableType;
   N: Integer;

{$I StrPak }
{$I GetWdPak }
{$I HashPak }
{$I MovePak }
{$I SortPak }
{$I PrintPak }

begin
   InitializeHashTable (HashTable);
   CreateStr (Word);

   while not EOF do
   begin
      GetWord (Word);
      if StrLength (Word) >= MinWordLength then
      InsertOrIncrement (HashTable, Word)
   end;
```

```
    MoveHighFreqWordsToSortTable (HashTable, SortTable, N);

    Sort (SortTable, N);

    PrintResults (SortTable, N);
end;


begin
    ReportWordFrequencies
end.
```

FIGURE 9.1

A main program and a procedure to report word frequencies, based on a hash table implementation.

"Getting" a word basically means *recognizing* a word, according to whatever definition of a word is to be used. We shall define a word to be any contiguous sequence of letters, terminated by a blank, any character other than a letter, or the end of the line.

Recognizing a word in a language, according to some definition or a word, is a classical problem in computer science. It occurs in the processing of almost any text—such as the text of a computer program. An early step in the work of a compiler is *lexical analysis,* in which the text is broken into *tokens* such as identifiers, operators, etc. One common way to approach the design of a word recognizer is with a *transition diagram* showing how the program moves from one *state* to another in the process of recognizing a word (or other token). Here is a transition diagram for our task:

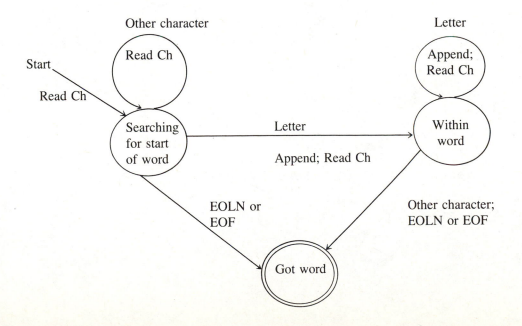

The circles designate states. At the start of the process we are looking for the start of a word, having read a character. If the character is a letter, as shown above the arrow going to the right, then we want to append it to the word we are building (which was empty), read another character, and move into a new state called `WithinWord`. If we encounter any character other than a letter while searching for the start of a word, we are still searching, so we get another character and return to the same state. If we should encounter the end-of-line or end-of-file signal, we go to the `GotWord` state, relying on the user of the recognize to check for zero length words. (Other applications could require alternative approaches to this issue of encountering the end of the input while still searching.)

Once we are within a word, we want to continue reading characters and appending them to the word that is being built up, until encountering anything except a letter.

`GotWord` is in a double circle, meaning that it an *accepting state*. We set out to recognize a word; if we reach the accepting state, we have found one.

`GetWdPak` includes a procedure named `GetWord` that implements this transition diagram, together with simple procedures to handle uppercase and lowercase letters. Here they are:

```pascal
function IsUpperCaseLetter (Ch: char): boolean;
begin
    IsUpperCaseLetter := Ch in ['A'..'I',
                                'H'..'R',
                                'S'..'Z']  { works for EBCDIC, too }
end;
```

```pascal
function IsLetter (Ch: char): boolean;
begin
    IsLetter := Ch in ['a'..'i',
                       'h'..'r',
                       's'..'z']
end;
```

```pascal
procedure GetWord (var Word: StrType);

const
    ASCIILowerCaseConvert = +32;

type
    StateVar = (SearchingForStartOfWord, WithinWord, GotWord);

var
    State: StateVar;
    Ch: char;
```

```
begin
    MakeStrEmpty (Word);
    State := SearchingForStartOfWord;

    while State <> GotWord do
    begin
        if EOLN then
            ReadLn;

        Read (Ch);
        if IsUpperCaseLetter (Ch) then
            Ch := Chr(Ord(Ch) + ASCIILowerCaseConvert);

        case State of

            SearchingForStartOfWord:
            begin
                if IsLetter (Ch) then
                begin
                    AppendChar (Word, Ch);
                    State := WithinWord
                end;
                if EOLN or EOF then
                    State := GotWord    { possibly empty }
            end;

            WithinWord:
            begin
                if IsLetter (Ch) then
                    AppendChar (Word, Ch)
                else
                    State := GotWord;
                if EOLN  or EOF then
                    State := GotWord
            end

        end    { case }

    end    { while }

end;    { procedure GetWord }
```

Observe how the case statement is a reasonably direct representation of the transition diagram. This makes it fairly easy to modify the program to recognize words according to different definitions than we are using. Exercise 19 asks you to explore this problem.

All that is left is the hash table management. It is difficult to predict distributions of words in the absence of even a statement of what language we are to process, so we chose chained hashing. This permits the program to keep working, even if the guess on hash table size should turn out to be badly wrong, while waiting for an opportunity to take the system off-line and make modifications. (Degraded performance is almost always preferable to a program crash.)

Initializing the chained hash table is done by the procedure already shown in Section 9.8, which will not be repeated.

The hash function is necessarily somewhat different because we have alphabetic data to deal with. It is not difficult to convert a letter to a numerical equivalent, of course, simply using the Pascal `Ord` function. Everything else depends on performance requirements, in other words, how crucial is it to be sure that the hashed addresses minimize clustering? This is rather difficult to quantify in the absence of more information about the data, and turns out not to be critical for this application.

We choose to multiply the numerical equivalent of every other character by a constant that will generate addresses covering the full range of a reasonable-sized hash table, but to put a limit on the number of letters to include in the hashing. The tradeoff, clearly, is between the time to hash in some elegant way—which takes time—and the time saved in reduced clustering. As shown in the following function, we hash only on the basis of the first three letters. Consequently, "imperial" and "implementation," for example, will both hash to the same location but, of course, the collision resolution method will insure that the two words will not be confused.

This is the hashing function:

```
function Hash (TextWord: StrType): integer;
const
   MaxCharsToHash = 3;
   HashMultiplier = 37;
var
   H, I, WordLength: integer;
begin
   H := 0;
   I := 1;
   WordLength := StrLength (TextWord);

   while (I <= WordLength) and (I <= MaxCharsToHash) do
   begin
      if Odd (I) then
         H := H + Ord (TextWord.Ch[I])
      else
         H := H + HashMultiplier * Ord (TextWord.Ch[I]);
      I := I + 1
   end;

   Hash := H mod HashTableSize
end;
```

The final procedure that we shall consider is the one that either inserts a word in the hash table if it doesn't exist there, or increments its count if it does. The choice between the two can be made only by going to the hash table; once there, we can either build a new record in the chain, or add 1 to the count.

It would be a nice touch, of course, to be able to draw on the linked list operations of Chapter 6 for processing the collision resolution chains. Regrettably, that is not possible, for the reason noted in Chapter 6. There, to keep things simple, we used a primitive (non-structured) `Item`. Now, as life will have it, we need both a field for the word and a field for the count, so the earlier operations are not suitable.

However, the explicit coding of the linked list operations we need is not complicated, as follows:

```
procedure InsertOrIncrement (var HT: HashTableType;
                                 TextWord: StrType);
var
   H: HashIndex;
   P: HashTablePtr;
   AlreadyInTable: boolean;

begin
   H := Hash (TextWord);
   P := HT[H];
   AlreadyInTable := false;

   while (P <> Nil) and (not AlreadyInTable) do
   if CompareStr (P^.Word, TextWord) = '=' then
      AlreadyInTable := true
   else
      P := P^.Next;

   if AlreadyInTable
   then
      P^.Count := P^.Count + 1
   else
   begin
      New (P);
      CopyStr (TextWord, 1, StrLength (Word), P^.Word);
      P^.Count := 1;
      P^.Next := HT[H];
      HT[H] := P
   end
end;
```

Here is the output when this program was run with the text of Sections 9.1 and 9.2 as input, with the minimum word length and minimum word frequency both set at five:

```
    20    table
    14    would
    12    there
     9    example
     8    information
     8    items
     7    shall
     7    search
     6    program
     6    storage
     6    number
     6    field
     6    primary
     5    which
     5    implementation
     5    searching
     5    design
```

When run with the same data but with the constants changed so that the minimum word length was three and the minimum word frequency was eight, this was the output:

```
83    the
23    and
20    table
19    are
18    that
14    for
14    would
13    with
12    there
11    this
10    not
10    one
10    key
 9    example
 8    item
 8    items
 8    time
 8    may
 8    information
```

The performance of the program easily falls within a "a second or so after completion of reading the input." That expectation was stated as a requirement in Chapter 2. On the other hand, the reading stage was somewhat slower than what we might expect from the program and the machine. A bit of experimentation showed that large amounts of time were being spent in executing procedures such as `IsLetter,` which is based on Pascal set operations.

In a real-life situation, the obvious solution would be to recode these in assembly language, taking advantage of whatever machine instructions were available to speed the work. In most higher-level languages intended for production programming (such as Ada, Modula-2, PL/I, or C), it would be possible to combine such assembly language routines with the rest of an ordinary program. It is quite common that a small percentage of the code uses a high fraction of the total time, and that the few critical pieces are not very complex and are easily coded in a lower-level language.

Exercises 16 and 17 ask you to see what you can do to improve performance while staying with Pascal.

9.13 CONCLUSION

In a certain sense, many important applications of computers boil down to search and retrieval. Obtaining one piece of data out of thousands, and doing it in two seconds instead of two minutes or two hours, is one basic reason people use computers. These kinds of applications require you to know much more than we can discuss here about the characteristics of external storage devices and the systems and programming techniques for using them effectively. That is an entire body of serious study. We have been able to do no more than give you a preview of this study.

On the other hand, many other applications demand high performance on search operations for tables held in internal storage, which was our chapter topic. And, these internal methods are also used in conjunction with external searching. If you have just brought in a 200-item index to a 500,000 item data base, for example, you need to be able to find the right place in the index in a hurry. This chapter has given you the tools to do that.

<hr>

EXERCISES

1.

Sequential search in an unordered table T can be speeded up in several ways:
- **(a)** If the search table is of size N, add an $N + 1$st record. Before beginning a search for `SearchArg,` copy `SearchArg` into `T[N+1]`. An unsuccessful search will then be indicated if the search index reaches $N+1$.
  - **(i)** Write an algorithm for sequential search with a dummy record.
  - **(ii)** Search is still an $O(N)$ operation. Why is it faster than sequential search without a dummy?
- **(b)** Another alternative is the insertion of a sentinel at the end of the table. (Recall that a sentinel is a value of the same type as the table items, but which is an impossible value of `SearchArg.`) How does this method compare with (a), above?
- **(c)** Still another possibility is to add a dummy, as in (a), but, to test two elements in the loop rather than one. An algorithm using the boolean `Found` is:

```
T[N+1] := SearchArg;
Found := false;
I := -1;

while (I < N) and (not Found) do
begin
    I := I + 2;
    if T[I] = SearchArg then
        Found := true
    else if T[I+1] = SearchArg then
        Found := true
end;

if I = N + 1 then
    Found := false;
```

  - **(i)** Trace this algorithm with tables where N is even and where N is odd.
  - **(ii)** Why is this algorithm faster than either of those in (a) or (b)?
- **(d)** Do any of the algorithms above fail if $N = 0$?
- **(e)** Code (a) through (c) and test them on the same data, comparing running times.

2. If the search table is ordered on the search key, the algorithms of Exercise 1 do not require a dummy record.
   (a) Does the algorithm of Exercise 1 (c) still work? If not, what changes must be made?
   (b) Are sequential search algorithms faster for an ordered search table than for one that is unordered:
   (i) For a successful search?
   (ii) For an unsuccessful search?

3. There are three abnormal situations where the binary search program of Section 9.4 will fail:
   - $N = 0$.
   - `SearchArg.Key` < `A[1].Key`, or `SearchArg.Key` > `A[N].Key`.
   - The table is not ordered on the `Key`.

   For each of these conditions, discuss:
   (a) How likely the condition is to occur, and whether the program should be expected to detect it.
   (b) If your answer for any of the conditions is that the program should be required to detect it and report the error, suggest ways to handle the problem. Consider program changes and turning off run-time checking. Discuss the effect on portability.
   (c) In terms of a few applications that you specify, discuss the design tradeoffs between the responsibility of the writer of a search routine to detect all abnormal conditions, versus the responsibility of the user of the routine to provide valid data.

4. Why is binary search unsuitable in a situation where insertions and deletions on the table occur fairly frequently?
   (a) Suggest a system for marking deleted records, with table reorganization occurring only at off-peak times, such as weekends or at night.
   (b) Could insertions be handled in a similar manner? If so, how?

5. Suppose characters are represented by ASCII codes. What value(s) of M, used to compute the hash function, $h(K) = K \bmod M$, would hash the identifiers `APTR`, `BPTR` and `CPTR` to the same location? What value(s) would hash `X1`, `Y1`, and `Z1` to the same location? Consider the following internal character representations:
   (a) Characters are represented by eight-bit codes, allowing for the full ASCII character set, both printing and non-printing.
   (b) Characters are represented as seven-bit codes, which do not include foreign letters or graphics symbols. (Character strings are packed.)
   (c) Characters are represented by six-bit codes. Here we might be limited to ASCII codes between 32 (blank space) and 95 (underscore). This character type would include no lowercase letters. Assume that strings are packed, so that, for example, `APTR` occupies 24 bits.

6. Another method for computing hash values, which is used on some com-

puters because of its speed, is based on the logical function XOR. If APTR is represented in six-bit code as 100001 110000 110100 110010, Hash (APTR) = (100001 XOR 110000 XOR 110100 XOR 110010) mod 64 = 010111 mod 64 = 10111.

(a) Why is 64 a reasonable modulus value here?

(b) What is the disadvantage to this method? (Hint: Compute the XOR of RAPT.)

(c) How would this hash function work if an identifier were limited to a single uppercase letter or a single uppercase letters followed by a digit, as in early Basic?

(d) Is *scattering* (the opposite of clustering) improved if the second digit of a six-digit character number is 0 instead of 1, as in the ASCII code? (For example, '1' is coded as 000001, rather than 010001.)

7. Both methods presented for rehashing NewKey on detecting a collision involve probing the table in increasing increments modulo the table size until an empty location is found. A third method for computing the increments *Inc*$_i$ is due to Morris (1968). It eliminates the clustering problem by picking the increments in a pseudorandom fashion, and works well when the hash table size is 2^k, for some $k > 0$. It is called RandomRehash, and works as follows:

- Initialize $R = 1$.

- To calculate each *Inc*$_i$, do the following:
    Let $R = R*5$.
    Mask out all but the low order $k+2$ bits of R, and place the result in R.
    Let *Inc*$_i$ be the result of shifting R right 2 bits.

For example, suppose $k = 8$, and $R_{i-1} = 308$. Then $R_i = R_{i-1} * 5 = 1540 = $ 0000 0110 0000 0100. Masking out all but the low-order $8 + 2 = 10$ bits, leaves $R_i = $ 0000 0010 0000 0100. *Inc*$_i = $ 0000 0000 1000 0001 $= 129$.

(a) Compute 10 increments beginning with $R = 1$. Do they appear to be pseudorandom?

(b) Write a Pascal RandomRehash function.

(c) When using RandomRehash for searching, a good estimate of the expected number of comparisons needed depends on the load factor, *LF*: $E(NumComparisons) = -(1/LF) \log(1-LF)$. Compute the expected number of comparisons for load factors of 0.1, 0.5, and 0.9. What happens to the expected number of comparisons if $LF = 1$, meaning that the hash table is full?

8. (For those who have had a little calculus.) A footnote in section 9.7 on quadratic hashing states that the loop

```
begin
    H := (H + Inc + 1) mod M;
    Inc := Inc + 2
end;
```

produces the successive squares of the integers if `Inc` is initialized to 0, because $d/dx \ x^2 = 2x$. Explain. Can you see a way to generate the cubes of the integers, using some variation of this technique?

9. Write a procedure, `ChainHashDelete,` to delete an item from a chained hash table. Why is this easier than deleting from a linear hash table?

10. When a program is compiled, several tables must be formed. These include a *symbol table,* which holds a list of identifiers along with their types and values. Use any of the hashing methods to construct a symbol table for the code of the procedure `QuadHashInsert`.

    Deciding which strings represent identifiers is the job of the parser. Assume the parse phase has been completed and use the identifiers as input to your program. (In actuality, of course, the symbol table would be constructed as the parsing was carried out.) Because identifiers in Pascal can be any length, the actual names can be kept in a separate `NameList,` with the symbol table holding a pointer to the name list. You may also assume that a `TypeTable` has already been constructed, and use it as input to your program. Use the following declaration for your hash table `InfoType`:

```
InfoType = record
   NamePtr: ^NameList;
   IdentType: TypeTableIndex;
   Value: integer    {Represents the starting address for the
                      memory location identified.}
end.
```

11. We discussed two implementations of sets in Chapter 3 and a linked list implementation in Chapter 6. For various reasons, all of these methods are awkward for large sets. Suppose a large set is maintained as a hash table.
    (a) Write algorithms for each of the set operations included in the ADT set, as shown in Section 3.2. Can `MakeUniversalSet` be implemented with a hash table? What about `Complement`?
    (b) What changes would you have to make in your algorithms of (a) to implement a bag?

12. An AVL, or height-balanced, tree was described in Section 9.9. Build an AVL tree from the input used in the text: 50, 45, 15, 10, 75, 55, 70, 80, 60, 32, 20, 40, 25, 22, 31, and 30.
    (a) Write the `BalanceFactor` beside each node and keep your tree balanced at each insertion.
    (b) What values of `BalanceFactor` signal the need for a right rotation? A left rotation? Both?
    (c) How far up the tree must one check balance factors to assure balance of the entire tree?
    (d) How and when should this checking be done? Is it necessary to check balance factors before an insertion? Is it necessary to check balance

factors after a balancing other than at the root? If not all balance factors need to be checked, which ones do?

13. Tree balancing can be done by *weight* instead of height. (Weight-balanced trees become especially important when nodes themselves are weighted; that is, some are more important than others, but they are still sometimes useful when nodes are of equal weight.) Consider a tree T_N, with N nodes of equal weight. The (weight) balance of T_N, $WB(T_N) = (L+1)/(N+1)$, where L is the number of nodes in the left subtree. (Do we prefer large or small values of *WB?*) Consider the 16-node tree of Section 9.9. Before height balancing, $WB(T_{16}) = 11/17$. After height balancing, $WB(T_{16}) = 10/17$.

   (a) Reorganize the structure of the tree discussed above to achieve a weight balance factor $WB = 8/17$ or $WB = 9/17$. Insert nodes into the weight-balanced tree in the order given, but adjust the organization after each insertion to optimize balance while maintaining the binary search tree characteristic of lexicographic ordering under an inorder traversal.

   (b) Draw a tree, T_{11}, such that $WB(T_{11}) = 1/3$, which is not height-balanced. Also draw a tree, T'_{11}, with $WB(T'_{11}) = 1/3$, where T'_{11} is height-balanced.

   (c) Draw a height-balanced tree, T''_{10}, such that $WB(T''_{10}) = 3/11$.

14. Consider the modified B-trees mentioned at the end of Section 9.11, used as the basis of the Indexed Sequential Access Method (ISAM).

   (a) Draw a diagram of such a tree as constructed from the data used in Section 9.9: 50, 45, 15, 10, 75, 55, 70, 80, 60, 32, 20, 40, 25, 22, 31, and 30.

   (b) Draw the tree resulting from your tree of (a) after inserting a record with key field of 56.

   (c) Continue (b) with the following insertions:
   47, 32, 16, 15, 12.
   Be sure to split nodes and rebalance the tree when necessary.

15. Basic operations implemented for an ISAM system are `Find`, `Get`, `GetNext`, `Insert`, and `Delete`. Assume the existence of two pointers to an ISAM-type B-tree: `Root` points to the root of the tree and `Current` points to the record most recently accessed. `Find` locates a record, given its key. `Get` moves a record into the user's workspace for processing after a `Find`. `GetNext` finds the next record after that pointed to by `Current` and moves it into the user's workspace. `Insert` inserts a record immediately after that pointed to by `Current`. `Delete` deletes a record, after a `Find`, and then sets `Current` to `Nil`.

   Redraw the tree of Exercise 14 (c) after each of the following operations has been executed, keeping track of the location of `Current`:

   (a) `Find (Key = 45)`
   (b) `Delete (Current)`
   (c) `Find (Key = 30)`

(d)

```
Current = Root;
Find (First);    {You can figure out what this means.}
Get (Current);
while (more data) do
begin
    Print          (Current^);
    GetNext (Current)
end;
```

16. In the procedures for `WordFrequency` of Section 9.12, see what you can do to speed up processing while the text is being read. For example, if you are working on an ASCII machine, the uppercase letters have consecutive ASCII codes, as do the lowercase letters. Thus, the function calls to `IsUpperCaseLetter` and `IsLetter` could be replaced by `if` statements with compound conditions. Make this change and compare run times for the two versions. Make your test runs on a sufficiently large sample of text so that time differences will be noticeable. (You may be astonished by the results.) Are there other changes, specific to your machine or Pascal implementation, that are worth trying?

17. As we noted in the chapter and in Exercise 6, there are several choices of useful hash functions. Some others can be found in the references at the end of the chapter. Experiment with the `WordFrequency` program to test various hashing strategies.
    (a) Change to a simpler hash function to reduce the time needed to compute the hash code for each word.
    (b) Use a different collision resolution scheme.
    (c) Use a hash function that scatters the hashed addresses better, such as the `RandomRehash` of Exercise 7.
    (d) Try some combination of the above.

18. (This is a quickie!) Modify the `WordFrequency` program so that for each group of words having the same frequency, the words are sorted alphabetically.

19. With appropriate changes, the procedure `GetWord` in the word frequency analysis program of Section 9.12 can recognize words under other useful definitions. For each of the following definitions of a word, draw a transition diagram and make the appropriate change to `GetWord`. (In each case, the terminating condition also includes `EOLN` or `EOF`.)
    (a) A word consists of one or more letters or digits, the first of which is a letter, followed by any character other than a letter or a digit. (This is a Pascal identifier.)
    (b) A word consists of one or more digits, followed by a decimal point, followed by one or more digits, followed by any character other than a digit. (This is a Pascal real constant without an exponent.)
    (c) A word consists of the letters `IF` in that sequence, or the letters `THEN`, or the letters `BEGIN`, or the letters `END`; in each case the word is to be accepted only if followed by a blank. (These are four of Pascal's special symbols. The transition diagram will have four accepting states.)

The next two exercises should be done by everyone!

20. In each of the following situations, state what table organization and search method you would use. Explain your choice, and suggest a situation where the conditions might prevail.

(a) There are 50 items. Once the table has been built, there are no insertions or deletions. You are in a big rush to get the program running, and it will run at most a dozen times.

(b) There are, potentially, 10,000 items. There are no deletions, and an insertion is always followed by a two-second "dead zone," during which a search is never required. At all other times, retrievals must be very fast.

(c) There can be as many as 100,000 items. You do not have enough memory to permit hashing. Average speed is important, but it is not catastrophic if on rare occasions a transaction takes considerably longer than average. Consider the cases where transactions distribute as follows:

    (i) Of every 1000 transactions, 998 are retrievals, one is an insertion, and one is a deletion.

    (ii) Of every 1000 transactions, 50 are insertions, 900 are retrievals, and 50 are deletions.

    (iii) Of every 1000 transactions, 900 are insertions, 50 are retrievals, and 50 are deletions.

(d) There are thousands of items. Speed is urgent and you have some memory space to waste.

(e) There are thousands of items. Speed is urgent, but you do not have memory space to waste. (Do you have enough information to answer this question? If not, what more would you need?)

(f) There are, potentially, about 2000 items, with insertions and updates intermixed. (Think of the word frequency analysis as a model.) Fifty percent of the transactions refer to one percent of the items, another 30 percent of the transactions apply to another one percent of the items, and 15 percent of the transactions apply to 10 percent of the items. The remaining transactions (five percent) apply to the other 88 percent of the items.

21. An application involves many tables, say 100 or so. Each table could have, potentially, as many as 10,000 items. If space were provided for this maximum size for all 100 tables, storage would be needed for a million items; you don't have anywhere near that much memory. However, you have an additional piece of information: it is impossible for all tables to reach their maximums simultaneously. The maximum is 100,000 items for all tables combined, and you do have that much space.

(a) How would you organize the tables and the search strategy if any one item could be in at most one table at a time?

(b) What would you do if an item could be in more than one table at a time?

SUGGESTIONS FOR FURTHER STUDY _____

The first description of binary search trees is in Windley (1960). The first published correct binary search for tables of all sizes (not just tables of size $2^k - 1$, representing complete trees) is Bottenbruch (1962). Reingold, Nievergelt, and Deo (1977) suggest, however, that the method must have been known earlier.

Indeed, McCracken (1957) contains a program for binary search, although for the special case of 65 items and coded without a loop " . . . because it will be simpler to follow if we write it out in straight-line fashion." I have no idea where I learned the method; it has the feel of something used as a coding example in programming courses for various machines that I had attended.

Bentley (1985) contains a version of binary search, including a good exposition of the use of pre- and post-conditions, in the "Programming Pearls" column of the *Communications of the ACM*. These columns are to programmers what the "Mathematical Puzzles" columns of *Scientific American* are to mathematics buffs—lots of fun and a storehouse of novel and clever small problems. Along the way, Bentley has presented many standard algorithms. Bentley (1986) collects and expands these columns.

The original paper discussing hashing is Peterson (1957). Later results are contained in Knuth (1973) and Morris (1968). Organization of symbol tables, including hash tables, can be found in Aho and Ullman (1977), Aho, Hopcroft, and Ullman (1982), Horowitz and Sahni (1984), and Batson (1965). Tutorials on hashing and table lookup techniques can be found in Maurer and Lewis (1975) and Price (1971).

The first issue of *Computing Surveys* contains an elementary discussion of compiler writing (Glass, 1969). It looks at a PL/I compiler, written in Fortran for the Univac 1108. Although actual practice has changed a great deal since 1969, the article provides an easily understood discussion of a compiler's chores.

Gonnet (1984) contains a remarkable collection of information about sorting and searching, with algorithms expressed as Pascal or C code. Performance of the algorithms is expressed both as formulas and as experimental results. All of the methods treated in this text are covered, as well as many more. The presentation is more terse, but should provide no serious problem to anyone who has completed a course such as this one. The *Handbook* is highly recommended.

The `RandomRehash` function of Exercise 7 is described in Gries (1971), as are others; the treatment of the compilation process is based on Algol. Aho and Ullman (1977) presents, in an appendix, suggestions for programming projects involving the interpreting or compiling of a subset of Pascal. Many of these projects are beyond the abilities of students who have completed only this course, but reading through the appendix will provide a good preview of what is to come.

B-trees and AVL trees are presented superbly in Kruse (1987). A student looking for a programming project involving either of these structures will find most, if not all, the help needed here. Another good source for material on B-trees, including the most common applications, is Comer (1979). Recent research on data bases has involved table lookups using more than one key (e.g., `Find` all women over age 30 with 3.2–4.0 GPAs). Bentley and Friedman (1979) provide a good explanation of the issues involved.

CHAPTER 10

GRAPHS

10.1 INTRODUCTION

Many problems can be naturally formulated in terms of graphs. What is the shortest distance between Boise, Idaho and Portland, Maine, flying scheduled airlines? Is there a way to drive from 43rd and Sixth to 39th and Fifth that is less than one-quarter of a mile, taking into account one-way streets? Is there a circuit path between resistor 46 and capacitor 119, taking into account diodes (which are like one-way streets)? What is the total length of the connectors in a particular integrated circuit layout? Can that circuit be laid out in such a way that no connectors cross? Is there a way to build a given manufacturing plant in less than 14 months, given the time required for each major activity and the required sequence of construction activities?

All of these examples involve practical application of computers, which is our primary interest in this book. Graphs also occur in many branches of applied and theoretical mathematics. Indeed, graph theory is a flourishing branch of mathematics in its own right.

Graphs have been studied by mathematicians for centuries. Today computer science builds on that deep and rich foundation, bringing to the task the algorithmic approach and an interest in problems that could not be attacked until the power of computers became available.

We can offer no more than a glimpse of of this fascinating and vibrant branch of computer science in this brief chapter. We choose to discuss a few topics that have application in their own right and which are building blocks for further work. And, because this is an overview chapter, we shall introduce the major implementation methods in parallel with the first few algorithms.

10.2 TERMINOLOGY AND NOTATION

There is a considerable vocabulary to the study of graphs, which we will present here, something in the manner of a glossary, even though some of the terms are not used until later in the chapter.

A *graph* is a collection of *vertices* and *edges*. Vertices are also called *nodes*. A graph is pictured in the plane with dots or circles for the vertices, and curves connecting pairs of vertices for the edges. Here is the graph that we will use to illustrate the first few algorithms:

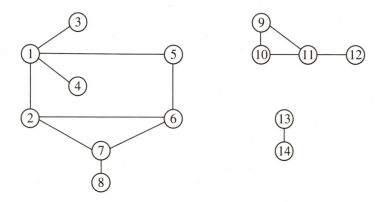

We define this graph by saying that it consists of the vertices 1 through 14, and the edges (1, 2), (1, 3), (1, 4), (1, 5), (2, 6), (2, 7), (5, 6), (6, 7), (7, 8), (9, 10), (9, 11), (10, 11), (11, 12), and (13, 14). In some application of graphs the shape of the picture we draw has some meaningful connection with what is being described; our airline and circuit cases are examples. In others, such as the manufacturing scheduling example, the picture is no more than a convenience, with no significance to the placement of vertices or the length of edges.

This definition of a graph does not permit *multiple edges* connecting a pair of vertices. It also does not permit a *loop*, an edge that connects a vertex to itself. An object with such edges is called a *multigraph;* we will not deal with multigraphs in this text.[1]

A *path* from vertex x to vertex y is a list of vertices in which successive vertices are connected by edges, such that it is possible to get from x to y. For example, in our sample graph (1, 2, 7, 8) is a path from 1 to 8; another is (1, 5, 6, 2, 7, 8). A graph is said to be *connected* if there is at least one path from every vertex to every other vertex. Our graph is clearly not connected. A graph that is not connected is composed of *connected components*. Our example has three connected components. A *cycle* is a path in which the first and last vertices are the same; (1, 5, 6, 7, 2, 1) is one example of a cycle, and (9, 10, 11, 9) is another. A graph with no cycles is said to be *acyclic*.

---

[1]As usual, there is alternative terminology. Some authors would refer to our graph as a *simple* graph, to signify the exclusion of multiple edges and loops.

An acyclic connected graph is a *tree*. (Binary trees and general trees, as studied in Chapter 7, are special cases under this definition.) A group of trees is a *forest*. A *spanning tree* of a graph is a subgraph that contains all the vertices but only enough of the edges to form a tree. One spanning tree of the component shown on the left in our example is as follows:

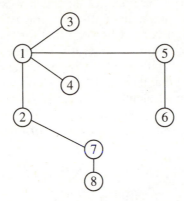

This spanning tree is hardly unique. Indeed, a spanning tree is not unique unless the graph was initially a tree.

The obvious and conventional terminology is to denote the number of vertices by V and the number of edges by E. The possible range of E is from zero, in the degenerate case, to $V(V-1)/2$. In the latter case, where all possible edges are present, the graph is said to be *complete*. A graph with relatively few edges is said to be *sparse*, and one with most edges present is said to be *dense*.

The choice of algorithm is sometimes dictated by whether the graph is sparse or dense. For example, if we have a choice between an algorithm that takes $O(V^2)$ time and another that takes $O((E+V) \lg E)$, we would prefer the former for a dense graph and the latter for a sparse one.

So far we have assumed that the edges are non-directional: (1, 2) is the same edge as (2, 1). These are *nondirected* graphs. Said otherwise, the two vertices that define an edge in a nondirected graph are unordered. When the defining vertices are ordered, we have a *directed graph,* often called a *digraph*. We draw the picture of a directed graph with arrows on the edges.

10.3 THE COMPUTER
REPRESENTATION OF GRAPHS

The first question when we work with a graph in a computer is how to represent it. There are several fairly standard ways and, as with most of the things we have studied, each has its advantages in certain circumstances.

Perhaps the most intuitive way to represent a graph is to establish a square boolean matrix (two-dimensional array) with a row and a column for each vertex. Then the element in row I, column J is `true` if there is an edge connecting vertex *I* and vertex *J,* and `false` if there is not. This is called an *adjacency matrix* representation because it shows which vertices are adjacent to each other. Alternatively, as we shall do in the program in this section, the elements of the array can be from an enumerated type having the values `Edge` and `NoEdge,` which may make the program easier to read.

The adjacency matrix of a nondirected graph is symmetric, i.e., $A_{ij} = A_{ji}$. This would seem to permit saving half the storage for the array by using techniques such as those discussed in Chapter 2, but for various reasons this is seldom done. With a directed graph, of course, it is not true, in general, that $A_{ij} = A_{ji}$. For some applications of multigraphs it is convenient for the diagonal elements to be `true,` indicating that there is an edge (loop) connecting a vertex to itself. In other cases the diagonal elements are never referenced by the algorithm and it makes no difference what is put there.

Here is the adjacency matrix representation of our sample graph:

	1	2	3	4	5	6	7	8	9	10	11	12	13	14
1	0	1	1	1	1	0	0	0	0	0	0	0	0	0
2	1	0	0	0	0	1	1	0	0	0	0	0	0	0
3	1	0	0	0	0	0	0	0	0	0	0	0	0	0
4	1	0	0	0	0	0	0	0	0	0	0	0	0	0
5	1	0	0	0	0	1	0	0	0	0	0	0	0	0
6	0	1	0	0	1	0	1	0	0	0	0	0	0	0
7	0	1	0	0	0	1	0	1	0	0	0	0	0	0
8	0	0	0	0	0	0	1	0	0	0	0	0	0	0
9	0	0	0	0	0	0	0	0	0	1	1	0	0	0
10	0	0	0	0	0	0	0	0	1	0	1	0	0	0
11	0	0	0	0	0	0	0	0	1	1	0	1	0	0
12	0	0	0	0	0	0	0	0	0	0	1	0	0	0
13	0	0	0	0	0	0	0	0	0	0	0	0	0	1
14	0	0	0	0	0	0	0	0	0	0	0	0	1	0

The adjacency matrix for a graph obviously has V^2 elements, or a minimum of V^2 bits. For a sparse graph this can represent a great deal of wasted storage: graphs of practical interest can easily have thousands of vertices, but far fewer than the maximum possible $V(V - 1)/2$ edges. For a sparse graph, most of the elements of the adjacency matrix say merely "No edge here." In such a case we prefer to store information about that edges that are present, and say nothing about those that are not.

This reasoning leads to the *adjacency list* representation: for each vertex, we create a linked list showing the vertices that are adjacent to it. For a nondirected graph, each edge is shown twice, once for each of the vertices it connects.

Whereas the adjacency matrix representation of a graph is unique, the adjacency list representation depends on the order in which the edges are presented to the program that builds that representation. The program shown later inserts new nodes at the head of a list, which is the fastest way to do it. If the edges of our sample graph are presented in the order in which they were listed in the matrix we just reviewed, the adjacency list representation would lead to the following output, which is part of the output of a program shown later.

```
Node    1 is adjacent to:        5      4      3      2
Node    2 is adjacent to:        7      6      1
Node    3 is adjacent to:        1
Node    4 is adjacent to:        1
Node    5 is adjacent to:        6      1
Node    6 is adjacent to:        7      5      2
Node    7 is adjacent to:        8      6      2
Node    8 is adjacent to:        7
Node    9 is adjacent to:       11     10
Node   10 is adjacent to:       11      9
Node   11 is adjacent to:       12     10      9
Node   12 is adjacent to:       11
Node   13 is adjacent to:       14
Node   14 is adjacent to:       13
```

A node in these linked lists simply contains, in its information field, the number of a vertex that is adjacent to the vertex for that list. The space required for this representation depends on the details of machine architecture, of course, but in any event it will be proportional to $(V + E)$, not V^2. There is a V term because there is one list for every vertex, and an E term because every edge is present in the representation. In one representative machine architecture, the adjacency list representation as implemented in the program shown later would take only about 20 percent as much space to hold our sample graph as the adjacency matrix representation.

In something of a change from topics we discussed earlier, we cannot very well speak of an ADT *graph* independent of the representation. This could be done, of course, but because performance of the various algorithms depends so heavily on the representation, it is necessary to choose both the representation and the algorithm to fit the application.

10.4 GRAPH SEARCH STRATEGIES: DEPTH-FIRST AND BREADTH-FIRST

Now we come to the first task dealing with a graph as well as the first algorithm.

For any of a variety of purposes, it can become necessary to *visit* all the vertices of a graph in a systematic manner. As with binary trees, there are several standard ways, each with advantages in given circumstances.

The two basic ways to visit all the vertices of a graph are with *depth-first search* and *breadth-first search*. Intuitively, the difference is as follows. We pick a vertex as the starting point and consider the vertices connected to it. With depth-first search we follow a path from a previous vertex as far as possible before moving on to the next neighbor of the starting vertex. With breadth-first search we look at all of neighbors of a vertex first, *then* follow the paths from each of those vertices to its neighbors, and so forth.

With a depth-first search starting at 1 in our sample graph, we would have the following picture. This can be viewed simply as a redrawing of the graph with three of the edges shown as dotted lines (these are edges that are in cycles) and with numbers written beside the vertices to show the order in which they are visited.

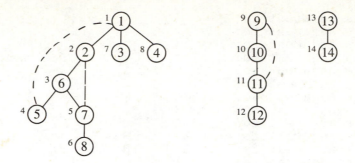

This order of visiting the vertices is not unique because it depends on the representation. An adjacency list representation of the graph could lead to many different orderings of the visits, depending on the sequence in which the edges are entered.

These graphs, if we disregard the dotted lines, are *spanning trees* for their connected components, i.e., trees made by selecting $V - 1$ edges from each component in such a way that all the vertices of the component are connected. The collection is a *spanning forest* for the graph. The spanning trees are not unique, except in the case of an acyclic component.

A breadth-first search could produce this redrawing of the same tree ("could" because, again, it is not unique).

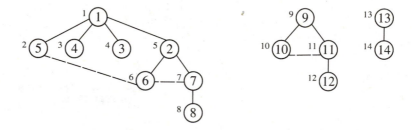

We see that the vertices were visited in a quite different order, and that the redrawn graph is somewhat "flatter" than the depth-first search version. This is another spanning forest for the original graph, again minus the dotted lines. Observe that the edges in this spanning forest are different from those in the spanning forest produced by the depth-first search.

10.5 A DEPTH-FIRST SEARCH ALGORITHM

Now let's see how a depth-first search algorithm works. Here is the procedure that does the work, taken from the complete program shown later:

```
procedure DepthFirstSearch (A: AdjacencyMatrix;
                            V: Index);
var
   K: Index;
   Visited: array [Index] of boolean;

   procedure Visit (K: Index);
   var
      J: Index;
   begin
      Write (K:4);
      Visited[K] := true;
      for J := 1 to V do
         if (A[K, J] = Edge) and (not Visited[J]) then
               Visit (J)
   end;

begin    { body of procedure DepthFirstSearch }

   WriteLn ('The nodes as traversed in a depth-first search:');
   WriteLn;

   for K := 1 to V do
      Visited[K] := false;

   for K := 1 to V do
      if not Visited[K] then
         Visit (K)
end;
```

This procedure contains another procedure named `Visit`, and a body consisting of two `WriteLn`s and two `for` statements. The first `for` statement "marks" all vertices as "unvisited," by setting the elements of the `boolean` array `Visited` to `false`. Then we examine each vertex in turn, by looking at its element in `Visited`: if it has not been visited yet, we do so.

"Visiting" a vertex means to invoke the nested procedure `Visit`, sending it a vertex number. The first action is to print the vertex number, so as to indicate that we have reached it in the depth-first search. Now we mark the vertex as having been visited, and then check all other vertices that have edges in common with this one, i.e., are connected to it. Whenever we find such an edge, we ask whether its other vertex has already been visited and, if not, we visit it.

`Visit` is recursive. This means that after it is called by the statement in the body of `DepthFirstSearch`, it will "stay within itself" so long as it can find vertices connected to the one for which it was invoked. If the graph is connected, `Visit` will be called by `DepthFirstSearch` only once. If the graph is not connected, it will be called as many times as there are connected components, three in our example.

The test `if not Visited[J]` in `Visit` comes into play in two different ways. First, when `Visit` is dealing with vertex X and finds that it has an edge in common with vertex Y, it immediately invokes itself to visit Y. In the course of that visit it will discover than Y is connected to X. But, of course, vertex X has already been visited, so it should not be reported. The second way this `if` statement works is with cycles. Consider vertex 5 in our example. It will be reached first in the depth-first search from 1 to 2 to 6 to 5; at that point `Visit` will discover that 5 is connected to 1, but that fact should not be reported because 1 has already been visited. Then, when the depth-first search that started at 1 finishes with vertices 2, 3, and 4, it will discover that 1 is connected to 5—but that should not be reported either because we have already seen 5. The dotted lines in the diagram thus correspond to edges for which both vertices had already been examined earlier in the search, i.e., edges that are in cycles.

Here are the declarations for the main program that calls the `Depth-FirstSearch` procedure:

```
program DepthFirstSearch (input, output);

const
    MaxVertices = 50;    { or whatever }

type
    Index = 1..MaxVertices;
    EdgeExistence = (Edge, NoEdge);
    AdjacencyMatrix = array [Index, Index] of EdgeExistence;

var
    A: AdjacencyMatrix;
    V: Index;    { number of vertices }
```

`Initialize` is a procedure that gives the value `NoEdge` to all elements of the adjacency matrix. The input data simply shows the edges, so all the edges for which there is no data need to be properly initialized. Note that this operation takes $O(V^2)$ time. For a graph with a large number of vertices but relatively few edges, this operation by itself could could take up most of the running time of an algorithm.

```
procedure Initialize (var A: AdjacencyMatrix;
                          V: Index);
var
    I, J: Index;
begin
    for I := 1 to V do
        for J := 1 to V do
            A[I, J] := NoEdge
end;
```

`ReadGraph` reads as many records as there are in the input, each record consisting of two numbers that identify the vertices connected by an edge. For a nondirected graph we enter each edge twice in the adjacency matrix.

```
procedure ReadGraph (var A: AdjacencyMatrix);
var
   I, J: Index;
begin
   while not EOF do
   begin
      ReadLn (I, J);
      A[I, J] := Edge;
      A[J, I] := Edge
   end
end;
```

The input begins with an integer that gives the number of vertices in the graph. This is read in the main program, since it is needed prior to initialization.

Next, `PrintGraph` writes a line for each vertex, showing the vertices connected to it. The assumption here is that the adjacency matrix is on the sparse side, meaning that there are far fewer than V^2 edges. If the matrix were dense, we might consider looking into printing a square picture in row-and-column format, although with realistic sized graphs this would normally be unmanageable.

```
procedure PrintGraph (A: AdjacencyMatrix;
                      V: Index);
var
   I, J: Index;
begin
   for I := 1 to V do
   begin
      Write ('Vertex ', I:4, ' is adjacent to: ');
      for J := 1 to V do
         if A[I, J] = Edge then
            Write (J:4);
      WriteLn
   end;
   WriteLn
end;
```

`DepthFirstSearch` would be placed next, followed by a simple main program that reads the number of vertices and invokes the procedures.

```
begin
   ReadLn (V);
   Initialize (A, V);
   ReadGraph (A);
   PrintGraph (A, V);
   DepthFirstSearch (A, V)
end.
```

Here is the output when this program is run with a data file describing the sample graph shown earlier.

```
Vertex    1 is adjacent to:    2    3    4    5
Vertex    2 is adjacent to:    1    6    7
Vertex    3 is adjacent to:    1
Vertex    4 is adjacent to:    1
Vertex    5 is adjacent to:    1    6
Vertex    6 is adjacent to:    2    5    7
Vertex    7 is adjacent to:    2    6    8
Vertex    8 is adjacent to:    7
Vertex    9 is adjacent to:   10   11
Vertex   10 is adjacent to:    9   11
Vertex   11 is adjacent to:    9   10   12
Vertex   12 is adjacent to:   11
Vertex   13 is adjacent to:   14
Vertex   14 is adjacent to:   13
```

The nodes as traversed in a depth-first search are as follows:

```
   1    2    6    5    7    8    3    4    9   10   11   12   13   14
```

Our discussion makes it clear that, with a minor modification, this program can identify the connected components of a graph. For any connected component, all invocations of `Visit`, except the first, are recursive. All we have to do is insert a statement before the (non-recursive) invocation of `Visit` in the body of `DepthFirstSearch`, stating that a new component is about to be produced. If the original graph is connected, there will, of course, be only one component. The program could readily be modified to report this fact. Here is the changed procedure:

```
procedure DepthFirstSearchComponents (A: AdjacencyMatrix;
                                       V: Index);
var
   K: Index;
   Visited: array [Index] of boolean;
   Component: integer;

   procedure Visit (K: Index);
   var
      J: Index;
   begin
      Write (K:4);
      Visited[K] := true;
      for J := 1 to V do
         if (A[K, J] = Edge) and (not Visited[J]) then
               Visit (J)
   end;
```

```
begin    { body of procedure DepthFirstSearchComponents }

    for K := 1 to V do
       Visited[K] := false;

    Component := 1;
    for K := 1 to V do
       if not Visited[K] then
       begin
           WriteLn ('Component ', Component,
                    ' consists of vertices:');
           Visit (K);
           WriteLn;
           WriteLn;
           Component := Component + 1
       end
end;
```

Here is the output of the modified procedure, for the same sample graph:

```
Component 1 consists of vertices:
    1    2    6    5    7    8    3    4

Component 2 consists of vertices:
    9   10   11   12

Component 3 consists of vertices:
   13   14
```

Depth-first search implemented with an adjacency matrix runs in $O(V^2)$ time because it examines every element of the adjacency matrix.

10.6 BREADTH-FIRST SEARCH

The recursive `Visit` procedure in a depth-first search involves an implicit stack, as we recall from Chapter 5. This stacking of vertices means that we follow each path from a vertex as far as possible. What would happen if we replaced the stack mechanism with a queue? That is, instead of following a path from the starting vertex as far as possible, using a stack mechanism, suppose we enqueue neighboring vertices until they have all been enqueued. At that point each of the vertices in the queue can be examined in turn. In brief, this is how breadth-first search works.

Let us look at a program for breadth-first search, using an adjacency list representation for the graph. The change from a depth-first to breadth-first search strategy is a matter of a few changes in the procedure `Visit,` but first let us consider the adjacency list representation.

Here are the declarations:

```
program BreadthFirstSearch (input, output);
{ Breadth-first search using an adjacency list representation. }

const
    MaxVertices = 50;

type
    Index = 1..MaxVertices;
    ItemType = Index;

    NodePtr = ^Node;
    Node = record
                Item: Index;     { A neighbor of this list's vertex }
                Next: NodePtr
            end;

    List = NodePtr;

    AdjacencyListArray = array [Index] of List;

    Queue = List;


var
    AdjList: AdjacencyListArray;
    V: Index;     { Number of vertices }


{$I ListPtr }
{$I QList }
```

This time the graph is represented by an array of linked lists, one list for each vertex. Each list shows all the vertices that are adjacent to that list's vertex. The queue and linked-list operations are those from Chapter 6. As usual, your compiler directives might be different.

Initialize now deals with a array of linked lists rather than a matrix of (essentially) boolean values. Creating the lists takes $O(V)$ time, rather than the $O(V^2)$ time for the adjacency matrix representation. This time difference in initialization has nothing to do with the search strategy but it is still an important consideration. In extreme cases, the execution time of the program could be dominated by the time to initialize the adjacency matrix.

```
procedure Initialize (var AdjList: AdjacencyListArray;
                           V: Index);
var
    I: Index;
begin
    for I := 1 to V do
        CreateList (AdjList[I])
end;
```

When `ReadGraph` gets the definition of an edge, say connecting vertices *X* and *Y*, it places vertex *X* on *Y*'s list, and places *Y* on *X*'s list. This assumes a nondirected graph. Changing the program to work with a directed graph could, in some simple cases, merely require modifying this routine.

```
procedure ReadGraph (var AdjList: AdjacencyListArray);
var
   I, J: Index;
begin
   while not EOF do begin
      ReadLn (I, J);
      InsertAtFront (AdjList[J], I);
      InsertAtFront (AdjList[I], J)
   end
end;
```

The modifications in `PrintGraph` are simple.

```
procedure PrintGraph (AdjList: AdjacencyListArray;
                      V: Index);
var
   I: Index;
   P: NodePtr;
begin
   for I := 1 to V do begin
      Write ('Node ', I:4, ' is adjacent to:   ');
      P := AdjList[I];
      while not ListIsEmpty (P) do
      begin
         Write (Item (P):4, '  ');
         Advance (P)
      end;
      WriteLn
   end;
   WriteLn
end;
```

The body of `BreadthFirstSearch` is the same as that for `Depth-FirstSearch`, except that here we add the creation of a queue. Otherwise, all the changes are in the procedure `Visit` (which is now somewhat different).

```
procedure BreadthFirstSearch (AdjList: AdjacencyListArray;
                              V: Index);
var
   K: Index;
   VertexQueue: Queue;
   Visited: array [Index] of boolean;

   procedure Visit (K: Index);
   var
      I: Index;
      P: NodePtr;
   begin
      Visited[K] := true;
      EnQueue (VertexQueue, K);
      while not QueueIsEmpty (VertexQueue) do
      begin
         DeQueue (VertexQueue, I);
         Write (I:4);
         P := AdjList[I];
         while not ListIsEmpty (P) do
         begin
            if not Visited[Item (P)] then
            begin
               Visited[Item (P)] := true;
               EnQueue (VertexQueue, Item (P));
            end;
            Advance (P)
         end
      end
   end;

begin   { body of procedure BreadthFirstSearch }

   WriteLn ('The nodes in the order visited',
            ' in a breadth-first search:');
   WriteLn;

   CreateQueue (VertexQueue);
   for K := 1 to V do
      Visited[K] := false;

   for K := 1 to V do
      if not Visited[K] then
         Visit (K)
end;
```

As before, we first mark vertex K as visited. But now we also immediately enqueue that vertex. This is essentially a way to get the major loop initialized, since its termination test is an empty queue. Within the `while` loop we dequeue a vertex, write a line showing that has been visited, then prepare to follow the linked lists of all the vertices adjacent to this one. As each neighbor is encountered, it is simply enqueued; nothing else is done at this time. When the end of the adjacency list has been reached, control reverts to the outer (while) loop, where the vertices that have by now been enqueued are dequeued. However, after each one has been dequeued, we again go into the loop that enqueues all its neighbors. By the FIFO action of a queue, all the neighbors of K will be written out before any of the neighbors of the neighbors, and similarly at all levels.

The main program is routine.

```
begin
    ReadLn (V);
    Initialize (AdjList, V);
    ReadGraph (AdjList);
    PrintGraph (AdjList, V);
    BreadthFirstSearch (AdjList, V);
end.
```

Here is the output when the program is run for our sample graph.

```
Node     1 is adjacent to:     5     4     3     2
Node     2 is adjacent to:     7     6     1
Node     3 is adjacent to:     1
Node     4 is adjacent to:     1
Node     5 is adjacent to:     6     1
Node     6 is adjacent to:     7     5     2
Node     7 is adjacent to:     8     6     2
Node     8 is adjacent to:     7
Node     9 is adjacent to:    11    10
Node    10 is adjacent to:    11     9
Node    11 is adjacent to:    12    10     9
Node    12 is adjacent to:    11
Node    13 is adjacent to:    14
Node    14 is adjacent to:    13
```

The nodes in the order visited in a breadth-first search:

```
    1   5   4   3   2   6   7   8   9  11  10  12  13  14
```

This output produces the breadth-first search tree shown earlier for our sample graph:

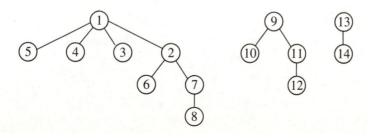

Can we make sense of the order in which the vertices were visited? We must know, so as to answer this question, the order in which the edges were entered, which was: (1, 2), (1, 3), (1, 4), (1, 5), (2, 6), (2, 7), (5, 6), (6, 7), (7, 8), (9, 10), (9, 11), (10, 11), (11, 12), and (13, 14). Now recall that the adjacency lists are built by placing each new vertex at the *beginning* of the list, so that the first vertex on 1's list is 5, then 4, then 3, and last 2. This is why 5 was the second vertex visited.

Can you see why 6 was visited before 7? One might think that, on the analogy with the treatment of 1's neighbors, 7 should have been visited before 6, because edge (2, 6) was entered before edge (2, 7), and so 7 should have been at the front of 2's adjacency list. And, in fact, that's where it is. But, 6 gets enqueued as a result of visiting 5, which occurs before 2 is visited.

An almost trivial modification of the program is to have it identify the trees in a spanning forest. Any new edge encountered while enqueueing vertices in the `while` loop is in the spanning tree for that component because the logic already rejects edges that are in cycles. The modified `while` loop is:

```
while not QueueIsEmpty (VertexQueue) do
begin
   DeQueue (VertexQueue, I);
   P := AdjList[I];
   while not ListIsEmpty (P) do
   begin
      if not Visited[Item (P)] then
      begin
         { this is a spanning forest edge }
         WriteLn (I:4, Item (P):4);
         Visited[Item (P)] := true;
         EnQueue (VertexQueue, Item (P));
      end;
      Advance (P)
   end
end
```

With this modification and some minor changes in the main program, the program produces this output:

```
The edges of a spanning forest:

    1    5
    1    4
    1    3
    1    2
    5    6
    2    7
    7    8
    9   11
    9   10
   11   12
   13   14
```

10.7 AN APPLICATION: SEARCHING A MAZE

One approach to solving a maze is to formulate the problem in graph theory terms, creating a vertex at every point where a decision is required. This means that every vertex will have at least three edges incident on it. Figure 10.1 shows a maze together with a corresponding graph.

We use this example to demonstrate how depth-first search and breadth-first search compare. Figure 10.2 shows for each method, a graph at a point in the process where half of the nodes have been visited. The difference between the two strategies is intuitively clear: depth-first search follows a given path as far as it can, whereas breadth-first search "fans out" from the starting point. In human terms, depth-first search would be appropriate for an individual, and breadth-first search appropriate for a group.

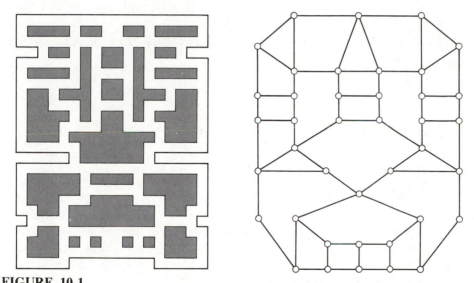

FIGURE 10.1
A maze used to demonstrate graph search algorithms, together with a graph that represents the maze.

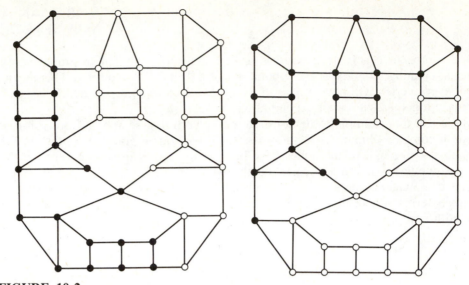

FIGURE 10.2
Depth-first and breadth-first searches of the maze of Figure 10.1, at the point where they are halfway through the search.

10.8 SHORTEST PATH IN A DIRECTED GRAPH: DIJKSTRA'S ALGORITHM

A frequent application of graphs is to find the shortest path between vertices in a weighted directed graph. The graph might represent a circuit, with edge weights being lengths of connectors in microns or inches; it might represent the phases of a construction project, with the edge weights being time in days. With the understanding that the edge weights are generalized ''costs'' in the application, the problem is often described as that of finding the minimum-cost path between one vertex in a graph and all others.

Edsgar W. Dijkstra is the discover of the method that we shall study; it is one of the earliest graph algorithms.

We use an adjacency matrix representation, in which the edge lengths are the costs (distances, times, or whatever) associated with the edges. We initialize this matrix, called `Edge` in our program, to very large values, indicating impossibly large costs where there are no edges. We then initialize an array called `Dist` to equal the first row of the edge matrix.

We now seek the shortest path from the first vertex to all others. Our approach is to identify a set of vertices for which we know the shortest possible distances from vertex 1; we call this ''special'' set `S`. The first vertex is the default first member of `S`; the shortest possible distance from vertex 1 to vertex 1 is, of course, zero.

Now we go through a two-step process, adding vertices to the set `S` until they are all in it:

1. Pick a vertex, call it `W`, that is not in `S`, and for which the distance from 1 to `W` is a minimum. Add `W` to `S`.

2. For every vertex still not in `S`, see whether the distance from vertex 1 to that vertex can be shortened by going through `W`. If so, update the corresponding element of `Dist`.

The first time we carry out the first step, it amounts to looking for the shortest edge from vertex 1 to another vertex. After that first time, the second step may have found a way to get from vertex 1 to some vertices by going through intermediate vertices, which is what the `Dist` array records. So the search in Step 1 is in the `Dist` array, not the `Edge` matrix. Additionally, an array `Path` holds, for each vertex, the vertex that is its predecessor on the shortest path from vertex 1.

Here is the algorithm in pseudocode form, not including the processing of `Path`:[2]

```
S := {1};

Initialize Dist to be the edges from vertex 1, = 1st row of Edge

for I := 1 to V - 1:
    choose a vertex W, not in S, for which Dist[W] is minimum;
    add vertex W to S;
    for each vertex J, still not in S:
        Dist[J] := min(Dist[J], Dist[W] + Edge[W, J];
```

To observe Dijkstra's algorithm in action, consider this directed graph (The edge weights here obviously do not correspond to geometric length; recall that the meaning of a graph is independent of how it is drawn.):

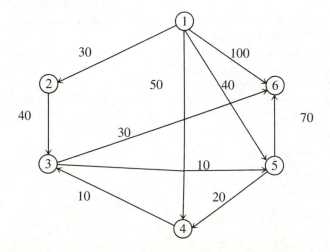

[2]Adapted from Alfred V. Aho, John E. Hopcroft, and Jeffrey D. Ullman, *Data Structures and Algorithms*, Addison-Wesley, Reading, MA, 1983.

Here are the values of the relevant variables as this algorithm executes.

Iter	S	W	Dist[2]	Dist[3]	Dist[4]	Dist[5]	Dist[6]
Initial	{1}	–	30	Infinite	50	40	100
1	{1, 2}	2	30	70	50	40	100
2	{1,2,5}	5	30	70	50	40	100
3	{1,2,5,4}	4	30	60	50	40	100
4	{1,2,5,4,3}	3	30	60	50	40	90
5	{1,2,5,4,3,6}	6	30	60	50	40	90

The initialization sets the elements of Dist equal to the edge weights from vertex 1 to each of the others. The weight of the non-existent edge from 1 to 3 is shown as infinity, which will force the desired actions from the algorithm. At this point the special set S = {1}.

The first iteration seeks a vertex not in S for which the corresponding element of Dist is a minimum. That is vertex 2, so S = {1, 2}. Now, in the second step of the first iteration, we check to see whether we can shorten the distance from vertex 1 to any other vertex, by going through the new "special" vertex. The answer is that we can. By going through 2 to get to 3, we shorten the distance from infinity to 70. Dist[3] is accordingly updated. No other distances can be shortened by going through 2.

The second iteration finds that, of the vertices not in S, element 5 in Dist is the smallest. Vertex 5 is therefore the new special vertex, so now S = {1, 2, 5}. No paths to other vertices can be shortened by going through 5.

The third iteration determines that vertex 4 has the smallest value in Dist of the vertices not in S, and now D = {1, 2, 4, 5}. And, now it turns out that we can shorten the path from 1 to 3 by going through 4.

In the fourth iteration vertex 3 is added to the special set, so S = {1, 2, 3, 4, 5}, and we discover that we can shorten the distance to 6 by going through 3 (which we get to by going through 4).

The last iteration adds 6 to S. All vertices are now "special," meaning that we have found the shortest paths from vertex 1, so it is no surprise that no paths may be shortened by going though 6.

Here is the output of the program shown below, run with data defining the illustrative graph we saw before:

```
Shortest paths between vertex 1 and all other vertices:

Vertex  Path Length  Predecessor

   2         30            1
   3         60            4
   4         50            1
   5         40            1
   6         90            3
```

Dijkstra's algorithm is an example of what is called a *greedy algorithm,* meaning that at each stage it simply does what is *locally* optimal. It turns out, in this case, that taking the local optimum produces a global optimum.

Here is a program that implements Dijkstra's algorithm. It includes an array named `Path` that is initialized to zero or one, depending on whether or not there is an edge from vertex 1 to another vertex, and which is updated any time a shorter way to a vertex is found after the selection of a new special vertex. When the algorithm terminates, `Path[J]` contains the predecessor to vertex `J`, in the shortest path from 1 to `J`. The entire path can be found by tracing backward through the entries in this array (or the program could be modified to do so). If a vertex is not reachable because no edges lead into it, its predecessor in `Path` will still be zero.

```
program Dijkstra (input, output);

{ For a weighted directed graph, find the minimum-cost
  paths between one vertex and all other vertices. }

const
   MaxVertices = 50;
   Infinity = 20000;    { means no edge -- see text }

type
   Index = 1..MaxVertices;
   EdgeMatrix = array [Index, Index] of integer;

var
   Edge: EdgeMatrix;
   V: Index;


procedure InitializeGraph (var Edge: EdgeMatrix;
                               V: Index);
var
   I, J: Index;
begin
   for I := 1 to V do
     for J := 1 to V do
        Edge[I, J] := Infinity
end;


procedure ReadGraph (var Edge: EdgeMatrix;
                         V: Index);
var
   I, J: Index;
begin
   while not EOF do
      ReadLn (I, J, Edge[I, J])
end;
```

(Continued)

(Continued)

```pascal
procedure PrintGraph (Edge: EdgeMatrix;
                      V: Index);
var
   I, J: Index;
begin
   WriteLn ('The edge matrix, with ',
            Infinity, ' meaning no edge:');
   WriteLn;
   for I := 1 to V do begin
      Write ('Row ', I:2, '    ');
      for J := 1 to V do
         Write (Edge[I, J]:8);
      WriteLn
   end;
   WriteLn;
   WriteLn
end;


procedure Dijkstra (Edge: EdgeMatrix;
                    V: Index);
var
   S: set of Index;    { the "special" vertices }
   I, J: Index;
   W: Index;
   MinDist: integer;
   Dist: array [Index] of integer;
   Path: array [Index] of integer;

begin
   { Make 1 the default first "special" vertex }
   S := [1];

   { Initialize shortest paths, so far, to be edges from 1 }
   for J := 2 to V do
   begin
      Dist[J] := Edge[1, J];
      if Edge[1, J] = Infinity then
         Path[J] := 0
      else
         Path[J] := 1
   end;

   for I := 1 to V - 1 do
   begin
      { choose a vertex W in V - S such that Dist[W] is a minimum }
      MinDist := Infinity;
      for J := 2 to V do
         if (not (J in S)) and (Dist[J] < MinDist) then
         begin
            MinDist := Dist[J];
            W := J
         end;
```

```
            { add W to the set of "special" vertices }
            S := S + [W];

            { adjust Dist array to reflect inclusion of W in S }
            for J := 2 to V do
                if (not (J in S)) and (Dist[W] + Edge[W, J] < Dist[J]) then
                begin
                    Dist[J] := Dist[W] + Edge[W, J];
                    Path[J] := W
                end
    end;    { for I := 1 to V - 1 }

    WriteLn ('Shortest paths between ',
                'vertex 1 and all other vertices:');
    WriteLn;
    WriteLn ('Vertex  Path Length  Predecessor ');
    WriteLn;
    for I := 2 to V do
        WriteLn ('   ', I,
                '        ', Dist[I]:5,
                '            ',  Path[I]);
end;


begin
    ReadLn (V);
    InitializeGraph (Edge, V);
    ReadGraph (Edge, V);
    PrintGraph (Edge, V);
    Dijkstra (Edge, V);
end.
```

The program follows the pseudocode closely, so only a little additional explanation is necessary. Pascal does not provide a function to find the minimum of its arguments, so that action is programmed. In doing so, we have to form the sum `Dist[W] + Edge[W, J]`. Due to this action we cannot use `MaxInt` to represent ''infinity'': the addition would lead to a value too large to hold in a word in the computer, leading, at least, to wrong results. The value used for ''infinity'' is, of course, highly machine-dependent.

It would not always be desirable to have the algorithm that does the central work also do the printing. It was done that way here because it permits us to keep things simple by making `Path` and `Dist` local to `Dijkstra`.

Here is the output when this program was run with data that defined the sample graph.

The cost matrix, with 20000 meaning no edge:

```
Row  1      20000         30     20000         50         40        100
Row  2      20000      20000         40      20000      20000      20000
Row  3      20000      20000      20000      20000         10         30
Row  4      20000      20000         10      20000      20000      20000
Row  5      20000      20000      20000         20      20000         70
Row  6      20000      20000      20000      20000      20000      20000
```

Shortest paths between vertex 1 and all other vertices:

Vertex	Path Length	Predecessor
2	30	1
3	60	4
4	50	1
5	40	1
6	90	3

For a more realistic application of Dijkstra's algorithm, consider the problem of finding the shortest paths between locations in a section of a city having one-way streets. Figure 10.3 is a map of a portion of midtown Manhattan.

All the streets in this grid are one-way except 42nd Street. Here is the output from the program after it was modified to handle vertex names in a meaningful

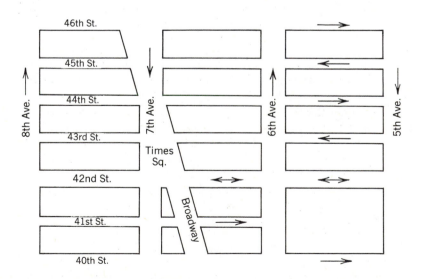

FIGURE 10.3
A map of a section of midtown Manhattan, showing the one-way streets. Used to demonstrate Dijkstra's algorithm.

way. (Facilities for converting between internal vertex numbers and external vertex names would be a requirement for any actual graph program. For our purposes, it is a nonessential detail.)

```
Shortest paths between  44th & 6th and all other intersections:
```

Vertex	Path Length	Predecessor
45th & 6th	250	44th & 6th
46th & 6th	500	45th & 6th
43rd & 6th	1850	43rd & 5th
42nd & 6th	2130	42nd & 5th
41st & 6th	3110	40th & 6th
40th & 6th	2860	Bway & 40th
46th & 5th	1300	46th & 6th
45th & 5th	1550	46th & 5th
44th & 5th	800	44th & 6th
43rd & 5th	1050	44th & 5th
42nd & 5th	1330	43rd & 5th
40th & 5th	1860	41st & 5th
46th & 7th	2900	Bway & 46th
45th & 7th	1050	45th & 6th
Bway & 44th	1300	45th & 7th
Bway & 43rd	1550	Bway & 44th
42nd & 7th	1830	Bway & 43rd
41st & 7th	2110	42nd & 7th
40th & 7th	2360	41st & 7th
Bway & 46th	2750	46th & 8th
Bway & 45th	1150	45th & 7th
Bway & 42nd	1830	Bway & 43rd
Bway & 41st	2110	Bway & 42nd
Bway & 40th	2360	Bway & 41st
46th & 8th	2100	45th & 8th
45th & 8th	1850	Bway & 45th
44th & 8th	2650	43rd & 8th
43rd & 8th	2400	Bway & 43rd
42nd & 8th	2630	42nd & 7th
41st & 8th	2910	41st & 7th
40th & 8th	20000	No path
41st & 5th	1610	42nd & 5th

10.9 THE MINIMUM COST SPANNING TREE: KRUSKAL'S ALGORITHM

Many applications require finding a minimum-cost spanning tree for a weighted nondirected graph. Circuit layout jobs are a prime example. Considering that sparse graphs with many thousands of vertices are not uncommon, finding methods that operate at high speed becomes worthwhile. Kruskal's algorithm[3], another of the early inventions in this field, does the job with the help of rapid means of implementing the two set operations that are needed.

[3]J.B. Kruskal, Jr., "On the Shortest Spanning Tree of a Graph and the Travelling Salesman Problem," Proc. of the AMS **7**, 1 (1956).

The key to the method is the following property of a minimum spanning tree: Given any division of the vertices of a graph into two sets, the minimum spanning tree contains the shortest of the edges connecting a vertex in one set to a vertex in the other set. The proof is by contradiction. Suppose we had a purported minimum spanning tree that did *not* contain this shortest edge, which we may call *s*. Then, adding *s* would create a cycle, which could be removed by deleting another edge connecting the two sets. Since this other edge is longer than *s*, removing it would reduce the total weight of the tree, which must therefore not have been at the minimum.

The strategy of Kruskal's algorithm is based on this fact. We sort the edges into increasing order of their weights, then build the minimum spanning tree by adding edges that do not create cycles until we have $V-1$ of them.

A fast implementation of this strategy depends on a clever way to recognize a cycle, as follows. We initialize the algorithm by making one-member sets of the vertices. When we begin by picking the shortest edge, the two vertices it connects become members of the same set. Any time a new edge is added that includes *one* of these vertices, the other vertex of that edge is added to the set. If a candidate edge turns out to have *both* of its vertices in the same set, we reject it because adding it would create a cycle.

In pseudocode form, Kruskal's algorithm is as follows:

```
Make one-element sets of all vertices
EdgesSoFar = 0
repeat
    Pick next edge in order of weight
    if its vertices are not in the same set, then
        Add the edge to the spanning tree
        Form the union of the two sets that its vertices are in
        EdgesSoFar = EdgesSoFar + 1
until EdgesSoFar = V - 1
```

To see Kruskal's algorithm in action, consider this graph:

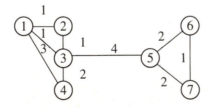

Suppose the edges have been sorted into the following order:

```
Vertex 1    Vertex 2    Weight

    1           2           1
    1           3           1
    2           3           1
    6           7           1
    3           4           2
    5           6           2
    5           7           2
    1           4           3
    3           5           4
```

(If the edges that have the same weight were sorted into a different sequence, we would get a different spanning tree.)

We initialize the process by making one-element sets of the vertices, {1}, {2}, {3}, {4}, {5}, {6}, {7}. The shortest edge will always be in the minimum spanning tree, so the first edge is added to what will eventually be the minimum-cost spanning tree. We form the union of the sets containing these two vertices, giving {1, 2}, {3}, {4}, {5}, {6}, {7}. The next edge (in order of weights) connects vertices 1 and 3. These are not in the same set, so we accept this edge and form the union of the sets connecting its vertices, giving {1, 2, 3}, {4}, {5}, {6}, {7}. The next edge connects vertices 2 and 3, which are in the same set, so it is rejected as an edge of the minimum spanning tree. The vertices of the next edge, 6 and 7, are not in the same set, so we accept that edge and form the union of the sets containing its vertices: {1, 2, 3}, {4}, {5}, {6, 7}. Now the edge connecting vertices 3 and 4 is accepted: {1, 2, 3, 4}, {5}, {6, 7}. Next come 5 and 6: {1, 2, 3, 4}, {5, 6, 7}. The edge connecting 5 and 7 is rejected, as is the edge connecting 1 and 4. Finally, the edge connecting 3 and 5 is accepted. All vertices are in one set, and we have $V - 1$ edges in a minimum spanning tree.

The key to making this algorithm work quickly is to have a fast way to determine whether two vertices are in the same set, and to form the union of the two sets if not. These are the only set actions we require, so we may combine the two actions into one procedure.

The set representation will be as a general tree, and the tree will be implemented with an array. The tree contains no information other than set membership, so there is nothing corresponding to what we have called the `Item` field in other tree applications. All we need is link showing the parent of a node. Since the elements of our set are the integers from 1 to the number of vertices, we can use an array implementation, as follows. We set up an array of integers named `Parent`. If element I is the root of a tree representing a set, then `Parent[I]` contains zero. Otherwise, `Parent[I]` contains the element number of the parent of `I`. Initialization of the vertices to a forest of one-node trees consists of setting all elements to zero.

Now we can watch the algorithm operate for our sample tree by showing the edges being added to the minimum spanning tree for the graph above, together with the vertex sets and the `Parent` array.

Initialization:

Parent: element

	1	2	3	4	5	6	7
link	0	0	0	0	0	0	0

Set trees: ① ② ③ ④ ⑤ ⑥ ⑦

Minimum spanning tree edges:

① ② ⑥

③ ⑤

④ ⑦

After accepting edge (1, 2), we have:

Parent: element

	1	2	3	4	5	6	7
link	0	1	0	0	0	0	0

Set trees: ① ③ ④ ⑤ ⑥ ⑦
            ②

Minimum spanning tree edges:

      1
①——②   ⑥

③   ⑤

④   ⑦

After accepting edge (1, 3), it looks like this:

Parent: element

	1	2	3	4	5	6	7
link	0	1	1	0	0	0	0

Set trees: ①   ④ ⑤ ⑥ ⑦

Minimum spanning tree edges:

Edge (2, 3) is rejected.
After accepting edge (6, 7), we have:

Parent: element 1 2 3 4 5 6 7
link | 0 | 1 | 1 | 0 | 0 | 0 | 6 |

Set trees:

Minimum spanning tree edges:

And, after accepting edge (3, 4), we have:

Parent: element 1 2 3 4 5 6 7
link | 0 | 1 | 1 | 1 | 0 | 0 | 6 |

Set trees:

Minimum spanning tree edges:

After accepting edge (5, 6), the situation is as follows:

Parent: element

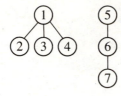

Set trees:

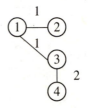

Minimum spanning tree edges:

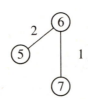

Edge (5, 7) is then rejected.
Edge (1, 4) is rejected.
After accepting edge (3, 5), we have the following solution:

Parent: element

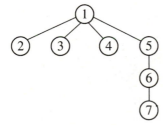

Set trees:

Minimum spanning tree edges:

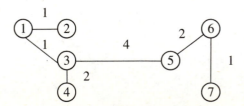

A program follows that consists of a main program—the procedure Kruskal—and various other service routines.

```pascal
program Kruskal (input, output);

{ Find the minimum-cost spanning tree for a weighted graph. }

{ Graph representation: one-dimensional array of edge records. }

{ Set representation: a general tree (array implementation),
  with nodes containing only links:
  Parent[I] = 0: the tree contains only the root,
                 i.e., the set has only one element.
  Parent[I] > 0: I is a non-root node; Parent[I] is its parent. }


const
   MaxVertices = 50;    { or whatever }
   MaxEdges = 2450;     { for MaxVertices = 50 }

type
   Index = 0..MaxEdges;

   EdgeRecord = record
                   Vertex1, Vertex2: Index;
                   Weight: -1..MaxInt
                end;

   EdgeArray = array [Index] of EdgeRecord;

   ParentIndex = 0..MaxVertices;

   ParentArray = array [0..MaxVertices] of ParentIndex;

var
   Edge: EdgeArray;
   Parent: ParentArray;
   V, E: Index;


procedure ReadEdges (var Edge: EdgeArray;
                     var E: Index);
var
   Vertex1, Vertex2: Index;
   Weight: 1..MaxInt;
begin
   E := 0;
   while not EOF do
   begin
      E := E + 1;
      ReadLn (Vertex1, Vertex2, Weight);
      Edge[E].Vertex1 := Vertex1;
      Edge[E].Vertex2 := Vertex2;
      Edge[E].Weight := Weight
   end
end;
```

(Continued)

(Continued)

```
procedure SortEdges (var Edge: EdgeArray;
                         E: Index);
{ Insertion sort of Edge array into increasing order of weights }
var
    I, J: Index;
    Temp: EdgeRecord;
begin
    Edge[0].Weight := -1;    { Sentinel }
    for I := 2 to E do
    begin
        Temp := Edge[I];
        J := I;
        while Edge[J - 1].Weight > Temp.Weight do
        begin
            Edge[J] := Edge[J - 1];
            J := J - 1
        end;
        Edge[J] := Temp
    end
end;


procedure InitializeParentArray (var Parent: ParentArray;
                                     V: Index);
{ Initializes the vertices to a forest of one-node trees. }
var
    I: Index;
begin
    for I := 1 to V do
        Parent[I] := 0
end;


procedure FindAndUnion (var Parent: ParentArray;
                        Vertex1, Vertex2: Index;
                        var SameSet: boolean);

{ SameSet indicates whether Vertex1 and Vertex 2 in same set.
  If not, Parent[J] becomes the Union set of their sets. }

var
    I, J: Index;
begin
    { Make I point to root of tree containing Vertex1 }
    I := Vertex1;
    while Parent[I] > 0 do
        I := Parent[I];

    { Make J point to root of tree containing Vertex2 }
    J := Vertex2;
    while Parent[J] > 0 do
        J := Parent[J];

    { If different sets, attach one set tree to root of other. }
    if I <> J then
        Parent[J] := I;
    SameSet := I = J
end;
```

```
Procedure Kruskal (Edge: EdgeArray;
                   V: Index);
var
   EdgesSoFar: Index;
   EdgeIndex: Index;
   I, J: Index;
   SameSet: boolean;
begin
   EdgesSoFar := 0;
   EdgeIndex := 0;
   repeat
      EdgeIndex := EdgeIndex + 1;
      I := Edge[EdgeIndex].Vertex1;
      J := Edge[EdgeIndex].Vertex2;
      FindAndUnion (Parent, I, J, SameSet);
      if not SameSet then
      begin
         WriteLn (I:5, J:5, ' ', Edge[EdgeIndex].Weight:5);
         EdgesSoFar := EdgesSoFar + 1;
      end
   until EdgesSoFar = V - 1
end;


begin
   ReadLn (V);
   ReadEdges (Edge, E);
   SortEdges (Edge, E);
   InitializeParentArray (Parent, V);
   WriteLn ('Minimum cost spanning tree by Kruskal''s algorithm:');
   Kruskal (Edge, V)
end.
```

The real work of the program, in terms of getting the job done quickly, is in the function `FindAndUnion`. The two `while` loops make `I` and `J` point to the roots of the trees containing the two vertices. If these are the same tree, we have established that the two vertices are in the same set. If not, forming their union is a matter of linking one of them to the root of the other.

The execution time of the algorithm is dominated by the time it takes to find the roots of the set trees. Consequently, it is clearly advantageous to take reasonable steps to keep these trees "bushy," that is, broad.

For an application of Kruskal's algorithm, consider the telephone network shown in Figure 10.4.

Let us suppose that a hypothetical company with manufacturing facilities in Georgia and California, plus offices in certain major cities, has a leased-line telephone system. Every location is connected to at least two others so as to provide backup communications in the event of temporary outages. Management has decided to investigate a cost-saving measure in which the double-links would be eliminated, at least part of the time. Now the question is, which of the intercity links should be maintained in such a way that all locations are still connected with a minimum mileage of telephone lines? This is precisely the minimum-cost spanning tree problem. Figure 10.5 shows the spanning tree produced by the program for Kruskal's algorithm.

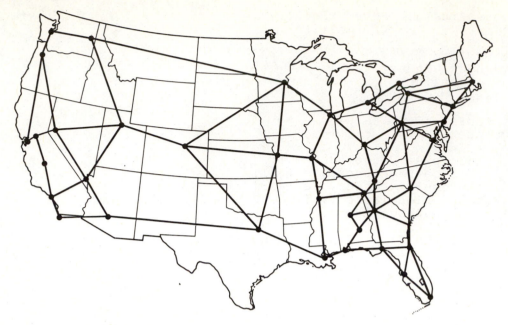

FIGURE 10.4
A hypothetical telephone network, used to illustrate Kruskal's algorithm for finding a minimum-cost spanning tree.

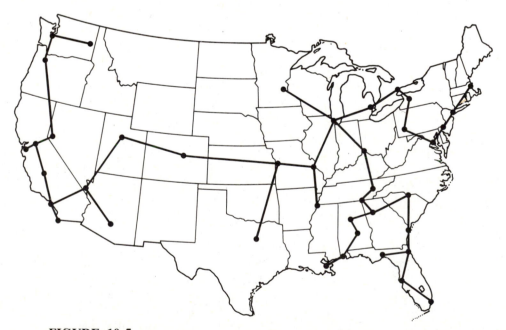

FIGURE 10.5
A minimum-cost spanning tree found by Kruskal's algorithm for the network of Figure 10.4.

10.10 CONCLUSION

We hope that this overview of graphs and graph algorithms has whetted your appetite for further study. The field is attractive for its mathematical challenges, the importance of its many applications, and the fascination of the combination of a centuries-old branch of mathematics with the power of the modern computer. The exercises and the bibliography will suggest a few paths of further investigation.

EXERCISES

1.
    Show that if V is the number of vertices and E the number of edges in a graph:
    (a) $O(V^2) < O((E + V) \lg E)$, if the number of edges, E, is maximal.
    (b) $O(V^2) > O((E + V) \lg E)$, if $E = O(V)$.
    (c) What is the relationship between $O(V^2)$ and $O((E + V) \lg E)$ if $E = O(V \lg V)$?

2. An undirected graph is *connected* if there is a path between any two vertices. What procedure of this text could be used to determine whether a graph is connected or not?

3. An edge, e, of a graph, is said to be *incident* on a vertex, v, if v is an endpoint of e. The *degree* of a vertex, $d(v)$, is the number of edges incident on v.
    (a) Determine the degree of each vertex of the graph shown at the beginning of Section 10.2.
    (b) Prove that the number of vertices of *odd* degree in a finite graph is even. (Note: If e is a self-loop, i.e., $e = (v_i, v_i)$, e is considered to be incident twice on v_i.)

4. A *path* in a graph is a sequence of alternating vertices and edges, such that all vertices are distinct. An *Euler path* in a graph is a path such that every edge is traversed exactly once.
    (a) Show that an undirected graph, G, contains an Euler path if $d(v)$ is even for every vertex v, of G.
    (b) Show that no Euler path exists if more than two vertices are of odd degree.
    (c) Euler's first paper on graph theory (1736) included a solution to the *Königsberg Bridge problem:* Two islands lie in the Pregel River in Kalingrad (formerly Königsberg), as shown in the sketch below. The problem is to determine a circuit (cycle) that crosses each bridge exactly once, or show that no such circuit exists. Use your answers to (a) and (b) above, to solve this problem.

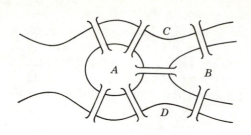

Konigsberg in 1736.

(a)

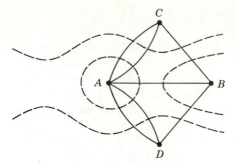

Euler's graphical representation.

(b)

5. An undirected graph that has an Euler path is called an *Euler graph*. It can be shown (can you?) that a connected undirected finite graph is an Euler graph if and only if exactly two vertices are of odd degree, or all vertices are of even degree.

(a) If v_1 and v_2 are the only two vertices of odd degree in graph G, convince yourself with diagrams that the only Euler paths in G begin at either v_1 or v_2, and end at the other. Can you see how an algorithm for finding an Euler path could be devised?

(b) If all vertices of G are of even degree, convince yourself that all Euler paths are circuits. Again, do you see how to construct an algorithm?

(c) Write a Pascal program to determine whether a graph is an Euler graph or not.

(d) Write a program to find an Euler path in an Euler graph.

6. In a digraph (directed graph) we define the *indegree* of a vertex, $d_{in}(v)$, to be the number of edges incident on v that terminate at v. The *outdegree*, $d_{out}(v)$, is the number of edges that have v as their starting vertex.

(a) Write down the adjacency matrix for the digraph, $G = <V, E>$, where $V = \{1, 2, 3, 4, 5, 6, 7, 8\}$, and $E = \{(2, 1), (3, 1), (4, 1), (5, 1), (5, 6), (6, 1), (6, 2), (6, 7), (7, 1), (7, 2), (7, 8), (8, 1)\}$.

(b) Draw the digraph for (a) above.

(c) What is the indegree and outdegree of each vertex? How can you compute these numbers from the adjacency matrix?

7. List the vertices in the order visited when performing `Breadth-FirstSearch` and `DepthFirstSearch` on the Königsberg Bridge graph, and on the graph of Exercise 6. Start at any vertex you choose.

8. Make the changes necessary in `DepthFirstSearch` if the graph is represented as an adjacency list instead of as an adjacency matrix.

9. Make changes necessary in `BreadthFirstSearch` if the graph is represented as an adjacency matrix instead of an adjacency list.

10. A *directed Euler path* is a directed path in which every edge appears exactly
     once. The *underlying graph* in a directed graph, G, is G with the directions
     ignored. A *directed Euler circuit* and a *directed Euler graph* are defined
     similarly. It can be shown that a finite digraph is an Euler digraph if its
     underlying graph is connected, and one of the following conditions holds
     (Even, 1979):

     - There are vertices v_1 and v_2, where $d_{out}(v_1) = d_{in}(v_1) + 1$, and $d_{out}(v_2)$
       $+ 1 = d_{in}(v_2)$. For all other vertices, v, $d_{in}(v) = d_{out}(v)$.
     - For all vertices $d_{in}(v) = d_{out}(v)$.

     (a) Draw digraphs satisfying each of these two conditions and locate the
              Euler paths.
     (b) Which paths are circuits?
     (c) What is the connection between the conditions necessary for the ex-
              istence of Euler paths in digraphs and those in undirected graphs?

11. An Euler circuit traverses each *edge* exactly once; a Hamiltonian circuit
     visits each *vertex* exactly once.
     (a) Find a Hamiltonian circuit, if there is one, in each of these graphs:

     i)   ii)

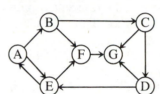
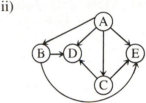

     (b) Finding a minimal Hamiltonian circuit in a weighted, undirected graph
              is sometimes called the *Traveling Salesman Problem* if we think of
              the vertices as cities that a salesman must visit. It is one of a class of
              problems for which no algorithm that runs in polynomial time is known.
              It could, however, be solved in polynomial time if we had multiple
              processors running at the same time, each investigating a possible
              circuit. Problems with this run-time behavior are called *NP-hard*.

              The first step in solving the Traveling Salesman Problem is to find
              all Hamiltonian circuits in a graph, $G = <V, E>$. Write an algorithm
              for finding a Hamiltonian Circuit, if there is one, starting and ending
              at a given vertex. (Hint: `DepthFirstSearch` can be made to do
              the job if the `Visit` procedure is changed to keep track of the
              number of nodes visited, and visited nodes are remarked unvisited if
              they lead to a dead end.)

12. Make the following modifications to the program `Dijkstra`:
     (a) Find the shortest paths from each vertex to all others.
     (b) Find the shortest path from a starting vertex, v_s, to a terminal vertex,
              v_t.

13. An alternative to Dijkstra's algorithm for finding all shortest paths in a directed graph is due to Ford (1956, 1962). Ford's algorithm finds the shortest distance of every vertex, v, from a starting vertex, s. (It cannot, however, be used for undirected graphs as can Dijkstra's.) Ford's algorithm is:

   - Make `Dist [s] = 0`. For all other vertices, $v \neq s$, make `Dist [v]` infinite.

   - As long as there is an edge, (u, v), such that `Dist [v] > Dist [u] + Edge [u, v]`, replace `Dist [v]` with `Dist [u] + Edge [u,v]`.

   Trace Ford's algorithm through the two graphs used to demonstrate Dijkstra's algorithm.

14. A *sink* in a digraph is a non-isolated vertex, v, with $d_{out}(v) = 0$ and $d_{in}(v) = V - 1$. In other words, an edge that terminates at v originates at every other vertex of G.
    (a) How many sinks can a simple graph have?
    (b) What characterizes the adjacency matrix for a graph that has a sink?
    (c) There is an obvious way to test an adjacency matrix for sinks if the sum of each row and column is available. What is the cost of computing these sums?
    (d) Can you write an $O(V)$ algorithm to find all sinks when the row and column sums are not known?
    (e) Write a Pascal program to find all sinks in a digraph, if there are any.

15. A *bipartite graph* is a graph, $G = <V, E>$, where the vertices can be partitioned into two disjoint sets, V_1 and V_2, such that every edge in E joins a vertex in V_1 to a vertex in V_2. Use depth-first search to partition the vertices of a bipartite graph, or to return a message if the graph is not bipartite.

16. A graph is said to be *k-colorable* if all the vertices can be colored, using k different colors, so that no two adjacent vertices are of the same color. The *chromatic number* of a graph is the least integer k, such that the graph is k-colorable.
    (a) Show that the chromatic number of a binary tree is, at most, 2. When is it less than 2?
    (b) Show that a bipartite graph is two-colorable.
    (c) Map-coloring problems have intrigued the mathematical community for many years. How can a map-coloring problem be represented as a graph-coloring problem?

17. Embedded in the `Kruskal` program of this chapter is the detection of a cycle (circuit) in a graph. *DAG* is the acronym for a *directed acyclic graph*. Using the program fragment suggested, write a procedure to decide whether a graph is a DAG or not.

SUGGESTIONS FOR FURTHER STUDY

Almost all discrete mathematics texts include material on graphs. One of the best sources for computer science students is Even (1979), because of its informal algorithmic approach. A survey of work done from 1960 through 1975, including reprints of seminal articles and applications of graphs in various fields, can be found in Fulkerson (1975).

Euler presented the Königsberg Bridge problem in his first paper on graph theory in 1736. It is reprinted with commentary in Newman (1953).

Dijkstra's shortest path algorithm was first published in Dijkstra (1959), and is applicable to undirected graphs as well as directed graphs with negative, as well as positive, weights. Ford's algorithm first appeared in Ford (1956) and is discussed in Ford and Fulkerson (1962). It applies only to directed, positively weighted graphs. The costs of finding the lengths of paths from all vertices to all vertices is $O(V^3)$ for Dijkstra's and $O(E * V^2)$ for Ford's algorithm. Another $O(V^3)$ algorithm is due to Floyd (1962).

An easily understandable discussion of NP-hard problems, as well as the class called *NP-complete,* can be found in Garey and Johnson (1979). Baase (1978) is also a source for examples in addition to explanations and theorems.

Networks are often used to model the flow of liquids through pipes, the current through electrical conduits or the number of vehicles on highways. The classic algorithm to find maximum flow is due to Ford and Fulkerson (1962). A good explication can be found in Even (1979).

Deo (1974) discusses applications for many engineering areas, as well as presenting the theory of graphs and a number of programs.

Surface-coloring problems date from the Four Color Conjecture of Francis Guthrie, a graduate student at University College, London, in 1852. Guthrie hypothesized that any planar map was four-colorable. (A planar map, or planar graph, is one where edges cross only at vertices.) Showing that any planar map is five-colorable is relatively easy, and examples of maps that are not three-colorable are not hard to draw. A description of the computer-generated proof of the Four Color Conjecture can be found in an article by its creators, Appel and Haken (1978). A history of coloring problems on non-planar surfaces and an interesting account of how mathematicians work is in Stahl (1985).

One application of DAGs, with starting and terminal vertices, is the *PERT chart,* an acronym for *Program Evaluation and Review Technique.* Weightings often represent times or costs, with the object being to minimize schedule time or cost. A related technique is called the *Critical Path Method* (CPM). Deo (1974) contains an overview.

BIBLIOGRAPHY

Aho, A. V., and Ullman, J. D. 1977. *Principles of Compiler Design*. Reading, MA: Addison-Wesley.

Aho, A. V., Hopcroft, J. E., and Ullman, J. D. 1982. *Data Structures and Algorithms*. Reading, MA: Addison-Wesley.

Amsterdam, J. 1985. "An analysis of sorts." *BYTE* **10**(9), 105–112.

Appel, K., and Haken, W. 1978. "The four color problem." In Steen, L. A. (Ed.), *Mathematics Today*. New York: Springer-Verlag. 153–180.

Baase, S. 1978. *Computer Algorithms: Introduction to Design and Analysis*. Reading, MA: Addison-Wesley.

Backus, J. 1978. "Can programming be liberated from the von Neumann style? A functional style and its algebra of programs." *Communications of the ACM* **21**(8), 613–641.

Batson, A. 1965. "The organization of symbol tables." *Communications of the ACM* **8**(2), 111–112.

Bentley, J. 1983. "Programming pearls: Writing correct programs." *Communications of the ACM* **26**(12), 1040–1045.

Bentley, J. 1984. "Programming pearls: How to sort." *Communications of the ACM* **27**(4), 287–291.

Bentley, J. 1985. "Programming pearls: Thanks, heaps." *Communications of the ACM* **28**(3), 245–250.

Bentley, J. 1986. *Programming Pearls*. Reading, MA: Addison-Wesley.

Bentley, J., and Friedman, J. H. 1979. "Data structures for range searching." *ACM Computing Surveys* **11**(4), 397–413.

Bird, R. S. 1977. "Notes on recursion elimination." *Communications of the ACM* **20**(6), 434–439.

Bird, R. S. 1980. "Tabulation techniques for recursive programs." *ACM Computing Surveys* **12**(4), 403–417.

Bitton, D., Dewitt, D. J., Hsaio, D. K., and Monon, J. 1984. "A taxonomy of parallel sorting." *ACM Computing Surveys* **16**(3), 287–318.

Bottenbruch, H. 1962. "Structure and use of Algol 60." *Journal of the ACM* **9**, 161–221.

Boyer, C. B. 1968. *A History of Mathematics*. New York: John Wiley & Sons.

Brinch-Hansen, P. 1973. *Operating System Principles*. Englewood Cliffs, NJ: Prentice-Hall.

Brooks, F. P. 1975. *The Mythical Man-Month*. Reading, MA: Addison-Wesley.

Cardelli, L., and Wegner, P. 1985. "On understanding types, data abstraction, and polymorphism." *ACM Computing Surveys* **17**(4), 471–522.

Chomsky, Noam. 1957. *Syntactic Structures*. The Hague: Mouton.

Cohen, D. I. A. 1986. *Introduction to Computer Theory*. New York: John Wiley & Sons.

Cohen, D. J., and Gotlieb, C. C. 1970. "A list structure form of grammers for syntactic analysis." *ACM Computing Surveys* **2**(1), 65–82.

Cohen, J. 1981. "Garbage collection of linked data structures." *ACM Computing Surveys* **13**(3), 341–368.

Cohen, L. W., and Ehrlich, G. 1963. *The Structure of the Real Number System*. Princeton: Van Nostrand Reinhold.

Comer, D. 1979. "The ubiquitous B-tree." *ACM Computing Surveys* **11**(2), 121–138.

Date, C. J. 1981. *An Introduction to Data Base Systems*, 3rd ed. Reading, MA: Addison-Wesley.

Deo, N. 1974. *Graph Theory with Applications to Engineering and Computer Science*. Englewood Cliffs, NJ: Prentice-Hall.

Dijkstra, E. W. 1959. "A note on two problems in connection with graphs." *Numerische Mathematik* **1**, 269–271.

Dijkstra, E. W. 1965. Cooperating sequential processes. Eindhoven, the Netherlands: Technological University. (Reprinted in Genuys, F. (Ed.) (1968). *Programming Languages*. New York: Academic Press).

Dijkstra, E. W. 1968. "Go to statement considered harmful." *Communications of the ACM* **11**(3), 147–148.

Dromey, R. 1983. *How To Solve It by Computer*. Englewood Cliffs, NJ: Prentice-Hall.

Even, S. 1979. *Graph Algorithms*. Potomac, MD: Computer Science Press.

Feuer, A. R. 1982. *The C Puzzle Book*. Englewood Cliffs, NJ: Prentice-Hall.

Floyd, R. W. 1962. "Algorithm 97: Shortest Path." *Communications of the ACM* **5**(6), 345.

Floyd, R. W. 1964. "Algorithm 245: Treesort 3." *Communications of the ACM* **7**(12), 701.

Ford, L. R., Jr. 1956. *Network Flow Theory*. (Report No. P-923), The Rand Corporation.

Ford, L. R., Jr., and Fulkerson, D. R. 1962. *Flows in Networks*. Princeton: Princeton University Press.

Fulkerson, D. R. (ed.). 1975. *Studies in Graph Theory* (Parts 1 & 2). *MAA Studies in Mathematics* **11–12**. Washington: The Mathematical Association of America.

Garey, M. R., and Johnson, D. S. 1979. *Computers and Intractability: A Guide to the Theory of NP-Completeness*. New York: W.H. Freeman.

Garland, S. J. 1986. *Introduction to Computer Science with Applications in Pascal*. Reading, MA: Addison-Wesley.

Gerstmann, H., and A. Ollongren. 1980. "Abstract objects as abstract data types." In D. Bjorner (Ed.), *Abstract software specifications. Lecture Notes in Computer Science 86*. New York: Springer-Verlag. 439–450.

Glass, R. L. 1969. "An elementary discussion of compiler/interpreter writing." *ACM Computing Surveys* **1**(1), 55–77.

Gleick, J. 1986. "Machine beats man on ancient front." *New York Times*. August 26, p. C1.

Gonnet, G. H. 1984. *Handbook of Algorithms and Data Structures*. Reading, MA: Addison-Wesley.

Graham, G. S. (ed.). 1978. "Queuing network models of computer system performance." [Special issue]. *ACM Computing Surveys* **10**(3).

Graham, N. 1982. *Introduction to Computer Science: A Structured Approach*. St. Paul, MN: West.

Gries, D. 1971. *Compiler Construction for Digital Computers*. New York: John Wiley & Sons.

Gries, D. 1981. *The Science of Programming*. New York: Springer-Verlag.

Hehner, E. C. R. 1984. *The Logic of Programming*. Englewood Cliffs, NJ: Prentice-Hall.

Hester, J. H., and Hirschberg, D. S. 1985. "Self-organizing linear search." *ACM Computing Surveys* **17**(3), 295–311.

Hoare, C. A. R. 1961. "Algorithm 63: Partition," and "Algorithm 64: Quicksort." *Communications of the ACM* **4**(7), 321.

Hoare, C. A. R. 1962. "Quicksort." *Computer Journal* **5**(1), 10–15.

Hoare, C. A. R. 1972. "Proof of correctness of data representations." *Acta Informatica* **1**, 271–281.

Hockey, S. 1980. *A Guide to Computer Applications in the Humanities*. Baltimore: The Johns Hopkins University Press.

Horowitz, E., and Sahni, S. 1984. *Fundamentals of Data Structures in Pascal*. Rockville, MD: Computer Science Press.

Huntington, E. V. 1904. *Transactions of the American Mathematical Society* **5**, 288–309.

Ide, N. M. 1987. *Pascal for Humanists*. Philadelphia: University of Pennsylvania Press.

Johnsonbaugh, R. 1984. *Discrete Mathematics*. New York: Macmillan.

Jouannaud, J. (ed.). 1985. *Functional Programming Languages and Computer Architecture. Lecture Notes in Computer Science 201*. New York: Springer-Verlag.

Kernighan, B. W., and Plauger, P. J. 1974. ''Programming style: examples and counterexamples.'' *ACM Computing Surveys* **6**(4), 303–319.

Kernighan, B. W., and Ritchie, D. M. 1978. *The C Programming Language*. Englewood Cliffs, NJ: Prentice-Hall.

Knuth, D. E. 1973a. *The Art of Computer Programming*. Volume 1: *Fundamental Algorithms,* 2nd ed. Reading, MA: Addison-Wesley.

Knuth, D. E. 1973b. *The Art of Computer Programming*. Volume 3: *Sorting and Searching*. Reading, MA: Addison-Wesley.

Knuth, D. E. 1974. ''Structured programming with go to statements.'' *ACM Computing Surveys* **6**(4), 261–301.

Knuth, D. E. 1981. *The Art of Computer Programming*. Volume 2: *Seminumerical Algorithms,* 2nd ed. Reading, MA: Addison-Wesley.

Knuth, D. E., Morris, J. H. Jr., and Pratt, V. R. 1977. ''Fast pattern matching in strings.'' *SIAM Journal on Computing* **6**(2), 240–267.

Koffman, E. B. 1985. *Problem Solving and Structured Programming in Pascal*. Reading, MA: Addison-Wesley.

Kruse, R. L. 1987. *Data Structures and Program Design*, 2nd ed. Englewood Cliffs, NJ: Prentice-Hall.

Ledgard, H. F. 1986. *Professional Pascal: Essays on the Practice of Programming*. Reading, MA: Addison-Wesley.

Lewis, H. R., and Papadimitriou, C. H. 1981. *Elements of the Theory of Computation*. Englewood Cliffs, NJ: Prentice-Hall.

Liskov, B., and Guttag, J. 1986. *Abstraction and Specification in Program Development*. Cambridge, MA: MIT Press.

Liskov, B., and Zilles, S. 1974. ''Programming with abstract data types.'' In *Preceedings of the ACM SIGPLAN Conference on Very High Level Languages. SIGPLAN Notices* **9**, 50–60.

Lueker, G. S. 1980. ''Some techniques for solving recurrences.'' *ACM Computing Surveys* **12**(4), 419–436.

Martin, W. A. 1971. ''Sorting.'' *ACM Computing Surveys* **3**(4), 147–174.

Maurer, W. D., and Lewis, T. G. 1975. ''Hash table methods.'' *ACM Computing Surveys* **7**(1), 5–20.

McCarthy, J. 1960. ''Recursive functions of symbolic expressions and their computation by machine.'' *Communications of the ACM* **3**(4), 184–195.

McCarthy, J. 1978. ''The history of Lisp.'' In *Proceedings of the ACM SIGPLAN Conference on the History of Programming Languages*.

McCracken, D. D. 1957. *Digital Computer Programming*. New York: John Wiley & Sons.

McCracken, D. D. 1961. *A Guide to Fortran Programming*. New York: John Wiley & Sons.

McCracken, D. D., and Jackson, M. A. 1982. "Life-cycle concept considered harmful." *ACM Software Engineering Notes*. **7**(2), 29–32.

Metz, J. R., and Barnes, B. H. 1977. *Decision Table Languages and Systems*. New York: Academic Press.

Mili, A. 1985. *An Introduction to Formal Program Verification*. New York: Van Nostrand Reinhold.

Moret, B. M. E. 1982. "Decision and diagrams." *ACM Computing Surveys* **14**(4), 593–623.

Morris, J. H., Jr., and Pratt, V. R. 1970. "A linear pattern-matching algorithm." *Technical reports 40*. Berkeley: University of California.

Morris, R. 1968. "Scatter storage techniques." *Communications of the ACM* **11**(1), 38–43.

Newman, J. R. (ed.). 1953. "Leonard Euler and the Koenigsberg bridges." *Scientific American*, July, 66–70.

Peano, G. 1894. *Formulaire de Mathematique*. Turin.

Peterson, W. W. 1957. "Addressing for random access storage." *IBM Journal of Research and Development* **1**(2), 130–146.

Pollack, S. 1982. *Studies in Computer Science. MAA Studies in Mathematics 22*. Washington: Mathematics Association of America.

Price, C. E. 1971. "Table lookup techniques." *ACM Computing Surveys* **3** (2), 49–66.

Reingold, E. M., Nievergelt, J., and Deo, N. 1977. *Combinatorial Algorithms*. Englewood Cliffs, NJ: Prentice-Hall.

Roberts, E. S. 1986. *Thinking Recursively*. New York: John Wiley & Sons.

Rohl, J. S. 1984. *Recursion Via Pascal*. New York: Cambridge University Press.

Samet, H. 1982. "The quadtree and related hierarchical data structures." *ACM Computing Surveys* **16**(2), 187–260.

Sandewall, E. 1978. "Programming in an interactive environment: The LISP experience." *ACM Computing Surveys* **10**(1), 35–71.

Sedgewick, R. 1978. "Implementing Quicksort programs." *Communications of the ACM* **21**(10), 847–857.

Sedgewick, R. 1983. *Algorithms*. Reading, MA: Addison-Wesley.

Shell, D. L. 1959. "A high speed sorting procedure." *Communications of the ACM* **2** (7), 30–32.

Shneiderman, B. 1984. "Response time and display rate in human performance with computers." *ACM Computing Surveys* **16**(3), 265–286.

Shortt, J., and Wilson, T. C. 1979. *Problem Solving and the Computer: A Structured Concept with PL/I (PL/C)*, 2nd ed. Reading, MA: Addison-Wesley.

Solow, D. 1982. *How to Read and Do Proofs*. New York: John Wiley & Sons.

Stahl, S. 1985. ''The other map coloring theorem.'' *Mathematics Magazine* **58**(3), 131–145.

Steele, G. L., Jr. 1984. *Common Lisp: Reference Manual*. Billerica, MA: Digital Press.

Suppes, P. 1960. *Axiomatic Set Theory*. Princeton: Van Nostrand Reinhold.

Tenenbaum, A. M., and Augenstein, M. J. 1986. *Data Structures Using Pascal,* 2nd ed. Englewood Cliffs, NJ: Prentice-Hall.

Tremblay, J., and Sorenson, P. 1984. *An Introduction to Data Structures with Applications*, 2nd ed. New York: McGraw-Hill.

Turner, D. 1981. ''The future of applicative languages.'' In *Proceedings of the 3rd European Conference on Informatics, Lecture Notes in Computer Science 123*. New York: Springer-Verlag. 334–348.

Ullman, J. D. 1982. *Principles of Database Systems*. Rockville, MD: Computer Science Press.

Vasta, J. A. 1985. *Understanding Data Base Management Systems*. Belmont, CA: Wadsworth.

Williams, R. 1971. ''A survey of data structures for computer graphics systems.'' *ACM Computing Surveys* **3**(1), 1–22.

Windley, P. F. 1960. ''Trees, forests and rearranging.'' *Computer Journal* **3**, 84–88.

INDEX OF FUNCTIONS, PROCEDURES, AND PROGRAMS

11

GENERAL INDEX